D1526139

THE CALL OF DUTY

MILITARY AWARDS AND DECORATIONS OF THE UNITED STATES OF AMERICA

BY JOHN E. STRANDBERG AND
ROGER JAMES BENDER

Published by R. James Bender Publishing,
P.O. Box 23456, San Jose, CA 95153

Printed in the United States of America

Designed by Roger James Bender and
Roger Waterman

ISBN No. 0-912138-54-8

Introduction

The awards illustrated in this book represent the dedication, devotion to duty, and sacrifices of millions of American soldiers, sailors, airmen and marines. These awards stand as a tribute to the American spirit and the individual stories they tell, and the history they represent are shaped as much by each recipient's story as by the official regulations.

This book began as the result of my enthusiasm for collecting American medals. That passion was first kindled in the late 1960s when my grandfather gave me the Purple Heart and World War I Victory Medal which he had earned a half century earlier. However, the book in this final form, truly would not have been possible without the generous assistance, support and encouragement of many other people.

By far the most important contribution came from Roger James Bender. Roger's enthusiasm for this project quickly transformed his role from that of publisher to one of coauthor. The contacts he has developed through his many years of publishing books for military hobbyists provided a gold mine of photographs showing recipients wearing their awards and decorations.

Both Roger and I would also like to thank those who contributed their time and expertise as well as opening their collections to our cameras. First we would like to thank both Todd Wheatly and Doug Boyce. These well - known collectors freely shared their knowledge and collections with us to help make this book possible. Their years of collecting experience and research added immeasurably to the depth of information and the quality of many of the medals illustrated here.

Our thanks also go out to John P. Mull, for allowing us to photograph dozens of medals in his collection and for his encouragement throughout this entire project; to Albert F. Gleim for his long hours of critiquing the original manuscript and providing information on many decorations and campaign medals; to Charles P. McDowell, for his information and photographs on Polar awards and NASA decorations; to Paul Nutting, for information and photographs on the Kearny Medal and Kearny Cross; and to Frank Paulus, for providing many valuable photographs on Medal of Honor variants.

Others who provided assistance in completing this project include:

Ed Anderson
LT Emily Beard, NOAA
CDR F.C. Brown, USN
Paul Caraher, Jr.
John Coy
Department of the Army
Ron Fischer
Lee Graves, GRACO Industries
Greg Gritsch
CDR Michael H. Hess, USPHS
Dawn Jackson
PNC Robert S. Jackson, USN
John Jensen
Gary Krug
John Langton
Ken Lazier
Legion of Valor
John E. Lelle
Allen Menke
Ralph McCleod
Carl Morcate
Thomas J. Nier
National Archives
CDR Thomas H. Perez, USPHS
George Petersen
Jim Phillips
Cindy Robinson, NASA
Adam Rohloff
Robert Schulman, NASA
Smithsonian Institution
Glenn A. Sousa
State Historical Society of North Dakota
Joe Stone
Roger Sullivan
Jerry Voigt

I would also like to thank my wife, Terri, for her endless encouragement and support during the more than three years that this project was in the works.

Like any hobbyist, the collector of American awards and decorations needs accurate information. The compilation of that information is not complete with the publication of this book. Roger and I encourage all serious collectors to share the information they acquire through the publication of journal articles, monographs, and books. Many excellent organizations exist for the collector, among the best for the collector of American awards is the Orders and Medals Society of America.

Authors' Comments

This book has been designed to provide the collector of American awards and decorations with a comprehensive reference source on the medals authorized for wear by members of the uniformed services of the United States. Every effort has been made to present the medals in their proper order of precedence as currently prescribed in Department of Defense regulations. In addition, the names used for each medal are their proper names as they appear in the appropriate regulations. Thus, the reader will find, for example, that the medal most commonly referred to as the Indian Wars Medal by collectors is titled the Indian Campaign Medal, which is its proper name as found in Army regulations.

Being a general reference guide, this book does not go into great detail discussing all manufacturer's variations. Generally the only time a variation of a particular medal will be discussed or illustrated is when the design change is the result of official regulations or changes in government specifications. Most medals are encountered with minor variations which are the result of die changes or the need to modify manufacturing techniques. The documentation of these many variations, while important to the collector, is better left to the journals and monographs.

Table of Contents

Awards for Valor and Meritorious Service

Medal of Honor 15
- Army 17
- Navy 42
- Air Force 56

Brevet Medal 58
Distinguished Service Cross 60
Navy Cross 68
Air Force Cross 73
Defense Distinguished Service Medal 75
Distinguished Service Medal
- Army 75
- Navy 80
- Air Force 82
- Coast Guard 83

Certificate of Merit 83
Silver Star 85
Defense Superior Service Medal 88
Legion of Merit 89
Distinguished Flying Cross 97
Soldier's Medal 100
Navy and Marine Corps Medal 102
Airman's Medal 103
Coast Guard Medal 103
Bronze Star Medal 104
Purple Heart 106
Defense Meritorious Service Medal 111
Meritorious Service Medal 111
Air Medal 113
Aerial Achievement Medal 115
Joint Service Commendation Medal 115
Commendation Medal
- Army 116
- Navy 117
- Air Force 117
- Coast Guard 118

Joint Service Achievement Medal ..119
Achievement Medal
- Army 120
- Navy 120
- Air Force 121
- Coast Guard 121

Gold Life Saving Medal 122
Silver Life Saving Medal 126

Good Conduct and Other Length of Service Medals

Combat Readiness Medal 131
Army Good Conduct Medal 132
Navy Good Conduct Medal 134
Marine Corps Good Conduct Medal 138
Air Force Good Conduct Medal 140
Coast Guard Good Conduct Medal 140
Army Reserve Components Achievement Medal
- Army Reserve 141

- Army National Guard 141
Naval Reserve Meritorious Service Medal 142
Air Reserve Forces Meritorious Service Medal 142
Selected Marine Corps Reserve Medal 143
Coast Guard Reserve Good Conduct Medal 144
Prisoner of War Medal 144

Campaign and Service Medals

Rim Numbering................................148
Suspension Brooch Styles..............150
Civil War Campaign Medal
- Army 154
- Navy 156
- Marine Corps 156
Indian Campaign Medal - Army 157
West Indies Campaign Medal
- Navy 161
- Marine Corps 161
Spanish Campaign Medal
- Army 162
- Navy 163
- Marine Corps 163
Spanish War Service Medal
- Army 165
Army of Cuban Occupation Medal 170
Army of Puerto Rican Occupation Medal 171
Philippine Campaign Medal
- Army 172
- Navy 174
- Marine Corps 174
Philippine Congressional Medal
- Army 177
China Campaign Medal - Army 178
China Relief Expedition Medal
- Navy 178
- Marine Corps 178
Army of Cuban Pacification Medal 181
Cuban Pacification Medal
- Navy 181
- Marine Corps 181
Nicaraguan Campaign Medal (1912)
- Navy 183
- Marine Corps 183
Mexican Service Medal
- Army 185
- Navy 186
- Marine Corps 186
Haitian Campaign Medal (1915)
- Navy 187
Mexican Border Service Medal
- Army 188
Dominican Campaign Medal
- Navy 189
- Marine Corps 189
World War I Victory Medal 191
- Army clasps 192
- Navy clasps 192
Texas Cavalry Congressional Medal 194
Army of Occupation of Germany Medal 194
Haitian Campaign Medal (1919-1920)
- Navy 195
- Marine Corps 195
Second Nicaraguan Campaign Medal
- Navy 198
- Marine Corps 198
Yangtze Service Medal
- Navy 200
- Marine Corps 200
Marine Corps Expeditionary Medal 201
Navy Expeditionary Medal 202
China Service Medal
- Navy 202
- Marine Corps 202
American Defense Service Medal ..203
-Army bars 204
- Navy bars 204
Women's Army Corps Service Medal 205

American Campaign Medal 205
European-African-Middle Eastern Campaign Medal 207
Asiatic-Pacific Campaign Medal ...207
World War II Victory Medal 208
Army of Occupation Medal 208
Navy Occupation Service Medal
- Navy 209
- Marine Corps 209
Typhus Commission Medal 210
Medal for Humane Action 210
Korean Service Medal 211
National Defense Service Medal 212
Armed Forces Expeditionary Medal 212
Vietnam Service Medal 213
Southwest Asia Service Medal 214
Antarctica Service Medal 214
Coast Guard Arctic Service Medal 215
Humanitarian Service Medal 216
Armed Forces Reserve Medal
- Army Reserve 216
- National Guard 216
- Navy Reserve 216
- Marine Corps Reserve 216
- Air Force Reserve 216
- Coast Guard Reserve 216
Naval Reserve Medal 218

Commemorative Medals

Andre Medal 222
Kearny Medal 223
Kearny Cross 224
Gilmore Medal (Sumter Medal) 225
Butler Medal (Army of the James Medal) 226
Ely Medal 227
Fort Sumter Medal 227
Fort Pickens Medal 228
Manila Bay Medal (Dewey Medal) 229
West Indies Naval Campaign Medal (Sampson Medal) 232
Specially Meritorious Medal - War With Spain 234
Cardenas Medal of Honor 236
Jeannette Arctic Expedition Medal 238
Byrd Antarctic Expedition Medal ..238
Second Byrd Antarctic Expedition Medal 239
NC-4 Medal 239
Peary Polar Expedition Medal 240
United States Antarctic Expedition Medal 241
American Field Service Medal 241

Proficiency Medals

Navy Expert Pistol Shot Medal 245
Navy Expert Rifleman Medal 246
Coast Guard Expert Pistol Shot Medal 246
Coast Guard Expert Rifleman Medal 247
U.S. Naval Academy Short Range Battle Practice Medal 247
Marksmanship Badge
-Navy and Marine Corps 248
-Revenue Cutter Service 250

Commendation and Service Ribbons

Combat Action Ribbon (Navy, USMC, USCG) 254
Coast Guard Commandant's Letter of Commendation Ribbon 254
Presidential Unit Citation (Army, Air Force) 254
Presidential Unit Citation (Navy, USMC, USCG) 254
Valorous Unit Award 254
Joint Meritorious Unit Award 255
Army Superior Unit Award 255
Navy Unit Commendation 255
Coast Guard Unit Commendation ..255
Coast Guard Bicentennial Unit Commendation Ribbon 255

Air Force Outstanding Unit Award 255
Air Force Organizational Excellence Award 256
Meritorious Unit Commendation (Army) 256
Meritorious Unit Commendation (Navy and Marine Corps) 256
Coast Guard Meritorious Unit Commendation 256
Navy "E" Ribbon 256
Reserve Special Commendation Ribbon (Navy, Marine Corps) 257
Outstanding Airman of the Year 257
Sea Service Deployment Ribbon (Navy, Marine Corps) 257
Coast Guard Special Operations Service Ribbon 257
Coast Guard Sea Service Ribbon 258
Coast Guard Restricted Duty Ribbon 258
Navy Arctic Service Ribbon 258
Naval Reserve Sea Service Ribbon 258
Marine Corps Reserve Ribbon 259
Air Force Recognition Ribbon 259
NCO Professional Development Ribbon (Army) 259
Army Service Ribbon 259
Air Force Overseas Ribbon - Short Tour 259
Air Force Overseas Ribbon - Long Tour 260
Air Force Longevity Service Award Ribbon 260
Overseas Service Ribbon (Army) 260
Navy and Marine Corps Overseas Service Ribbon 260
Navy Recruiting Service Ribbon 261
Navy Fleet Marine Force Ribbon 261
NCO Professional Military Education Graduate Ribbon (Air Force) 261
USAF Basic Military Training Honor Graduate Ribbon 261
Coast Guard Basic Training Honor Graduate Ribbon 261
Coast Guard Reserve Meritorious Service Ribbon 262
Army Reserve Components Overseas Training Ribbon 262
Small Arms Expert Marksmanship Ribbon (Air Force) 262
Distinguished Marksman, Distinguished Pistol Shot Ribbon (Navy) 262
Distinguished Marksman, Distinguished Pistol Shot Ribbon (USCG) 262
Distinguished Marksman Ribbon (Navy) 263
Distinguished Pistol Shot Ribbon (Navy) 263
Air Force Training Ribbon 263

Appurtenances

Oak Leaf Cluster 266
Bronze Numerals 266
Gold Numerals 266
"V" Device 267
Service Stars 267
Arrowhead 268
Berlin Airlift Device 268
Ten-Year Device (Bronze Hour glass) 268
Antarctic Wintering Over Devices 268
Clasps 268
Bronze Maltese Cross 271
Silver W 271
Bronze A 271
Gold and Silver Stars 271
Silver E 272
Navy "E" Device 272
Silver S 272
Fleet Marine Force Combat Operations Insignia 272
Operational Distinguishing Device 272
Gold N 272
Bronze Globe 273

Silver Sea Horse 273
Planet 273
Lifesaving Medals 273

Presentation Cases and Boxes of Issue 275

Order of Precedence 287

Non-Military Governmental Awards and Decorations

Merchant Marine

Distinguished Service Medal 296
Meritorious Service Medal 297
Mariner's Medal 297
World War II Victory Medal 298
Expeditionary Medal 298
Gallant Ship Unit Citation Bar 299
Merchant Marine Combat Bar 299
Merchant Marine Defense Medal ...300
Atlantic War Zone Medal 300
Mediterranean Middle East War Zone Medal 301
Pacific War Zone Medal.................302
Korean Service Medal 302
Vietnam Service Medal 303

United States Public Health Service

Distinguished Service Medal 308
Meritorious Service Medal 308
Surgeon General's Medallion 309
Surgeon General's Exemplary Service Medal 310
Outstanding Service Medal 310
Commendation Medal 311
Achievement Medal 311
PHS Citation 312
Outstanding Unit Citation 312
Unit Commendation 312
National Emergency Perparedness Award 312
Foreign Duty Award.......................313
Hazardous Duty Award 313
Isolated/Hardship Award 314
Special Assignment Award.............315
Smallpox Eradication Campaign Ribbon....................................315
Regular Corps Ribbon 315

National Oceanic and Atmospheric Administration

NOAA Administrator's Award Medal....................................319
NOAA Corps Commendation Medal..................................319
NOAA Special Achievement Award Medal 320
NOAA Corps Director's Ribbon 320
NOAA Unit Citation Ribbon 320
NOAA ACO Awards Medal 321
NOAA Corps Atlantic Service Ribbon 321
NOAA Corps Pacific Service Ribbon 322
NOAA Corps Mobile Duty Service Ribbon 322
NOAA Corps International Service Ribbon 323
NOAA Corps Rifle Ribbon 323
NOAA Corps Pistol Ribbon 323
Coast and Geodetic Survey Distinguished Service Medal 324
C & GS Meritorious Service Medal....................................325
C & GS Good Conduct Medal 325
C & GS Defense Service Medal 326
C & GS Atlantic War Zone Medal .326
C & GS Pacific War Zone Medal ...327

National Aeronautics and Space Administration

Congressional Space Medal of Honor 331
Distinguished Service Medal (1st Design) 332
Distinguished Service Medal (Current Design) 333
Distinguished Public Service Medal 334
Outstanding Service Medal 334
Exceptional Service Medal 335
Outstanding Leadership Medal 335
Exceptional Scientific Achievement Medal 336
Exceptional Bravery Medal 336
Exceptional Engineering Achievement Medal 337

Public Service Medal 337
Exceptional Achievement Medal 338
Equal Employment Opportunity Medal 338
Space Flight Medal 340
NACA Distinguished Service Medal 340
NACA Exceptional Service Medal 341

Appendices

Navy Campaign Medal Eligibility Rosters
1. Philippine Campaign Medal 343
2. China Relief Expedition Medal ..345
3. Cuban Pacification Medal 345
4. Nicaraguan Campaign Medal 345
5. Mexican Service Medal 345
6. Haitian Campaign Medal (1915).347
7. Haitian Campaign Medal (1919 - 1920) 347
8. Dominican Campaign Medal 348
9. Second Nicaraguan Campaign Medal 349
10. Yangtze Service Medal 350
11. China Service Medal 353
Army/Navy WW I Victory Medal clasps eligibility roster 356
Qualifying Expeditions for Navy and Marine Corps Expeditionary Medals 357
US Army campaign designations for WW II campaign medals 359
Navy, USMC, and USCG campaign designations for WW II campaign medals (service stars)...360
Qualifying Operations for the Armed Forces Expeditionary Medal .364
Army, Navy, and USMC campaign designations for theVietnam Service Medal 365
Qualifying Operations for the Humanitarian Service Medal 366
Navy Clasps for the World I Victory Medal 368
West Indies Naval Campaign Medal (Sampson Medal) eligibility roster for Engagement Bars ..377
Manila Bay Medal (Dewey Medal) eligibility roster 379
Specially Meritorious Medal eligibility roster 381
Bibliography 383

Awards for Valor and Meritorious Service

Awards for military achievement have been as much a part of the history of warfare as the development of weaponry. Their use as a means of recognizing bravery in combat and service to the nation has long been acknowledged by generals and statesmen alike as a vital part of the esprit de corps of military service.

The history of American military awards and decorations can be traced back to the first desperate months of the American Revolution. In 1776 General George Washington received the nation's first medal, in appreciation for driving the British out of Boston. However, this first gold medal was not intended for wear on the uniform.

Our nation's first award designed for wear on the uniform appeared on 7 August 1782, when General Washington established the Badge of Military Merit. This first badge was made of purple cloth or silk. Heart-shaped, with a narrow lace border, the badge was intended to be sown to the left lapel of the uniform, over the heart.

The Badge of Military Merit was intended as a permanent order to recognize and foster "every species of military merit". The badge was to recognize both acts of unusual gallantry as well as extraordinary fidelity and service. It was General Washington's wish that the Badge of Merit show the citizens of the colonies that "the

Inset: This New Jersey doughboy wears the Type III Army Medal of Honor, the French Croix de Guerre with Palms and a Montenegrin decoration.

road to glory in a patriot army and a free country is thus opened to all."

To determine the validity of claims for award of the Badge of Merit a Board of Officers was appointed to consider requests for the award. Despite General Washington's wish that the Badge of Military Merit be permanent, the Board of Officers met only one time, on the 24th of April 1783. That board recommended approval of two awards, which were approved by General Washington in General Orders dated 27 April 1783 and awarded 3 May 1783.

The report of the Board of Officers recommended Sgt. Elijah Churchill and Sgt. William Brown for award of the Badge of Merit. Sergeant Churchill served with the 4th Troop of the 2nd Regiment of Light Dragoons and received his Badge for "conspicuous gallantry, firmness and address" in the attacks on Fort St. George and Fort Slongo on Long Island. Sergeant Brown served with Cpt. Samuel Comstock's Company, 5th Connecticut Regiment of the Continental Line, earning his Badge for leading a "forlorn hope" against the left British Redoubt at Yorktown on 14 October 1781.

The third and final recipient of the Badge of Military Merit was Sergeant Daniel Bissell of Cpt. David Humphrey's Company, 2nd Connecticut Regiment of the Continental Line. Sgt.Bissell's "fidelity, perseverance and good sense" came to the personnel attention of General Washington, who ordered that he be awarded the Badge on 10 June 1783.

Following the end of the Revolutionary War, with the size of the Army reduced to fewer than one thousand men, the Badge of Military Merit lapsed into disuse. However the deeds of the soldiers who continued to serve did not go unrecognized.

In keeping with its heritage as a citizen army, the first medals to be issued to American servicemen on a large scale were state issued medals for volunteer service. It was not until sixty-six years after General Washington announced the Badge of Military Merit that the first federal award for military achievement was established. The Certificate of Merit, created in 1847, was a printed certificate which recognized the military merit and heroism of enlisted soldiers. American servicemen would have to wait until the Civil War, and the introduction of the Medal of Honor, before a medal intended for wear would be available.

The Medal of Honor remained our nation's only military medal for over forty years, until 1905, when the Army authorized a medal to be awarded to all recipients of the Certificate of Merit. With the United States' entrance into the First World War it became apparent that the Medal of Honor and Certificate of Merit were inadequate to recognize the wide range of heroism and military achievement which the war in Europe was witness to. To solve this problem, Congress discontinued the Certificate of Merit in 1918 and authorized the Distinguished Service Cross and the Distinguished Service Medal to take its place. These awards became the framework for what has come to be known as the Pyramid of Honor. The awards and decorations that have followed in the years since the First World War are our nation's tribute to the service and heroism of her soldiers, sailors, airmen and marines.

The Medal of Honor

On a September day in 1862, near Sharpsburg, Maryland, along the tree lined banks of the Antietam Creek, General George McClellan and his Army of the Potomac met General Robert E. Lee's Army of Virginia. The bloody battle that followed left the fields and woods of the Maryland countryside littered with the dead and wounded of both sides. That day, amidst the terrible noise and smoke of battle a few special men earned everlasting glory.

One of those men was Private William Hogarty of the 23rd New York Infantry. Pvt. Hogarty was serving that 17th day of September with the 4th U.S. Artillery, its ranks withered from weeks of combat. As the fighting raged, Hogarty watched as one cannon crew was devastated by musket fire. On his own initative, he ran through the hail of gun-fire to the now silent cannon. Unaided, Pvt. Hogarty trimmed the shell's fuse, rammed it home, primed the cannon, aimed and fired the gun into the advancing Confederate infantry.

More than one hundred years later in the jungles of Vietnam Corporal Larry Maxam, USMC, was serving as a fire team leader. His company was guarding the Military District Headquarters when it came under heavy attack. The attacking enemy poured coordinated fire from automatic weapons, rockets, artillery and mortars into the defensive perimeter. Seeing that enemy fire had knocked out a vital machinegun position, Cpl. Maxam placed his assistant team leader in charge of his team and raced across the fire swept compound to the gun position. Completely exposed to enemy fire, Cpl. Maxam was wounded as he raced to man the machinegun. Upon reaching the gun position, Cpl. Maxam, ignoring his wounds, quickly placed the gun into action, pouring devastating fire into the attacking Viet Cong. For the next 1 1/2 hours, although being wounded by a rocket propelled grenade and again by small-arms fire, Cpl. Maxam continued to deliver intense machinegun fire into repeated enemy assaults. After his wounds made him too weak to reload the machinegun, Cpl. Maxam continued his defensive fire with his M-16. After successfully defending his position, Cpl. Maxam succumbed to his wounds.

These two narratives of Medal of Honor action, seperated by more than a century, exemplify the spirit of courage and tenacity under fire that have come to be associated with our nation's highest award for valor.

As the United States began to honor the valor and achievements of its fighting men, the criteria for award of the Medal of Honor changed. Originally awarded only to enlisted personnel for exemplary soldier-like qualities, eligibility was soon expanded to include commissioned officers. Over time, the addition of other awards elevated the importance of the Medal of Honor and narrowed the scope of its award to any person who, while a member of the armed forces of the United States, distinguishes themselves conspicuously by gallantry and intrepidity at the risk of their life above and beyond the call of duty.

Just as the criteria have changed with time, so has the actual design of the medal itself. Counting changes in ribbon design, there have been six different Army Medal of Honor designs, ten different Navy designs and one Air Force design.

Because of federal statutes, the different Medal of Honor designs for the Army, Navy, and Air Force are all referred to as the Medal of Honor. These different designs should not be officially referred to as the Army Medal of Honor, Navy Medal of Honor, or Air Force Medal of Honor. Instead, at least officially, they should be referred to as "Medal of Honor-Army design" and so on. However, as this reference book is directed at the collector of awards and decorations, these awards shall be referred to by their more common or unofficial names.

Medal of Honor - Army

The Army Medal of Honor was approved by President Lincoln on 12 July 1862. Originally intended to recognize "gallantry in action, and other soldier-like qualities" among enlisted personnel, the law was amended by an act of Congress on 3 March 1863 to include officers. This amendment also made the award of the Medal of Honor retroactive to the beginning of the Civil War. On 25 March 1863 the first Army Medal of Honor was issued. In the years since its inception the standards for the Army Medal of Honor have become more demanding so as to place it at the top of a Pyramid of Honor created by Congress in 1918.

On 9 July 1918 Congress passed an act which established criteria for the award of the Medal of Honor as being incontestable proof of acts of heroism so unique, and above and beyond the call of duty as to clearly distinguish the soldier from his comrades.

Additional amendments by Congress reserve the awarding of the Medal of Honor for the President and restrict its award to members of the United States Army who are citizens of the United States.

One of the most controversial figures to earn the Medal of Honor was Mary Edwards Walker. After graduating from medical school in 1855 she became one of the first female doctors in the country. At the outbreak of the Civil War she applied for a commission as an army surgeon but was turned down because of her sex. Undaunted, Mary Walker worked as a volunteer tending the wounded on the front lines during the battles of Fredericksburg and Chickamauga. Throughout her services Walker continued to attempt to gain a commission. After her capture while serving as an assistant surgeon for the 50th Ohio Infantry she spent four months in a Confederate prison. Following her release, she was given a contract at $100 a month plus back pay and continued to serve with the 52nd Ohio, although as a civilian.

Mary Walker wearing her Medal of Honor.

Mary Walker was presented her MoH in January 1866 by President Andrew Johnson. The Army Review Board of 1916-1917 recinded her MoH due to her civilian status. However, in 1978 her MoH was restored by President Carter.

Since its inception, there have been 2,348 Army Medals of Honor awarded. A breakdown by wars or campaigns is as follows:

CIVIL WAR	1861-1865	1,196
THE INDIAN CAMPAIGNS	1861-1898	423
SPANISH-AMERICAN WAR	1898	30
PHILIPPINES/SAMOA	1899-1933	70
THE BOXER REBELLION (CHINA)	1900	4
PEACETIME	1899-1916	1
WORLD WAR I	1914-1918	95

PEACETIME	1920-1940	2
WORLD WAR II	1941-1945	294
KOREAN WAR	1950-1953	78
VIETNAM WAR	1964-1973	155

Unlike most other decorations, the Army Medal of Honor, which was originally designed by Christian Schussel and engraved by Anthony C. Paquet, has undergone a number of changes since it was first approved by Congress on 12 July 1862.

The first change came on 2 May 1896 when Congress authorized a change in the ribbon design. The first ribbon was a variation of the American flag. The second ribbon was composed of a white vertical center stripe flanked on either side by a wide blue stripe and a wide red stripe. The third change was the adoption, by Congress, on 23 April 1904 of a totally new design by Major General George L. Gillespie. This third Medal Of Honor design incorporated a totally new medal pendant with a new ribbon design of 13 stars on a sky blue ribbon. The next change to the Army Medal of Honor was the incorporation of a small ring on the back of the brooch. This addition in 1917 allowed the medal to be worn from a cravat. Beginning in 1944 the Medal of Honor was permanently suspended from a neck cravat, similar to the design adopted by the Navy in 1943, which incorporated the field of 13 stars on a small pad sewn to the cravat immediately above the medal pendant. The sixth and final change was the adoption of a larger cravat pad on 25 July 1963.

Army Medal of Honor, Type I (1862-1896)

John Langton

Colonel M. Emmet Urell.

Captain Thomas Custer, a multiple Medal of Honor recipient.

State Historical Society of North Dakota

John Langton

From 1907 until 1947 the Air Force was a branch of the Army and personnel of the Army Air Corps received the Army type decoration. In all 46 airmen have won Army Medals of Honor; 4 during WW I, 38 during WW II, and 4 during the Korean War.

Captain George E. Albee.

John Langton

Sergeant Louis J. Bruner.

John Langton

James P. Miller.

John Langton

Sergeant James L. Carey.

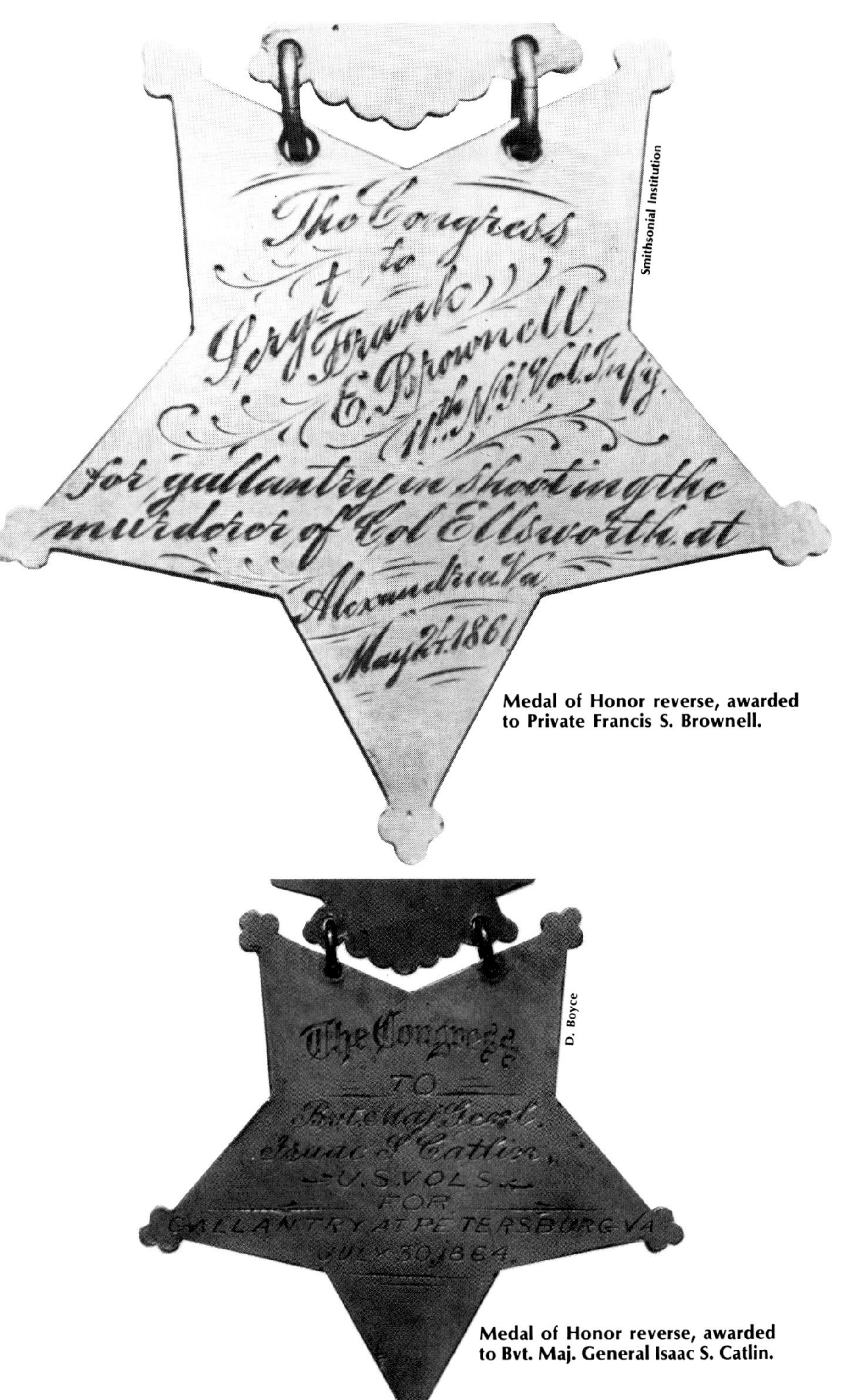

Smithsonian Institution

Medal of Honor reverse, awarded to Private Francis S. Brownell.

D. Boyce

Medal of Honor reverse, awarded to Bvt. Maj. General Isaac S. Catlin.

Paul Caraher, Jr.

Army Medal of Honor, Type I, and presentation case, awarded to Private George G. Creanor, Co. K, 27th Maine Volunteers. Given enmass, the Maine Volunteers recipients were later striken from the rolls.

Paul Caraher, Jr.

Note the recipient's name was affixed to the bottom of the presentation case.

Above: Army Medal of Honor, Type I, awarded to Private Kosoha, Indian Scout, for gallant conduct during campaigns and engagements with Apaches, winter of 1872-73.

R. Sullivan

General Frank D. Baldwin wearing both of his MoH awards, one for Peach Tree Creek, Georgia, on 12 July 1864, and one for McClellan's Creek, Texas, on 8 November 1874.

Army Medal of Honor, Type II (1896-1904), in a maroon "Tiffany" presentation case. Above right: Reverse of the medal presented to Hospital Steward William C. Bryan.

81987 A.G.O. Adjutant General's Office, June 18/97.

MEMORANDUM:

The Secretary of War has directed the issue of a medal of honor to Mr. William C. Bryan, of Evanston, Illinois, the medal to be engraved as follows:

THE CONGRESS

To

William C. Bryan,

Hospital Steward, U. S. Army,

for distinguished gallantry on Powder River, Wyoming Territory, March 17, 1876.

H. A. Kimfson

Assistant Adjutant General.

For the Supply Division,
War Department.

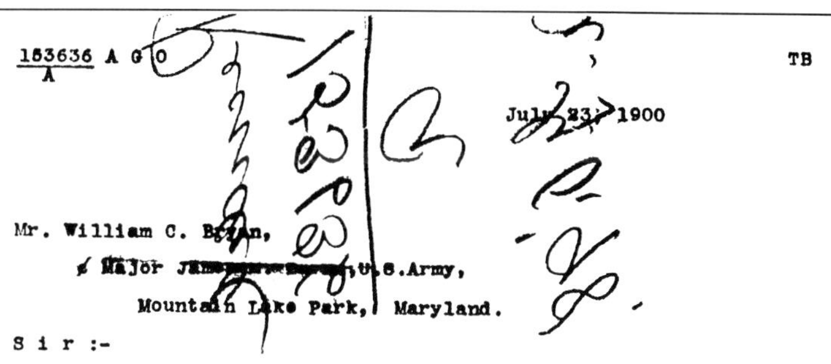

163636 A G O
A

TB

July 23, 1900

Mr. William C. Bryan,
Major [illegible], U.S.Army,
Mountain Lake Park, Maryland.

S i r :-

Inclosed herewith I forward you medal of honor (with bow-knot), awarded you"for distinguished gallantry on Powder River, Wyoming Territory, March 17, 1876", while serving as Hospital Steward, U.S. Army, together with your Army papers as requested in your indorsement of the 7th instant.

Very respectfully,

[signature]

Assistant Adjutant General.

With the introduction of the new 1904-style Medal of Honor, recipients had the option of retaining their old style or exchanging it for the new one, which Bryan did (see below).

CG

916949

WAR DEPARTMENT,
THE MILITARY SECRETARY'S OFFICE
WASHINGTON.

One inclosure.

September 28, 1904.

Mr. William C. Bryan,
521 Fourteenth Street, N. W.,
Washington, D. C.

Sir:

Referring to your request for information relative to the exchange of the Congressional medal of honor heretofore issued to you for the medal of new design, and the rosette, under the provisions of the act of Congress approved April 23, 1904, and War Department Circular No. 36 of August 22, 1904, I am directed by the Secretary of War to inform you that the inclosed blank form of application should be filled up, subscribed and attested in accordance with the instructions printed thereon and returned to this office.

The medals and bowknots of the old design will be destroyed as soon as the medals and rosettes of the new design shall have been issued to replace them.

Very respectfully,

[signature]

Assistant Adjutant General.

MILITARY SECRETARY'S OFFICE ... Secretary, War Department, Washington, D.C."

1034662

APPLICATION

FOR

MEDAL OF HONOR OF NEW DESIGN AND FOR ROSETTE,

under the provisions of the act of Congress approved April 23, 1904, and War Department Circular No. 36 of August 22, 1904,

and a. OF

William C. Bryan

FORMERLY A

Hospital Steward Regiment

of U.S.A.

Old medal 156 } July 12-05
mems supply dir }
medal sent Aug 18-05

(1.) The identity of the applicant must be established by the testimony of witnesses who have had a personal acquaintance with him for at least five years immediately preceding the date of their testimony. Officers or enlisted men of former company or regiment are preferable as identifying witnesses. If the witnesses are of that class, or were of the military service in any organization, the fact should be stated, with statement of rank, company and regiment.

(2.) To receive the consideration of the War Department any affidavit must bear the official seal of the officer administering the oath, if he uses an official seal.

(3.) If the oath is administered by an officer not using a seal, a certificate of his official capacity, made under seal by an officer authorized to make such certificate, must be furnished.

The principal object of the requirements in this blank form of application is to establish the identity of applicants, and thus prevent the issuance of the Medal to persons not entitled to receive it.

(a. s. o. 53)

1034662

WAR DEPARTMENT,

THE MILITARY SECRETARY'S OFFICE

WASHINGTON.

August 18, 1905.

Mr. William C. Bryan,

63 N Street, N.W.,

Washington, D. C.

Sir:

I am directed by the Acting Secretary of War to inform you that, in accordance with the act of Congress approved April 23, 1904, a medal of honor of new design has this day been issued to you, to replace the medal of honor awarded you June 15, 1899.

The medal, the rosette to be worn in lieu thereof, and the medal of honor ribbon have been forwarded to you under separate cover by registered mail. Please acknowledge their receipt.

Very respectfully,

Military Secretary.

Public resolution, approved on February 27, 1907, stated that holders of Medal of Honors were now not required to surrender their old style medals when requesting the new style. Both, however, could not be worn at the same time.

1034662

WAR DEPARTMENT,

THE ADJUTANT GENERAL'S OFFICE,

WASHINGTON.

March 29, 1907.

Mr. William C. Bryan.

416 Jackson Block,

Denver, Colorado.

Sir:

I am directed by the Acting Secretary of War to inform you that, pursuant to the provisions of the joint resolution of Congress approved February 27, 1907, the medal of honor and the bow-knot surrendered by you in order to receive the medal and the rosette provided for by the act of Congress approved April 23, 1904, have this day been returned to you by registered mail.

Please acknowledge their receipt.

Very respectfully,

Adjutant General.

John Langton

Major General Wm. R. Shafter.

John Langton

General Francis S. Dodge.

Colonel Alfred J. Sellers.
(worn with unofficial Type II neck cravat)

John Langton

Sergeant Wallace W. Johnson.

John Langton

Army MoH, Type II, obverse.

The Congress
to
Artf. Joseph A. Nolan,
Co. E. 45th Inf. U.S. Vols.
for gallantry near Labo
Luzon P.I.
May 29
1900.

Reverse.

Prototypes (left and center) of the Army Medal of Honor, Type III (1904-1913), and the accepted design (right).

National Archives

Sergeant Alvin York wearing a Type III (1904-1913).

Cased Medal of Honor, Army Type III.

Shortly after World War I, a redesign of the Army Medal of Honor was contemplated. Medalists saw the existing Type III MoH as finished on only one side with a cheap and insignificant appearance. Also, the star hung from two points which was considered not proper, and the green oak leaves on the star conflicted with the laurel leaves of the surrounding wreath and confused the general design. A new design by Paul Manship (right) was submitted to the Secretary of War in which the star hangs from one point. A head of Columbia, the emblem of liberty, replaced that of Minerva. A reverse was made to the medal, having for its chief feature a simple American shield. The new design was to strengthen the character of this highest award for American valor. It was, however, never adopted.

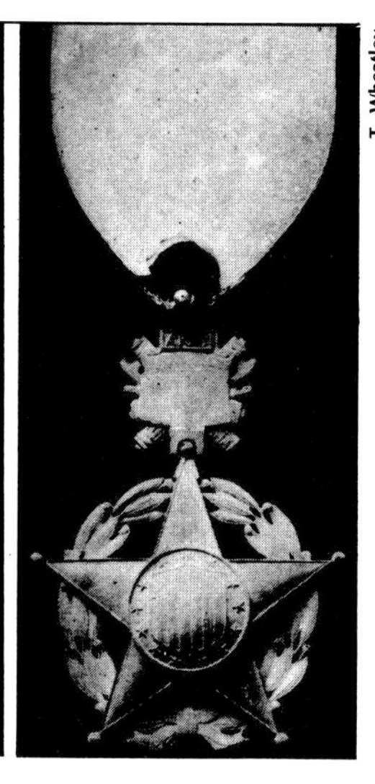

T. Wheatley

State Historical Society of North Dakota

Army Type III MoH awarded to Private Gotfred Jensen for action at San Miguel de Mayumo, Luzon, Philippine Islands, 13 May 1899.

Army Medal of Honor, Type IV (1913-1944). It differs from the Type III only in that it has a small ring soldered to the back of the brooch allowing the entire medal to be suspended from a cravat.

Legion of Valor

Sergeant Louis van Irsel.

Legion of Valor

Sergeant Philip C. Katz.

USMC Captain Louis Cukela received both the Army and Navy Medal of Honor for the same action in WWI. Note he is wearing the Army version around his neck and the Navy "Tiffany Cross" Medal of Honor on the left breast of his Marine Corps uniform. Photo dated October 1930.

Type IV with cravat.

Sergeant Anthony J. Carson wears his medal with cravat plus the ribbon pinned over his right breast pocket.

Legion of Valor

Legion of Valor

Legion of Valor

Major Richard I. Bong.

Sgt. Arthur Beyer earned the MoH on 15 January 1945, when, as a member of a tank destroyer battalion in the Battle of the Bulge, killed eight Germans, captured 18 more, and destroyed two machine guns near Arloncourt, Belgium.

Pfc. Lloyd C. Hawks was the first medical aid man in World War II to receive the MoH when he crawled into a hail of enemy fire on the Anzio beachhead in Italy in January 1944, to rescue three wounded comrades, though critically wounded himself.

Above: Sgt. John A. Pittman receives his MoH from President Truman for heroism near Kujangdong, Korea, on 26 November 1950. During a counterattack, although already wounded by mortar fragments, he threw himself on a grenade thrown in the midst of his squad, absorbing the burst with his body.

Right: Lt. Donald E. Rudolph was awarded his MoH for action on Luzon on 5 February 1945. He tore a hole in the roof of a Japanese pillbox with his bare hands and tossed a grenade inside. He then went on to destroy seven more while exposed to enemy fire.

Type V
(1944-1964)

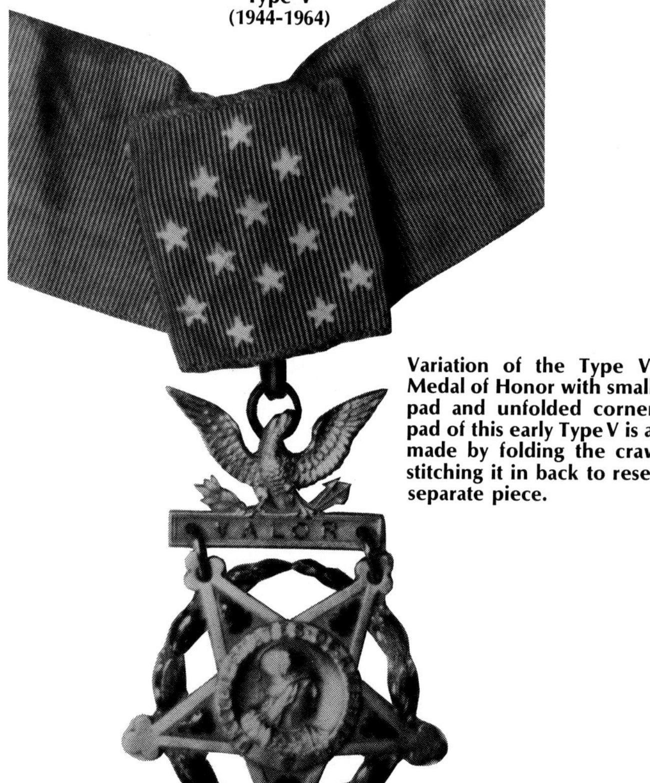

Variation of the Type V Army Medal of Honor with small cravat pad and unfolded corners. The pad of this early Type V is actually made by folding the cravat and stitching it in back to resemble a separate piece.

Type VI (1964-present), note larger pad size.

Ken Lazier

Major General Charles C. Rogers. Note: This photo shows the early practice of wearing oakleaves on the Air Medal as opposed to bronze numerals now used, and also the oakleaves on the National Defense Service Medal as apposed to the 3/16″ stars as currently used.

Medal of Honor - Navy

The Navy Medal of Honor came into being during the winter of 1861. During those months the Union was hard pressed for victories but there was no lack of gallantry among her fighting men. Senator Grimes, of Iowa, took the lead as chairman of the Senate Naval Committee and introduced a bill authorizing a Navy medal. The bill, signed by President Lincoln on 21 December 1861, established a Medal of Honor for enlisted men of the Navy and Marine Corps (officers in the Navy and Marine Corps were not eligible for the Medal of Honor until 1915). This was the first decoration authorized by Congress to be worn on the uniform.

Navy Medal of Honor, Type I, with first style ribbon and fouled anchor (1862-1882).

As soon as the Navy Medal of Honor was authorized, James Pollock, Director of the U.S. Mint was asked to submit designs for the medal. After several designs were submitted, the Navy approved one on 9 May 1862. By the time the final design was approved by the Secretary of the Navy, the Army design of the Medal of Honor had also been approved. As a result, the Secretary of War, Edwin Stanton, directed the medals be of the same design; the only difference between the Army and Navy medals was that the Army medal, instead of being attached to its ribbon by an anchor, was attached by means of the American Eagle symbol perched atop crossed cannons and cannon balls.

On 3 April 1863 the first Navy design Medal of Honor was awarded "in the name of the Congress of the United States". During its history, the Navy Medal of Honor design has been awarded only 1,039 times, less than half the number of Army awards. A breakdown by wars or time periods is as follows:

PERIOD	NAVY	MARINE CORPS	COAST GUARD
CIVIL WAR	310	17	-
KOREA - 1871	9	6	-
SPANISH-AMERICAN WAR	66	15	-
PHILIPPINES	9	9	-
BOXER REBELLION (CHINA)	22	33	-
SAMOA	5	0	-
MEXICAN CAMPAIGN	46	9	-

Navy Medal of Honor, Type I, awarded to Seaman John Andrews on board the U.S.S. Benicia for action against Korean forts on 9 and 10 June 1871.

HAITI - 1915	-	6	-
DOMINICAN REPUBLIC	-	3	-
WORLD WAR I	21	7	-
HAITI - 1919-1920	-	2	-
NICARAGUA - 1927-1933	-	2	-
PEACETIME - 1865-1940	177	5	-
WORLD WAR II	57	81	1
KOREAN WAR	7	42	-
VIETNAM WAR	15	57	-
TOTAL	744	294	1

John Langton

Sergeant John F. Mackie, USMC.

Of those 1,039 awards, one stands out as unique, not because of the circumstances of its award, but rather because it is the only award to a member of the United States Coast Guard.

On 27 September 1942, after making preliminary plans for the evacuation of nearly 500 beleaguered Marines from the beaches of Point Cruz on Guadalcanal, Petty Officer Douglas Munro, USCG, led a group of Higgins boats toward shore. Under constant fire from enemy machineguns on the island, Munro led a group of five boats onto the beach. As four of the craft loaded Marines for evacuation, he placed his craft, with its two machineguns further up the beach between the Japanese guns and the heavily loaded evacuation craft. While engaged in a valiant duel with the enemy guns and with the perilous task of evacuation nearly finished his craft was raked with automatic weapons fire and Munro was instantly killed. The crew of Munro's craft, two of whom were wounded, continued to provide covering fire until the last of the boats had cleared the beach.

During World War I Marines serving in France were under the command of the Army. Under these circumstances they were eligible for both the Army and the Navy Medal of Honor. In a place known as Belleau Wood, Gunnery Sergeant Charles Hoffman became the first Marine to be so recognized. Others recognized for acts of bravery and awarded both the Army and Navy Medal of Honor were Sgt. Louis Cukela, Sgt. Matej Kocak, Cpl. John Pruitt, and Pvt. John Kelly.

Like its counterpart, the Navy Medal of Honor has undergone many design changes, ten in all, since its inception. These ten design changes often parallel changes in the Army ribbon design. The first design change

Type II with first style ribbon and unfouled anchor (1882-1904).

John Davis, USN, wearing his Medal of Honor and Good Conduct Medal with an unusually long ribbon.

John Langton

John Langton

Above: Thomas C. Cooney, Chief Machinist, earned his Medal of Honor for actions during the battle at Cardenas, Cuba, 11 May 1898. Cooney is wearing the Navy Type II Medal of Honor and also the Sampson Medal with the "USS Winslow" top bar.

John Langton

William Halford, USN.

was the elimination of the rope fouling the anchor from which the pendant was suspended. The Navy Type III Medal of Honor is the same as the Type II but uses the second Army style ribbon. The Navy Type IV medal is the same as the Type II and III but uses the new style ribbon adopted for the Army Type III Medal of Honor. The

Men of the "U.S.S. Marblehead" wearing the Navy Medal of Honor for action on 11 May 1898. Two boatloads of her crew worked for 80 minutes under fire from infantry trenches ashore cutting the underwater telegraph cable leading from Cienfuegos, Cuba. Three men from the

Navy Type V Medal of Honor (1913-1942) was the first Navy style to be suspended from a cravat. This style uses the standard pendant suspended from the unfouled anchor, and is attached directly to the cravat by a large loop.

In 1919 a decision was made by the Secretary of the Navy to adopt separate

R. Sullivan

ship later earned the MoH for a mine-clearing operation at the approaches to Caimanera, Guantanamo Bay, Cuba, during the period of 26 and 27 July, which resulted in the clearing of 27 contact mines.

John Langton

John S. Lawson, USN, wears the Type III Navy Medal of Honor (1896-1904). Note ribbon colors. He earned his MoH on 5 August 1864 while serving on board the USS Hartford during the attack on Fort Morgan.

Type IV Navy Medal of Honor (1904-1913).

Type III Navy Medal of Honor (1896-1904).

Type V Navy Medal of Honor (1913-1942).

T. Wheatley

Above: Shortly after World War I the Navy Department requested that a new design for the Navy Congressional Medal of Honor be submitted. Paul Manship and James E. Fraser developed a design based on the compass, as it appeared on ancient maps. A model was prepared but rejected since it was un-American in appearance and resembled a French or Belgian medal.

Legion of Valor

Lieutenant John Davis.

Legion of Valor

Rear Admiral William A. Moffett.

designs for the Navy Medal of Honor to distinguish those medals awarded for combat heroism from those awarded for non-combat heroism. The new Medal of Honor also came to be known as the *Tiffany Cross* because it was designed by Tiffany & Company of New York. The first style of the *Tiffany Cross* is known as the Navy Type VI and is different from the Type VII in that the suspension ring is soldered directly to the top arm of the cross on the Type VII and the Type VI has a small finger cast to the top arm of the cross to which the suspension ring is attached.

The Navy continued to award the Type V Medal of Honor for noncombat heroism during the period from 1919-1942 when it awarded the *Tiffany Cross* for combat heroism.

On 7 August 1942 Congress discontinued use of the *Tiffany Cross* and returned to a single Medal of Honor. The design of the 1942 Navy Medal of Honor is referred to by collectors as the Navy Type VIII. This Medal of Honor uses the standard planchet and anchor suspender but the cravat has the addition of a narrow cravat pad with unfolded corners. The Navy Type VIII was used for only one year and was replaced by the Type IX (1944-1964) which is identical to the Type VIII except the corners of the cravat pad are folded. The final design change to the Navy Medal of Honor resulted in the Type X (1964-present). The Navy Type X uses the same large cravat pad found on the Army Type VI Medal of Honor.

Multiple Medal of Honor recipient, Sergeant-Major Daniel J. Daly. Daly won his first MoH as a private while serving during the battle of Peking, China, 14 August 1900, and his second MoH in Haiti, while serving in the 15th Company of Marines as a Gunnery-Sergeant on 22 October 1915.

Legion of Valor

Multiple recipient, Lt. John McCloy. Note both pendants are suspended from the same ribbon.

The specimen shown was presented to Boatswain's Mate 2nd Class John Otto Siegel.

Type VI (1919-1927). Note the suspension ring is soldered to a small finger cast on the cross.

Type VIII (1942-1943). Note the cravat pad is constructed by folding and stitching the actual cravat.

Navy "Tiffany Cross" Medal of Honor (also known as the new Navy Medal of Honor "Gold Cross" or as Navy type VII (1927-1942)). The suspension ring is soldered to the top arm of the cross.

Above and right: Navy Medal of Honor, Type VIII (1942-1943), awarded to PFC Henry Gurke, USMC. He was attached to the 3rd Marine Raider Battalion and killed in action against Japanese forces in the Soloman Islands on 9 November 1943.

State Historical Society of North Dakota

Major Archie Van Winkle, USMC, wearing Type IX cravat with small pad (1944-1964).

Type X with large cravat pad (1964-present).

Medal of Honor - Air Force

The current and only style of the Air Force Medal of Honor was authorized by Congress on 6 July 1960. The medal was designed by the U.S. Army Institute of Heraldry and replaced the Army design of the Medal of Honor as the award given to members of the Air Force after 1 November 1965.

As with all other Medals of Honor, the Air Force design of the Medal of Honor is awarded for acts of personal bravery or self-sacrifice during combat that are so conspicuous as to clearly distinguish the individual for gallantry and intrepidity above his comrads.

The Vietman War is the only conflict in which Air Force personnel have been awarded the new Air Force design of the Medal of Honor. In that war only 12 airmen were awarded the Air Force Medal of Honor.

The Air Force design Medal of Honor is a gold finished five point star 2 inches in diameter, with one point down. Its points are tipped with trefoils and joined by a green enamel laurel wreath. In the center is the likeness of the head of the Statue of Liberty surrounded by an amulet of 34 stars representing the number of states in 1862. The star is suspended from a gold design of thunderbolts which is attached to a horizontal bar bearing the word "Valor".

Obverse.

Major Bernard F. Fisher was the first recipient of the Air Force Medal of Honor. His citation, awarded for action on 10 March 1966 for conspicuous gallantry and intrepidity at the risk of his own life above and beyond the call of duty, reads that on that date, the special forces camp at A Shau was under attack by 2,000 North Vietnamese Army regulars. Hostile troops had positioned themselves between the air strip and the camp. Other hostile troops had surrounded the camp and were continuously raking it with automatic weapons fire from the surrounding hills. The tops of the 1,500-foot hills were obscured by an 800 foot ceiling, limiting aircraft maneuverability and forcing pilots to operate within the range of hostile gun positions, which often were able to fire down on attacking aircraft. During the battle, Maj. Fisher observed a fellow airman crash land on the battle-torn airstrip. In the belief that the pilot was seriously injured and in imminent danger of capture, Maj. Fisher announced his intention to land on the airstrip to effect a rescue. Although aware of the extreme danger and likely failure of such an attempt, he elected to continue. Directing his own air cover, he landed his aircraft and taxied almost the full length of the runway, which was littered with battle debris and parts of an exploded aircraft. While effecting a rescue of the downed pilot, heavy ground fire was observed, with 19 bullets striking his aircraft. In the face of the withering ground fire, he applied power and gained enough speed to lift-off at the overrun of the airstrip. Maj. Fisher's profound concern for his fellow airman, and at the risk of his life above and beyond the call of duty, are in the highest traditions of the U.S. Air Force and reflect great credit upon himself and the Armed Forces of his country.

D. Boyce

Reverse.

Major Bernard F. Fisher (left) and Lt. Col. (then Major) Dafford W. Myers after the dramatic rescue at A Shau that won Major Fisher the Air Force Medal of Honor.

Captain Gerold O. Young wearing the Air Force Medal of Honor.

Brevet Medal

From 1861 until 1915 the Navy and Marine Corps had few means of rewarding the heroism of officers other than the Brevet Commission (the Navy Medal of Honor being restricted to enlisted personnel until 1915).

Following the Civil War, with its flagrant abuse of the Brevet Commission by the Army, Congress passed an act on 15 July 1870 which forbid the wearing of an officer's Brevet rank. This essentially sounded the death knell for the Brevet Commission. The last Marine Corps Brevet Commissions were given for the Boxer Rebellion in 1900.

Because there was no medal or special badge to signify the commission, holders of a Brevet after the Civil War received only the Brevet certificate as a sign of their heroism in battle. Following World War I, with the introduction of many new awards, the distinction of the Brevet Commission was often over shadowed or unnoticed.

Major General John A. Lejenne, Commandant of the Marine Corps from 1920 until 1929, believed that those officers recognized by a Brevet Commission should also receive an appropriate medal to serve as a distinction for their bravery and heroism.

In a directive dated 7 June 1921, the Secretary of the Navy authorized the Brevet Medal to be awarded to those Marine Corps officers whose Brevet Commissions were confirmed by the Senate.

Obverse and reverse of Percival C. Pope's Brevet Medal (courtesy Navy Memorial Museum).

At the time of its authorization, the Brevet Medal was awarded to twenty officers. This select fraternity represented the elite of the Marine Corps and are the only recipients of this rare award.

The original order for the Brevet Medal specified that it should be worn immediately after the campaign medal for which the Brevet Commission was earned. Shortly after its inception, the Brevet Medal was elevated to a position immediately following the Distinguished Service Medal, thus elevating its importance to rank as a decoration. The status of the Brevet Medal was further enhanced on 15 April 1929, when it was elevated to a position immediately following the Medal of Honor in the Navy's Pyramid of Honor.

Several factors combine to make the Brevet Medal one of the rarest of all U.S. decorations. First, the Brevet Medal was not awarded posthumously and second, by 1921 the Brevet Commission had lapsed into disuse with the introduction of the Navy Cross and the broadening of the award criteria for the Navy Medal of Honor in 1915, to include officers. In reality, the Brevet Medal was obsolete from the day it was first awarded.

Right: 1973 strike, the last official striking of the medal. Note silkscreened stars on ribbon.

John Lelle

R. Fischer

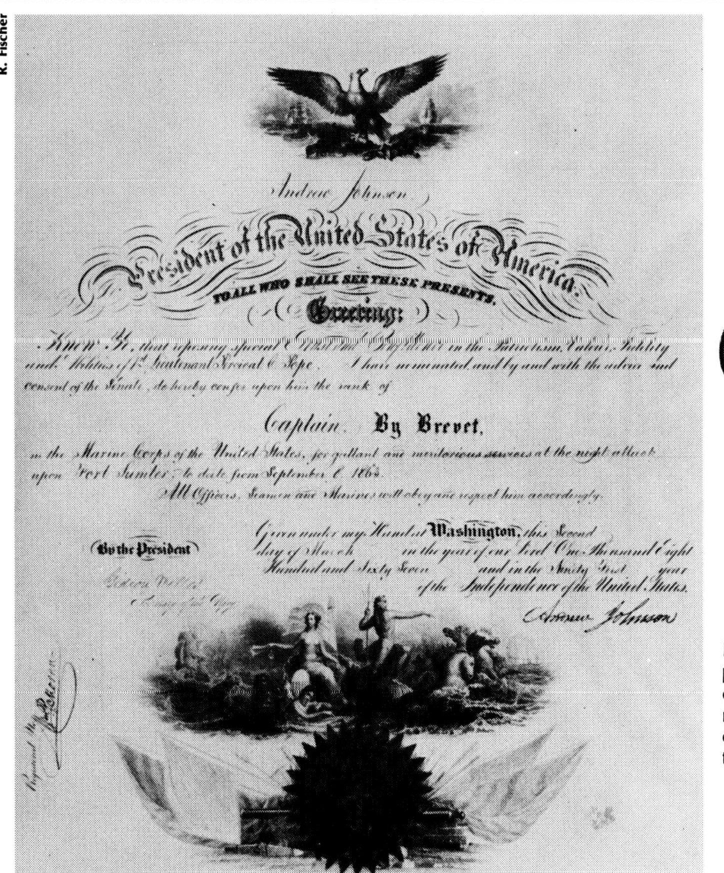
Andrew Johnson,

President of the United States of America,

To all who shall see these presents, Greeting:

Know Ye, that reposing special Trust and Confidence in the Patriotism, Valour, Fidelity and Abilities of 1st Lieutenant Percival C. Pope, I have nominated and by and with the advice and consent of the Senate, do hereby confer upon him the rank of

Captain By Brevet,

in the Marine Corps of the United States, for gallant and meritorious services at the night attack upon Fort Sumter, to date from September [illegible] 1863.

All Officers, Seamen and Marines will obey and respect him accordingly.

Given under my Hand at Washington, this Second day of March in the year of our Lord One Thousand Eight Hundred and Sixty Seven and in the Ninety First year of the Independence of the United States.

By the President

Andrew Johnson

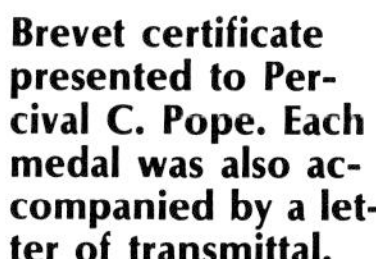

Brevet certificate presented to Percival C. Pope. Each medal was also accompanied by a letter of transmittal.

Distinguished Service Cross - Army

The Army Distinguished Service Cross was established by an Act of Congress on 9 July 1918 and amended by an Act of 25 July 1963. The Distinguished Service Cross was instituted to recognize any person, who while serving in any capacity with the Army, distinguishes himself by extraordinary heroism in combat.

The degree of heroism, while of a lesser degree than would justify the Medal of Honor, must be so extraordinary as to clearly distinguish the soldier from his comrads.

The Distinguished Service Cross also stands as this nation's highest award for valor for civilians serving with the Army. Award of the Distinguished Service Cross may be made to civilians serving in any capacity with the Armed Forces during wartime only. Circumstances for such an award must be clearly of an exceptional nature and the award must be approved by the President of the United States.

Current style DSC.

National Archives

Major General B.B. Buck, 3rd Div.

The idea for a medal to recognize distinguished service which did not warrant the Medal of Honor was first proposed by Major General Leonard Wood. In July 1911, while serving as the Army's Chief of Staff, MG Wood brought his idea to the attention of Secretary of War Henry L. Stimson. The proposal for an award which could be presented to both officers and enlisted personnel met with little support.

With the United States' entry into World War I, the idea was again brought up, this time, by General John J. Pershing in November 1917. The result of General Pershing's proposal was the creation of a Distinguished Service Medal and a Distinguished Service Cross.

Since the inception of the Distinguished Service Cross, there have been approximately 13,500 awarded. A breakdown of DSC awards by war, or action, is as follows:

*INDIAN WARS	6
*SPANISH-AMERICAN WAR	30
*PHILIPPINE INSURECTION	60
*BOXER REBELLION	6
*MEXICAN BORDER SERVICE	5
^*MISCELLEANOUS	97
WORLD WAR I	6,481
WORLD WAR II	4,696
KOREA	805
VIETNAM	1,100

* Retroactive awards

^ Includes conversions of Certificate of Merit

Note: There were no awards of the DSC for operations in Grenada, Panama, or Desert Shield/Storm.

Oakleave cluster indicates an additional award. Large size used until 1932.

Early DSC awarded to Pvt. Edward W. Burton, Machine Gun Co., 364th Inf. Rgt., 91st Div., for action near Eclisfontaine on 4 October 1918.

As with all military awards, there are some interesting facts associated with the history of the Distinguished Service Cross. Famous World War I ace Eddie Rickenbacker recieved the award with seven oakleaf branches. The Pattons are perhaps the most famous father and son recipients. General George S. Patton Jr. won the Distinguished Service Cross in both WW I and WW II, while his son won two Distinguished Service Crosses for heroism in Vietnam.

During WW I, members of the Marine Corps serving in Europe were under the command of the Army and they were awarded Army decorations for valor. One such example occurred on 5 October 1918, in a shell cratered field near St. Etienne, France, when a young U.S. Marine Corps 2nd Lieutenant raced forward of his regiment's trench line 800 meters. Under constant shellfire, 2Lt Cecil Widdifield picked his way through the craters and debris to rescue a wounded comrade. The heroics of this young Marine also earned him the Navy Cross for the same action.

Another example of DSC action occurred a half century later, during the Vietnam War. When a terrorist grenade landed in their midst, U.S. Army Captain Eugene Banks threw himself on the grenade. When it failed to explode immediately, Cpt. Banks shouted a warning, jumped to his feet and threw the grenade in the direction of the terrorist. The grenade exploded without any injury. Captain Banks' quick reactions saved the lives of at least 11 of his men and earned him the DSC.

First style American-made DSC, numbered "78."

The Army Distinguished Service Cross was originally designed by Lieutenant Andre Smith and the first 100 serially numbered crosses were of his design. However, production was quickly modified to a slightly more simple design, submitted by Captain Aymar Embury. Interestingly, both Lt. Smith and Cpt. Embury were both assigned to B Company, 40th Engineers, Camouflage Section, which was located at Camp American University in Washington D.C.

The first 102 Distinguished Service Crosses incorporated the use of oak leaves to ornament the arms of the cross as well as a diamond shaped plaque behind the eagle and the words E Pluribus Unum on the scroll below the eagle. The wings of the eagle were also smaller and less upswept on the original design.

In addition to the two distinctly different American made variants, two French made copies of the DSC also exist. The first French variety is similar to the first style American but the overall size of the planchet is smaller. The First Style American made DSC measures 45.9mm x 53.0mm while the First Style French made DSC measures 40.8mm x 47.7mm. In addition to the size difference, the words "For Valor" on the reverse of the planchet are proportionally smaller on the French variety than on the American variety.

The second type American and French varieties of the DSC are also similar in design, with the French planchet being slightly smaller than the American made planchet. The measurements are 46.3mm x 51.5mm for the American made second style DSC and 42.2mm x 49.2mm for the French made second style DSC. In addition to the size difference, the inscription on the obverse of the scroll reads "E Pluribus Unum" on the French made type and "For Valor" on the American made second type Distinguished Service Cross.

D. Boyce

First style French-made DSC. Note size of "For Valor" on the reverse.

At left is an original design of the cross. The initial production run was done at the United States Mint in Philadelphia and consisted of 102 pieces. They are numbered "1" to "100" on the right side rim of the lower arm. Two were unnumbered. Upon examination it was determined a design change was necessary, but due to General Pershing's immediate needs the first style crosses were shipped to France for presentation. They were to be replaced upon delivery of the new or current design. Similar crosses were struck in France shortly after the end of World War I, and were unnumbered. These French versions are smaller and thinner than the US design.

Left: Second style, American made DSC, with "For Valor" on the obverse scroll. Note the first style oak "branch" on ribbon. Below: Second style, French made DSC.

George Petersen

Note French style of suspension on the DSC.

Lowell Jackson

Second style, French made DSC, with "E Pluribus Unum" on the obverse scroll.

T. Wheatley

Note thinness of the second style, French made DSC.

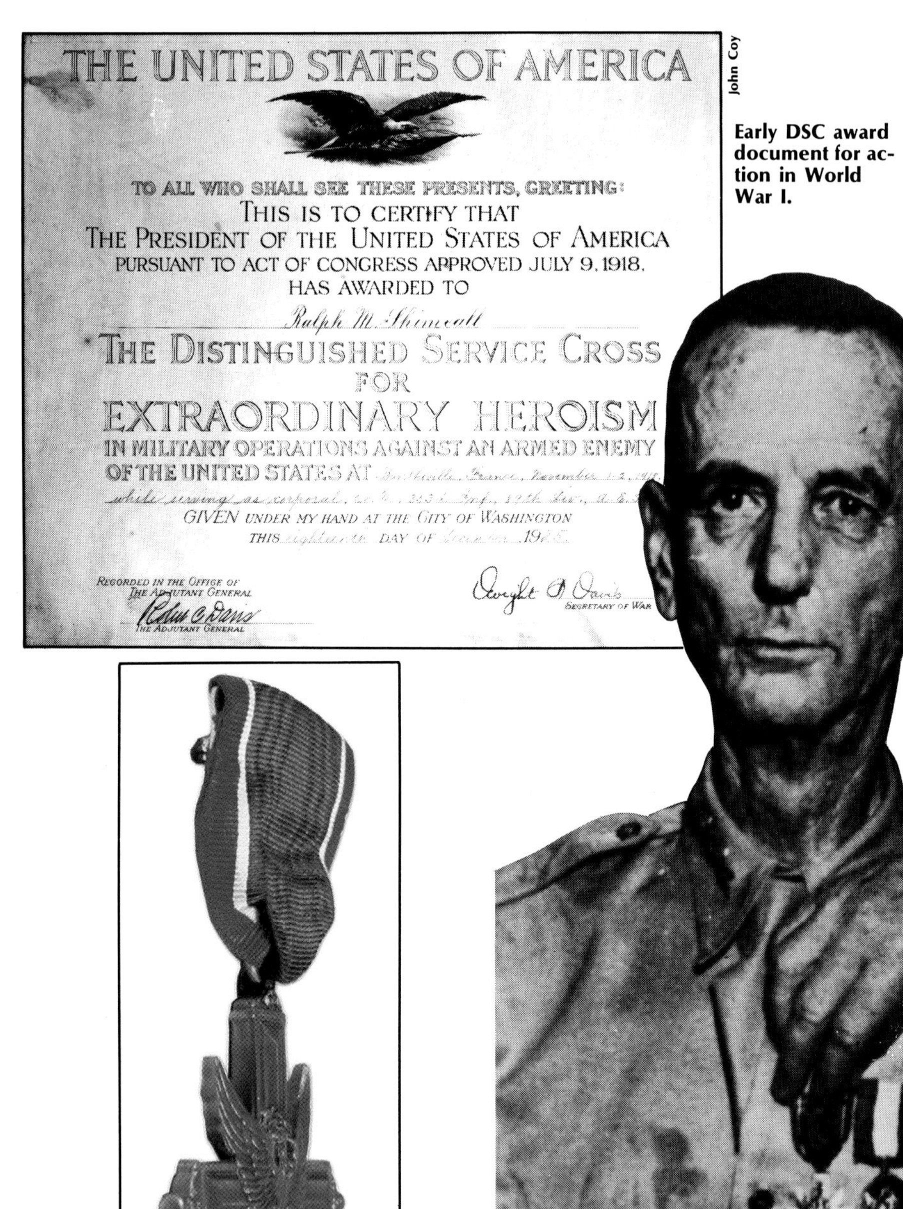

THE UNITED STATES OF AMERICA

TO ALL WHO SHALL SEE THESE PRESENTS, GREETING:

THIS IS TO CERTIFY THAT

THE PRESIDENT OF THE UNITED STATES OF AMERICA

PURSUANT TO ACT OF CONGRESS APPROVED JULY 9, 1918,

HAS AWARDED TO

Ralph M. Shimeall

THE DISTINGUISHED SERVICE CROSS

FOR

EXTRAORDINARY HEROISM

IN MILITARY OPERATIONS AGAINST AN ARMED ENEMY

OF THE UNITED STATES AT *[illegible], France, November 1-2, 1918,*

while serving as corporal, [illegible]

GIVEN UNDER MY HAND AT THE CITY OF WASHINGTON

THIS *[illegible]* DAY OF *[illegible]* 192*[illegible]*

RECORDED IN THE OFFICE OF THE ADJUTANT GENERAL

[signature]

THE ADJUTANT GENERAL

Dwight F. Davis

SECRETARY OF WAR

John Coy

Early DSC award document for action in World War I.

Ken Lazier

Early version of the current style DSC with serial number "10553."

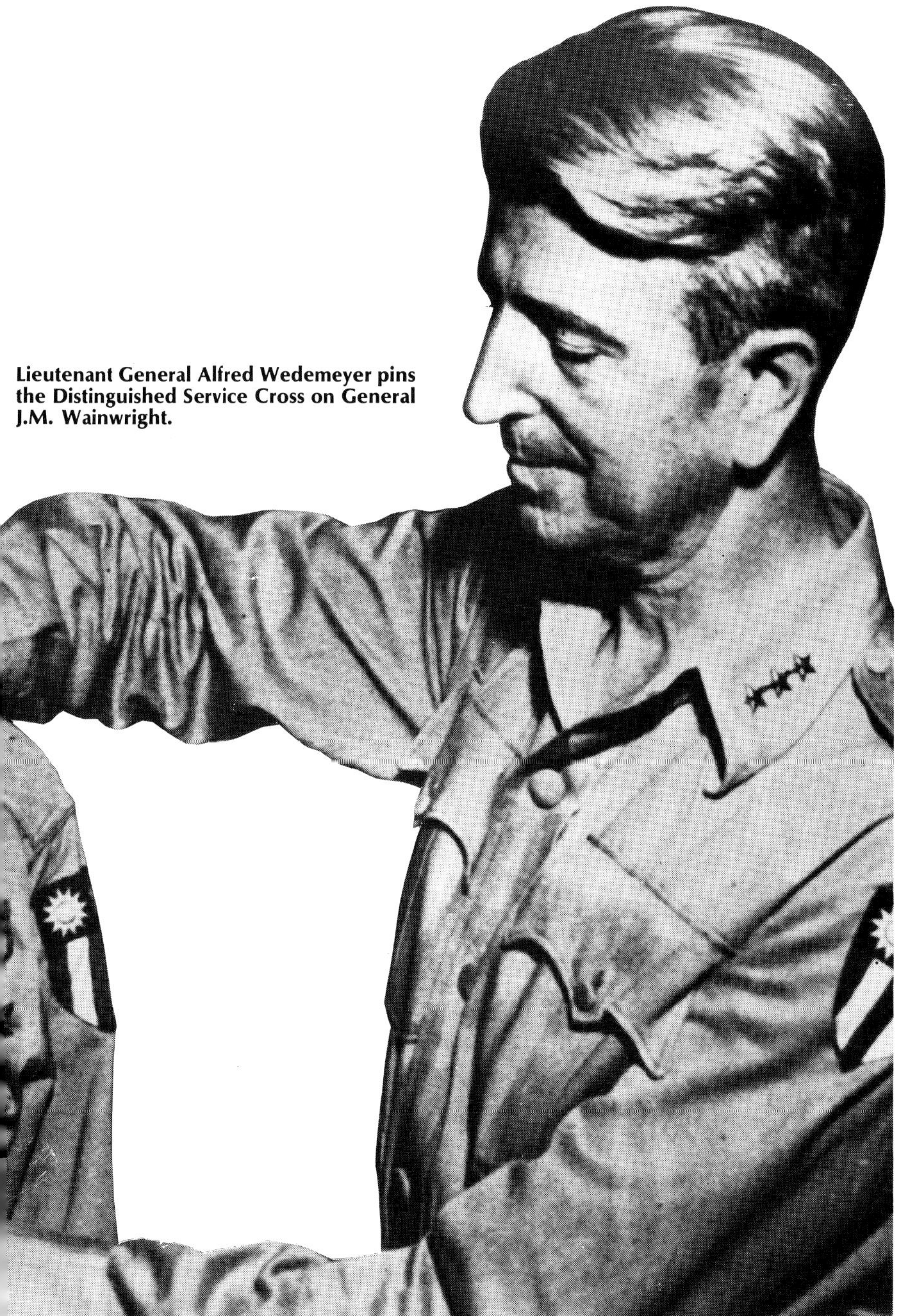

Lieutenant General Alfred Wedemeyer pins the Distinguished Service Cross on General J.M. Wainwright.

Navy Cross

The Navy Cross was created by an Act of Congress on 4 February 1919. The orginal wording of the Act, which was established by Public Law 253, outlined the requirements for award of the Navy Cross as "...extraordinary heroism or distinguished service in the line of his profession, such heroism or distinguished service not being sufficient to justify a Medal of Honor or Distinguished Service Medal." This wording of the law created a problem for commanders in that the same law restricted award of the Distinguished Service Medal to meritorious service to the Government in a duty of great responsibility.

By its wording the law seemed to indicate that the Navy Cross was inferior in order of precedence to the Navy DSM. However, only the Navy Cross could be awarded for acts of heroism. This confusion was cleared up by the passage of Public Law 702 on 7

Ken Lazier

Admiral William D. Leahy.

August 1942. This Act of Congress restricted the Navy Cross to acts of combat heroism and placed it above the Navy DSM in precedence. Under current regulations the Navy Cross is intended to recognize acts of heroism by any person serving in any capacity with the naval service of the United States.

The Navy Cross, or Distinguished Service Cross as it was called at the time of its design by James E. Fraser, appeared shortly after World War I. The first issue was of three-piece construction (front and back discs separately attached). Also, the ribbon was approximately ⅛″ wider than the later issue and had a narrower white center stripe.

Type I Navy Cross awarded to Captain Frank Whitehead, USMC. Note the 1 9/16″ wide original ribbon with 1/8″ narrow center stripe.

The so-called "Black Widow" Navy Cross is an early World War II issue with oxidized finish.

R. Fischer

Original ribbon (1 9/16″) with a 3/8″ gold star.

Post-1948 ribbon (1 3/8″) with a 5/16″ gold star.

Navy Cross second award devices.

R. Sullivan

Captain Lamar R. Leahy.

During World War II, early awards of the Navy Cross had a very dark finish caused by oxidation of the metal used for the pendant. Because of the unique finish and the fact that many of the initial World War II awards were posthumous, the "legend" of the "Black Widow" Cross began. While the "Black Widow" variety of the Navy Cross is rare, there is no indication in official Navy records that such a version was designed to indicate a posthumous award.

Richard Mundhenk

Sergei Kurzenov, fighter pilot of the Northern Fleet and Hero of the Soviet Union, was awarded the Navy Cross on 20 October 1944. Note he wears the "Black Widow" version.

Air Force Cross

Award of the Air Force Cross was made effective 1 November 1965 by 10 U.S.C. 8742. The Air Force Cross is intended to recognize the valor of any individual serving in any capacity, civilian or military, with the Air Force. To merit award of the Air Force Cross, the individual must distinguish himself by extraordinary heroism in connection with military operations against an armed enemy. The degree of heroism, while of a lesser degree than that required for award of the Medal of Honor must never the less be so notable and involved the risk of life so extraordinary as to set the individual apart from his comrads.

Up until its organization as a separate branch of the service, the Air Force was a part of the U.S. Army and as such its members received the Army designs of the Medal of Honor, Distinguished Service Cross, and Distinguished Service Medal. Even with the establishment of the Air Force as a separate branch of the service on 18 September 1947, members of the Air Force continued to receive Army decorations throughout the 1950s. After the Korean war efforts were begun to select different designs to parallel the Army Medal of Honor, Distinguished Service Cross, and the Distinguished Service Medal for award to Air Force personnel.

State Historical Society of North Dakota

Upon his return from Vietnam this Air Force colonel is officially awarded all of his earned decorations at one ceremony.

A 1956 Air Staff Study began the ground work for the creation of new Air Force medals to replace the Army design awards. On 6 July 1960 the Congress of the United States acted to establish distinctive awards for heroism and valor for the fledgling United States Air Force.

The Air Force Cross ranks second in the Air Force Pyramid of Honor and was designed by Eleanor Cox, Awards Division, Headquarters United States Air Force. To date, less than 200 Air Force Crosses have been awarded.

The Distinguished Service Medal represents our nation's highest award for meritorious service or achievement. All the major branches of our country's Armed Forces have their own distinctive design for the Distinguished Service Medal. However, all are officially referred to as simply the Distinguished Service Medal. Within the collector community the different designs are referred to by branch of service; such as Navy Distinguished Service Medal or Army Distinguished Service Medal. While such names are unofficial, except for the main headings, these names will be used in this reference.

General March wears the Army Distinguished Service Medal.

K. Lazier

Defense Distinguished Service Medal

The Defense Distinguished Service Medal (DDSM) was established by Executive Order 11545, on 9 July 1970. The award is presented at the sole discretion of the Secretary of Defense to any military officer of the United States who is assigned to joint staffs or other joint activities of the Department of Defense and who distinguishes himself by exceptionally meritorious service in a position of unique and great responsibility.

The Defense Distinguished Service Medal takes precedence over the Distinguished Service medals of the individual branches of service. It is not intended for award to any individual for a period of service for which a military department's Distinguished Service Medal or similar decoration has been awarded.

Award of the DDSM is limited to individuals who have made significant contributions to DoD operations. The first award of the Defense Distinguished Service Medal was to Chairman of the Joint Chiefs of Staff, General Earle G. Wheeler. General Wheeler was presented his DDSM by Secretary of Defense Melvin R. Laird. Past recipients also include Alexander Haig Jr., Elmo Zumwalt and Creighton Abrams.

Distinguished Service Medal - Army

The Army Distinguished Service Medal (DSM) was established by Presidential Order on 2 January 1918 and confirmed by Congress on 9 July 1918. However the roots of the DSM can be traced to a report, submitted on 5 July 1911 by MG Leonard Wood, to Secretary of War Henry L. Stimson. In his report MG Wood suggested that the Army extablish a medal for distinguished service. General Wood (who erned the Medal of Honor in 1886 during the Indian Campaigns) felt that the lack of a lesser award had led to the awarding of the Medal of Honor to officers whose service did not really justify the award.

The Secretary of War was interested in the proposal and on 7 August 1912 asked the Quartermaster General to come up with an appropriate design for a distinguished service medal. However no further progress

The above, early DSM is serial numbered "99" and was issued to General McCaw, a World War I surgeon who became Assistant Surgeon General of the Army in the late 1920s.

was made on selecting a design until after the United States entered the First World War.

The First Distinguished Service Medals were presented on 21 October 1918, and were awarded to: Marshall Foch (France), Marshall Joffre (France), General Petain (France), Field Marshall Sir Douglas Haig (England), Lieutenant General Diaz (Italy), Lieutenant General Gillian (Belgium), and General John J. Pershing (United States).

Ken Lazier

A. Rohloff

Army DSM awarded to Clinton A. Pierce, #2507. He was commanding officer of the 26th Cavalry when it covered the retreat to Bataan. His wife received the medal in 1942 while he was a POW. Pierce survived 3½ years in Japanese captivity.

General Eisenhower pins the Army Distinguished Service Medal on Major General Doolittle's shirt.

Catherine G. Sinnott graduated from the St. Thomas School of Nursing in Nashville, Tennessee in 1910. Answering the call to duty when World War I broke out, she enlisted in the Army Nurse Corps, serving in France as part of the American Expeditionary Force.

As a Second Lieutenant she became one of only twenty-two Army Nurses to earn the DSM for service during the war. General Order 9, 1923, which includes her DSM citation, reads in part: "...as Chief Nurse of the Nurses' Concentration Camp at Savenay, France, she managed the affairs of nearly 1000 nurses with exceptional tact, industry, and good judgement." In addition to her duties at the embarcation camp at Savenay, she served at Camp Hospital 28 near Nevers, France. The "Meuse-Argonne" and "Defensive Sector" battle clasps on her World War I Victory Medal indicate that she also saw her share of combat.

2LT Sinnott's care and concern for America's soldiers led her to continue her service in the U.S. Army. LTC Catherine G. Sinnott died in 1946, while still on active duty, and is buried at the Presidio in San Francisco.

Catherine Sinnott's DSM, serial numbered "1958."

Under current regulations the Distinguished Service Medal is awarded to any person who, while serving in any capacity with the United States Army, shall distinguish himself by exceptionally meritorious service to the government on a duty of great responsibility. For service during peacetime the term duty of great responsibility applies to a narrower range of positions than in actual time of war and requires evidence of conspicuously significant achievement.

Awards of the DSM may be made to persons other than members of the Armed Forces for wartime service only, under exceptional circumstances, and only with the approval of the President. The Army Distinguished Service Medal was designed by Captain Aymar Embury.

Above right: The Army Distinguished Service Medal is awarded by the Secretary of War, Newton D. Baker, to men for their part in winning World War I.

Right: Major General Keith L. Ware, MoH, is awarded his DSM by Secretary of the Army, Stanley R. Resor (21 November 1967).

Dept. of the Army

Distinguished Service Medal - Navy

The Navy Distinguished Service Medal was authorized by Congress on 4 February 1919 and made retroactive to 6 April 1917. The Navy Distinguished Service Medal ranks third in order of precedence in the Navy Pyramid of Honor and is designed to recognize any person serving in any capacity with the U.S. Navy who distinguishes himself by exceptionally meritorious service to the government in a duty of great responsibility.

Two basic styles of Navy Distinguished Service Medals exist; the current style, which has been awarded since 1919, and an earlier style. Few examples of the early style Navy Distinguished Service Medal have been encountered, and those medals which have been observed have unprefixed rim numbers below 100.

This early style of the Navy DSM features a circular planchet. Centered on the planchet is a large fouled anchor. Behind the anchor is an ocean scene with waves and a setting sun on the left horizon. At the bottom right of the planchet is a spray of laurel. The words "Distinguished Service" surmount the entire scene. This style DSM features an elaborate suspension bar in the form of an eagle with outstreached wings and a scroll bearing the date "1917-18". Many first style Navy DSMs were awarded to flag officers of friendly foreign navies for WWI service. Fifteen were known to be awarded to officers of the Imperial Japanese Navy, among them #83 to Vice Admiral Ide and #61 to Admiral Kato. The ribbon for the early style DSM is the same style as that used on the current medal.

In general the Distinguished Service Medal is awarded only to those officers in principal commands at sea or in the field whose service contributes materially to the success of a major command or project. The Navy Distinguished Service Medal was designed by Paul Manship.

The first style Navy Distinguished Service Medal.

T. Wheatley

The original design for the Navy DSM (above) was initially accepted, but later the acceptance was withdrawn. With an alteration to the suspension it was resubmitted and accepted, resulting in the style illustrated at left.

Major General Logan Feland, USMC, wears an early Navy DSM.

Distinguished Service Medal - Air Force

The Air Force Distinguished Service Medal was authorized by Congress on 6 July 1960, to replace the Army Distinguished Service Medal which had previously been awarded to Air Force personnel. However, delays in selecting a final design and drafting the appropriate Air Force regulations postponed adoption of the new Air Force DSM until 1 November 1965.

The award of the Air Force Distinguished Service Medal follows the same guidelines as for the Army Distinguished Service Medal in that the conditions for which the award is made must involve exceptionally meritorious service to the government in a duty of great responsibility. The Air Force Distinguished Service Medal was designed by the U.S. Army Institute of Heraldry.

Members of the Air Force who were awarded the original Distinguished Service Medal design prior to 1 November 1965 continue to wear the original (Army) award. Those who receive the DSM after that date are awarded the new Air Force design. In addition, personnel who are awarded a second DSM after 1 November 1965 wear both the original and the new design, with the new design taking precedence (in wear only) over the old design.

Distinguished Service Medal - Coast Guard

The United States Coast Guard was established by an Act of Congress on 28 January 1915, which consolidated the former Revenue Cutter Service and the Life-Saving Services under the control of the Treasury Department. Later, on 1 July 1939 control of the Bureau of Lighthouses which was formerly under the Department of Commerce was passed to the Coast Guard.

The Coast Guard Distinguished Service Medal was established in 1962 to replace the Navy Distinguished Service Medal which, up to that time, had been awarded to Coast Guard personnel. The award criteria remained the same as for the Navy Distinguished Service Medal. However, the adoption of the Coast Guard Distinguished Service Medal, with its portrait of the "Massachusetts" under full sail on the obverse of the planchet, gave members of the Coast Guard a distinctive award to recognize the exceptionally meritorious service of its members.

Certificate Of Merit

The Certificate of Merit was originally established by Congress on 3 March 1847. This certificate, signed by the President, was initially awarded only to privates, for gallantry in action or meritorious service. In 1854 eligibility was expanded to include sergeants.

The first conflict in which soldiers were eligible for award of the Certificate of Merit was the Mexican War. Certificates issued for the Mexican War were engraved by J.V.N. Throop of Washington D.C. and measured 9 3/4 inches by 15 3/4 inches. In all 539 Certificates of Merit were awarded for the Mexican War.

In the years following the Mexican War commanders continued to recommend soldiers for Certificates of Merit. However, the War Department continued to turn down these recommendations because it had interpreted the Act of 3 March 1847 to restrict award to the Mexican War period.

Certificate of Merit.

Last awarded Certificate of Merit "No. 357" to Paul Scalletta.

D. Boyce

D. Boyce

ARMY OF THE UNITED STATES.

Certificate of Merit.

Know all whom it may concern, That PRIVATE Michael Dailey of Company H. of the 3d Regiment of Artillery having DISTINGUISHED HIMSELF in the SERVICE of the United States, on the twelfth day of September 1847 in the Battle of San Antonio, on the recommendation of Bvt Major Sherman, the Commanding Officer of his Regiment. I do hereby award to the said PRIVATE Michael Dailey this Certificate of Merit, which under the provision of the 17th section of the Act [illegible]

Given under my hand at the City of Washington this first day of March in the year of our Lord one thousand eight hundred and fifty one.

Geo. Conrad
Secretary of War

Millard Fillmore
President of the United States

An original Certificate of Merit for the Mexican War.

In 1874 the laws of the United States were codefied in what is known as the Revised Statutes. Section 1216 of the Revised Statutes provided field commanders with the ammunition they needed to persuade Secretary of War George McCrary to reinstitute the Certificate of Merit. In War Department General Orders 110 dated 6 December 1877 eligibility for the Ceritificate of Merit was reinstituted and backdated to 22 June 1874, the date the Revised Statutes were issued.

On 11 January 1905 a medal was authorized to be worn by previous recipients of the Certificate of Merit. The Certificate of Merit was discontinued by Act of Congress on 9 July 1918, following introduction of the DSM and Distinguished Service Cross. A total of 1,206 Certificates of Merit were issued, the last being to Cpl. Paul Scaletta, Co. B, 159th Infantry on 5 May 1918 for saving the lives of four fellow soldiers from drowning at Ocean Beach, California.

T. Wheatley

Certificate of Merit "No. 234" issued to Paul Glad as a lifesaving award.

Silver Star

The history of the Silver Star can be traced back to 9 July 1918 when Congress approved the Citation Star which was promulgated in War Department Bulletin No. 43 of that same year. The Citation Star was a star measuring 3/16 of an inch in diameter that was attached to the suspension ribbon of the campaign medal for which the individual was cited, in official orders, for gallantry in action.

The Citation Star was not presented in a formal ceremony. It was left up to the individual soldier to verify his eligibility and affix the star to his campaign medal.

In its present form, the Silver Star was approved by the Secretary of War on 16 July 1932. Before soldiers could wear the new Silver Star, they were required to present a copy of the orders which made them eligible for the old Citation Star. The criteria for the award of the Silver Star were amended by an act of Congress on 15 December 1942 to include civilians serving with the armed forces. While the degree of heroism required for the award is of a lesser degree than that required for the Medal of Honor or Distinguished Service Cross it must nevertheless be performed with marked distinction. The Silver Star ranks third in the Congressional Pyramid of Honor for combat bravery.

D. Boyce

Above: John P. Goodman's WWI Victory Medal with silver Citation Star. Goodman was given his Silver Star (right) after presenting a copy of orders making him eligible for the Citation Star for gallantry in action at Belleau Bois, France, 27-28 October 1918.

World War II Navy issue Silver Star (note thickness). See Bronze Star section for comparison photos.

Ed Anderson

A Silver Star marked "BBB Co/Phil.," manufactured by the Bailey, Banks & Biddle firm.

Below: Marine PFC Jack W. Kelso is presented with the Silver Star by his commanding officer, Colonel Thomas C. Moore, Jr. Korea, 24 September 1952.

The ironies of war! Silver Stars awarded to Sgt. Archie W. Vaughn (left) and PFC. Otis W. Vaughn (right), twin brothers killed in action in France on 11 September 1944. These Ipava, Illinois boys were squad leader and gunner of a machinegun section who held their position against a severe enemy counterattack, while their company was withdrawing. They remained at their position until one gun jammed and the ammunition supply of the other became exhausted. (Also see Purple Heart section of this book.)

John Coy

John Coy

John Coy

HEADQUARTERS

104TH (*Timberwolf*) INFANTRY DIVISION

SILVER STAR MEDAL CITATION

Technical Sergeant Paul Shinkevich (Then Staff Sergeant) (Army Serial Number 36 437 207), Infantry, Company D, 413th Infantry, United States Army, is awarded the Silver Star Medal for gallantry in action in Germany on 23 February 1945. After returning to friendly shores to administer first aid to a wounded man, Sergeant Shinkevich led a second successful assault crossing over a fast-flowing river. When rifle elements failed to appear at a rallying point, he tenaciously and aggressively led his section forward in the face of withering enemy fire. So brilliantly did he employ his men as rifle troops that they overran and captured the objective with a minimum of loss. Sergeant Shinkevich's singular gallantry and superb leadership contributed materially to the success of a difficult mission and exemplified the finest traditions of the American soldier and combat leader. Entered military service from Kewanee, Illinois.

SEAL

BY COMMAND OF THE DIVISION COMMANDER

GENERAL ORDERS No.153 1945

AG 104th Inf. Div. 12-5-45 (1000)

A non-regulation Silver Star citation issued by the 104th Infantry Division. During WWII the official War Department certificate was not always available so some organizations created their own.

Defense Superior Service Medal

The Defense Superior Service Medal was established by Executive Order 11904 on 6 February 1976. This award is presented by the Secretary of Defense to any member of the Armed Forces of the United States who has rendered superior meritorious service in a position of significant responsibility with the Office of the Secretary of Defense, the Organization of the Joint Chiefs of Staff, a specified or unified command, a Defense agency, or such other joint activity as may be designated by the Secretary of Defense.

Below: Chairman of the Joint Chiefs of Staff, Colin Powell, presents the Defense Superior Service Medal to Admiral James R. Hogg.

Ken Lazier

Legion of Merit

The Legion of Merit came into being on 20 July 1942 as a result of Public Law 671. Executive Order 9260 in October of that same year and War Department Bulletin 54 the following month completed the necessary steps to establish the Legion of Merit as the nations second highest award for service or achievement.

The Legion of Merit was developed to serve several distinct purposes which came about as the nation became more deeply involved in the Second World War. President Roosevelt and the War Department wanted an award to honor foreign military personnel without diluting the importance of the Distinguished Service Medal. There was also an increasing need to recognize members of the United States Armed Forces for a wide range of outstanding contributions to America's increasing war effort. To serve such a variety of needs the Legion of Merit was created in four degrees: Chief Commander, Commander, Officer and Legionnaire. On the recommendation of the War Department, award criteria were later modified to award only the Legionnaire degree to members of the U.S. Armed Forces.

Chief Commander, the highest degree of the Legion of Merit was intended for heads of foreign militaries. Among the first awarded was to Generalissimo Chiang Kai-shek of China. The Chief commander grade of the Legion of Merit is in the form of a three-inch diameter breast star, worn on the left side. The service ribbon for the Chief Commander degree features a gold miniature of the pendant set on a gold-colored bar engraved with two rows of stylized arrow feathers.

In the degree of Commander, the LoM was first awarded to Brigadier General Amaro Soares Bittencourt of Brazil. The Commander degree of the Legion of Merit is suspended from a neck ribbon of the same color and design as the suspension ribbons for both the Officer and Legionnaire grades. The service ribbon for the Commander degree features a silver minature of the pen-

National Archives

Colonel General Alexander v. Govbat, commander of the Soviet 3rd Army is decorated by Lieutenant General William Simpson with the Commander Grade of the Legion of Merit (28 May 1945).

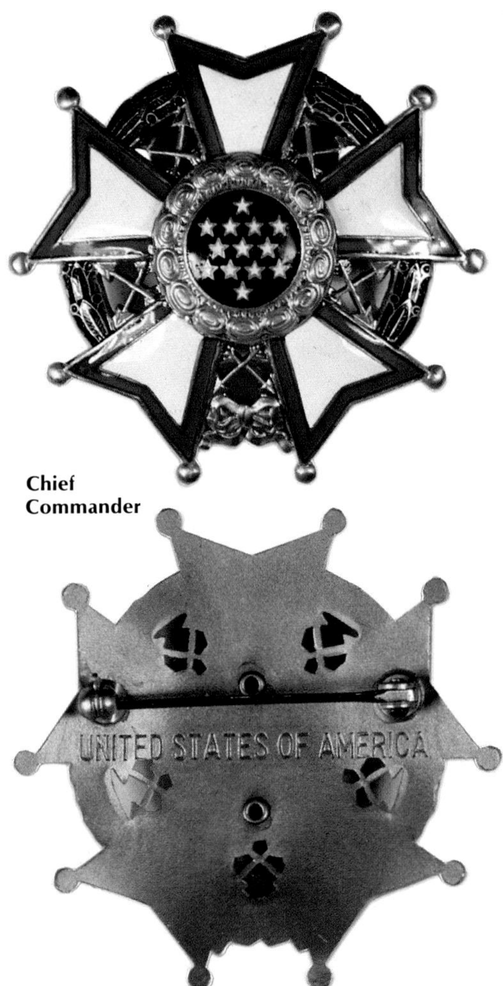

Chief Commander

dant set on a silver bar with two rows of stylized arrow feathers.

For award to field grade officers of friendly foreign nations the Officer degree was established. First to receive it was Col. Meijer of the Royal Netherlands Army. The Officer degree of the Legion of Merit is identical to the Legionnaire grade with the addition of an 11/16th inch gold miniature of the planchet attached to the suspension ribbon and a similiar 5/16th inch device attached to the service ribbon.

The Fourth degree, the Legionnaire, is conferred upon foreign service members and U.S. personnel. The first award was to Lt. Ann A. Bernatitus. Lt. Bernatitus, a U.S. Navy nurse, won her LoM for heroic performance of duty on Bataan and Corregidor.

During World War II and the Korean War use of the Legion of Merit changed very little. During this time the majority of awards were given for achievement. Following the Korean War it became apparent that changes in the criteria for award would be necessary if the Legion of Merit was to continue as an effective means of recognizing peacetime service. As a result, award criteria were changed in 1957 to allow the medal to be presented for exceptionally meritorious service in a succession of difficult and increasingly important duty positions.

Following the end of the war in Vietnam, the Legion of Merit has become the award of choice to recognize field grade officers and Sergeants Major upon their retirement. Currently, awards of the LoM for retirement comprise three fourths of all the medal's presentations.

Despite the changes in the award criteria, the Legion of Merit continues as the nation's second highest peacetime award, behind only the Distinguished Service medals of the various branches of the Armed Forces. It remains one of the most prestigious awards a soldier, sailor, airman or marine can earn. Those who wear it are recognized as having made a significant contribution to the mission of the Armed Forces of the United States.

The first 800 of the Commander's grade were serial numbered on the reverse of the suspension ring. Illustrated is #184.

A. Menke

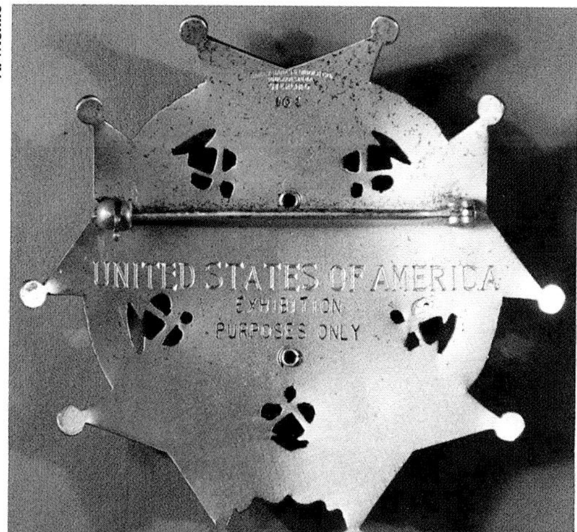

First production style Legion of Merit Chief Commander made by BB & B. Numbers 1 through 101 were serial numbered and maker marked at the 12 o'clock position on the reverse.

Obverse of serial number 200.

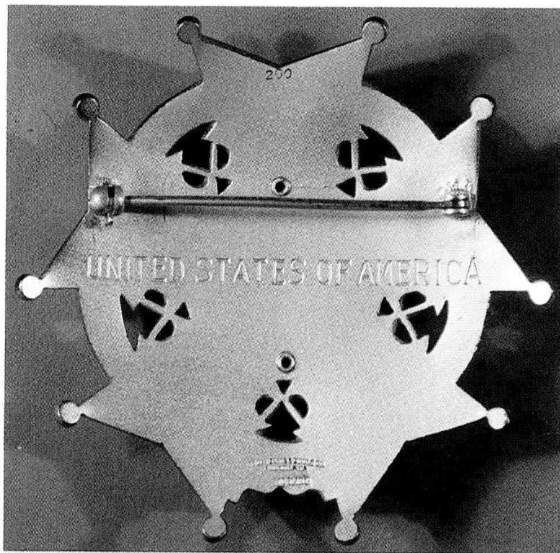

Numbers 102 through 200 were serial numbered at the 12 o'clock position but maker marked at the 6 o'clock position.

J. Mull

Commander

A. Menke

LoM Commander grade presented to British general Sir Brian Robertson.

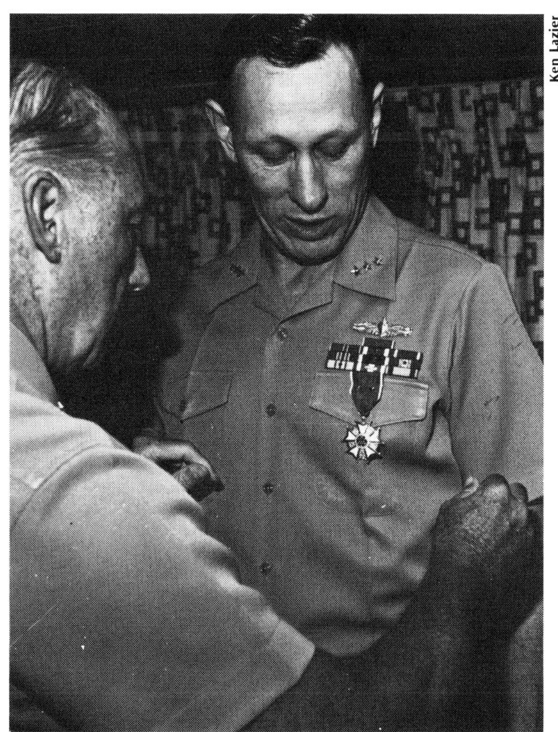

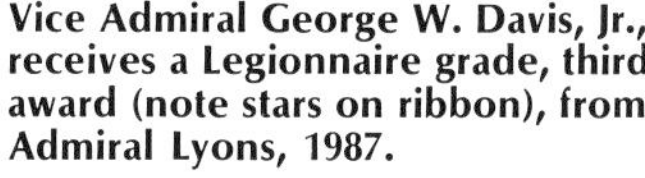

Vice Admiral George W. Davis, Jr., receives a Legionnaire grade, third award (note stars on ribbon), from Admiral Lyons, 1987.

Original example of the first LoM Officer grade commissioned by General Hurd (note three white enamel stars on suspension loop). Only six examples of each LoM grade were commissioned by General Hurd and produced by George Meele of Bailey, Banks and Biddle. Note the "United States of America" is engraved on the reverse of these examples rather than being in raised letters as on production versions. Also, note the enamel work on the reverse. The LoM Legionnaire grade has two white enamel stars on the suspension loop.

LoM Legionnaire grade awarded to Major Edward J. Flemming, US Army Chemical Corps, has a WWII wrap brooch. The LoM awarded to Howard A. York, USMC, has a Korean War issue slot brooch.

LoM Legionnaire grade, #3446, awarded to Colonel Randolph P. Williams, US Army Air Corps, is a posthumous award for WWII service as Chief of Staff of the 19th Tactical Air Command.

A. Menke

Officer

Commander

Chief Commander

Devices for the Legion of Merit ribbon.

BB & B LoM Legionnaire grade, #70, with pierced arrows.

D. Boyce

Early issues of the Officer and Legionnaire grade were serial numbered on the brooch. Serial numbers were assigned to each contract issued by the government, but not all manufacturers actually stamped the assigned numbers on their product, thus, there were breaks in the observed number sequences.

D. Boyce

Legionnaire.

Above: Captain Jesse Hicks Carter, USN, receives the Legion of Merit on 13 June 1945 for exceptionally meritorious conduct as commander of a destroyer squadron.

Distinguished Flying Cross

The Distinguished Flying Cross (DFC) was established by Act of Congress on 2 July 1926. From that time until the outbreak of World War II the DFC was used primarily to recognize aviation pioneers.

During the late 1920s, when aviation feats captured the imagination of the country in much the same way as the space race did half a century later, the Distinguished Flying Cross was awarded to some of the most famous names in aviation history. The first DFC issued was awarded to Captain Charles Lindbergh for his solo flight across the the Atlantic in 1927. That same year Commander Richard E. Byrd became the first member of the U.S. Navy to earn a DFC. Byrd was award his DFC for the 1926 flight to the North Pole. When Amelia Earhart was awarded her DFC she became the only female civilian to be honored with the Distinguished Flying Cross, as the award criteria for the DFC were amended on 1 March 1927 to restrict its award to members of the Armed Forces.

Current award criteria for the Distinguished Flying Cross clearly delineate the circumstances under which award may be made. The DFC is awarded to any person who, while serving in any capacity with the Armed Forces of the United States, distinguishes himself by heroism or extraordinary achievement while participating in aerial flight. Simply establishing a new aerial record does not necessarily qualify as an extraordinary achievement.

When the Distinguished Flying Cross is awarded for heroism the Combat Distinguishing Device, or bronze "V" device is worn on the suspension ribbon and the ribbon bar by members of the Navy and Marine Corps only.

Richard Mundhenk

Captain Edward M. O'Donnell, Jr., 121st Liaison Squadron attached to the Fifth Air Force (6 June 1945).

DFC awarded to W.N. Davis, USAAC, for action against Japanese forces in the battle of the Aleutian Islands, serial number "194."

DFC awarded to Lt. (jg) Frederick R. Horgan posthumously. The Navy was traditional in its presentation engraving. Navy issue DFCs were thicker and had a frosted finish (see comparisons at right). Also note wrap brooch.

DFC awarded to William L. DeVinney, USMC, for action in Korea during the Chosin Reservoir operation.

Navy issue.

Army Air Corps issue.

Soldier's Medal

Shortly after the end of the First World War, the War Department identified the need to recognize soldiers for acts of bravery during peacetime. Unlike the Navy, which awarded the Medal of Honor for acts of bravery above and beyond the call of duty during peacetime, the Army restricted award of the MoH to wartime acts of valor.

As a result, the Soldier's Medal was established by Act of Congress on 2 July 1926, for award to any member of the Armed Forces of the United States or of a friendly foreign nation who, while serving in any capacity with the Army of the United States, distinguishes himself by heroism not involving actual conflict with an enemy.

The degree of heroism, while of a lesser degree than that required for the Silver Star, must be above the call of duty and clearly set the individual apart from his comrads. Award of the Soldier's Medal is not intended to be made solely on the basis of having saved a life. For acts of lifesaving, or attempted lifesaving, it is required that the action be performed at the risk of one's own life.

The Soldier's Medal is given for a wide range of heroic acts. However, inherent in all approved cases is the element of risk of life to the person performing the act and to other persons. Many recommendations are down-graded to an Army Commendation Medal when this element of risk is not present.

Another test for award of the Soldier's Medal is whether the individual voluntarily placed himself in a position of great risk, or whether he was performing a duty which, although dangerous, was the reason for his presence at the scene.

The most common example that illustrates this distinction involves soldiers who serve as instructors on hand grenade ranges. Whcn a traincc mishandlcs a livc grcnadc on the throwing range, instructors have often saved the trainee's life by picking up the grenade and throwing it out of the throwing pit, throwing the trainee and themselves out of the pit or otherwise protected the trainee. Because the instructors are expected to take these actions and they are trained to react in this manner, their actions usually do not meet the criteria for award of the Soldier's Medal.

As a result of the high standards of heroism required for an award of the Soldier's Medal, it is little wonder that a 1984 Concepts Analysis Agency study on U.S. Army awards showed that soldiers who have won the Soldier's Medal prize it above many combat decorations.

A. Menke

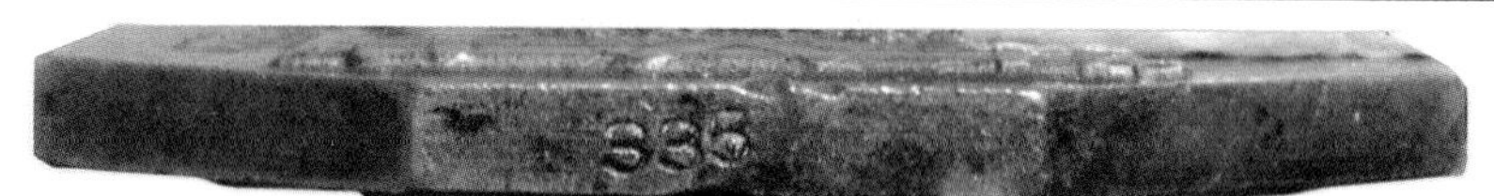

Soldier's Medal, #335, awarded to John R. Welker in 1939 for a lifesaving act.

Navy and Marine Corps Medal

The Navy and Marine Corps Medal was established on 7 August 1942 to recognize noncombat heroism and meritorious service. Awarded along the same lines as the Soldier's Medal, the Navy and Marine Corps Medal is a highly prized symbol of courage and devotion to duty.

The most famous recipient of the Navy and Marine Corps Medal was then Lt. (jg) John F. Kennedy. Kennedy was awarded the medal for his efforts in rescuing fellow crewmen after the sinking of his boat, the P.T. 109. His citation reads, in part, "His outstanding courage, endurance, and leadership contributed to the saving of several lives."

A. Menke

A. Rohloff

US Mint production Navy and Marine Corps Medal, privately engraved. It was awarded to a crew member of the "USS Hammond" which was sunk at Midway while trying to assist in the saving of the "USS Yorktown."

Airman's Medal

The Airman's Medal was established by Congress on 6 July 1960 to take the place of the Soldier's Medal which, up until that time, had been awarded to Air Force personnel. Award criteria for the Airman's Medal are the same as for the Soldier's Medal.

The pendant design for the Airman's Medal was originally selected for the Air Force Distinguished Service Medal. The pendant itself is unique for an American military decoration in that it is circular rather than being a distinctive shape as are other U.S. military decorations.

Coast Guard Medal

The Coast Guard Medal was first authorized by 14 U.S.C. 493 in 1949. However the medal was not struck until 1958 and the first awards of the Coast Guard Medal occurred that same year.

Like its counterparts for the other branches of the service, the Coast Guard Medal specifically recognizes noncombat acts of bravery which are of a voluntary nature and far exceed normal expectations. These acts must have placed the individual in great personal danger to qualify for award of the Coast Guard Medal. Coast Guard regulations equate the degree of heroism involved as being equal to the standards for the Gold Lifesaving Medal for civilians or military personnel in a liberty or leave status.

Bronze Star Medal

In a memorandum for President Roosevelt dated 3 February 1944, General George C. Marshall wrote; "The fact that the ground troops, infantry in particular, lead miserable lives of extreme discomfort and are the ones who must close in personal combat with the enemy, makes the maintenance of their morale of great importance." General Marshall went on to plead for the establishment of a Bronze Star decoration to fill this need.

The following day, President Roosevelt signed Executive Order 9419 authorizing the Bronze Star Medal to any person who, while serving in the armed forces of the United States on or after 7 December 1941, distinguishes himself by heroic or meritorious achievement or service, not involving aerial flight in connection with military operations against an armed enemy.

In 1947 award of the Bronze Star Medal was authorized retroactively to soldiers who had received the Combat Infantryman Badge or the Combat Medical Badge during the war. The basis for doing this was that these badges were awarded to soldiers who had borne the hardships which had initially been the basis for General Marshall's recommendation for the adoption of the Bronze Star Medal.

Bronze Star with "V" device for valor in combat.

SFC Gary D. Crossman, 10th SF is presented the Bronze Star by Col. Vernon E. Greene, 10th SFGA commander, October 1969.

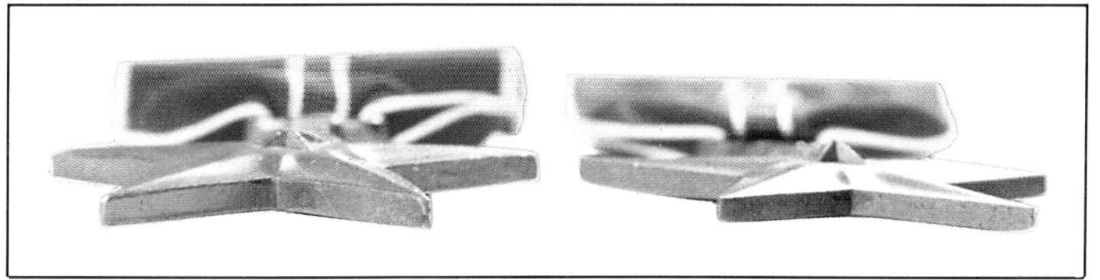

The Bronze Star at left is a WWII US Navy example. It is distinguished by its thickness and wrap brooch. The medal at right is a WWII Army Bronze Star with a slot brooch. The medal is noticably thinner than the Navy version.

The "V" device, called the Combat Distinguishing Device by Naval regulations, distinguishes the Bronze Star award for heriosm in combat against an armed enemy. The "V" device was first authorized in December 1945 and is not authorized for World War II conversions of the CIB or CMB.

Navy issue Bronze Star with wrap Brooch.

Dept. of the Army

This Special Forces Lieutenant has just been awarded the Bronze Star and Purple Heart.

Purple Heart

The Purple Heart was revived by presidential order in War Department Orders No. 3, dated 3 February 1932. The announcement of this new Purple Heart medal coincided with the 200th anniversary of George Washington's birthday. General George Washington established the original heart-shaped Badge for Military Merit on 7 August 1782. Only three NCOs are known to have received the original award which was a patch of purple cloth with a lace or binding border.

John Langton

Original Purple Heart.

The initial orders authorizing the Purple Heart applied only to Army personnel. Award of the Purple Heart to Navy and Marine Corps personnel would not be authorized until President Roosevelt signed Executive Order No. 9227 on 3 December 1942.

The Purple Heart was revived as a result of a War Department study and review of all military decorations. The Purple Heart was initially awarded to those soldiers and civilian personnel who were wounded in the First World War and earlier wars. However, from 7 December 1941 until 2 September 1942, the Army also awarded the Purple Heart for meritorious service. Following the adoption of the Legion of Merit, the Army discontinued this policy. Although it was not mandatory, Army personnel who were awarded the Purple Heart for meritorious service were encouraged to apply for a more appropriate award. Since that time the Purple Heart has been used solely to recognize wounds received in combat.

When the award was instituted, the War Department never intended that every war injury be recognized with a Purple Heart. The wound for which the award is made must be a direct result of enemy action, must have required treatment by a medical officer and the medical treatment must be recorded as part of official record.

D. Boyce

1st Lieut. John P. Goodman's Purple Heart for a leg wound received while directing flanking rifle fire on an advancing enemy at Belleau Bois, France, 28 October 1918.

With the increasing use of the US Armed Forces in a peace-keeping role, award of the Purple Heart was modified on 28 March 1973 to include service members who are wounded in military operations outside the of the United States as part of a peace-keeping force. Executive Order 12464, dated 23 February 1984 also authorized award of the Purple Heart to service members and civilian military employees who are wounded as a result of an international terrorist attack. To qualify, the attack must be identified with a recognized international terrorist group and the injuries received must be consistent with the requirements for war related wounds.

When the Purple Heart was initially introduced, it ranked below all other decorations for valor or meritorious service. However, in 1985 Congress elevated it to a position immediately behind the Bronze Star. This change occurred because of a widely held belief among members of the armed forces that wounds received in combat deserved more recognition than honors for peacetime achievement.

The original U.S. Army contracts for the Purple Heart specified that the heart-shaped purple center be enameled. During World War II the government let two contracts for numbered medals. These contracts were awarded on 1 July 1942 to Rex Products for numbers 100,000 to 400,000 and to the Robbins Company for numbers from 400,001 to 600,000. Both Rex Products and the Robbins Co. soon fell behind in their production due to the time consuming enamelling process. Rex Products produced about 124,000 enamelled Purple Hearts before switching to a lacquering technique for about 90,000 medals and finally converted to the polished phenolic center. Robbins Co. produced less than 90,000 medals with enamelled centers before switching directly to polished phenolic centers.

Unlike the Army, the Navy relied on the U.S. Mint to supply its demand for medals.

Elizabeth Will, who assisted in the design of both the Purple Heart and the Distinguished Flying Cross.

The Navy's initial requisition from the Mint called for 135,000 medals with split brooches. Due to the need to conserve metals such as copper and brass, the initial order of Purple Hearts from the Mint were manufactured from sterling silver and gold

A Rex Products Purple Heart serial numbered "327493."

plated. Due to the need to use such valuable metals, the Navy's first order of Purple Hearts cost just over $2.56 each as compared to about $1.76 each for those the Army had ordered with gold plated bronze pendants. Subsequent Navy requisitions for Purple Hearts which were given to the Mint in 1944 and 1945 were not subject to restrictions on the use of copper and brass and were able to be produced in bronze at a much lower cost.

Of interest to the collector is the fact that the Navy Purple Hearts were not numbered. However, due to the Mint's inability to meet its promised production schedule, the Navy submitted a request to the Army in early 1945 for 60,000 Purple Heart medal sets. This request was quickly approved and these slot brooch style medals were the only numbered Purple Hearts issued by the Navy.

John Coy

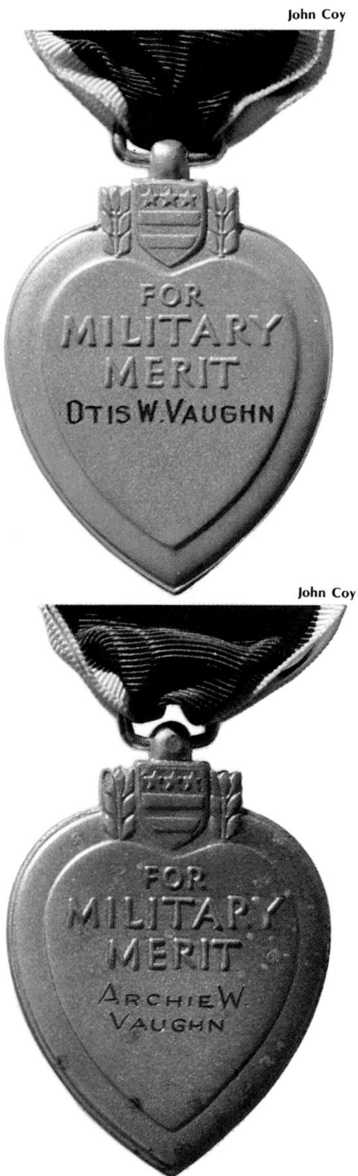

John Coy

Purple Hearts awarded posthumously to twin brothers, Otis and Archie Vaughn, killed on the same day in the same action (see Silver Star section). Their award documents are at right.

Legion of Valor

Sergeant Frederick R. Cushing. Note two first style oakleaf clusters on the Purple Heart ribbon which denote subsequent awards of the same decoration.

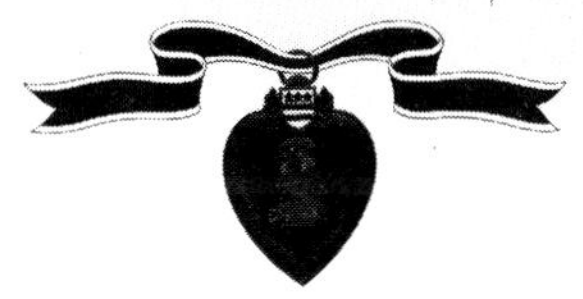

THE UNITED STATES OF AMERICA

TO ALL WHO SHALL SEE THESE PRESENTS, GREETING:

THIS IS TO CERTIFY THAT
THE PRESIDENT OF THE UNITED STATES OF AMERICA
PURSUANT TO AUTHORITY VESTED IN HIM BY CONGRESS
HAS AWARDED THE

PURPLE HEART

ESTABLISHED BY GENERAL GEORGE WASHINGTON
AT NEWBURGH, NEW YORK, AUGUST 7, 1782
TO
Private First Class Oits W. Vaughn, A.S.No. 36051897,

FOR MILITARY MERIT AND FOR WOUNDS RECEIVED
IN ACTION
resulting in his death September 11, 1944.

OFFICIAL: GIVEN UNDER MY HAND IN THE CITY OF WASHINGTON
THIS 22nd DAY OF December 1944

MAJOR GENERAL
THE ADJUTANT GENERAL

Henry L Stimson
SECRETARY OF WAR

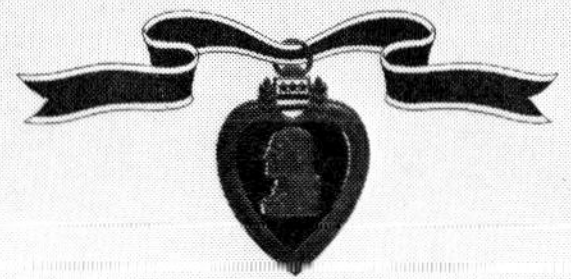

THE UNITED STATES OF AMERICA

TO ALL WHO SHALL SEE THESE PRESENTS, GREETING:

THIS IS TO CERTIFY THAT
THE PRESIDENT OF THE UNITED STATES OF AMERICA
PURSUANT TO AUTHORITY VESTED IN HIM BY CONGRESS
HAS AWARDED THE

PURPLE HEART

ESTABLISHED BY GENERAL GEORGE WASHINGTON
AT NEWBURGH, NEW YORK, AUGUST 7, 1782
TO
Sergeant Archie W. Vaughn, A.S.No. 36051926,

FOR MILITARY MERIT AND FOR WOUNDS RECEIVED
IN ACTION
resulting in his death September 11, 1944.

OFFICIAL: GIVEN UNDER MY HAND IN THE CITY OF WASHINGTON
THIS 19th DAY OF December 1944.

MAJOR GENERAL
THE ADJUTANT GENERAL

Henry L Stimson
SECRETARY OF WAR

T. Wheatley

Purple Heart awarded to Pvt. Ernest Marino, 35th Inf. Rgt., stationed at Schofield Barracks on December 7, 1941. Serial number "74007."

John Coy

T. Wheatley

Purple Heart awarded posthumously to Pfc. Allen R. Bresnahan, USMC, killed in action on Guam. Unnumbered.

Far right: This is a sterling silver example as can be seen in the engraving (silver highlights and blackened tarnish).

Defense Meritorious Service Medal

The Defense Meritorious Service Medal (DMSM) was established by Executive Order 12019 on 3 November 1977 for award during peacetime to recognize noncombat meritorious service or achievement. This award is given under similar circumstances to the Defense Superior Service Medal when the meritorious service or achievement is of a lesser degree than that required for the DSSM. However, while the service or achievement required is of a lesser degree than that required for the DSSM, it still must be incontestably exceptional and of a degree that clearly places the individual above his peers.

The Defense Meritorious Service Medal takes precedence over the Meritorious Service Medal and is awarded to any active member of the Armed Forces assigned to a qualifying joint activity. Individuals on temporary duty for at least 60 days are also eligible for this award.

Meritorious Service Medal

Conditions within the armed forces of the United States in the 1930s reflected America's increasing role as a global power. In the years following the First World War the War Department continued to analyze the importance of recognizing military achievement and service. The results of these studies led to the development of a series of awards for both valor and meritorious achievement or service.

By 1938 the Army had identified the need for an award to recognize meritorious service or achievement without lessening the prestige of the Distinguished Service Medal. It was not until the outbreak of the Second World War that the requirements for the new medal crystallized. Finally in 1942 the new medal was established, however not as the Meritorious Service Medal, but as the Legion of Merit.

It was not until the height of the Vietnam War that the military identified the need to establish an award to upgrade the image of the Legion of Merit, whose prestige had been slipping because it was the only peace-

Rear Admiral James R. Hogg wearing the Meritorious Service Medal next to the Legion of Merit (third award - note stars).

time achievement award between the Commendation medals and the Distinguished Service medals.

The Meritorious Service Medal appeared to be an award whose time had finally come. Congress approved the MSM on 16 January 1969 and award approval for the MSM was delegated at the two-star level because Major Generals already had approval authority for the Bronze Star.

To earn the Meritorious Service Medal, the acts or service must be comparable to that required for the Legion of Merit but in a duty of lesser responsibility. This similarity between the MSM and the Legion of Merit is paralleled in the ribbon design which is maroon and white for both awards.

The Meritorious Service Medal is one of only two awards which cannot be given for service in a combat zone, the other being the Army Achievement Medal. The decision to reserve the MSM for peacetime achievement or service was affirmed during the Vietnam War, because the Bronze Star already served basically the same function, in that it can also be awarded for meritorious service or achievement in a combat zone. Although the MSM is considered of equal precedence to the Bronze Star it is worn after the Bronze Star.

For company grade officers and enlisted personnel below the rank of Sergeant Major, the MSM usually represents the highest peacetime award for service or achievement that they have the opportunity to earn. As such, the MSM serves as a reminder that those who have earned it have contributed measurably to the effectiveness of their units.

Air Medal

The Air Medal was established on 11 May 1942 by Executive Order 9158. This award was created specifically to protect the prestige of the Distinguished Flying Cross which was being awarded in increasing numbers as America took the offensive in the Pacific and other theaters of World War II.

Currently the Air Medal is awarded to any person who, while serving with the Armed Forces of the United States distinguishes himself by meritorious service while engaged in military operations involving aerial flight. It is specifically intended to recognize personnel who serve on crew or non-crewmember status which requires regular participation in aerial flight on a frequent basis.

During WW II commanders in the field viewed the Air Medal as a junior DFC and a number of formulas were developed whereby Air Medals could be earned for completion of a specific number of combat sorties. Additional directives by theater commanders dictated the number of Air Medals needed to "trade up" to a DFC. Both of these policies violated the intent of the Air Medal.

By 1943 the War Department became concerned enough about the "trade up" policies and the vast differences between theaters in terms of the number and types of qualifying sorties that they ordered an end to the "automatic" DFCs. This issue would later resurface during the Vietnam War when Air Medals were again given out on the basis of hours and missions.

Following the Vietnam War the Army adopted revised criteria which eliminated qualification for the award based on sorties or hours flown. The Navy, on the other hand, still retains a complicated and exacting system for awarding the Air Medal based upon a strike/flight basis.

The Navy strike/flight basis requires an individual to earn 20 points, based on the following formula, for award of an Air Medal:

1. 10 strikes (1 strike = 2 points), or
2. 20 flights (1 flight = 1 point), or
3. 50 missions (1 mission = .4 points), or
4. 250 flight hours in direct combat support that do not encounter enemy opposition, or
5. Any combination of the above.

According to Naval regulations a strike is a sortie which delivers ordnance against the enemy which encounters opposition and a flight is a sortie which delivers ordnance against the enemy but encounters no opposition.

In addition, the Navy distinguishes between award of the Air Medal on a strike/flight basis and those awarded for heroism or achievement. This is done by the use of Gold Block Numerals placed on the left-hand orange stripe (as seen by the viewer) to denote awards for meritorious achievement or heroism. Awards made on a strike/flight basis are denoted by placing Bronze Block Numerals on the right-hand orange stripe. Both systems use the numeral "1" to denote the initial award of the medal.

Joe Stone

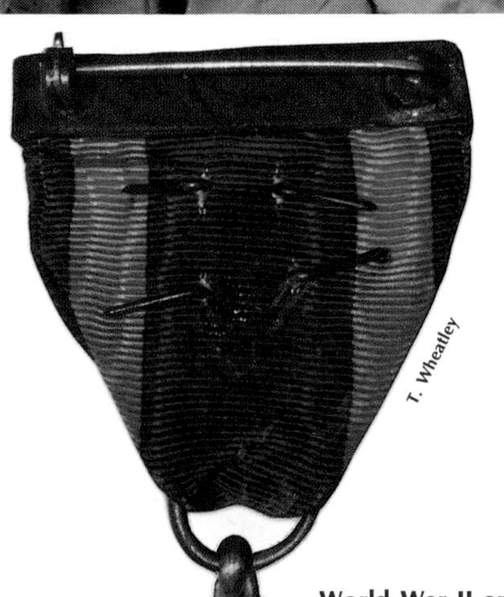

T. Wheatley

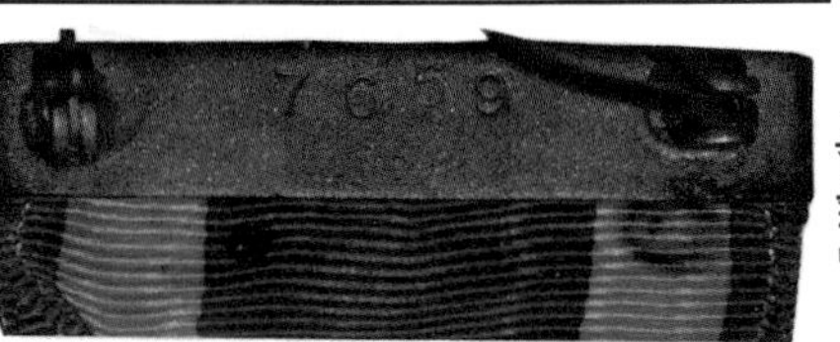

T. Wheatley

Early, numbered example of the Air Medal, "7659" on brooch.

World War II era Air Medal named to 2d Lt. Timothy J. Cavanaugh, A.C. (Air Corps).

Aerial Achievement Medal - Air Force

The Aerial Achievement Medal (AAM) is the newest decoration adopted by the Armed Forces. Authorized by the Secretary of the Air Force on 3 February 1988, the AAM is intended to recognize sustained meritorious achievement while participating in aerial flight. The AAM is authorized for award to US military personnel and civilians whose conduct while participating in aerial flight is above and beyond that normally expected of professional airmen.

The Aerial Achievement Medal represents a departure from the normal military procedure of establishing a specific set of criteria for award of a decoration. Because the various Major Air Commands fly different types of aircraft and perform different missions, it was decided that each MACOM would publish its own criteria for the award. All published criteria conform to the general theme of sustained achievement or performance.

Joint Service Commendation Medal

The Joint Service Commendation Medal was authorized by the Department of Defense in a directive dated 17 May 1967. This decoration is intended to recognize any member of the Armed Forces who distinguishes himself while assigned to a DoD recognized joint activity. Award of the JSCM was made retroactive to 1 January 1963.

The Joint Services Commendation Medal takes precedence with the Commendation medals for the various branches of the service. However, when worn in conjunction with another Commendation Medal it is worn first.

The required achievement or service, while of a lesser degree than that required for award of the Meritorious Service Medal must nevertheless have been accomplished with distinction. Awards made for acts of heroism in combat are signified by the addition of the "V" device on the service ribbon and suspension ribbon.

Army Commendation Medal

The Army Commendation Medal (ARCOM) is perhaps one of the most frequently seen decorations in the military today. The ARCOM was established by the War Department on 18 December 1945 as the Army Commendation Ribbon. It was to be awarded to junior soldiers for acts of achievement or meritorious service. Later, criteria for its award specifically precluded award of the Army Commendation Medal to general officers during peacetime.

In 1948, the Army Commendation Ribbon was renamed the Commendation Ribbon in order to allow its use by the newly created Air Force. In 1950 the award was renamed the Commendation Ribbon with Metal Pendant and finally in 1960 the current designation of Army Commendation Medal was adopted in conjunction with a new design created for the Air Force Commendation Medal.

Awards made for acts of heroism in combat are signified by the addition of the "V" device on the service ribbon and suspension ribbon.

Below: This Special Forces SFC is awarded the Army Commendation Medal.

Dept. of the Army

Navy Commendation Medal

Like its Army counterpart, the Navy Commendation Medal began as a ribbon not a medal. Navy Regulations dated 11 January 1944 authorized the Navy Commendation Ribbon, and on 22 March 1950, the Secretary of the Navy established the addition of a metal pendant for the ribbon. The medal took its final form on 21 September 1960 when the name was officially changed to the Navy Commendation Medal.

Although the metal pendant is identical to that of the Army Commendation Medal and the ribbon colors are the same, the ribbon pattern of the Navy Commendation Medal differs from that of the ARCOM.

While the decoration, and its name have changed over the years, its use today more accurately reflects the intention behind its establishment; that is to recognize the service, achievements and contributions of junior officers and enlisted personnel.

Awards made for acts of heroism in combat are signified by the addition of the "V" device on the service ribbon and suspension ribbon.

Air Force Commendation Medal

The roots of the modern United States Air Force go back to the leather flight jackets of the Army Air Force. Even after it was designated a seperate branch of service following the Second World War, members of the Air Force continued to receive Army decorations until 1959.

The Air Force Commendation Medal was authorized by the Secretary of the Air Force on 28 March 1959 and its award was made retroactive to 24 March 1958. Criteria for award of the AFCOM parallel that of the various commendation medals for the other branches of the Armed Forces.

The obverse of the pendant for the AFCOM portrays the seal of the Air Force topped by an American eagle perched atop a torse with clouds behind it.

Awards made for acts of heroism in combat are signified by the addition of the "V" device on the service ribbon and suspension ribbon.

Coast Guard Commendation Medal

As with its counterparts for the other branches of service, the Coast Guard Commendation Medal (CGCM) began its history as a ribbon when it was authorized by the Secretary of the Treasury on 26 August 1947.

The hexagonal pendant, designed by the U.S. Army Institute of Heraldry, was added on 5 July 1951 and the official name changed to the Coast Gaurd Commendation Ribbon with Metal Pendant. The name was again changed on 2 October 1959 to the Coast Guard Commendation Medal.

2nd Design.

McDowell

1st Design.

The original CGCM design features an American eagle with the seal of the Treasury Department surrounded by the inscription "United States Coast Guard — 1790."

The current design of the CGCOM came about as a result of the Treasury Department turning over control of the Coast Guard to the Department of Transportation. As a result, the original design, with the Department of the Treasury seal incorporated into the design, became obsolete.

During the transition from the orignal style to the current style medal an interim style planchet was used. This interim planchet was the same design as the original but used a three ring suspension system rather than the knob and ring style found on both the original and current style planchets. The second design, approved by the Commandant of the Coast Guard on 11 June 1968, retains the same ribbon as the original however the design on the pendant was changed and the eagle and Department of

J. Strandberg

Interim style, note ring attachment. Only about 200 were produced of this variation.

the Treasury seal was replaced with the Coast Guard seal.

When multiple awards of the CGCM occur, the bronze "V", when worn, is to the left of the 5/16th inch stars which are used to denote subsequent awards. Coast Guard regulations also authorize the Operational Distinguishing Device or Silver "O" to be worn on the ribbon when appropriate.

Awards made for acts of heroism in combat are signified by the addition of the "V" device on the service ribbon and suspension ribbon.

Joint Service Achievement Medal

The Joint Service Achievement Medal was authorized in Department of Defense Directive 1348.28 dated 29 March 1984. This directive authorized the Joint Service Achievement Medal to be presented in the name of the Secretary of Defense to military personnel assigned to one of a number of specified joint activities.

The JSAM is specifically intended to provide recognition to junior enlisted personnel and junior officers for their service and achievement. Award of the Joint Service Achievement Medal is restricted to peacetime and excludes general officers.

The Joint Service Achievement Medal takes precedence before the Achievement Medals of the military departments.

The initial production run of the JSAM was issued with a different reverse. The die used for the first reverse also included "For Presentation Only" in three lines in the center of the pendant. Intended only for use in awards ceremonies, 1000 medals of this type were produced and distributed to major commands. Once production of the issue medals reached appropriate levels these medals were recalled. However, it is doubtful that many were actually returned or destroyed.

McDowell

Army Achievement Medal

Recommendations for the establishment of the Army Achievement Medal date back to 1975. However, it was not until 2 March 1981 that the Secretary of the Army approved the AAM.

The spirit behind the establishment of the Army Achievement Medal was the general feeling among commanders that award criteria for the Army Commendation Medal and the Meritorious service medal placed them beyond the reach of most junior enlisted members (Staff Sergeants and below) and company grade officers because these awards were aimed at a level of responsibility which they could not, by definition, achieve.

The AAM follows the Army Commendation Medal in order of precedence. However, unlike the ARCOM, the AAM cannot be awarded in a combat zone. With an estimated twenty percent of all soldiers receiving the Army Achievement Medal it has become the most visible symbol of the Army's Pyramid of Honor.

Navy Achievement Medal

The Navy Achievement Medal was originally authorized by the Secretary of the Navy on 1 May 1961. Initially designated as the Secretary of the Navy Commendation for Achievement, the award was in the form of a ribbon only. On 17 July 1967 the award was redesignated the Navy Achievement Medal and the unique square metal pendant added.

Unlike the Army Achievement Medal, the Navy Achievement Medal can be given for meritorious service or achievement in a combat or non-combat situation. In addition, Navy regulations permit the "V" device for combat heroism in conjunction with the Navy Achievement Medal.

Air Force Achievement Medal

The Air Force Achievement Medal (AFAM) was established by the Secretary of the Air Force on 12 October 1980 to recognize the achievements of junior officers and enlisted personnel. To emphasis this fact, award of the AFAM is restricted to the grade of Major and below.

Award of the Air Force Achievement Medal may be made for outstanding achievement or courage. Unlike the Army Achievement Medal, the AFAM may awarded in a combat zone.

Designed by CPT Robert Bonn in 1978, the AFAM was the first Air Force decoration that was not based on an Army decoration.

Coast Guard Achievement Medal

The Coast Guard Achievement Medal (CGAM) was initially established as the Secretary of the Treasury Commendation for Achievement on 29 January 1963. When control of the Coast Guard passed to the Department of Transportation the award was renamed. Although the design remained the same, the award was renamed the Secretary of Transportation Commendation for Achievement on 13 March 1967. The CGAM received its final name change on 11 June 1968 when it was redesignated as the Coast Guard Achievement Medal by the Commandant of the Coast Guard.

The Coast Guard Achievement Medal is intended to recognize the outsanding performance and superior achievement of junior commissioned officers and enlisted personnel. For officers, award of the CGAM is restricted to the ranks of Lieutenant Commander and below.

Gold Lifesaving Medal

Established by an Act of Congress on 20 June 1874, the Gold Lifesaving Medal is awarded by the Department of Transportation to both civilians and members of the military who risk their lives to save others from the "perils of the sea," within the United States, or upon any American vessel.

Originally the Gold Lifesaving Medal was a 1 3/4" medal and not designed for wear. Known as the Life Saving Medal of the First Class, the first awards were made to Lucien M. Clemons, A.J. Clemons, and Hubbard M. Clemons, of Marblehead, Ohio, for rescuing two men from the wreck of the schooner Consuello, in Lake Erie, on 1 May 1875. The medals were awarded on 19 June 1876 and forwarded to the recipients by Acting Secretary of the Treasury, Charles F. Conant on 30 June 1876.

medal was also officially changed at that time to the Gold Lifesaving Medal.

On 4 August 1949, acting on a suggestion from Admiral Farley, Commandant of the Coast Guard, the Congress approved a new ribbon design and slightly smaller planchet for the Gold Lifesaving Medal to make it "present a more harmonious appearance" when worn with other medals. Both the original and new designs of the Gold Lifesaving medal are struck in 99.9% pure gold. The planchet is 1 7/16 inches in diameter and the current ribbon is the standard 1 3/8th inches wide and is composed of a wide gold center stripe flanked by a thin white stripe and a red stripe on each end.

From its inception in 1874 until the end of 1991, 645 Gold Lifesaving Medals have been awarded. Only four individuals have

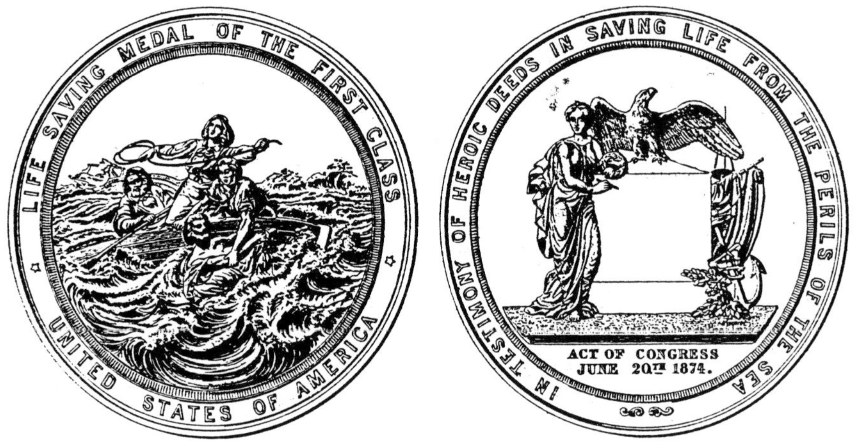

The Type I Lifesaving Medal of the First Class, without ribbon (1874-1878). The Type II was slightly smaller with a wording change on the obverse (1878-1882).

Congress approved a design change on 18 June 1878, slightly downsizing the medal and changing the wording on the obverse, but the medal was still not designed for wear. On 4 May 1882 Congress approved further changes to the Lifesaving Medal, approving a suspension bar and ribbon to make the medal adaptable for wearing. The new medal was suspended from a 2 inch wide scarlet red ribbon. The name of the

received a second award of the Gold Lifesaving Medal.

An ornate gold pin-back clasp is awarded in lieu of a second Gold Lifesaving Medal. The clasp is a straight bar upon which is engraved "SECOND SERVICE." A ribbon bearing the inscription "Act of Congress May 4th 1882" flows beneath the bar while a branch of leaves arches above the bar. The clasp for the current Gold Lifesaving Meda

The Type III Gold Lifesaving Medal (1882-1949) was awarded for "rescuing or endeavoring to rescue any other person from drowning, shipwreck or other peril of the waters."

is slightly smaller and the date on the ribbon has been changed to August 4th, 1949. The reverse of the clasp is engraved with the recipient's name and a brief account of the rescue and the date the rescue occurred.

For the collector, acquiring a pure gold example of the Lifesaving Medal is virtually impossible.

Legion of Valor

President Coolidge decorates Chief Gunner's Mate Frank W. Crilley with the Medal of Honor. He also received the Gold Lifesaving Medal for the same action.

Thomas Ryan

Type III Gold Lifesaving Medal (Tiffany & Co.-all capital letters) awarded to Delos Hayden for heroic daring in rescuing the crews of three vessels - October 31, November 1, and November 11, 1883. Written on the inner top lid: "Presented by Capt. B.P. Dobbins at the Cleveland Lite Boat Station - July 8, 1885." Note the additional chain supports.

Type IV Gold Lifesaving Medal approved on 4 August 1949.

R. Sullivan

Captain Harry Manning, "SS America," wearing his Gold Lifesaving Medal in 1929.

Gary Krug

"New Gold Lifesaving Bar" (24K) given in lieu of a second Gold Lifesaving Medal.

Silver Lifesaving Medal

Awarded under the same circumstances as the Gold Lifesaving Medal, the Silver Lifesaving Medal recognizes heroism of a lesser degree. The design changes in the Silver Lifesaving Medal parallel those of the Gold Lifesaving Medal.

Originally known as the Life Saving Medal of the Second Class, the first awards occurred on 23 June 1876. John O. Philbrick and Otis N. Wheeler of Cape Elizabeth, Maine were awarded the medals for rescuing two men wrecked on Watts Ledge, Maine on 30 November 1875.

Type I Lifesaving Medal of the Second Class, without ribbon (1874-1878).

When the initial approval of the wearable design was given by Congress in 1882, the 2-inch wide ribbon was light blue moire. This was changed on 4 August 1949 to a wide silver center strip flanked by a thin stripe of white and a slightly wider stripe of blue. At the same time the width of the ribbon was changed to 1 3/8th inches and the pendant reduced slightly in size.

An ornate silver pin-back clasp is awarded in lieu of a second Silver Lifesaving Medal. The clasp is a straight bar upon which is engraved "SECOND SERVICE." A ribbon bearing the inscription "Act of Congress May 4th 1882" flows beneath the bar while a branch of leaves arches above the bar. The clasp for the current Silver Lifesaving Medal is slightly smaller and the date on the ribbon has been changed to August 4th 1949.

Type III Silver Lifesaving Medal (1882-1949) (see "Gold" section for details on first two types).

Thomas Ryan

Type III Silver Lifesaving Medal (Tiffany & Co.-all capital letters) inscribed: "To Frank Waters for heroic service in rescuing the crew of the schooner "Jane" - February 29, 1884."

National Archives

George S. Patton proudly displays his Silver Lifesaving Medal next to his DSC and DSM. The last medal on the first row is the 1912 Stockholm olympic participation medal given by the King of Sweden. Patton placed 5th in the pentathlon.

Type IV Silver Lifesaving Medal approved on 4 August 1949. Note new ribbon colors.

Note the various engraving styles on the seven reverses of the Type III Silver Lifesaving Medals illustrated.

Gary Krug

The "New Silver Lifesaving Bar" (99% pure silver) given in lieu of a second Silver Lifesaving Medal.

Good Conduct and Other Length of Service Medals

Combat Readiness Medal - Air Force

The Combat Readiness Medal (CRM) was established by the Secretary of the Air Force in 9 March 1964 and further amended on 28 August 1967. The CRM is awarded for two years of service in a combat or mission ready status for direct weapons employment. To qualify an individual must meet several requirements:

- Be a member of a unit which is subject to combat readiness reporting; and
- Be individually certified as combat or mission ready and have been continuously subject to an individual positional evaluation program according to a higher headquarters standard; and
- Complete 24 months of sustained combat or mission readiness with no more than a 120 day break.

This MoH recipient wears the Army Good Conduct Medal.

Good Conduct Medal - Army

The Army's Good Conduct Medal was established by Executive Order 8809 (War Department Bulletin 17, 1941) on 28 June 1941 and further amended by Executive Order 9323 (War Department Bulletin 6, 1943) and Executive Order 10444 (Department of the Army Bulletin 4, 1953).

The Good Conduct Medal (GCM) was developed to regognize exemplary behavior, efficiency, and fidelity while serving on active Federal military duty in an enlisted grade throughout a qualifying period of time.

Any one of several periods of continuous active Federal military can qualify enlisted personnel for award of the GCM. These qualifying periods are:

- Each 3 years completed on or after 27 August 1940.
- For the first award only, one year served entirely during the period 7 December 1941 and 2 March 1946.
- For the first award only, upon completion of service on or after 27 June 1950 of less than 3 years but more than one year.

First style Army Good Conduct Medal with large ring mount, serial numbered "208."

For the first award only, upon termination of service on or after 27 June 1950 of less than one year when final separation was due to a physical disability incurred in the line of duty.

For the first award only, for those individuals who were killed in action or who died of wounds prior to the completion of one year of active Federal military service.

Subsequent awards of the Good Conduct Medal are indicated by a clasp attached to the suspension ribbon and the service ribbon. The clasp is in the form of a stylized rope with a knot representing each successive award. The clasp is in bronze for the 2nd through 5th award, silver for the 6th through 10th award, and gold for the 11th through 15th award.

The initial strike of Army GCMs were serial numbered in a manner similar to the early campaign medals. However, the size of these serial numbers is quite small when compared to the numbers which appear on campaign medals.Serial numbered Army Good Conduct Medals were awarded prior to World War II and all were originally suspended from a Full-Wrap brooch.

An early strike of the Army GCM with wrap brooch and serial number "16763."

An Army Good Conduct Medal named to Mary V. Baker, probably of the Women's Army Corps (unnumbered).

Navy Good Conduct Medal

The Navy Good Conduct Medal is our country's second oldest medal and has been in continuous use since 26 April 1869. Initially called the Good Conduct Badge, the medal was established by the Secretary of the Navy for award to any man holding a Continuous Service Certificate, who had distinguished himself for obedience, sobriety, and cleanliness, and who had demonstrated proficiency in gunnery and seamanship. The Good Conduct Badge was awarded upon completion of the term of enlistment. Any seaman who qualified for three awards under consecutive re-enlistments was promoted to Petty Officer.

The Good Conduct Badge was a Maltese cross design of nickel with a circular medallion in the center. The medallion itself had a rope border and the words "Fidelity Zeal Obedience" inscribed around the rim and the initials "U.S.N." in the center. The cross was suspended from a 1/2 inch wide ribbon composed of three equal stripes of red, white and blue.

D. Boyce

Navy Good Conduct Badge issued from 1869-1884.

By 1880 the Navy had recognized the need to redesign the Good Conduct Badge to make it more suitable for wear as the narrow ribbon and lack of a brooch made the original difficult to wear. The new design for the pendant , proposed by Commodore Winfield Scott Schley, was adapted from the design which appeared on the letterhead of the Navy Department's Bureau of Equipment and Recruiting, of which Schley was the head. The new circular planchet was suspended from a 1 5/8th inch wide ribbon with a wide red center stripe flanked by narrow stripes of white and blue.

On 21 November 1884 Navy Department General Order 327 authorized a new design. The name was subsequently changed to the Good Conduct Medal on 26 April 1896. Award criteria were also modified to fix the time requirement at three years continuous active duty.

The new Good Conduct Medal was suspended from a maroon ribbon and was circular in design. The design for the new medal retained the pendant designed in 1880 by Commodore Schley who was the head of the Navy's Equipment and Recruiting Bureau. However, the pendant of the "new" Good Conduct Medal was attached to the suspension ribbon by a straight bar clasp.

Legion of Valor

MoH recipient Herbert L. Foss wears the "new" Good Conduct Medal.

Subsequent enlistments were recognized by the addition of a clasp attached to the suspension ribbon. These clasps had rounded ends and rope borders and were engraved on the front with the duty station or ship upon which the recipient served and the discharge date and Continuous Service Number on the reverse. During the 1930's the name of the ship or duty station was replaced with the discharge year and the

R. Sullivan

The newly designed 1880 pendant suspended from the first style ribbon.

G. Sousa

Reverses of Navy Good Conduct bars.

"USS Nitro" on obverse.

"1938" on obverse.

J. Voigt

Current issue.

recipient's name was engraved on the reverse. Early enlistment claps were pinned to the suspension ribbon. In approximately 1942 the enlistment clasps were changed and were converted to a slide on variety similar to WW I Navy victory clasps. These later enlistment clasps had the enlistment number; i.e. "SECOND AWARD", "THIRD AWARD" etc. in raised lettering on the front and were not engraved on the reverse. Following World War II, 3/16th inch bronze stars were used in place of the enlistment bars to denote subsequent enlistments, and the bottom suspension bar was dropped in favor of the standard ring suspension.

After WWII, 3/16 inch bronze stars denoted subsequent enlistments, in this case, four reenlistments.

Marine Corps Good Conduct Medal

The Marine Corps Good Conduct Medal, designed by Major General Charles Heywood, was established by the Secretary of the Navy by Special Order No. 49 on 20 July 1896. The medal is intended to recognize good behavior and faithful service in the Marine Corps by enlisted personnel.

Old style top suspension bar.

Qualifying service consists of uninterrupted service where the individual has no convictions by courts-martial, not more than one non-judicial punishment under U.C.M.J. article 15, and no lost time by reason of sickness-misconduct or injury-misconduct.

For the first award only, the GCM may be awarded to the next of kin in those cases where the individual is killed in combat or dies of wounds received in combat. In addition, the Marine Corps Good Conduct Medal is authorized for personnel who are separated from service as a result of physical disabilities incurred in combat action.

Legion of Valor

Note additional bar on this sergeant's Good Conduct Medal ribbon.

Second style.

The Marine Corps Good Conduct Medal has undergone slight design modifications since its inception. As originally established, the GCM incorporated a suspension bar bearing the words "U.S. Marine Corps" through which the suspension ribbon was draped and a bronze rifle attached to the bottom of the suspension ribbon to which the medal pendant was attached. Following World War II, the top suspension bar was eliminated.

In addition to the slight design changes that the Marine Corps Good Conduct Medal has undergone, there have also been variations in the style of engraving used to record the recipients name and service information on the reverse of the medal.

In general, prior to World War I Marine Corps GCMs were engraved with the recipient's enlistment number, name (on one line), and date span. Due to the dramatic increase in the size of the Marine Corps during World War I, most MCGCMs from this period are impressed with rim numbers in the 20000 to 70000 range. These were issued, unnamed, to those Marines who had enlisted only for the duration of the war. Career enlisted personnel continued to receive hand-engraved and hand-numbered medals.

Following the Second World War the Marine Corps changed from engraving to stamping the recipient's information on the reverse. This information was also reduced to the recipient's name (on two lines) and the year of issue. The Marine Corps officially stopped naming the Good Conduct Medals in 1951. However, a few stamped examples do exist from 1952 and 1953.

Additional awards were indicated by the addition of clasps with the number of the award inscribed. These clasps were attached to the suspension ribbon and bronze arabic numerals were used on the service ribbon. Currently both the clasps and numerals have been replaced by the use of 3/16th inch bronze stars.

Gunnery Sergeant Jimmie E. Howard, USMC, MoH, wears the current Good Conduct Medal with three bronze stars.

Air Force Good Conduct Medal

From its inception as a branch of the armed forces in 1947, until 31 May 1963, qualifying Air Force enlisted personnel were awarded the Army's Good Conduct Medal (GCM).

The Air Force Good Conduct Medal (AFGCM) was established for award to enlisted Air Force personnel on or after 1 June 1963. In the circumstances where a service member qualifies for award of the Good Conduct Medal prior to 1 June 1963 and later qualifies for a subsequent award, the subsequent award would be made using the AFGCM. In these cases, the AFGCM would take precedence over the GCM.

Current award criteria for the AFGCM include not only a minimum of three years continuous active duty, but also the stipulation that the individual must have demonstrated a positive attitude towards the Air Force and their job. Merely staying out of trouble for three years is not considered basis for award of the Air Force Good Conduct Medal.

Coast Guard Good Conduct Medal

The Coast Guard Good Conduct Medal (CGGCM) was first authorized on 12 December 1923. Intended to recognize superior performance of duty during a four year period of service, the time requirement was shortened on 30 June 1934 to conform to the three year term in effect for the Navy and Marine Corps Good Conduct Medals.

As initially awarded, the CGGCM was attached to a 1 1/2 inch wide maroon ribbon with a single white center stripe suspended from a rectangular top bar bearing the inscription "U.S. Coast Guard". The metal pendant was 1 7/16 inches in diameter with the likeness of a cutter in the center sur-

rounded by the motto SEMPER PARATUS. The pendant is suspended from a straight crossbar looped through the bottom of the suspension ribbon. Subsequent awards of the CGGCM were indicated by the addition of bronze Good Conduct Bars. These bars were attached to the suspension ribbon by means of a flat hinged-back clasping bar which allowed the bar to be easily removed. Good Conduct Bars were engraved on the front with the recipients ship or duty station and the date of award on the reverse.

Both the suspension top bar and the Good Conduct Bars were discontinued following the Korean War. The current Coast Guard Good Conduct Medal is suspended from a 1 3/8th inch wide ribbon and the planchet has been reduced to 1 1/4th inches. The new planchet also features the Coast Guard insignia in the center rather than the small ship. The current CGGCM also does not incorporate the use of the bottom crossbar and is attached directly to the suspension ribbon by means of a suspension ring.

Army Reserve Components Achievement Medal

The Army Reserve Components Achievement Medal (ARCAM) was established by the Secretary of the Army in DA General Orders 30, 1971. The ARCAM is awarded to any member of the Army Reserve or Army National Guard, in the grade of Colonel or below, who successfully completes four years of qualifying service with a Troop Component Unit on or after 3 March 1971.

The ARCAM comes in two different designs, one for the Army Reserve and one for the Army National Guard. The front of the pendant is the same for both designs. However, the reverse of the National Guard versions bears the inscription "Army National Guard" and the Army Reserve version is inscribed "United States Army Reserve". Personnel who qualify for both versions are authorized to wear only one award.

Second and successive awards of the ARCAM are indicated by the addition of bronze Oak Leaf Clusters to both the suspension and service ribbon.

Army Reserve version.

National Guard version.

Naval Reserve Meritorious Service Medal

The Naval Reserve Meritorious Service Medal (NRMSM) was initially proposed by the Naval Reserve Policy Board on 26 June 1962. The proposal of the Board was approved by the Secretary of the Navy on 22 June 1964 with eligibility back-dated to 1 July 1958.

The NRMSM is awarded to any enlisted member of the Naval Reserve who completes four years of qualifying service on or after 1 July 1958. Qualifying service includes, but is not limited to, attending 90 percent of all scheduled reserve drills and four Annual Training periods during the four year period. In addition, the individual must receive no evaluation less than 3.0 (if marks are assigned) on any evaluation.

Subsequent awards of the Naval Reserve Meritorious Service Medal are indicated by the addition of bronze 3/16th inch stars to both the service and suspension ribbons of the medal.

Air Reserve Forces Meritorious Service Medal

The Air Reserve Forces Meritorious Service Medal (ARFMSM) was established on 7 April 1964 for award to qualifying personnel on or after 1 April 1965. Initially awarded as a ribbon only, the medal pendant was added on 2 November 1971.

For service before 1 July 1975 the minimum time requirement was four years of qualifying service. Award of the ARFMSM after that date is based on three years of service. The time requirements for qualifying service begin anew if the individual has more than a 24 hour break in servic. Airmen who accrue at least one year of qualifying service and terminate their enlisted Reserve status by accepting a commission as an officer or warrant officer are awarded the ARFMSM.

AFR 900-48 describes qualifying service as "exemplary behavior, efficiency, and fidelity while serving in an enlisted status in the Air Reserve forces." During the period considered for award, the individual must have no convictions by courts-martial and no punishment under Article 15 of the U.C.M.J.

Selected Marine Corps Reserve Medal

This medal was established by the Secretary of the Navy on 19 February 1939 as the Fleet Marine Corps Reserve Medal. However the organizational name was officially changed on 1 July 1938 to the Organized Marine Corps Reserve. The name was again changed to the Selected Marine Corps Reserve in the late 1980s.

Two styles of this medal exist. The ribbon and reverse of both medals are identical. However, the name on the obverse of the pendant reads "Fleet Marine Corps Reserve" on the first variety and "Marine Corps Reserve" on the second variety. Because the designation of the Marine Corps Reserve organization had officially been changed prior to final approval of the medal, the first variety was technically obsolete when it was struck and only very limited examples exist today.

Award of the Selected Marine Corps Reserve Medal is made to any member of the Marine Corps Reserve who, subsequent to 1 July 1925, and prior to 24 April 1961, has attended 80 percent of all scheduled drill periods within a period of four consecutive years. Attendance requirements were raised to 90 percent for all qualifying periods after 24 April 1961.

A bronze 3/16th inch star is worn on the suspension ribbon and ribbon bar to denote subsequent awards.

First variety.

D. Boyce

Coast Guard Reserve Good Conduct Medal

The Commandant of the Coast Guard established the Coast Guard Reserve Good Conduct Medal on 1 February 1963. The CGRGCM was established to recognize enlisted members of the active reserve in much the same manner as the Coast Guard Good Conduct Medal recognizes active duty enlisted personnel.

Formerly known as the Coast Guard Reserve Meritorious Service Ribbon, the CGRGCM is awarded for three consecutive years of creditable service under conditions similiar to those for award of the Coast Guard Good Conduct Medal.

Prisoner Of War Medal

The Prisoner of War Medal was authorized by Public Law 99-145 on 8 November 1985 and is awarded to any person who served with the United States Armed Forces and was taken prisoner and held captive on or after 5 April 1917.

To qualify for award of the POW Medal the individual's service while held captive must have been honorable. Hostages of terrorists and persons detained by governments with which the United States is not actively engaged in armed conflict are not eligible for the POW Medal.

Americans surrendering to members of the 1st SS-Panzer Division during the early stages of the Battle of the Bulge.

Campaign and Service Medals

The collector of United States campaign medals soon discovers that America's military history encompasses much more than the major conflicts of the Revolutionary War, Civil War, World War I, World War II, Korean War, and the Vietnam War. One soon discovers that some of our nation's early heros emerged from battles in Cardenas, Cuba; Peking, China; Port - au - Prince, Haiti; or Bluefields, Nicaragua. Long before Marines spoke in hallowed terms of places like Guadalcanal, Tarawa, Iwo Jima and the "Frozen Chosin"; there was the "Citadel", Peking, Veracruz, Fort Riviere, and Quilali.

These "little wars" helped define America as a world military power and provided the esprit-de-corps and traditions that would steel our soldiers, sailors and marines for World War I and the horrors of Belleau Wood, Verdun, and the Somme.

General John Pershing wears four Army campaign medals on his dress uniform.

Rim Numbering on Campaign Medals

European countries have long recognized the service of their soldiers and sailors by awarding campaign medals. In the United States, several states, veteran's organizations, and even unit commanders carried on this tradition and began issuing medals for military service before the Civil War.

However, federal military campaign medals for service with the Armed Forces of the United States did not make their first appearance until shortly after the turn of the twentieth century.

The movement towards government-issued campaign medals was begun by Major General Adna R. Chaffee while he was serving as the commander of the American forces involved in the China relief expedition. Later while serving as the Chief of Staff of the Army in 1904, Chaffee directed a study aimed at developing a proposal for a series of Army campaign medals.

Chaffee's proposal was accepted by the Secretary of War on 5 January 1905. Shortly thereafter, on the 11th and 12th of January 1905, War Department General Orders 4 and 5 announced five Army campaign medals; the Civil War Campaign Medal, Indian Campaign Medal, Spanish Campaign Medal, Philippine Campaign Medal, and the China Campaign Medal.

In 1908 the Navy followed suit by authorizing their own Civil War Campaign Medal design for issue to members of the Navy and Marine Corps.

Prior to the First World War all Navy and Marine Corps campaign medals shared the same reverse designs adopted for the Navy or Marine Corps Civil War Campaign Medals.

In the early 1920s the Navy stopped contracting with private manufacturers for the production of its campaign medals. However, the US Mint found the reverse design used on the pre-WW I Navy and Marine Corps campaign medals to be objectionable from an artistic standpoint. As part of its efforts to refine the reverse design, the Mint opted to place the "For Service" in two straight lines rather than two curved lines, which had been the previous design used by private manufacturers. Beginning with the Dominican Campaign Medal, established in 1921, the Navy and Marine Corps instituted a new reverse design which was used until World War II. Beginning with the Second World War campaign medals, American campaign medals were standardized for all branches of the service and each has a unique reverse design which compliments the obverse design.

Prior to World War I the Navy and Marine Corps contracted with private sources for the production of their campaign medals and most were issued with unprefixed, rim-stamped serial numbers. After WW I the Navy and Marine Corps contracted with the U.S. Mint for their medal needs. As part of its contracting with the US Mint, the Navy had additional supplies of pre-WW I campaign medals produced. Of these early campaign medals, only the Navy Philippine Campaign and the Navy Mexican Service medals were struck with "M No." serial numbers. These are the only numbered Navy or Marine Corps campaign medals produced with the straight "For Service" on the reverse. The policy of numbering Navy and Marine Corps campaign medals continued until the 1930s when the size of both services swelled on the eve of the Second World War, making the numbering system impractical.

Army campaign medals after the Civil War Campaign Medal share the reverse of either the Indian Campaign Medal or the Spanish War Service Medal, with the exception of the Philippine Congressional Medal which has its own unique reverse design.

Army campaign medals produced prior to WW I were all manufactured by the U.S. Mint and are identified by either "No." or "MNo." serial numbers. The "No." numbered medals were the first issued and in general they were awarded only to active duty or retired personnel. In December 1913, bowing to pressure from the many veterans organizations, the Army authorized the issue of campaign medals to qualified veterans who were honorably discharged, these were the "MNo." serial numbered medals. Following the First World War, some additional stocks of older campaign medals were ordered from various private sources. The initial orders of these "contract" medals were distinguished by the use of unprefixed serial numbers. Although the "No." and "MNo." prefixed serial numbers start with the number "1", the contract medals generally continue the sequence of the "No." numbering series. Unlike the Mint num-

bered campaign medals, the dies used for numbering Army campaign medals made under private contract varied from company to company and contract to contract.

As with any rule, there are exceptions to the norm with regards to the numbering of Army campaign medals. It should be noted that the Spanish War Service and Mexican Border Service Medals were all made under private contract and issued with unprefixed serial numbers. Additionally, the Philippine Congressional Medal exists with only "No." prefixed serial numbers, while some stocks of the Army of Cuban Occupation Medal were issued from the U.S. Mint and bear "MNo." prefixed serial numbers.

The issue records of numbered campaign medals were kept by the Quartermaster Medal and Badge Office until December 1925. These records still exist today and medals issued prior to this date with "No." serial numbers or unprefixed serial numbers can usually be traced.

With the issuing of the World War I Victory Medal to literally millions of Army veterans, the practice of numbering Army campaign medals was suspended.

Suspension Brooch Styles

The collector of American medals is faced with a situation that is unique when compared with, say, collecting Third Reich awards; because most American medals are currently being manufactured by the government for issue to veterans as replacement pieces. These currently manufactured medals are not reproductions, but they do differ from the original issue examples. In some cases the difference between a current issue replacement medal and the original issue strike may be quite pronounced; in other cases the only difference may be in the style of brooch used.

Most collectors will attempt to acquire an original strike, or one of the same time period, of each particular medal they are seeking. To assist the collector, the following photographs illustrate the four types of brooches used on American medals. It is important to understand that a definitive beginning and ending date for the use of each brooch style is impossible to calculate. Some overlap of styles inevitably occurred when new brooch styles were adopted.

Brooch styles were usually not specified in government contracts. Therefore, manufacturers, either the U.S. Mint or private companies, used the type they had in stock when the contract was produced. For example, the private companies which supplied the Army with its medals introduced the slot brooch which was so common among World War II awards. However, the US Mint, which supplied medals to the Navy and Marine Corps did not adopt this style until late in the war. Thus, many World War II Navy awards are found with the wrap brooch while many Army awards for the same time period are found with slot brooches.

In addition to the interservice differences, each branch of the Armed Forces must issue medals from on-hand stock. In

USMC Expeditionary Medal suspended from a Split Brooch.

most instances a medal may actually have been produced several years before it is issued. In many cases this fact alone accounts for much of the time overlap from one brooch style to the next.

Generally speaking, the first style brooch adopted for use on American medals was the split brooch style. This style was used from about 1898 until 1920 on Army medals and until about 1932 on Navy and Marine Corps medals. The split brooch allowed the ends of the suspension ribbon to be sewn together before the ribbon was attached to the brooch. Because the back of the brooch did not extend the full width of the the ribbon, this style did not provide a good base for the pin back, allowing the base of the pin and the catch to become misaligned.

The wrap brooch, sometimes called the full-wrap brooch, was the second type of brooch used on American medals. This style of brooch first appeared in about 1917 and was used until about 1943. There is a variation of the wrap brooch in which the brooch is slit in the center to allow the ends of the suspension ribbon to be sewn together

Yangtze Service Medal (Navy) suspended from a Full-Wrap Brooch.

before it is sliped onto the brooch. This variation often goes undetected since the slit is hidden once the suspension ribbon is slipped onto the brooch. This is the most common version of the wrap brooch.

Following the introduction of the Bronze Star Medal in 1944, the Army began wide spread use of the slot brooch style, although the Navy continued to use the full-wrap brooch style on its medals until 1945. The slot brooch allowed the brooch to be stamped from a single flat piece of metal, usually brass. The brooch pin was then soldered to the back of the brooch. One end of the suspension ribbon was slipped through the slot in the brooch and folded over the top of

American Defense Service Medal suspended from a Slot Brooch.

the brooch. The suspension ribbon was then sewn to the brooch through two small holes on either side of the bottom of the brooch. The slot brooch continued to be used on medals produced until approximately 1960.

The fourth, and current style brooch used on American medals is the crimp brooch. In all three previous brooch styles the suspension ribbon must be sewn together by hand. The crimp brooch eliminates the need for this laborious process by crimping the ends

Major General William P. Upshur, USMC. A MoH recipient for action in the Haitian campaign in 1915, he is wearing his Cuban Pacification, MC Expeditionary, Haitian Campaign, Dominican Campaign and WWI Victory Medals. He also wears the Dominican Republic's Order of Juan Pablo Duarte.

Navy Expeditionary Medal suspended from a Crimp Brooch.

of the suspension ribbon between the two brooch pieces.

The crimp brooch consists of two pieces; the base forms a channel into which the two ends of the suspension ribbon are placed. The top plate, which holds the pin back, is placed in the base on top of the suspension ribbon. With the top plate in place, the edges of the base are crimped over the top plate, securing the suspension ribbon in place. During the transition period between the slot brooch and the crimp brooch, many manufacturers used up their supply of slot brooches by substituting them for the top plate in the crimp style brooch. These odd variations are most often found on World War II campaign medals, Army Good Conduct Medals, Army and Navy Commendation Medals, and some Armed Forces Reserve Medals. In use since about 1960, a few medals with crimp brooches are encountered with clutch backs, however the crimp brooch is usually found in a pin back style.

The collector who is seeking an original strike of a particular medal must be aware of the brooch styles used during the time when a medal was first struck and issued. For example, a collector who sees an Army of Cuban Occupation Medal suspended from a slot brooch should immediately realize that it is not an original strike but one that was produced in the late 1940's or 1950's for reissue, or that a brooch has been replaced. Likewise, by knowing that the Army Good Conduct Medal was first struck in 1941, the collector who is aware of when brooch styles were used, would know that the first strikes of the Army GCM were mounted on a wrap brooch. And, since the wrap brooch was superseded by the slot brooch shortly after the introduction of the Army GCM, the knowledgeable collector would also be aware that Army GCMs with wrap brooches are worth more than slot brooch Army Good Conduct Medals.

Being aware of brooch styles, and when they were used, is another tool the collector can use to enhance the joy of collecting American medals.

Civil War Campaign Medal - Army

The Civil War Campaign Medal was authorized 11 January 1905. However the final design for the Civil War Campaign Medal was not approved and adopted by the Army until the publication of War Department General Order 12, 1907. In that year, War Department General Order 12 authorized the Civil War Campaign Medal for active federal service between 15 April 1861 and 9 April 1865, or service in Texas between 15 April 1861 and 20 August 1866.

The Army's Civil War Campaign Medal was initially issued with a ribbon that had a narrow white center stripe, flanked on either side by equal stripes of red, white and blue. This ribbon was changed to a blue and grey ribbon in 1913 to match the ribbon used on the Navy and Marine Corps versions of the Civil War Campaign Medal.

Because of the extremely long delay in authorizing this medal only about 9,500 of the over two million Union soldiers who fought in the Civil War received the medal. Civil War Campaign Medals were originally issued with serial numbers stamped on the rim. The first issue of numbered medals used the prefix "No.". Later issues were prefixed with "MNo." and still others had no prefix. After the last contract of numbered medals was exhausted, additional orders were placed for medals without serial numbers.

First style ribbon - serial number "No.340."

State Historical Society of North Dakota

Brigadier General J.W. Scully wears the first style ribbon on his Civil War Campaign Medal.

D. Boyce

Second style ribbon.

Army Civil War Campaign Medals numbered "M.No. 3420" and "3086" (the unprefixed stamping is a private contract strike).

State Historical Society of North Dakota

John Piatt Dunn wears the second style ribbon on his Army Civil War Campaign Medal.

Civil War Campaign Medal - Navy and Marine Corps

The Civil War Campaign Medal for Navy and Marine Corps personnel was authorized on 27 June 1908. While Congress had previously authorized commemorative medals for naval actions during the Spanish American War, the Civil War Campaign Medal was the first campaign medal authorized for personnel of the Navy or Marine Corps.

The Navy and Marine Corps Civil War Campaign Medals share a common design on the obverse of the pendant. This design depicts the naval battle between the Monitor and the Merrimac off Newport News, Virginia on 9 March 1862. The reverse of the pendant features an eagle, with wings spread, perched atop an anchor and chain. For Naval personnel the inscription surmounting the design reads "United States Navy" and for Marines the inscription is "United States Marine Corps". In both designs the words "For Service" appear in two curved lines beneath the eagle and anchor.

The pendant is suspended from a ribbon composed of two equal stripes of blue and gray.

Navy issue.

Navy Civil War Campaign Medal numbered "2585."

The initial issue of Civil War Campaign Medals were issued with serial numbers stamped on the rim. There were approximately 2,700 Navy CWCMs issued and 180 Marine Corps medals.

Marine Corps Civil War Campaign Medal, numbered "77."

Indian Campaign Medal

Following Congressional approval on 11 January 1905, the Indian Campaign Medal was authorized for wear by Army personnel by General Order 12 in 1907. The medal was awarded for service in a variety of campaigns and engagements against indian tribes throughout the western states between 1865 and 1891. Personnel qualified for award of the Indian Campaign Medal under one of the following conditions:

- Service in southern Oregon, Idaho, northern California, and Nevada between 1865 and 1868.
- Campaigns against the Comanches and confederated tribes in Kansas, Colorado, Texas, New Mexico and the Indian Territory between 1867 and 1875.
- Modoc War in 1872 and 1873.
- Apaches in Arizona in 1873.
- Northern Chyennes and Sioux in 1876 and 1877.

The original silk moire ribbon was red with darker red edges. It was changed in 1917 to distinguish it from the French Legion of Honor.

The redesigned ribbon was red with two 3/16 inch black stripes.

- Nez Percee War in 1877.
- Bannoc War in 1878.
- Northern Cheyennes in 1878 and 1879.
- Sheep-Eaters, Piutes, and Bannocks in June-October 1879. Utes in Colorado and Utah, Sept. 1879 to Nov. 1880.
- Apaches in Arizona and New Mexico in 1885 and 1886. Sioux in South Dakota, Nov. 1890 to Jan. 1891.
- Any action against hostile indians between 1865 and 1891 in which United States troops were killed or wounded.

The Indian Campaign Medal is more commonly referred to as the Indian Wars Medal by collectors. However, in Army Regulations 672-5-1 the medal is officially designated as the Indian Campaign Medal.

The U.S. Mint produced approximately 2,000 Indian Campaign Medals in the "No."

prefixed run and Army records recorded the issue of No.1 through No. 1927. To satisfy the demand from various veterans organizations, the government authorized the Mint to produce about 1,750 medals with "MNo." numbers. A further 250 medals were produced under private contract with unprefixed numbers.

Indian Campaign Medal awarded to John Q.A. Norton, Capt., Co. D, M.No. 327, 19th Kas. Cavalry. A militia soldier, Norton's regiment was mustered for six months for the campaign against the Commanches and Arapahoes, in support of the 7th Cavalry. The regiment's most prominent action was at Black Kettle's village on the Wachita River, Indian Territory (now Oklahoma), on November 27, 1868. During the six months of active service the regiment was in Kansas, Indian Territory, and Texas.

Left and below: A unique cavalry-related group consisting of an Army Civil War and Indian Campaign Medal. When issued, the recipient's name was authorized to be engraved on the rims of early campaign medals.

Army Civil War Campaign Medal awarded to John Q.A. Norton, Orderly Sgt., M.No. 2713, Co. E, 7th Ohio Cavalry. John Quincy Adams Norton participated in 24 engagements during the Civil War.

Spanish-American War

In the latter part of the nineteenth century the United States began to emerge as a new power in world politics. Beginning in the late 1880's more and more Americans began to support imperialistic ventures in the Pacific and Caribbean. The expansion of American interests into these areas would have, with time, led inevitably to a conflict with Spain. The spark which ignited the war between Spain and the United States was the rebellion, in 1895, of Cubans against the repressive policies of the Spanish regime controlling the island.

During 1896 and 1897 Congress attempted to mediate a peaceful settlement to the Cuban rebellion and persuade Spain to grant the island independence. Had it not been for the mysterious sinking of the battleship U.S.S. Maine in Havana harbour on 15 February 1898, with a loss of 260 lives, the United States might have been successful in avoiding a war with Spain.

While the Navy was well prepared for such a conflict the Army was far from prepared to do battle with a global power such as Spain. Suffering from decades of neglect following the Civil War, the U.S. Army numbered less than 26,000 and was ill prepared in both equipment and manpower for the conflict. As a result, combat actions had to wait until June 1898. By 14 June the invasion force destined for Cuba was ready to sail from Tampa, Florida. On 22 June, after heavy shelling, the 5th Corps, under General Shafter, began landing at Siboney and Daiquiri.

Shafter's plan for the attack on the Spanish defenses of Santiago was a simple frontal assault up San Juan Hill and Kettle Hill. The assaults scheduled for dawn on 1 July, were badly coordinated. In the face of stiff resistance both objectives were eventually captured, but at a cost of nearly 1,700 casualties.

With conditions in Santiago deteriorating rapidly the Admiral of the Spanish fleet attempted to break out of Santiago harbour, hoping to reach Cienfuegos on the south coast of Cuba. The American fleet immediately gave chase and in less than two hours destroyed Admiral Cevera's fleet.

A few days later, on 16 July the Spanish leaders in Santiago signed the unconditional surrender of all troops in Cuba. This surrender freed American troops for conquest of the Spanish garrison on Puerto Rico. On 21 July, General Miles sailed from Guantanamo, which had been captured by U.S. Marines in the first land skirmish of the war. On 25 July General Miles landed his 3,000 troops first at Guanica and then at Ponce against only light resistance. In August, with the arrival of an additional 10,000 troops from the United States, General Miles began his drive on the capital city of San Juan. The campaign ended on 13 August when word reached the island that Spain had signed a peace protocal. The campaign in Puerto Rico ended with fewer that fifty casualties.

In another tropical setting halfway around the world Admiral Dewey led his fleet against the Spanish squadron off the coast of Manila on 1 May 1898 and completely anniliated the Spanish forces in what became known as the Battle of Manila Bay. Despite this early success, the efforts of Admiral Dewey and General Merritt to secure a peaceful surrender of the Spanish garrison at Manila failed. On the morning of 13 August, General Merritt's 8th Corps attacked Manila supported by the guns of Admiral Dewey's fleet. The fighting was over in less than a day and the Spanish surrendered at a cost of just 17 Americans killed and 105 wounded.

America has recognized service in the Spanish-American war with several campaign medals. Army personnel were eligible for the Spanish War Service Medal, Spanish Campaign Medal, Army of Cuban Occupation Medal and the Army of Puerto Rican Occupation Medal. Navy and Marine Corps personnel were eligible for two congressionally authorized commemorative medals; the Dewey Medal and the Sampson Medal, as well as the West Indies Campaign Medal and the Spanish Campaign

Medal. Additionally, Navy and Marine Corps personnel who performed acts of bravery or meritorious service which did not rate the Medal of Honor were eligible for the Specially Meritorious Service Medal.

West Indies Campaign Medal

The West Indies Campaign Medal was authorized in 1908 for Navy and Marine Corps personnel who participated in the West Indies Naval Campaign. Veterans of the U.S. Naval Campaign in the West Indies had previously been awarded the "Sampson Medal" in 1901. However, the "Sampson Medal" was officially a commemorative medal and not a campaign medal. About 4,000 West Indies Campaign Medals were issued to Naval personnel and 400 to Marine Corps personnel.

In 1910 procurement of the West Indies Campaign Medal was terminated and replaced with issue of the Spanish Campaign Medal.

The West Indies Campaign Medal is identical in design to the Spanish Campaign Medal for Navy and Marine Corps personnel with the exception of the inscription on the obverse of the pendant, which reads "West Indies Campaign" rather than "Spanish Campaign".

The ribbon of the West Indies Campaign medal is yellow with two wide red stripes.

Marine Corps issue.

G. Sousa

Navy issue.

Because the West Indies Campaign Medal was replaced with the issue of the Spanish Campaign Medal, and because the Spanish Campaign Medal underwent a ribbon change in 1913, many West Indies Campaign Medals are encountered reribboned with second style Spanish Campaign suspension ribbons.

D. Boyce

Spanish Campaign Medal - Army

The Spanish Campaign Medal was established by War Department General Order 5 in 1905. It was awarded for service ashore or on the high seas enroute to any of the following countries:

- Cuba between 11 May and 17 July 1898
- Puerto Rico from 24 July to 13 August 1898
- Phillippine Islands between 30 June and 16 August 1898

The original ribbon for the Spanish Campaign Medal was yellow with two wide red stripes with narrow borders of blue. Because yellow and red were the national colors of Spain, the ribbon was changed in 1913 to yellow with wide blue stripes, in deference to the peaceful relations that had been reestablished with Spain. The Army issued about 18,400 Spanish Campaign Medals (8,000 No. numbered medals, 6,400 MNo. numbers, and about 4,000 unprefixed serial numbered medals).

Second style ribbon.

First style ribbon.

D. Boyce

Major Harold Sorenson wears the Spanish Campaign Medal with second style ribbon.

Spanish Campaign Medal - Navy and Marine Corps

The Spanish Campaign Medal was established by Special Order No. 81 on 27 June 1908 for issue to Navy and Marine Corps personnel who had participated in the Pacific Naval Campaign of the Spanish-American War. Award criteria were relaxed in the early 1920's to allow issue of the medal to all Navy and Marine Corps personnel who served during the Spanish War. Medals issued after this change were issued unnumbered and are not included in the issue totals. Approximately 6,000 Naval personnel received the medal along with 500 Marines.

The original ribbon for the Spanish Campaign Medal was identical to that of the West Indies Campaign Medal. However, in 1913 the ribbon was changed to coincide with the yellow and blue ribbon adopted by the Army.

First style ribbon for the Navy Spanish Campaign Medal.

First style ribbon for the Marine Corps Spanish Campaign Medal. Note "For Service" is in an arc.

Second style ribbon, Navy issue. Note triple-ring suspension authorized in 1923. (Bastian Brothers contract.)

D. Boyce

D. Boyce

Second style ribbon, Marine Corps issue.

Spanish War Service - Army

This medal was created by Act of Congress on 9 July 1918 and was intended to recognize the service of the many Spanish American War Volunteers who did not qualify for the Spanish Campaign Medal. Originally the Spanish War Service Medal was issued only to members of the National Guard who served on active federal duty for at least 90 days during the period from 20 April 1898 to 11 April 1899. Regulations were relaxed in the early 1920s to include any person on active federal duty with the Army during the same period who was not eligible for the Spanish Campaign Medal.

Because of the broad eligibility requirements the Spanish War Service Medal is fairly common. In all approximately 31,000 medals were issued. Initial issue medals were rim stamped with unprefixed numbers and those numbered through 16,650 can be traced through official records.

Note wrap brooch.

Legion of Valor

Captain Ralph W. Robart, DSC, wears the Army Spanish War Service Medal.

Note split-back brooch.

Note the size and spacing differences on the four examples illustrated below.

Spanish War Service Medal awarded to Alice G. L. Ryan (unnumbered) with "U.S. Army Nurse Corps" engraved on reverse scroll.

T. Wheatley

This uniquely mounted group awarded to Col. John Cocke consists of a Spanish War Medal No. 14709, Cuban Pacification Medal No. 868, Philippine Campaign Medal No. 1951, Mexican Border Service Medal No. 33201, and a WWI Victory Medal with "Meuse-Argonne" and "Defensive Sector" bars.

T. Wheatley

WAR DEPARTMENT

THE ADJUTANT GENERAL'S OFFICE nbb-595

WASHINGTON

IN REPLY REFER TO AG 201 Lowe, Arthur
(5-25-26) Ex

May 28, 1926.

Mr. Arthur Lowe,
159-22 - 88th Avenue,
Jamaica, L. I., N.Y.

Dear Sir:

Receipt is acknowledged of your application of the 25th instant for the Spanish War service and Philippine Campaign medals on account of service as private, Battery I, 7th Artillery and Company F, Signal Corps, from April 19, 1898, to April 17, 1901.

Your service as stated above, with the organizations named, entitles you to the desired medals, and I have this day approved your application for the Spanish War service medal and forwarded it to The Quartermaster General of the Army, this city, for issuance of the medal. A blank application is inclosed for your use in applying for the Philippine Campaign medal which should be filled up and returned to this office. Upon receipt of this application the matter will receive prompt consideration.

Very truly yours,

Robert C Davis
Major General,
The Adjutant General.
By

1 Incl.
(Form 0714)

Application, acceptance and shipping tickets for the Spanish War Service and Philippine Campaign Medals. (Next page) Rejection of application for the Philippine Congressional Medal.

Arthur Lowe.

WAR DEPARTMENT
Q. M. C. Form 260
Approved Oct. 1, 1918
Revised June 28, 1922

SHIPPING TICKET

CONSIGNOR: Phila. Q. M. I. Depot

CONSIGNOR'S VOU. NO. 13183
CONSIGNEE'S VOU. NO.
NO. OF SHEETS 1
SHEET NO. 1

FROM WAREHOUSE: Mr. Kemp

DATE: Invoiced 6/29/26.

Rqn.No.8443

SHIP TO Arthur Lowe, Captain, Reserve C.E., 159-22 - 88th Ave., Jamaica, Long Island, N.Y.

AUTHORITY OR REQ. NO. LTR/OQMG.6-1-26 file - QM 422 G-C Medals.Auth.#17078

TRANSPORTATION COST OF $ .... CHARGEABLE TO P/A NO.

ROUTING Franked Mail.

DATE SHIPPED OR DELIVERED 6/28/26.

B/L NO.	DATE	MADE BY	CAR NO.	CAR SEALS NO.

QUANTITY ORDERED	QUANTITY SHIPPED	UNIT	ARTICLES AND CONDITION	UNIT COST	TOTAL COST	PURPOSE NO.
			DAS.6-7-26 stock aom P-4712-A-7-6			
1	1	ea.	Medal, Spanish War Service Serial No.17078 Pkg. B-3173 Shipment Complete. (Rel. 6-24-26)			

ARTICLES LISTED IN COLUMN "SHIPPED" HAVE BEEN RECEIVED 19

(NAME) (RANK) (ORGANIZATION)

POSTED TO STOCK ACCOUNT OF CONSIGNOR BY	CONSIGNEE BY	SELECTED BY	CHECKED BY	PACKED BY	SHIPPING CLERK
		B.K.G.,		Perry	
DATE	DATE	DATE 6/25/26.	DATE	DATE	
THIS COPY FOR	CONSIGNEE TO RETAIN	CONSIGNEE TO SIGN AND RETURN	FINANCE OFFICER	WAREHOUSE	

WAR DEPARTMENT
Q. M. C. Form 260
Approved Oct. 1, 1918
Revised June 28, 1922

SHIPPING TICKET

CONSIGNOR: Phila. Q.M. I. Depot

CONSIGNOR'S VOU. NO. 13453
CONSIGNEE'S VOU. NO.
NO. OF SHEETS 1
SHEET NO. 1

FROM WAREHOUSE: Mr. Klingler
DATE: Invoiced 6/30/26.

Req 9948

SHIP TO Captain Arthur Lowe,
Engr.Res. 159-22-88th Ave.
Jamaica, L.I.N.Y.

AUTHORITY OR REQ. NO. Letter Q.M.G.O. 6/5/26 file QM 422 G-C Medals Auth #32946
TRANSPORTATION COST OF $ .... CHARGEABLE TO P/A NO.

ROUTING Franked Mail

DATE SHIPPED OR DELIVERED 6/30/26.

B/L NO.	DATE	MADE BY	CAR NO.	CAR SEALS NO.

QUANTITY ORDERED	QUANTITY SHIPPED	UNIT	AB 6/25/26 ARTICLES AND CONDITION Stock acm	UNIT COST	TOTAL COST	PURPOSE NO.
			A 7-6.			4712
1	1	Ea.	Medal Philippine Campaign Serial #23312	$.45	.45	
			Pkg. B-3245			
			Bills made 6/25/26.			
			Shipment Complete.			

ARTICLES LISTED IN COLUMN "SHIPPED" HAVE BEEN RECEIVED , 19

(NAME) (RANK) (ORGANIZATION)

POSTED TO STOCK ACCOUNT OF CONSIGNOR BY	CONSIGNEE BY	SELECTED BY	CHECKED BY	PACKED BY	SHIPPING CLERK
		B.K.G.		Perry	
DATE	DATE	DATE 6/28/26.	DATE	DATE	
THIS COPY FOR	CONSIGNEE TO RETAIN	CONSIGNEE TO SIGN AND RETURN	FINANCE OFFICER	WAREHOUSE	

REFER TO AG 201 Low, Arthur (2-3-32)Ex

February 9, 1932.

SUBJECT: Service Medals.

TO: Captain Arthur Lowe, Eng-Res.,
115-22 - 173rd Street,
Saint Albans, L.I., N.Y.

1. Receipt is acknowledged of your letter of February 3d making application for lapel buttons for the Spanish War service and Philippine campaign medals previously issued to you and also making application for the Philippines Congressional medal.

2. The Quartermaster General of the Army, this city, has been directed to issue the desired lapel buttons to you free of charge.

3. The Philippines Congressional medal is authorized for issue to those who, having entered the service under a call of the President for the War with Spain, served beyond the date on which they were entitled to their discharge, to help to suppress the Philippine insurrection, and were subsequently honorably discharged from the Army. Service as an enlisted man in the Regular Army, to count, must have been under an enlistment entered into between April 21, and October 26, 1898. The War with Spain closed on April 11, 1899.

4. In view of the fact that you did not enlist for service in the War with Spain between April 21, and October 26, 1898, it is regretted that you are not entitled to the Philippines Congressional medal.

By order of the Secretary of War:

Adjutant General.

Left: Original design for the Army Spanish War Service Medal which was submitted by BB & B but not accepted. It is shown next to the production variety to illustrate the size difference of the pendant and the ribbon color.

Occupation of Cuba

With the signing of the peace treaty on 10 December 1898, the United States successfully concluded the Spanish-American war and forced Spain to give up claims to Cuba, Puerto Rico, the Philippine Islands and Guam. American occupation troops, under the command of General Wood, remained in control of Cuba until May 1902 and assisted the new republic with drafting a constitution and electing a government. On 20 May 1902, General Wood formally transferred power to the newly elected president, Estrada Palma, formally ending the military occupation of Cuba.

President Estrada's first term in office was marked by significant social and economic gains in Cuba. However, corruption was wide spread within the Estrada government. The elections of 1905 were boycotted by the Liberal Party and Estrada won a second term but was forced to request American aid to put down the ensuing Liberal revolt and resign his presidency.

To restore peace and stability, William Howard Taft, the U.S. Secretary of War, went to Cuba on 9 September 1906. Finding the country in total disarray, Taft ordered 200 Marines and 5,600 Army troops to Cuba on 29 September to restore order and establish a provisional government. Taft remained as acting governor until 13 October 1906, when he was replaced by a Nebraska lawyer named Charles E. Magoon.

Magoon's administration brought prosperity, order and a return to democratic elections. The 1908 elections sponsored by Magoon brought Jose Miguel Gomez and Alfredo Zayas to power and on 28 January 1909 Magoon transferred control of the government to them, thus ending the United States occupation.

Army personnel who served in Cuba prior to 20 May 1902 were eligible for the Army of Cuban Occupation Medal while personnel who served in Cuba during the Liberal revolt were awarded the Army of Cuban Pacification Medal. Navy and Marine Corps personnel were eligible for award of the Cuban Pacification Medal.

Army of Cuban Occupation Medal

The Army of Cuban Occupation Meda (ACOM) was established by War Department General Orders 40, in 1915. Awardec for service in Cuba between 18 July 189 and 20 May 1902, it was primarily intendec to recognize the service of personnel sent tc Cuba after the close of hostilities. Despite the original intent, vertually all Cubar veterans who were eligible for the Spanish Campaign Medal also received the Army of Cuban Occupation Medal.

The ACOM was originally issued with "No." serial numbers on the rim and these numbers through No. 4102 can be traced. Other issues bore "MNo." serial numbers as well as unprefixed serial numbers. Later replacement issues of the ACOM were issued unnumbered. In all, about 13,50C numbered Army of Cuban Occupation medals were issued.

"No. 654."

Army of Puerto Rican Occupation Medal

The Army of Puerto Rican Occupation Medal (APROM) was first authorized on 4 February 1919. However adoption by the Army was delayed by World War I and the APROM was not officially approved until 4 February 1919. The Army of Puerto Rican Occupation Medal was awarded for service in Puerto Rico between 14 August and 10 December 1898. Because of the long delay in authorizing the APROM, only about 3,000 medals were issued and records exist for only 10 percent of those issued.

D. Boyce

"M.No. 183"

A. Menke

"No. 351"

A. Menke

Above: Private contract die used on unprefixed numbers "1 to 200," which has smaller letters and numbers on the obverse design.

Philippine Insurrection

After some hesitation, President McKinley bowed to public pressure and supported the view that the Philippine islands ought to be retained by the United States. After the United States officially proclaimed possession of all the Philippine islands in January 1899, Philippine insurgents under General Aguinaldo proclaimed independence, ratified their own constitution and prepared to do battle against the Americans.

U.S. troops on the island soon found themselves under heavy attack on the night of 4 February 1899 by 40,000 insurgents under the command of Auginaldo. This assault was repelled and after a few battles the contest evolved into a bloody guerrilla war which eventually saw the commitment of more than 100,000 troops between February 1899 and July 1902. Unrest among the Moros was still not quelled when President Theodore Roosevelt announced the formal end of the Philippine Insurrection on 4 July 1902.

Service in the Philippine Insurrection by Navy and Marine Corps personnel was recognized by the Philippine Campaign Medal. Army personnel were eligible for their own design of the Philippine Campaign Medal as well as the Philippine Congressional Medal.

Philippine Campaign Medal - Army

The Philippine Campaign Medal was authorized for Army personnel in War Department General Orders 5, on 11 January 1905. The medal was awarded for service in the Philippine Islands under any of the following conditions:

- Ashore between 4 February 1899 and 4 July 1902.
- Ashore in the Department of Mindanao between 4 Feb. 1899 and 31 Dec. 1904.
- Against the Pulajanes in Leyte between 20 July 1906 and 30 June 1907, or on Samar between 2 August 1904 and 30 June 1907.
- With any of the following expeditions:
- Against Pala on Jolo, April - May 1905.

A. Menke

An unusual campaign grouping to an Army/Marine Corps veteran. The medals are Army Spanish Campaign (M.No. 5321), Army Philippine Campaign (M.No. 7742), Marine Corps Cuban Pacification (1351), and the Marine Corps Philippine Campaign (1275).

- Against Datu Ali on Mindanao, October 1905.
- Against hostile Moros on Mt. Bud-Dajo, Jolo, March 1906.
- Against hostile Moros on Mt. Bagsac, Jolo, Jan. - July 1913.
- Against hostile Moros on Mindanao or Jolo, 1910 - 1913.
- Any action against hostile natives in wich U.S. troops were killed or wounded between 4 February 1899 and 31 December 1913.

There were about 44,000 Philippine Campaign Medals issued to Army personnel. Examples exist with both "No." and MNo." prefixed serial numbers stamped on the rim. Rim numbers are usually stamped at about the 6 o'clock position. Additional contracts were let for unprefixed numbers as well as unnumbered medals.

Ken Lazier

Right: Brig. Gen. Henry W. Lawton.
Below: Serial numbers "28630" and "No. 14402."

National Archives

Lt. Col. Benjamin A. Poore, G.S. Corps.

T. Wheatley

Army Philippine Campaign Medal, numbered "26444" with "1913" engraved under "For Service" on the reverse. Dating was authorized by the Army on only the Philippine Campaign Medal and the Mexican Service Medal. 1913 was the last year the Philippine Campaign Medal was authorized for issue.

Philippine Campaign Medal - Navy and Marine Corps

The Philippine Campaign Medal for Navy and Marine Corps personnel was authorized on 27 June 1908. Award of the Philippine Campaign Medal was limited to Navy and Marine Corps personnel serving on 64 ships stationed in Philippine waters and four shore stations during specific periods between 4 February 1899 and 10 March 1906.

The original ribbon was red with a single wide center stripe of yellow. In 1913 this ribbon was changed to the blue and red ribbon used on the Army medal.

Examples of the Navy issue medal exist with both unprefixed and "MNo." prefixed serial numbers. Marine Corps issue medals exist with only unprefixed numbers. In all, approximately 4,300 Navy and 1,200 Marine Corps medals were issued.

First style ribbon - Navy.

D. Boyce

Navy Philippine Campaign Medal with first style ribbon, numbered "1912," with recipient's name, position and ship engraved on rim.

D. Boyce

First style ribbon - Marine Corps.

D. Boyce

D. Boyce

Second style ribbon - Navy.

D. Boyce

Second style ribbon - Marine Corps.

Philippine Congressional Medal

The Philippine Congressional Medal was established on 29 June 1906 to recognize those individuals who entered the Army between 21 April and 26 October 1898 and fulfilled both of the following requirements:

- Served beyond the date on which they were eligible for discharge.
- Were ashore in the Philippine Islands between 4 February 1899 and 4 July 1902.

Congress authorized the procurement of 11,500 medals out of which approximately 6,200 were issued. All medals in the initial order were rim stamped with "No." serial numbers.

Serial numbers "No. 9674" and "No. 6230."

Boxer Rebellion

By the turn of the 20th century China found itself faced with extensive exploitation by foreign enterprises. Younger Chinese began to express their resentment at this situation with increasing acts of violence aimed at foreign influences and foreigners. These young people formed a secret society called the Fists of Righteous Furry. The sect, called the Boxers by Westerners, also found an ally in the Dowager Empress. When these acts of violence resulted in the murder of the German Minister on 20 June 1900 most remaining foreigners took refuge in the foreign legations area of Peking. Besieged by an overwhelming force, the legations appealed for help.

Using Manila as a base, the United States assembled a force of 2,500 soldiers and marines under the command of Maj. Gen. Adna R. Chaffee. On 13 July elements of this force, officially designated the China Relief Expedition, participated with troops of several other nations in the successful attack on Tientsin, China.

By early August, the allied forces amounted to more than 18,000 troops from England, France, Japan, Russia, Austria, Italy, and the United States. Fighting a number of sharp skirmishes en route, this force reached Peking on 12 August. On 15 August, Cpt. Henry J. Reilly's Light Battery F of the U.S. 5th Artillery shattered the gates leading to the Inner City and allied troops scattered the final remnants of the Boxer resistance.

Following the defeat of the Boxers in Peking all resistances was slowly eliminated and the Dowager Empress sued for peace in October. During the peace negations, which dragged on for almost a year the United States maintained a small contingent in north China. This force was withdrawn in September 1901 and the American presence in China was limited to a small legation guard in Peking and a garrison along the Tientsin-Peking railway.

For their service in the China Relief Expedition, soldiers of the U.S. Army received the China Campaign Medal. Sailors and U.S. Marines received the China Relief Expedition Medal.

China Campaign Medal - Army

Authorized 11 January 1905 by War Department General Orders 5, 1905, the China Campaign Medal was awarded for service ashore in China with the Peking Relief Expedition between 20 June 1900 and 27 May 1901.

Approximately 2,300 China Campaign Medals were awarded to eligible participants. The China Campaign Medal is found with both "No." and "MNo." prefixed serial numbers, as well as unprefixed serial numbers, stamped on the medal's rim. Unnumbered replacement issues also exist.

Awarded to Pvt. Elma Uhl, 6th Cavalry, numbered "746."

T. Wheatley

T. Wheatley

China Relief Expedition Medal - Navy and Marine Corps

The China Relief Expedition Medal was authorized on 27 June 1908 for award to Navy and Marine Corps personnel who served ashore in China or as crew members of 11 specific ships in China waters between 24 May 1900 and 27 May 1901.

The original striking of 400 Navy medals reads "China Relief Expedition 1901" around the obverse of the medal. However, due to a faulty die a new die was cut, and on subsequent Navy medals and all Marine Corps medals, the date reads "1900."

Both Navy and Marine Corps China Expedition Medals were issued with unprefixed serial numbers rim-stamped on the pendant.

First style ribbon - Navy (yellow with black stripes) used from 1908-1913.

D. Boyce

D. Boyce

First style ribbon - Marine Corps.

D. Boyce

Second style ribbon - Navy (yellow with blue edges) introduced in 1913.

D. Boyce

Second style ribbon - Marine Corps.

Some of the Marine contingent who took part in the relief of Tientsin in China.

Army of Cuban Pacification Medal

Following the end of the Spanish American War, American troops occupied Cuba. This occupation lasted for four and a half years, ending when a Cuban republic was established under President Thomas Estrada Palma. Political, social, and economic difficulties led to Palma's resignation on 29 September 1906 and the United States established a provisional government to quell the insurection then sweeping the country. A new government was formed under General Jose Miguel on 28 January 1908. The last American troops were withdrawn on 1 April 1908.

On 11 May 1909, in War Department General Orders 96, qualified Army personnel were awarded the Army of Cuban Pacification Medal. The medal was authorized for all personnel who served in Cuba between 6 October 1906 and 1 April 1909.

The Army of Cuban Pacification Medal was initially awarded with "No." and "MNo." prefixed serial numbers. Additional stocks ordered following World War I were issued with unprefixed serial numbers, while later replacement issue medals were issued without serial numbers.

D. Boyce

The above is an official 1940s reissue (note brooch), and should not be considered a reproduction.

Cuban Pacification Medal - Navy and Marine Corps

The Cuban Pacification Medal for Navy and Marine Corps personnel was authorized on 13 August 1909. Originally

Navy issue.

D. Boyce

intended to recognize the service of Navy and Marine Corps medical personnel who served ashore in Cuba from 6 October 1906 to 1 April 1909, eligibility was later extended to personnel aboard 24 ships which served in Cuban waters during specific periods between 12 September 1906 and 1 April 1909.

The Cuban Pacification medal was initially issued with unprefixed serial numbers. Approximately 2,100 Navy personnel and 1,500 Marines were awarded the medal.

Marine Corps issue.

D. Boyce

Nicaraguan Campaigns

American military actions in Nicaragua first began in August 1912 with the landing of US Marines and sailors at Corinto and Bluefields. President Diaz, whose government was heavily in debt to US banks, was besieged by two Liberal forces under the command of Presidential hopeful Mena and General Zeledon. Within a few days US Marines and Naval personnel supported by Nicaraguan government troops captured Zeledon and forced Mena into exile.

With the exception of a brief nine month period in 1925-1926, the US maintained troops in Nicaragua from 1912 until 1933. Over 2,700 sailors and Marines had taken part in the 1912 intervention. Most were quickly withdrawn, but a 100 man Marine legation guard was maintained in Managua until 1925.

Elections in January 1925 ended the Conservative monopoly on the presidency. However, the defeated Conservitive candidate Emiliano Chamorro succeeded in gaining control of the presidency one year later through a series of political deals and outright threats. US refusal to recognize the Chomorro government led to a Liberal uprising led by exiles operating from Mexico. By September 1926 the fighting had left the country bankrupt and the U.S. government, forced to recognize the new govenment of conservative President Diaz, sent in the Marines in efforts to suppress the Liberal revolutionaries.

Peace was officially declared on 16 May 1927, but one renegade Liberal, General Augusto Cesar Sandino and his band of Sandinistas, led US Marines on a six-year odyssey that reads like a prelude for the Vietnam war.

Navy and Marine Corps personnel who served in Nicaragua during the initial intervention in 1912 were eligible for the Nicaraguan Campaign Medal. Service in Nicaragua against the Sandino rebels from 1926 until 1933 was recognized by award of the Second Nicaraguan Campaign Medal.

Nicaraguan Campaign Medal (1912)

The Nicaraguan Campaign Medal was authorized on 22 September 1913 for award to Navy and Marine Corps personnel who served ashore or on eight specific ships in Nicaraguan waters between 29 July and 14 November 1912.

Approximately 1,400 Navy and 1,000 Marine Corps personnel were awarded the Nicaraguan Campaign Medal. The original issue medals were produced under private contract and were rim-stamped with unprefixed serial numbers.

A. Menke

Navy issue.

Marine Corps issue.

D. Boyce

The Mexican Campaign

America's southern neighbor had been at peace with itself and the United States for over half a century when revolution began to rock Mexico in 1910.

President for Life, Don Porfirio Diaz announced free elections and Francisco Madero, and American-educated liberal, took up the challenge to run against Diaz. Diaz, having second thoughts about his "free election" promise, jailed Madero and won the election in landslide fashion.

Released after the elections, Madero fled to the United States and organized a revolt which began on 18 November 1910 and succeeded in forcing Diaz to flee to France on 25 May 1911. Madero ascended to the Presidency the following day and began the insurmountable task of reunifying the country.

Madero's government was besieged by Emiliano Zapata in the south and Pancho Villa in the north. In an effort to quell the bandit uprisings Madero hired General Victoriano Huerta to lead the Mexican Army. However, Huerta quickly turned on Madero, murdering both Madero and his vice-president on 22 February 1913 and installed himself as president. The bandit opposition soon forced Huerto to follow Diaz into exile and Venustiano Carranza, Villa's ally in the war against Huerto, installed himself as president.

Carranza sooned turned on Villa and in a series of bloody campaigns against Villa's Division del Norete, Carranza smashed the once vaunted Division of the North and won recognition from President Woodrow Wilson. Pancho Villa's night raid on 9 March 1916 against the New Mexico town of Columbus and neighboring Camp Furlong was Villa's response to Wilson's recognition of the Carranza government. Suddenly, Mexico's bloody Civil War had spilled over onto American soil killing nine U.S. civilians and eight troopers of the 13th Cavalry.

On 16 March 1916, under the command of General John "Black Jack" Pershing, the black troopers of General Pershing's crack 10th Cavalry formed the western column of a two-pronged attack into Mexico with the troopers from the 13th Cavalry forming the east column. On the morning of 29 March, Custer's old regiment, the 7th Cavalry also joined the Punitive Expedition.

The Expedition achieved stunning victories over the villistas at Guerrero, Parral, and Ojos Asules but was never able to capture Villa. By late May Mexico and the United States were exchanging diplomatic salvos over the continued presence of U.S. troops on Mexican soil. Finally, on 21 June soldiers of Troops K and C of the 10th Cavalry fought a bloody skirmish at Carrizal with Mexican Army troops under the command of General Gomes.

The furious exchange of gunfire at Carrizal left both General Gomez and the commander of the American cavalrymen, Captain Charles Boyd dead. Mexican President Carranza then made major diplomatic overtures on 4 July to attempt a negotiated end to the Punitive Expedition.

As the prospects for American entry into the war in Europe increased, President Wilson began to withdraw the troops of

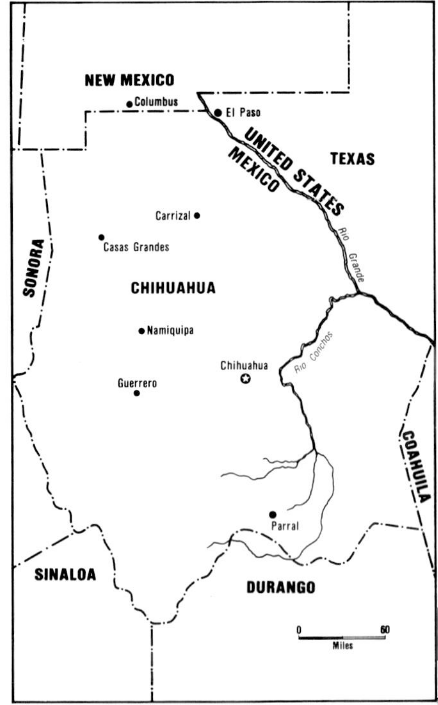

Pershing's expedition in January 1917. The last trooper crossed the Mexican-American border during the afternoon of 5 February 1917, just south of Columbus.

Over 100,000 National Guard troops from as far away as Oregon, North Dakota and New York served on the Mexican border during the Punitive Expedition, gaining valuable military experience which aided in the rapid deployment of U.S. troops following America's entry on 6 April 1917 into World War I.

Soldiers from the U.S. Army campaigning in Mexico against Pancho Villa were awarded the Mexican Service Medal while soldiers of the Regular Army and National Guard serving on the Mexican Border during 1916 and 1917 received the Mexican Border Service Medal. Navy and Marine Corps personnel were eligible for their own design of the Mexican Service Medal.

Mexican Service Medal - Army

The Mexican Service Medal was authorized 12 December 1917 to recognize the service of Army personnel in any of the following engagements or expeditions:

- Vera Cruz Expedition in Mexico between 24 April and 26 November 1914.
- Nogales, Arizona, 1-5 November 1915.
- Punitive Expedition in Mexico between 14 March 1916 and 7 February 1917.
- Buena Vista, Mexico 1 December 1917.
- San Bernardino Canon, Mexico, 26 December 1917.
- Le Grulla, Texas, 8-9 January 1918.
- Pilares, Mexico, 28 March 1918
- Nogales, Arizona, 27 August 1918.
- El Paso, Texas and Juarez, Mexico 15-16 June 1919.
- Any action against hostile Mexicans in which United States troops were killed or wounded between 12 April 1911 and 7 February 1917.

About 15,000 Mexican Service Medals were originally issued. The original U.S. Mint contract pieces were awarded with "No." or "MNo." serial numbers. Following WWI an additional commercial contract was let and these pieces were produced with unprefixed serial numbers. Replacement issue medals also exist without any serial numbers.

Serial numbers "No. 698" and "13075."

Mexican Service Medal - Navy and Marine Corps

The Mexican Service Medal for Navy and Marine Corps personnel was originally authorized 11 February 1918 for award to officers and men who served ashore during the Vera Cruz expedition between 21 April and 23 April 1914. Eligibility was quickly expanded to include personnel who served aboard 121 ships during specified periods from 21 April to 26 November 1914 and from 14 March 1916 to 7 February 1917. Navy and Marine Corps personnel who participated in engagements against hostile Mexican forces outside of these specific time periods were also eligible for award of the Mexican Service Medal.

The Mexican Service Medal is one of the few Navy and Marine Corps campaign medals issued with "MNo." serial numbers as well as the more common unprefixed serial numbers. In all about 16,000 Navy and 2,500 Marine Corps personnel received Mexican Service Medals.

D. Boyce

Navy issue.

Marine Corps issue.

D. Boyce

Haitian Campaigns

American military involvement in Haiti began the afternoon of 28 July 1915 with the landing of two companies of US Marines and three companies of Naval personnel from the USS Washington at Port-au-Prince.

This uninvited intervention began as a result of the high amount of debt the country had incurred to US banks and the total breakdown of law and order in the country. Beginning in 1912 the officially recognized path to the presidency of Haiti was by murdering the incumbent president. In 1912 President Leconte had been blown up in the National Palace. In 1913 President Auguste was poisoned. During 1914 three separate revolutions ousted Presidents Oreste, Zamor, and Theodore. Finally, on 27 July 1915, when President V.G. Sam murdered 167 of his political opponents in the Port-au-Price jail, he was murdered in the French Embassy by an angry mob and his dismembered body dragged through the streets. Seeing that law and order had totally broken down, Adm. William B. Caperton led two companies of Marines and three companies of sailors from the USS Washington into Port-au-Prince, thus beginning two decades of U.S. occupation.

During the first two years of occupation events on the island were fairly quiet and US Marines recruited and trained a 2,400 man Gendarmerie d' Haiti. Led by Marine Corps officers, the Gendarmerie became a well-disciplined force. Two-time Medal of Honor winner Major Smedley Butler became the first Commandant.

Revolutionary activity picked up again in September 1918 when a large force of Cacos, led by Charlemagne Peralte began raiding towns and Gendarmarie barracks. The so-called Cacos War ended in January 1920 shortly after the death of Charlemagne. Marine occupation in Haiti ended on 21 August 1934 when the last detachment of US Marines left the country.

The Navy and Marine Corps recognized service in Haiti during 1915 with the Haitian Campaign Medal. For service during the Cacos uprising, Navy and Marine Corps personnel received the Haitian Campaign Medal 1919-1920.

Haitian Campaign Medal (1915)

The Haitian Campaign Medal was established 22 June 1917 for issue to Navy and Marine Corps personnel who served ashore in Haiti between 9 July and 6 December 1915 or on board 14 specific ships operating in Haitian waters during the same time period.

Unlike earlier Navy and Marine Corps campaign medals, numbered Haitian Campaign medals were produced with only Navy reverses. About 5,200 medals were issued, generally those numbered in the 3,000 range were awarded to Marine Corps personnel.

Navy and Marine Corps issue.

A. Menke

Above: Bailey, Banks & Biddle (BBB) designed and produced the initial run of medals, with no Marine Corps reverse. Unnumbered pieces with Marine Corps reverses do exist and may have been produced at a later date for exhibition purposes or to fill demands from qualified Marine recipients.

Mexican Border Service Medal

The Mexican Border Service Medal was first authorized by Act of Congress 9 July 1918. This medal was created to specifically recognize the thousands of National Guard troops federalized for service during the Mexican War who did not qualify for award of the Mexican Service Medal. Eligibility for the Mexican Border Service Medal was extended to Army and National Guard personnel for service between 9 May 1916 and 24 March 1917, or for service with the Mexican Border Patrol between 1 January 1916 and 6 April 1917.

Serial number "23254."

Legion of Valor

Lt.Col. Thomas E. Swan, DSC, and a chaplain.

All Mexican Border Service Medals were produced under private contract and were issued with unprefixed serial numbers. About 34,000 of the 41,000 Mexican Border Service medals issued can be traced to specific receipiants.

Dominican Campaign

The political unrest in Haiti spilled over into the neighboring Dominican Republic, and by May 1916 fighting between rival political factions in that tiny country seriously threatened American financial interests. With the the Dominican government unable to protect the American and Haitian legations on the island, two companies of Marines were landed to protect the legations and a company of sailors was landed to capture Ft. San Geronimo.

Although fighting was limited and order quickly restored, American forces remained until December to solidify the control of the new Dominican government.

Service by Navy and Marine Corps personnel in the Dominican Republic during 1916 was recognized by the Dominican Campaign Medal.

Dominican Campaign Medal

The Domician Campaign Medal was issued to Navy and Marine Corps personnel for service in Santo Domingo between 16 May and 4 December 1916 or on board twenty-six specific ships operating in Dominican waters during the same time period. Authorized on 29 December 1921, the Dominican Campaign Medal introduced a new reverse design which would be used on all future Navy and Marine Corps campaign medals until WW II.

The Dominican Campaign Medal was issued to approximately 3,700 Navy personnel and about 2,700 Marines. As with previous campaign medals, the Dominican Campaign Medal was issued with unprefixed serial numbers, although subsequent contracts for replacement issue medals were placed for unnumbered medals.

D. Boyce

Navy issue.

D. Boyce

Navy issue Dominican Campaign Medal with recipient's name, rank and ship engraved on rim, number "69."

D. Boyce

Marine Corps issue.

World War I Victory Medal

With the United States' entry into the First World War the Army, Navy and Marine Corps swelled under the rapid influx of volunteers and draftees to their highest numbers since the Civil War. By the end of the war more men had served in uniform than in any other conflict up to that time.

Prior to World War I, the Army and Navy issued their own campaign medals to recognize active federal military service during war or in campaigns against hostile forces. However, the unprecedented size of the Armed Forces during WW I necessitated a rethinking of the manner in which the war time service of millions of World War I veterans would be recognized. Because of the long duration of the war and the large number of significant campaigns which were conducted, Congress authorized a war service medal, which was termed a Victory Medal, for award to all personnel who served on active duty with the Armed Forces.

The design of the World War I Victory Medal was the same for all branches of

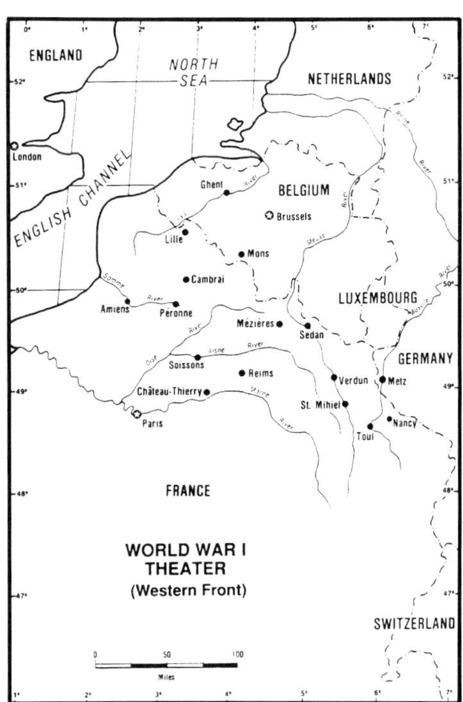

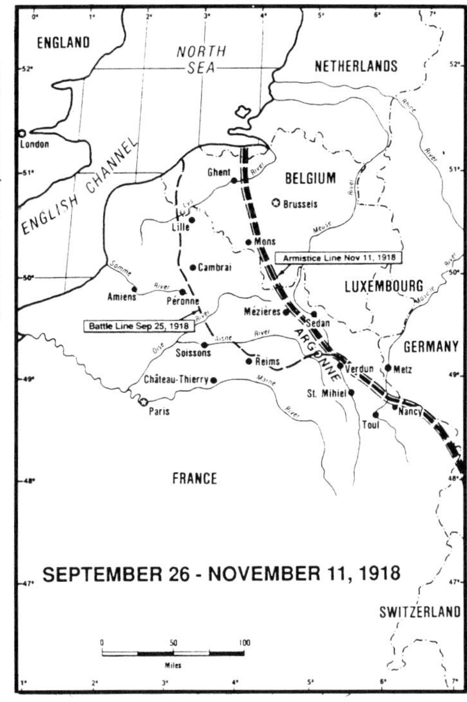

State Historical Society of North Dakota

Lt.Col. Frayne Baker.

D. Boyce

Victory Medal with Naval "Atlantic Fleet" clasp.

Legion of Valor

This Navy MoH and Navy Cross recipient wears the Victory Medal with single clasp.

service. Service in specific campaigns, countries or duty stations was signified by the attachment of clasps to the suspension ribbon.

Clasps for Army personnel, bearing the name of a specific campaign or country are 1/8th wide by 1 1/2 inches long with rounded ends. Clasps for Navy personnel are 5/16 inches wide with squared ends and a rope-like border.

Army personnel were authorized 13 Battle Clasps for participation in specific battles and a "Defensive Sector" clasp for service in the Defensive Sector. In addition, Army personnel who did not qualify for either a Battle Clasp or the "Defensive Sector" clasp could qualify for award of a Service Clasp for service in one of five specific countries. No service member was authorized more than one Service Clasp.

Navy personnel were authorized 19 Service Clasps for service in specific duty stations or countries. In addition, Marine Corps and Navy personnel who served with the American Expeditionary Forces in France or Siberia were eligible for appropriate Army Battle Clasps and Service Clasps. As with Army personnel, naval

Victory Medal with "Siberia" service clasp.

Legion of Valor

Above(Sergeant Henry B. Hallowwell, USMC, was the oldest "leather-neck" after WWI at 85 years-of-age. He served in the White House under President James Buchanan, served in the Civil War and was still recruiting in 1918.

Left: Sergeant Hubert H. Kidwell, DSC, wears the Victory Medal with six clasps.

personnel were authorized only award of one Service Clasp.

Both Army and Navy personnel were authorized to wear a bronze 3/16th inch star on the service ribbon to denote award of Battle Clasps. Service Clasps were not represented by stars on the service ribbon.

For a complete list of clasps see Appendix B.

Texas Cavalry Congressional Medal

This medal was authorized by Act of Congress on 16 April 1924 for award to the officers and enlisted personnel of the two Texas Cavalry Brigades raised by the State of Texas on 8 December 1917. These units were used to relieve Regular Army regiments then serving on the Mexican Border and were not eligible for the World War I Victory Medal.

D. Boyce

Ribbon colors: Yellow for cavalry, white for congressional nature of award, and green for the proximity to the Mexican border.

6000 were produced but as of April 1937 only 840 were issued by the Militia Bureau. The remainder were turned over to the US Property and Disbursing Officer of Texas.

Army of Occupation of Germany Medal

The Army of Occupation of Germany Medal was not established until 21 November 1941. War Department Bulletin 34, 1941 authorized award of the medal to any member of the Army who served in Germany or Austria-Hungary between 12 November 1918 and 11 July 1923. Navy and Marine Corps personnel who were attached to shore duty during those same dates were also eligible for award of the Army of Occupation of Germany Medal.

The original ribbon was of silk moire with a wide black center stripe flanked by stripes of red, white, and edged with a wavy blue stripe. The design was changed soon after the initial issue to a straight blue stripe.

Due to production scheduling, the pendant design for the Army of Occupation of Germany medal was not approved until after the change in the ribbon design. It is doubtful if any of the issued medals were suspended from the first style ribbon.

T. Wheatley

First style.

Second style.

Haitian Campaign Medal 1919 - 1920

Following the withdrawal of the bulk of American Navy and Marine Corps personnel from the first campaign in Haiti in 1915, the Gendarmerie d'Haiti was organized under control of the Marine garrison and assumed military and police duties on the island. In 1919 native Cacos under the leadership of chief Charlemagne Perlate began an intensive campaign of violence to overthrow the government.

The Haitian Campaign Medal 1919-1920 was authorized to recognize the service of Navy and Marine Corps personnel who reinforced the Marine garrison on the island and waged a prolonged and intensive campaign to restore order to Haiti. Awarded to Navy personnel of specific ships which operated in Haitian waters between 1 April 1919 and 15 June 1920 and to Marine Corps personnel who served ashore during that same time, this medal is identical to the first Haitian Campaign Medal with the exception that the date on the bottom of the obverse of the medal has been changed from "1915" to "1919-1920".

Navy issue Haitian Campaign Medal 1919-1920 with recipient's name and ship engraved on rim.

Note:
All Navy issues were unnumbered, whereas, all Marine Corps issues were numbered.

Navy issue.

D. Boyce

Marine Corps issue.

D. Boyce

D. Boyce

Personnel who were awarded the first Haitian Campaign Medal and subsequently qualified for the second Haitian Campaign medal were awarded a clasp, which was inscribed "1919-1920", for attachment to the suspension ribbon.

D. Boyce

D. Boyce

Most of the Haitian Campaign Medals were produced by Whitehead & Hoag Co. of Newark, New Jersey.

A. Menke

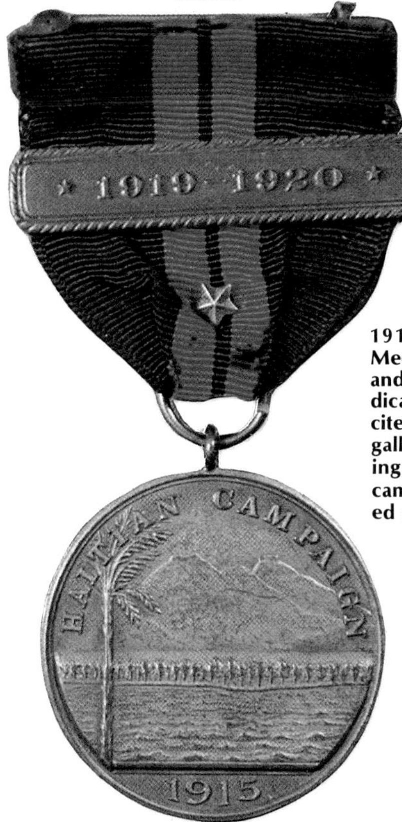

1915 Haitian Campaign Medal with "1919-1920" bar and a silver Citation Star indicating an individual was cited, in official orders, for gallantry in action. The wearing of Citation Stars on early campaign medals is considered uncommon.

A. Menke

A Joseph Mayer of Seattle production of an unaccepted design for the second Haitian Campaign Medal featuring the date "1919" on the obverse. Although not accepted by the Navy Department, this medal was produced by Mayer in limited quantity for purchase by qualified veterans. The actual design accepted by the Navy was submitted and produced by BB & B.

Second Nicaraguan Campaign Medal

In 1925 a coup d'etat by Emiliano Chamorro forced the leader of the Nicaraguan Liberal party, Juan Sacasa, to flee the country. After Washington refused to recognize Sacasa as President of Nicaragua he turned to Mexico for support. Mexican recognition of Sacasa led to nation wide revolution in Nicaragua. In a move to protect American interest and put an end to the violence, American Marines were sent to Nicaragua in January 1927. The American occupation of Nicaragua was essentially over in 1928 but the last contingent of Marines did not leave the country until 1933.

The Second Nicaraguan Campaign Medal was first authorized by Navy Department General Orders on 8 November 1929. It was awarded to Navy and Marine Corps per-

This China Marine wears the WWI Victory, Second Nicaraguan, Expeditionary and Good Conduct Medals.

Navy issue.

Marine Corps issue.

A. Menke

D. Boyce

sonnel who served in Nicaragua and its surrounding waters between 27 August 1926 and 2 January 1933. A few Army personnel also qualified for award of the Second Nicaraguan Campaign Medal and they were issued the Marine Corps version.

All initial issues of the Second Nicaraguan Campaign Medal had M.No. prefixed serial numbers and subsequent contracts for replacement issue medals were unnumbered.

Above: This Marine contingent repulsed an attack by General Augusto Sandino on Ocotal. Sandino was a rebel officer who took refuge in the jungle and held out there during the entire intervention, confining himself to irregular warfare and ambushes. Below: Sandino's flag was captured in his Ocotal repulse.

Yangtze Service Medal

In 1924 a new wave of nationalism began to sweep China and threatened to drive foreign business out of the country. The situation slowly escalated until 1927 when the United States dispatched a contingent of five thousand Marines to protect the International Settlement of Shanghai and several other cities with sizeable American businesses. While the fighting was not as serious as that which occurred during the Boxer Rebellion, the Marine presence in China continued until the outbreak of the Second World War.

The Yangtze Service Medal was authorized on 28 April 1930 by Navy Department General Orders No. 205. Navy and Marine Corps personnel who served in the Yangtze River Valley, Shanghai, China, or the surrounding waters between 3 September 1926 and 21 October 1927 or from 1 March 1930 to 31 December 1932 were eligible for award of this medal. Members of the US Army's 31st Infantry who were stationed in China were awarded the Yangtze Service Medal with the Marine Corps reverse.

Produced by the U.S. Mint the initial issue medal bore M.No. prefixed serial numbers while later replacement pieces have no serial numbers.

Navy issue.

D. Boyce

Legion of Valor

Marine Corps issue.

D. Boyce

Gunnery Sergeant John Hamas, USMC. Note this Navy Cross recipient wears the Yangtze Service Medal on the top row, second from right.

Marine Corps Expeditionary Medal

The Marine Corps Expeditionary Medal came about as a result of a proposal by Maj. William C. Wise, Jr. Major Wise presented a proposal to the Commandant of the Marine Corps on 5 April 1919 that the Marine Corps adopt a series of seven ribbons to recognize service in various expeditionary landings.

Major Wise's proposal met with a favorable response and was modified to allow a single ribbon. The resulting Marine Corps Expeditionary Ribbon was authorized by Marine Corps General Order No. 33 on 8 May 1919. The medal pendant was added on 28 July 1921 by Executive Order 3524. The main purpose of the Marine Corps Expeditionary Medal is to recognize Marine Corps personnel who have actually landed on foreign territory and engaged in operations against an armed opposing force. In addition, the action must also not qualify for any other campaign medal.

The Marine Corps Expeditionary Medal was originally produced using M.No. prefixed serial numbers. Newer strikes of the medal were produced without serial numbers.

To date more than sixty operations have qualified for award of the Marine Corps Expeditionary Medal, the latest being Persian Gulf operations prior to Operation Desert Shield / Desert Storm. A complete list of operations qualifying for the Marine Corps Expeditionary Medal is included in Appendix C.

With "Wake Island" clasp.

(See Appurtenances chapter for details.)

D. Boyce

This "China Marine" wears the Expeditionary Medal next to his WWII Victory Medal.

Navy Expeditionary Medal

The Navy Expeditionary Medal was authorized by Navy Department General Orders No. 84 on 5 August 1936. The medal is awarded to Naval personnel who have actually landed on foreign territory and engaged in operations against armed opposition or operated under circumstances which are deemed to merit special recognition and for which no service or campaign medal exists.

Naval personnel who served in defense of Wake Island during the period 7 - 22 December 1941 are authorized to wear a bronze "Wake Island" clasp on the suspension ribbon of the medal and a silver "W" on the service ribbon

Most recently, operations in Libya and the Persian Gulf have qualified Naval personnel participating in those operations for award of the Navy Expeditionary Medal.

A. Rohloff

China Service Medal

The China Service Medal was authorized by Navy Department General Orders No. 135 on 23 August 1940. Eligibility for the medal extended to personnel for service during two seperate periods. The first period of eligibility extended from 7 July 1937 to 7 September 1939. During that time the China Service Medal was awarded to personnel of the Navy and Marine Corps who served ashore in China or who were attached to any of the vessels which operated in support of operations in China during that time frame.

The second period of eligibility extended from 2 September 1945 to 1 April 1957. During this second time frame, personnel of the Navy, Marine Corps, and Coast Guard who were present for duty during operations in China, Taiwan, and the Matsu Straits were awarded the China Service Medal.

Navy issue.

D. Boyce

The Secretary of the Navy was authorized to award the China Service Medal to personnel of other Armed Forces of the United States for service performed in China during the period from 1945 to 1957.

Personnel who were awarded the China Service Medal for service during the period 1937 to 1939 and were also eligible for the award for the period 1945 to 1957 were awarded a 3/16th inch bronze star for attachment to the service and suspension ribbons of the initial award in lieu of a second medal.

Marine Corps issue.

D. Boyce

The China Service Medal was the last Navy and Marine Corps medal to be issued with rim numbers. However, only the first production run of medals for the 1937-1939 period were rim numbered, and these used unprefixed numbers. These medals were also issued with ring suspensions rather than the later issue knob suspensions.

American Defense Service Medal

From 8 September 1939 to 7 December 1941 members of the United States Armed Forces were serving during a state of limited emergency. Many members of the military, including the Army's Chief of Staff, felt that some kind of medal should be issued to servicemen to boost morale during this time.

On 28 February 1941, the Secretary of War's proposal for an American Defense Service Medal won the support of President Roosevelt. Executive Order 8808, issued on 28 June 1941, officially established the medal.

The Army implemented award of the American Defense Service Medal through War Department Circular 44, dated 13 February 1942. Navy authorization followed on 20 April 1942 via Naval Department General Order Number 172.

The American Defense Service Medal (ADSM) was awarded to Army personnel for 12 months honorable federal service during the state of limited emergency. Naval qualifications were less restrictive and allowed award of the ADSM to persons serving at least 10 days active duty between 8 September 1939 and 7 December 1941.

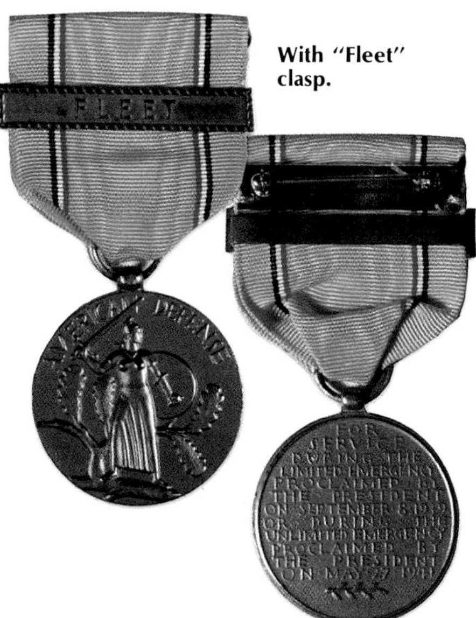

With "Fleet" clasp.

Both the Army and the Navy authorized service clasps to be worn on the suspension ribbon to denote service outside the Continental United States (CONUS) . The clasps are as follows:

FOREIGN SERVICE — Issued by the Army to personnel for service outside CONUS as a crew member of a vessel or aircraft, or as an assigned member if an organization assigned outside the continental limits of the United States.

BASE — For service on shore at bases and naval stations outside CONUS including Alaska and Hawaii.

FLEET — For service on the high seas while regularly attached to any vessel or aircraft squadron in the Atlantic, Pacific, or Asiatic Fleet.

SEA — For service by members of the Coast Guard on vessels making regular patrols at sea and who do not qualify for the FLEET clasp. The SEA clasp was originally authorized in Coast Guard General Order No. 10 dated 20 June 1942. Current Coast Guard Regualtions (COMDTINST 1650.25 Chapter 5-B-6-c) contain no reference to the SEA clasp.

Additionally, the Navy authorized a bronze "A" Device for wear on the service ribbon by personnel who served on board vessels operating in actual or potential contact with axis forces in the Atlantic.

Legion of Valor

This officer wears his American Defense Service Medal directly below his DSC.

Women's Army Corps Service Medal

The Women's Army Corps Service Medal (WACSM) was established by Executive Order No. 9365 on 29 July 1943. The medal was awarded for service in the Women's Army Auxiliary Corps between 10 July 1942 and 31 August 1943 or service in the Women's Army Corps between 1 September 1943 and 2 September 1945.

American Campaign Medal

The enormous scope of the Second World War made the concept of one single medal seem inadequate to recognize the global nature of the war and the hundreds of engagements and campaigns which would be fought by American servicemen. With this in mind, President Roosevelt signed Executive Order 9265 on 6 November 1942, which divided the globe into three separate Theaters of Operation and established a different campaign medal for Armed Forces personnel serving in each of the three Theaters.

The American Campaign Medal was awarded for service within the American Theater between 7 December 1941 and 2 March 1946 under any of the following conditions:

- On permanent assignment outside the continental limites of the United States (CONUS)
- Permanently assigned as a crew member of a vessel sailing ocean waters for 30 consecutive or 60 nonconsecutive days. Outside CONUS on temporary duty for 30 consecutive or 60 nonconsecutive days.
- Awarded a combat decoration while involved in active combat against the enemy.
- Within CONUS for an aggregate period of one year.

American Theater.

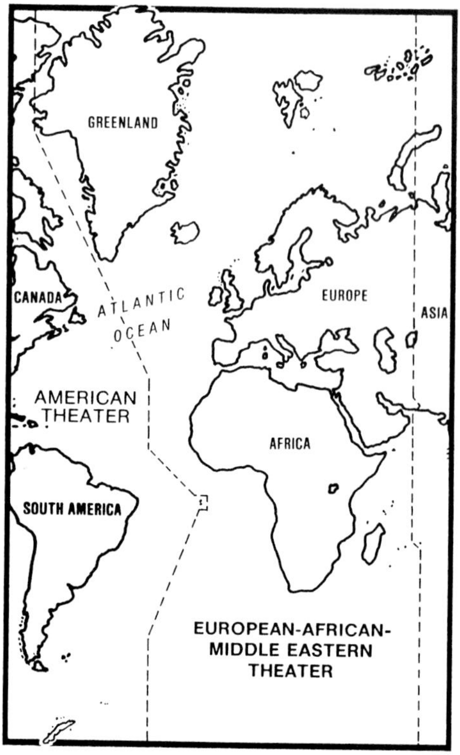

European-African-Middle Eastern Theater.

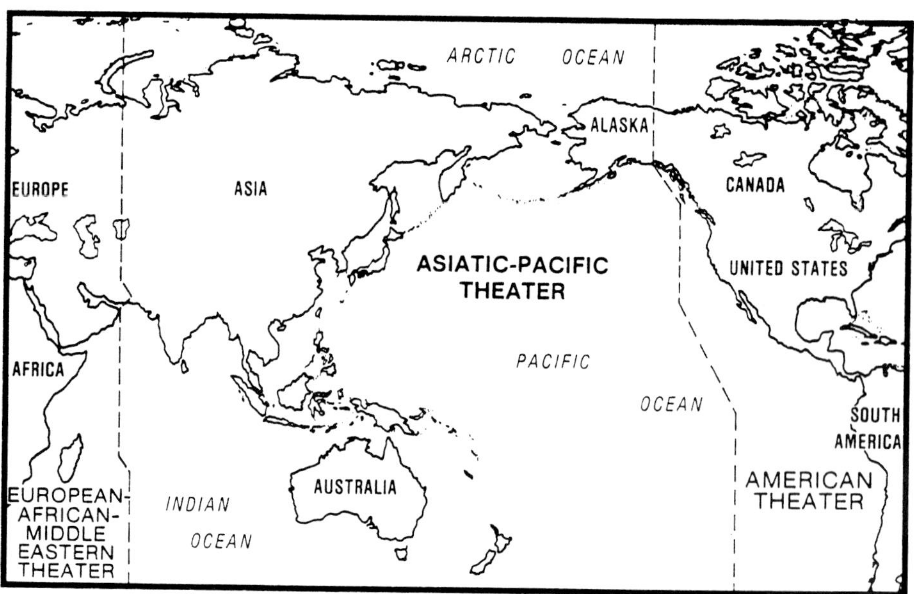

Asiatic-Pacific Theater.

European - African - Middle Eastern Campaign Medal

The European-African-Middle Eastern Campaign Medal (ETO Medal) was awarded for service within the EAME Theater between 7 December 1941 and 8 November 1945 under any of the following conditions:

- On permanent assignment within the Theater of Operations.
- On temporary duty within the Theater for 30 consecutive or 60 nonconsective days.
- Awarded a combat decoration while involved in active combat against the enemy.

Participation in one or more operation or engagement was signified by a 3/16th inch bronze star attached to both the service ribbon and the suspension ribbon. A silver star was worn in lieu of five bronze stars. An arrowhead was used to signify participation in a beach or airborne landing.

Asiatic - Pacific Campaign Medal

The Asiatic-Pacific Campaign Medal, also established by Executive Order on 6 November 1942 was awarded for service in the Asiatic-Pacific Theater between 7 December 1941 and 2 March 1946. The conditions for award of the Asiatic-Pacific Campaign Medal were the same as for award of the ETO Campaign Medal.

As with the ETO Campaign Medal, bronze and silver 3/16th inch stars were used to recognize multiple operations and arrowheads were used to recognize participation in beach or airborne landings.

World War II Victory Medal

The World War II victory medal was awarded by Act of Congress 6 July 1945 to all members of the armed forces who served at least one day active federal service between 7 December 1941 and 31 December 1946.

Army of Occupation Medal

The Army of Occupation Medal was established by War Department General Orders No. 32 in 1946 for award to members of the Army and Air Force (formally Army Air Corps) who served for 30 consecutive days at a normal place of duty while assigned to any of the following:

- Army of Occupation of Germany between 9 May 1945 and 5 May 1955.
- Service for which an individual qualified for the Berlin Airlift Device.
- Army of Occupation of Austria between 9 May 1945 and 27 July 1955.
- Army of Occupation of Berlin between 9 May 1945 and a date yet to be determined.
- Army of Occupation of Italy between between 9 May 1945 and 15 September 1947.
- Army of Occupation of Japan between 3 September 1945 and 27 April 1952.
- Army of Occupation of Korea between 3 September 1945 and 29 June 1949.

Individuals qualifying for the Army of Occupation Medal wear a bar attached to the suspension ribbon which is similar to those of the American Defense Service Medal to denote service in Germany or Japan. The bars are not worn on the service ribbon and are not denoted by the addition of stars to the service ribbon. The Berlin Airlift Device is authorized for wear on both the suspension and service ribbons by qualified personnel.

Navy Occupation Service Medal

The Navy Occupation Service Medal was authorized by NDGO No. 10 on 28 January 1948. This medal is awarded under much the same conditions as the Army of Occupation Medal for service under any of the following conditions:

- Germany from 8 May 1945 to 5 May 1955.
- Italy from 8 May 1945 to 15 December 1947.
- Trieste from 8 May 1945 to 25 October 1955.
- Austria from 8 May 1945 to 25 October 1955.
- Berlin from 8 May 1945 to a future date.
- Occupation duty in Japan from 2 September 1945 to 27 April 1952.
- Occupation duty in Korea from 2 September 1945 to 27 April 1952 except when such service also qualified an individual for the Korean Service Medal.

Appropriate clasps, similiar to those for the WW I Victory Medal, marked "EUROPE" and "ASIA" are authorized for wear on the suspension ribbon only. No device is authorized for wear on the service ribbon to denote award of one of these clasps. Qualified personnel may wear both clasps.

Personnel who served 90 consecutive days duty in direct support of the Berlin Airlift between 26 June 1948 and 30 September 1949 are authorized to wear the Berlin Airlift Device on both the service and suspension ribbon of the Navy Occupation Service Medal.

The reverses of the Navy Occupation Medal are different for Marine Corps personnel and Navy personnel and follow the same design as the Dominican Campaign Medal.

Navy issue.

Marine Corps issue.

Typhus Commission Medal

The Typhus Commission was conceived and established under the guidance of Captain (later Rear Admiral) Charles S. Stephenson. A medal recognizing meritorious service in connection with the work of the Commission was established by Executive Order on 24 December 1942. The first awards of the Typhus Commission Medal occurred early in 1944 and were of the service ribbon only since the medals themselves were not yet available.

Because members of the Typhus Commission were serving with both the Army and the Navy as well as the U.S. Public Health Service, the medal was ordered with the different service ribbon styles of that time. The original order consisted of 85 sets made up with the 1/2 inch wide Navy style service ribbon and 165 sets were ordered with the 3/8 inch wide Army style service ribbon.

The Typhus Commission Medal was first adopted into the Army's award regulations with Change 10 to AR 600-45 on 17 January 1946. However, because the Commission was disbanded in June 1946, the Army removed all reference to the award in the next Change to AR 600-45 which was published on 19 May 1947.

D. Boyce

Medal for Humane Action

On 23 June 1948 the Soviet-controlled government of East Germany announced that all traffic in and out of West Berlin would be suspended indefinitely. Faced with overwhelming Soviet forces in and around Berlin, President Truman endorsed a plan, proposed by Lt. General Wedemeyer, to supply West Berlin by air. The action of the United States in flying over one million tons of supplies into blockaded West Berlin during 1948 and 1949 prevented the starvation of thousands of civilians. Faced with their failure to force an end to the Allied occupation of West Berlin, the Soviets reopened the city to road, rail and water traffic on 12 May 1949.

To honor the more than 50,000 service personnel who had operated in direct support of the 276,926 airlift flights and the 28 servicemen who died in aircraft crashes, Congress authorized the Medal for Humane Action on 29 July 1949. The medal was authorized for award to any member of the Armed Forces of the United States who served for 120 consecutive days with or in direct support of the Berlin Airlift. Personnel who were killed while participating under the qualifying conditions were automatically awarded the medal posthumously.

Korean Service Medal

Service in the Korean War was recognized by award of the Korean Service Medal to qualifying members of all branches of the Armed Forces. The Korean Service Medal was authorized by Executive Order No. 10179 on 8 November 1950 and was awarded for service between 27 June 1950 and 27 July 1954. Personnel were required to serve for 30 consecutive or 60 nonconsecutive days during the period of eligibility to qualify for the Korean Service Medal.

Service during one of the following operations qualified an individual for a bronze engagement or battle star, a silver battle star was worn in lieu of five bronze stars:

- North Korean aggression, 2 Jun - 2 Nov 1950
- Communist China aggression, 3 Nov 1950 - 24 Jan 1951
- Inchon landing, 13 Sep - 17 Sep 1950
- 1st U.N. counteroffensive, 25 Jan - 21 Apr 1951
- Communist China spring offensive, 22 Apr - 8 Jul 1951
- U.N. summer-fall offensive, 9 Jul - 27 Nov 1951
- 2nd Korean winter, 28 Nov 1951 - 30 Apr 1952
- Korean defensive 1952 , 1 May - 30 Nov 1952
- 3rd Korean winter, 1 Dec 1952 - 30 Apr 1953
- Korea, summer-fall 1953, 1 May - 27 Jul 1953

Army personnel were authorized to wear an Arrowhead device for participation in an airborne or beach landing. Navy personnel who participated in ground combat were authorized to wear the Fleet Marine Force Combat Operation Insignia on the suspension and service ribbon.

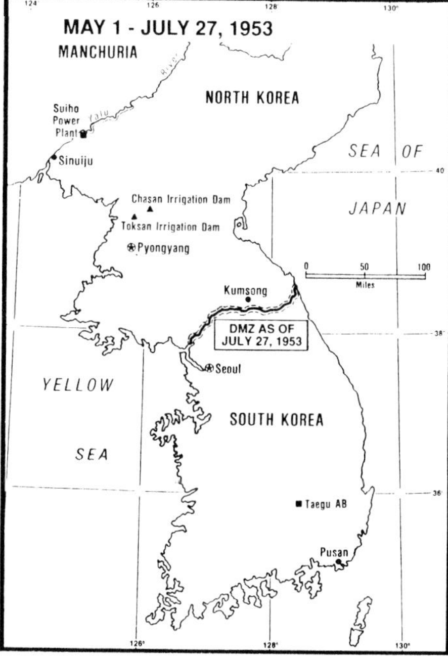

SEPTEMBER 16 - NOVEMBER 2, 1950

U.S.S.R.

MANCHURIA

Chosan

U.N. FORCES OCTOBER 26, 1950

SEA OF JAPAN

Sunchon

Sukchon

Pyongyang

Wonsan

0 50 100 Miles

NORTH KOREA

Kaesong

Seoul

Inchon

Suwon

U.N. FORCES OCTOBER 1, 1950

YELLOW SEA

SOUTH KOREA

Pohang

Taegu AB

U.N. FORCES SEPTEMBER 15, 1950

Pusan

National Defense Service Medal

The National Defense Service Medal (NDSM) was authorized by Executive Order No. 10488 on 22 April 1953. The NDSM was awarded to all members of the Armed Forces for any active federal service performed as part of normal extended active duty.

The initial period of eligibility for the NDSM was from 27 June 1950 to 27 July 1959. This period was first modified by Executive Order No. 11265 on 11 January 1966 to include the period 1 January 1961 to 14 August 1974. After a sixteen year hiatus, the Defense Department again reinstituted the National Defense Service Medal on 21 February 1991. This third period of eligibility, prompted by Operation Desert Storm, was made retroactive to 2 August 1990 through a date yet to be determined, and includes all active duty personnel as well as members of the active reserve.

Personnel who are authorized the NDSM for more than one covered period of service wear a bronze engagement star for service during subsequent periods of eligibility.

Armed Forces Expeditionary Medal

The Armed Forces Expeditionary Medal (AFEM) was established by Executive Order No. 10977 on 4 December 1961. The AFEM is awarded to any member of the Armed Forces of the United States who participates in or is involved in the direct support of any of the following types of operations; U.S. Military Operations, U.S. operations in direct support of the United Nations, or U.S. operations of assistance to friendly foreign nations.

A minimum of 30 days consecutive or 60 days nonconsecutive service is required. When the full period of an operation is less than 30 days participation for the entire period is required. In addition, personnel engaged in combat, or a duty which is equally as hazardous qualify for award of the AFEM without regard for time in the area.

Personnel who qualify for award of more than one AFEM are awarded a bronze service star for each successive qualifying period, a silver service star is worn in lieu of five bronze stars. A list of operations and time periods is included in Appendix F.

Vietnam Service Medal

The Vietnam Service Medal was established by Executive Order 11231 on 8 July 1965. The Vietnam Service Medal design is the same for all branches of the service and was awarded to all members of the Armed Forces of the United States who served in Vietnam and contiguous waters or airspace between 3 July 1965 and 28 March 1973. In addition, personnel serving in Thailand, Laos, or Cambodia in direct support of operations in Vietnam during the same time period are also eligible for this medal.

Award requirements were very lax, to be eligible an individal serving in any of the areas mentioned must:

- Be regularly assigned to an organization for 1 day which participates in or operates in direct support of military operations.
- Be regularly assigned to or attached to a naval vessel under the same conditions as above.
- Actually participate as an aircraft crewmember in at least one flight into airspace above Vietnam in support of military operations.
- Serve for 30 consecutive days or 60 nonconsecutive days on temporary duty in the qualifying areas.

There are 17 campaign stars authorized for the Vietnam Service Medal, personnel are authorized one bronze campaign star for each qualifying campaign with a silver star worn in lieu of five bronze stars. In addition, Navy personnel involved in ground combat are authorized the Fleet Marine Force Combat Operations Insignia. A complete list of campaigns is included in Appendix G.

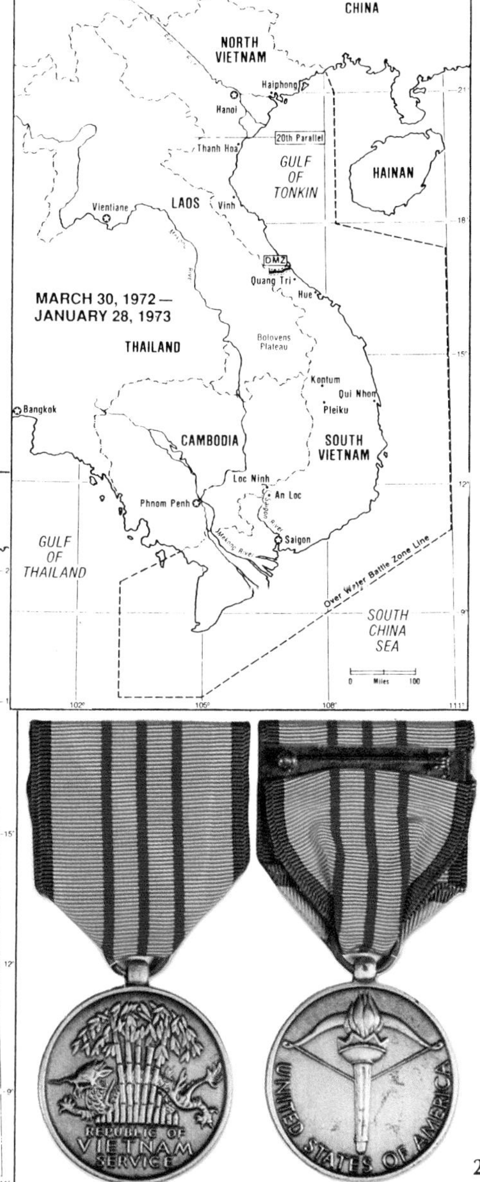

VIETNAM THEATER

Southwest Asia Service Medal

The Southwest Asia Service Medal was established by executive order of President George Bush on 15 March 1991. The medal was awarded to any member of the Armed Forces of the United States for service in the Middle East during Operations Desert Shield and Desert Storm.

Dates of qualifying service are from 2 August 1990 to a date yet to be determined. Three battle stars are authorized, one for the period from 2 August 1990 to 16 January 1991, a second star for the period 17 January to 11 April 1992, and the third star for the period 12 April 1992 to a date yet to be determined.

The reverse of the planchet shows an upraised sword entwined by a palm frond surrounded by the words "UNITED STATES OF AMERICA" and symbolizes military might and preparedness in defense of peace.

Antarctic Service Medal

With the outbreak of the Second World War research in the Antarctic came to a virtual stand still. However, the successful conclusion of the war brought renewed interest in Antarctic research to the scientific community in America.

With the establishment of permanent research stations, the Government soon realized that the past method of designing individual medals for each Antarctic expedition was now impractical. Rather than cease the recognition of service in the harsh Antarctic; Congress directed on 7 July 1960, through Public Law 86-800 (DA Bul. 3, 1960), that an appropriate medal be designed and award criteria be established for an Antarctic Service Medal.

The broad award criteria under which the Antarctic Service Medal is awarded extend retroactively to 1 January 1946. For those personnel who participated in a qualifying activity prior to 1 June 1973 no minimum time of service is required. However, subsequent to 1 June 1973, a minimum of 30 days duty at sea or ashore south of latitude 60 degrees south are required. Each day of service on the Antarctic Continent counts as two days when determining award eligibility.

Personnel who spend the winter months on the Antarctic continent are eligible to wear a bronze clasp inscribed "WINTERED OVER" on the suspension ribbon. A 5/16th inch disk bearing an outline of the Antarctic continent is authorized for the service ribbon. Similar gold clasps and disks are awarded for the second winter and silver clasps and disks represent three or more winters spent on the Antarctic continent. The winter months on the Antarctic are from mid-March through October.

Coast Guard Arctic Service Medal

The Coast Guard Arctic Service Medal (CGASM) was authorized by the Commandant of the U.S. Coast Guard on 20 May 1976. The CGASM is awarded retroactively to 1 Jan 1946 for 21 days consecutive service aboard a Coast Guard vessel north of the arctic from 1 May through 31 October or 21 days consecutive service north of 60 N from 1 November through 30 April. Service at any of the following Coast Guard Stations for the required 21 days will also qualify:

- Loran Station, Cape Athol, Greenland
- Loran Station, Cape Christian, Baffin Island, Canada
- Loran Station, Port Clarance, Alaska
- Radio Station, Barrow, Alaska
- Loran Station, Bo, Norway
- Loran Station, Jan Mayen Island, Norway

Currently the following eighteen Coast Guard vessels have met the eligibility criteria for award of the Coast Guard Arctic Service Medal:

Balsam (Coastal Tender)
Northwind (Icebreaker)
Blackhaw (Coastal Tender)
Polar Sea (Icebreaker)
Bramble (Seagoing Tender)
Polar Star (Icebreaker)
Burton Island (Icebreaker)
Sedge (Seagoing Tender)
Citrus (Seagoing Tender)
Southwind (Icebreaker)
Eastwind (Icebreaker)
Spar (Seagoing Tender)
Edisto (Icebreaker)
Staten Island (Icebreaker)
Evergreen (Icebreaker)
Storis (Utility Icebreaker)
Glacier (Icebreaker)
Westwind (Icebreaker)

There are no devices worn with the CGASM and it is awarded only once for single or multiple periods of service.

Humanitarian Service Medal

The Humanitarian Service Medal (HSM) was established by Executive Order 11965 on 1 April 1975. Army personnel became eligible for the medal for participation in Department of Defense recognized humanitarian service operations on or after 1 April 1975. Air Force personnel are eligable on the same bases for participation in operations subsequent to 1 April 1979.

To be eligible, the individual must have directly participated in a DOD recognized operation. In this context, direct participation is defined as "hands-on" participation within the specific geographic area prescribed in DOD Manual 1348.33 for each humanitarian operation. Personnel assigned to various staff functions at military headquarters which are geographically seperated from the operation are excluded from eligibility for the HSM.

Subsequent awards of the Humanitarian Service Medal are recognized by a 3/16th inch bronze star attached to both the suspension and service ribbons. A silver star is worn in lieu of five bronze stars. For a list of qualifying operations see Appendix H.

Armed Forces Reserve Medal

The Armed Forces Reserve Medal (AFRM) was established by Executive Order 10163 on 25 September 1950 and further amended by Executive Order 10439 on 19 March 1953. The AFRM is awarded to any officer or enlisted member of the Reserve Components of the Armed Forces of the United States who completes ten years of qualifying service. The ten years of service need not be continuous provided they are completed within twelve years.

The obverse design of the Armed Forces Reserve Medal and the ribbon are the same for all services. However there are distinctive reverse designs for the major Reserve Components. The designs are as follows:

Army Reserve - A Minute Man from the Organized Reserve Crest.
National Guard - National Guard Insignia.
Air Force Reserve - Eagle in the Clouds.
Naval Reserve - Sailing ship behind an eagle perched on an anchor.
Coast Guard Reserve - Coast Guard Insignia.
Marine Corps Reserve - Marine Corps Insignia.

An hourglass device is authorized for both the suspension and service ribbons to denote subsequent awards of the AFRM.

Army Reserve.

National Guard.

Air Force Reserve.

Naval Reserve.

Naval Reserve Medal

The Naval Reserve Medal was established by the Secretary of the Navy on 12 September 1938 for award to any member of the Naval Reserve who completed ten years on honorable service, either continuous or broken, prior to 12 September 1958. The ten year period of service is not confined to a twelve year period as for the Armed Forces Reserve Medal. Service after 12 September 1958 is credited towards award of the AFRM and must meet eligibility requirements for that award.

Coast Guard Reserve.

Marine Corps Reserve.

Mint strike with ring suspension and wrap brooch.

D. Boyce

T. Wheatley

An early issue Naval Reserve Medal with slot brooch.

Later issue (note ball suspension).

Outstanding Volunteer Service Medal

The Outstanding Volunteer Service Medal (OVSM) was established by Executive Order 12830, on 9 January 1993.

The OVSM is intended to recognize outstanding volunteer support of activities within the *civilian community*, by either Active Duty or Reserve military personnel.

To qualify for award of the OVSM, the service must be civilian in nature and reflect sustained, and direct individual involvement in the activity.

The Outstanding Volunteer Service Medal is not intended to recognize a single act, but reward significant support over an extended period of time.

Note:
As of this printing, individual military departments have not established specific award criteria or order of precedence.

Commemorative Medals

Prior to 1907 service members had no federally authorized medals to recognize service or participation in significant campaigns. As a result, many unit commanders paid for the manufacture of privately issued medals for award to troops under their command. The following chapter contains a few of the more historically important examples of these privately issued medals. In addition to those illustrated here, many units had, and continue to have, commemorative medals privately manufactured and issued.

Congress also authorized medals for issue to participants in historic events or campaigns. These were usually in the form of table medals, although some were of the same size as the standard issue service medals. Those Congressional medals illustrated here are the most historically important. Congress authorized many other commemorative table medals for award to specific Army and Navy commanders. However, because these were intended only for a specific individual, they have not been included in this book.

Sergeant Joseph Franklin, USMC, wears his Medal of Honor and Sampson Medal.

André Medal

On 3 November 1780 Congress directed that an award be developed for presentation to three enlisted men who had captured the British Adjutant-General, Major John André.

The medal is in the form of a large oval measuring 1 3/4th by 2 1/4th inches with the words "Amor" at the top and "Patriae Vincit" below with a flowering plant at both sides joined at the bottom by a bow. In the center were engraved the initials of the recipient. The obverse of the medal featured similiar designs with the word "Fidelity" at the top.

Three American militiamen, John Paulding, Isaac Van Wart, and David Williams were awarded the medal in an official ceremony by General Washington.

New York Historical Society

Facsimile of the Andre Medal.

Kearny Medal

Established by the officers of Kearny's command on 29 November 1862 the Kearny Medal is one of the most sought after and seldom seen medals. Conceived to honor their fallen commander, the medal was originally issued to the officers who served under Major General Philip Kearny in the 1st Division, 3rd Corps.

National Archives

Major General Phil P. Kearny.

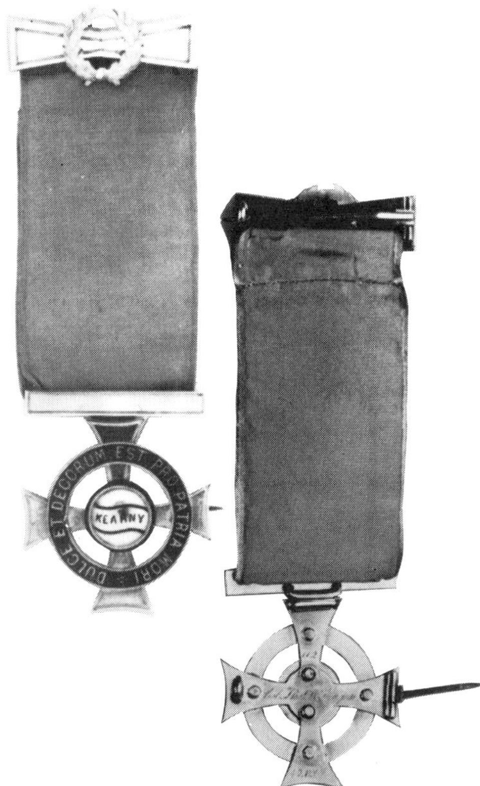

A committee of officers was elected to order 320 medals at a cost of $15.00 each from the firm of Ball, Black & Company of New York City. All the medals were numbered with the exception of those presented to Major Generals, Birney, Berry, and Major DeLacy who headed the committee.

The Kearny Medal is a gold cross patee 31mm in diameter. The center of the cross is a 10mm diameter circle bearing the name "KEARNY". Surrounding the center medallion is a gold-edged enameled ring bearing the Kearny motto "DULCE ET DECORUM EST PRO PATRIA MORI" which translates "It is fitting and proper to die for your country." The entire planchet is rivited three-piece construction; the cross, center medallion and enameled ring each being cast separately and riveted together.

The cross planchet is suspended from a red silk ribbon 30mm wide. Both the cross and the gold brooch are fitted with pin clasps.

Major General D.B. Birney.

The medal presented to Maj. Gen. Birney features a black enameled center set with 20 brilliants and the arms of the cross are elaborately engraved whereas those on the other medals are simple.

Kearny Medal presented to General Birney. Note the brilliants and black enamel center.

Reverse of above showing a different style of engraving than on other Kearny Medals. Also, the suspension ring, pin and clasp are unique to this medal.

The Kearny Cross

On 13 March 1863, Major General David B. Birney, who had succeeded Kearny followed the lead of Major De Lacy and ordered a second style bronze cross 42mm in diameter to be struck for award to enlisted personnel of the 1st Division, now called Birney's Division, for distinguished conduct in battle.

The Kearny Cross featured the words "Kearny Cross" engraved in a flowing ribbon which runs horizontally across both

arms of the cross. The reverse of the cross is engraved with the words "Birney's Division". The Cross is suspended from a red ribbon in much the same manner as the first style Navy Medal of Honor.

There were 463 recipients of the Kearny Cross, including two women, Mrs. Anne Etheridge, 5th Mich. Vols., and Mrs. Mary Tepe, 114th Pa. Vols.

Gilmore Medal (Sumter Medal)

Major General Quincy A. Gilmore, commanding officer of the Department of the South, ordered this medal on 28 October 1863 to commemorate the operations against Charleston.

The obverse of the medal features a fort surmounted by the words "Fort Sumter" with the date "Aug. 23d 1862" below. Thirteen stars encircle the entire design. The reverse of the medal bears the inscription "For Gallant and Meritorious Conduct" around the edge with three stars at the bottom. In the center are the words "Presented by" and a facsimile of the General's signature, "Q.A. Gilmore, Maj. Genl." in two lines.

The bronze 35mm planchet is suspended directly from a metal brooch on which the recipient's name is engraved.

General Gillmore had 400 of these medals produced. However, official records show only 20 recipients. This small number of recipients was due to the fact that company officers were supposed to recommend not more than three percent of their troops for the medal, and faced with this limitation declined to nominate anyone on the basis that every man performed in a gallant and meritorious manner.

D. Boyce

Note: Pin and catch are missing on the above example. See left for pin style utilized.

Butler Medal (Army of the James Medal)

In a speech to the solders of the Army of the James on 11 October 1864, the commanding officer, Major General Benjamin F. Butler, announced that a special medal would be struck to honor colored soldiers of his command for gallantry in action during the assault on New Market Heights, 29 September 1864.

The Butler Medal was struck in silver. The obverse of the 40mm planchet shows a fort being charged by two colored soldiers and bears the inscription "Ferro iis libertas perveniet" in a flowing ribbon. Below the soldiers are the words "U.S. Colored Troops."

The reverse of the medal bears the inscription "Campaign before Richmond 1864" surrounded by oak leaves and surmounted by the words "Distinguished For Courage."

The planchet is suspended from a red, white, and blue ribbon by an elaborate eagle's claw grasping a ball to which the suspension ring is attached. The brooch is a large oak leaf upon which is inscribe "Army of the James" in plain block letters.

General Butler had 197 medals struck at his own expense and it is known that he sent 46 of these medals to Major General Weitzel, who took over command of the 25th Corps from General Butler, on 25 May, 1865 for award to qualifying soldiers who were still serving with the 25th Corps at that time.

Butler Medal, obverse and reverse.

Ely Medal

Following the battle of Mine Run, Colonel John Ely, commander of the 23rd Penn. Vol. Inf ., was forced to resign because of wounds and sickness. While recovering from his injuries he commissioned a commemorative medal for award to selected troops who had participated in the battle of Marye Heights on 3 May 1863.

The medal measures 1 15/16th inches in diameter and is suspended from a blue silk ribbon separating two copper rectangular bars. These suspension bars are similiar to those found on the Kearny Cross. The obverse of the planchet is engraved with the inscription "Marye Heights, Fredericksburg, Va." in two lines above two clasped hands. Below the hands is the date "MAY 3rd 1863" in a straight line and below that in a curved line is the unit designation "23rd Reg: P.V." The reverse of the planchet featured a likeness of lady liberty seated and the inscription "Liberty and Union Now and Forever" above in two curved lines and "One and Inseparable" in one curved line below.

Fort Sumter Medal

On 6 June 1861 the Chamber of Commerce of the state of New York approved the issue of a bronze medal to honor Major Robert Anderson and the officers and men who defended Fort Sumter. The medals were designed and struck by New York City sculpter Charles Muller in four sizes to represent four different classes.

Fort Sumpter Medal
3rd or 4th Class.

The first Class Medal was six inches in diameter and featured a profile of Major Anderson facing right. Around the bust was the inscription; "Robert Anderson 1861". The reverse of the medal had the inscription; "The Chamber of Commerce, NewYork, Honors the Defenders of Fort Sumter — The Patriot, The Hero, and The Man." surmounting the figure of a female figure holding the American flag in her left hand and the flaming torch of war in her right hand. Below the figure is a representation of the ramparts of Fort Sumter. The Second Class Medal, as awarded to the officers of Major Anderson's command, is identical to the First Class Medal but having a diameter of four inches. Noncommissioned officers received a medal 3 1/2 inches in diameter with the same obverse but a different reverse. The reverse of the Third Class Medal bears the inscription "The Chamber of Commerce, New-York, Honors the Defenders of Fort Sumter- First to Withstand Treason." in two lines surmounting a representation of Fort Sumter and a depiction of Peter Hart raising the Stars and Stripes. The Forth Class Medal issued to Privates was 2 1/2 inches in diameter and identical to the Third Class Medal.

There was one First Class Medal issued, ten Second Class Medals awarded, 24 Third Class Medals issued, and 51 Fourth Class Medals presented.

Fort Pickens Medal

The Fort Pickens Medal was conceived and presented at the same time as the Fort Sumpter Medal. Also awarded in four classes, the obverse of all medals featured a bust of 1LT Adam J. Slemmer with his name and the date 1861 inscribed around the bust. The reverse of the six inch diameter First Class Medal, which was presented to First Lieutenant Slemmer, featured a representation of Cerberus as the monster of war chained to Fort Pickens. The inscription "The Chamber of Commerce, New York, honors, Valor, Forbearance, and Fidelity." above the monster and "Fort Pickens 1861" below. The Second Class Medal, which was presented to 2LT Jeremiah H. Gilman, was identical to the First Class Medal but only four inches in diameter. Twelve noncommissioned officers received the Third Class Medal which was 3 1/2 inches in diameter. The reverse of the Third Class Medal featured the inscription "The Chamber of Commerce, New York, Honors the Defenders of Fort Pickens" above a view of Fort Pickens and "Far Off But Faithful." below the fort. There were 39 Fourth Class Medals presented to the Privates of Slemmer's command. These medals were identical to the Third Class Medals but measured two inches in diameter.

As with the Fort Sumter Medal, the Fort Pickens Medal was cast in bronze for all classes.

Fort Pickens Medal
3rd or 4th Class.

Manila Bay Medal (Dewey Medal)

The Act of Congress on 3 June 1898 authorized the presentation of a sword of honor to Admiral Dewey for his stunning defeat of the Spanish Navy at Manila Bay on 1 May 1898. This Act also authorized the presentation of bronze commemorative medals for the officers and men of the Navy and Marine Corps who served on the ships under Admiral Dewey's command during the battle.

Any person who was attached to one of the following ships on 1 May 1898 was eligible for the medal:

USS Olympia
USRC McCulloch
USS Concord
USS Baltimore
USS Boston
USS Petrel
USS Raleigh

The original order for the Dewey Medal was placed with Tiffany & Co. of New York. There were approximately 1,800 medals in the initial order and all were issued with the recipient's name and rank stamped on the rim of the medal.

D. Boyce

Typical impressed name of edge of a Dewey Medal.

Details of Manila Bay Medal (Dewey Medal) reverse.

Aboard the US Navy battle-force flagship "California," Admiral Claude C. Bloch (left) replaces Admiral W.D. Leahy as commander of the battle-force. His is congratulated by Vice Admiral F.J. Horne (center), commander aircraft battle-force, and Vice Admiral W.T. Tarrant (right), commander of the scouting force, US Fleet, 1 February 1937. Note the wear of the West Indies Naval Campaign Medal.

R. Sullivan

West Indies Naval Campaign Medal (Sampson Medal)

The Act of Congress on 3 March 1901 authorized the Secretary of the Navy to award bronze medals to personnel of the Navy and Marine Corps to commemorate the naval and other engagements in the waters of the West Indies and on the shores of Cuba during the war with Spain.

The obverse of the medal shows a bust of Admiral William T. Sampson, hence the nick-name "Sampson Medal", surrounded by the inscription "U.S. Naval Campaign - West Indies 1898".

On first issues of the medal the pendant and ribbon were suspended from bronze engagement bars with the ship upon which the recipient served being the top bar. In 1908 the suspension ribbon was attached directly to the ship bar and campaign or engagement bars were clasped to the ribbon in much the same manner as used for the World War I Victory Medal.

D. Boyce

Thomas J. Nier

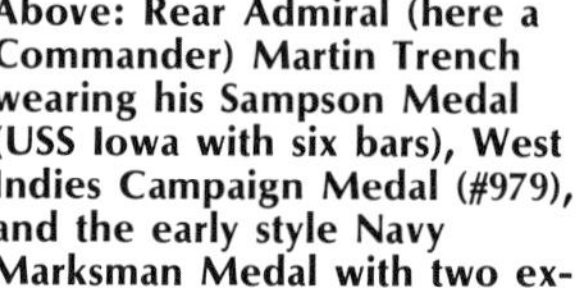
Above: Rear Admiral (here a Commander) Martin Trench wearing his Sampson Medal (USS Iowa with six bars), West Indies Campaign Medal (#979), and the early style Navy Marksman Medal with two expert bars and three silver date ovals (sharpshooter). Trench was later awarded the Navy Cross for meritorious service as the Commanding Officer of the Naval Torpedo Station, Newport, R.I.

G. Sousa

Detail photo of a Sampson Medal top bar.

Engraved naming on edge of first issue Sampson Medal.

D. Boyce

First issue with ribbon and pendant suspended from an engagement bar.

G. Sousa

Typical impressed naming on edge of Sampson Medal.

Second issue style.

Specially Meritorious Medal

The Specially Meritorious Medal was authorized by Congress on 3 March 1901 and was conferred upon officers and men of the Navy and Marine Corps for specially meritorious service other than in battle during the War with Spain.

With only 93 known awards of this medal, the Specially Meritorious Medal is among the rarest U.S. decorations. A list of recipients is presented in Appendix L.

D. Boyce

Specially Meritorious Medal awarded to Patrick Lynch, Coxwain, for rescuing crews from, and in close proximity to burning ships after the battle off Santiago, Cuba, 3 July 1898.

G. Sousa

Specially Meritorious Medal awarded to Nicholas Calango, Water Tender, for rescuing crews from, and in close proximity to burning ships after the battle off Santiago, Cuba, 3 July 1898.

C.D. Bloch wearing the Specially Meritorious Medal.

The following eight "unofficial" Specially Meritorious Medal recipients did not appear on the original 30 January 1904 letter to the US Mint which listed the original 71 recipients, or are among the 22 additional recipients listed in a letter to the US Mint dated 22 August 1904. Evidence, however, does exist that they were also awarded the medal.

Ensign Henry Ward
Ensign William Henry Buck
Ensign Rochester Cumings - "U.S.S. Harvard"
Lieutenant Hilary Williams - "U.S.S. Iowa"
Gunner C.D. Holland - "U.S.S. Iowa"
Lieutenant Commander C.D. Bloch
John Bradshaw - "U.S.S. Harvard"
William J. Roberts

Cardenas Medal of Honor

Authorized by a Joint Resolution of Congress on 3 May 1900, the Cardenas Medal of Honor was originally presented as a 3 1/8th inch table medal to the officers and crew of the Revenue Cutter Hudson. Later, as other wearable medals were adopted, a smaller version of the medal was designed. The smaller version of the Cardenas Medal of Honor was 1 1/4th inches in diameter and suspended from a ribbon designed with a wide center stripe of yellow-gold flanked by wide blue stripes. The ribbon and planchet are suspended from a rectangular brooch made of the same metal as the planchet and inscribed with the name "CARDENAS" in large capital letters.

The Cardenas Medal of Honor was awarded exclusively to First Lt. Frank H. Newcomb and his men aboard the Hudson for gallantry in action while towing a disable ship, the Winslow, to safety during the battle at Cardenas harbor on 11 May 1898.

The medal, designed by the U.S. Mint, was awarded in gold to Newcomb, in silver to his officers, and in bronze to the men of

John Langton

R. Sullivan

the Hudson. The obverse of the medal features a winged female figure with a winged helmet. The figure holds a sword in her right hand and a palm branch in her left hand. In the background is a depiction of the Hudson towing the Winslow. Below this scene is the inscription "Cardenas, May 11, 1898." The reverse features a nude female figure chiseling the inscription "Joint Resolution of Congress approved May 3, 1900, in recognition of the Galantry of the Officers and Men of the Hudson, Who in the face of a Galling Fire Towed the Winslow out of the Range of the Enemy's Guns." The reverse decorations also feature a palm branch and wreaths.

The Hudson and other ships of the Revenue Cutter Service, which later became the Coast Guard, performed gallant service during the Spanish-American War. The Cardenas Medal of Honor was the first award authorized solely for members of the Coast Guard.

John Langton

Large and small versions of the Cardenas Medal of Honor.

Jeannette Arctic Expedition Medal

Throughout the last one hundred years explorers from the United States have been drawn to the North Pole. The first of these expeditions to be commemorated by a Congressionally authorized medal was the ill-fated Arctic expedition lead by Lt. George DeLong, USN. This expedition, aboard the *Jeannette*, left San Francisco on 8 July 1879. All hope of success vanished on 13 June 1881 when the Jeannette, which had become trapped in pack ice 21 months earlier, was crushed and sank. Of the 33 members of the expedition only 12 survived to return to the United States.

Bowing to public pressure, Congress passed an act authorizing the medal on 30 September 1890. However it was not until 6 April 1892 that Secretary of the Navy, B. F. Tracey approved the final design of the medal.

In all, 33 medals were produced. Eight "Jeannette" Medals were produced in gold for the officers and senior members of the expedition and 25 medals were produced in silver for the other members of the expedition.

Like other Naval commemorative medals of the 19th century, the Jeannette Arctic Expedition Medal is suspended from a brooch bearing the ship's name. However, in this case the broach is very ornate, having an eagle with wings spread surmounting a bar bearing the name "Jeannette".

McDowell

Byrd Antarctic Expedition Medal, 1928-1930

Rear Admiral Richard Byrd, USN (retired) was the United States' most famous Antarctic explorer, leading several expeditions to the South Pole beginning in 1928.

The first expedition was successful in establishing the base camp which became known as "Little America". It was from this camp in 1929 that Byrd made the first flight over the South Pole, the feat for which he was promoted to Rear Admiral on the Navy's retired list.

Upon their return to the United States, Byrd and his expedition members were hailed as national heroes. Congress established the first Byrd Antarctic Expedition Medal on 23 May 1930. The medal was issued in three degrees; gold, silver, and bronze. In all, there were 66 gold medals awarded, 7 silver, and 9 bronze.

McDowell

Second Byrd Antarctic Expedition, 1933-1935

The second Antarctic expedition lead by Rear Admiral Richard Byrd, reoccupied "Little America" in 1933, expanding and improving its facilities. Included in the scientific agenda were plans for a two-man meteorological station to be located 100 miles south of the base camp. When events limited the station to a one-man outpost, Byrd decided to occupy the station himself rather than order one of his men to endure the hardships of a 200 day isolation.

Upon return to the United States in 1935, Byrd and his expedition were again honored by Congress when, on 2 June 1936, Congress directed that silver medals should be authorized for "deserving personnel of the Second Byrd Antarctic Expedition."

The first of 57 Second Byrd Antarctic Expedition Medals was presented to Rear Admiral Byrd by the Secretary of the Navy on 15 October 1937.

McDowell

NC-4 Medal

The NC-4 Medal was first awarded as a non-portable medal on 9 February 1929 to the crew of the NC-4 flying boat for their successful completion of the first transAtlantic airplane flight. This medal measured 2 1/2 inches in diameter and was struck in 14 karat gold. Later on 25 April 1935 a bronze "miniature", the same size as a full-size campaign medal, was authorized for wear on the uniform.

The Navy Curtiss flying boats were organized as a Division and placed under the command of Commander John H. Towers. The three planes were scheduled to attempt the first transAtlantic airplane flight on 8 May 1919. Navigational errors and rough seas prevented NC-1 and NC-3 from completing the flight from Rockaway Beach, Long Island to Plymouth, England. However, NC-4 under the command of Lieutenant-Commander Albert C. Read was able

to complete the journey, landing in Plymouth on 31 May 1919.

The NC-4 medal was awarded as follows:

Commander John H. Towers, USN
Lt. Commander Albert C. Read, USN
Lt. Elmer F. Stone, USCG
Lt. Walter Hinton, USN
Lt. James L. Breese, USN
Ensign Herbert C. Rodd, USNRF
Chief Machinist Mate Eugene S. Rhodes, USNRF

NC-4 miniature.

R. Sullivan

Albert C. Read, pilot of the NC-4.

Peary Polar Expedition Medal

The Peary Polar Expedition Medal was authorized by Congress on 28 January 1944. The award was intended to recognize the achievements of Admiral Robert E. Peary's successful expedition to reach the geographic North Pole on 6 April 1909.

The medal was designed by John Sinnock, chief artist for the U.S. Mint at Philadelphia and awarded to six of the 24 members of the 1908-1909 expedition. It is an interesting fact that Admiral Peary himself was not one of the members of the expedition to be selected for the award. The six personnel selected for the award were:

1. Cpt. Robert Bartlett, Peary's second in command
2. George Borup (posthumously)
3. Dr. John Goodsell
4. Matthew A. Henson, Peary's sledge assistant, a black man and the only other member of the expedition to reach the pole with Peary.
5. Comdr. Donald MacMillan
6. Ross Marvin (posthumously)

McDowell

United States Antarctic Expedition Medal

The United States Antarctic Service was a short lived organization. Headed by Rear Admiral Richard E. Byrd, the USAS was founded in 1939 to promote the continued exploration of the South Pole. The Second World War forced the demise of the USAS after only one expedition, that being the 1939-1941 expedition for which the medal was created.

The U.S. Antarctic Expedition Medal was created by an Act of Congress on 24 September 1945 and was awarded in three degrees; gold, silver, and bronze. In all 160 medals were authorized, of which 60 were gold, and 50 each were silver and bronze. Rear Admiral Byrd received one of the medals in gold.

McDowell

American Field Service Medal

The American Field Service (1914-1917) was a volunteer ambulance corps staffed by men from the United States who offered their services in support of France during World War I. The AFS evolved from the American Ambulance Hospital in Paris. By the time the American Field Service was absorbed into the U.S. Army in the Fall of 1917, 2,437 American volunteers had served in the AFS and 127 gave their lives during their service.

The origins of the American Field Service Medal remain a mystery. Most American Field Service Medals were mailed to recipients in the United States by Registered Mail from AFS offices in Boston. From the fact that the transmittal letter is dated 3 January 1919, we can surmise that the medals were distributed during that year.

Although the AFS Medal and the accompanying letter of transmittal bear the name of Louis Maurier, the French Minister of War, there is no known documentary evidence that the medal was an award of the French government. As a result, the medal was treated as a quasi-governmental war service medal and not authorized for wear on the military uniform.

The AFS medal is bronze 37mm (1 7/16th inches) in diameter with a round suspension knob at the top. The obverse of the medal features a raised block bearing the words "FIELD SERVICE" surmounted by a flaming bomb upon which is the letter "A" (the collar insignia of the French Automobile Service to which the AFS was attached). The flaming bomb is flanked on the left by a perched eagle (symbol of the U.S.) and on the right by a crowing rooster (symbol of France).

The reverse was blank and featured a multi-line engraving which read "Presented to, (recipients name in all capitals), by, LOUIS MOURU, French Minister of War, for services rendered, French Army, 1917-1918-1919. The ribbon featured a wide center stripe of buff flanked on either side by tri-color bands on each edge, from the outside toward the center being blue, white and red.

Captain Thomas Cassiday, DSC, scored eight air victories in WWI. Note he wears the American Field Service Medal.

Stretchers slung between two wheels on their way from the trenches to waiting American ambulances.

As the quick transportation of wounded — from the front to the nearest hospital — is so great a factor in saving their lives, the American Ambulance Field Service was organized soon after the beginning of the war, and during the subsequent two years its achievement has fully demonstrated the value of its purpose. It has now in the field more than 200 motor ambulances. These are driven by young American volunteers, most of whom are graduates of American universities. *To them has been successfully entrusted the vitally important matter of bringing the wounded in the shortest possible time from the trenches to places where the first surgical help can be given. Upon this first surgical help largely depends, naturally, the chance of the wounded surviving long enough to reach the base hospitals.* These ambulances are grouped in sections of twenty to thirty cars, and attached to the French Armies. *They carry wounded between the front and the Army Hospitals within the Army Zone.* So valiantly has their work been done that in each section a number of these men have been given the *croix de guerre* for gallantry under fire.

This service with the French Armies at the front is maintained through a special FIELD SERVICE FUND, and those desiring to give to it should send their contributions as directed below. Curtailing expenses to the lowest point consistent with efficiency, a monthly expenditure of approximately $11,000.^00 is now found requisite. This amount is being raised by single gifts — or by monthly subscriptions for any number of months, or the duration of the war. These monthly contributions of course vary greatly, according to the means of those who are kind enough to help; in two or three cases extraordinarily generous amounts being given, and in many instances monthly sums ranging from $5.^00 up to $100.^00 having been promised. Needless to say contributions of *any* size — monthly or single — will be most gratefully received. Guarantees for the year at present amount to about $5000.^00 monthly. As this sum — even with numerous additional gifts — is insufficient for current needs it is very keenly hoped that those who during the past year have been so generous as to contribute to the purchase of the ambulances in use, and others who can now perhaps more fully appreciate the true worth of this work to France, may feel willing to do what they are able toward guaranteeing its continuation.

Cheques may be made payable to

"Am. Am. Field Service Fund"

and sent to Lee, Higginson & Co., State St., Boston, Mass.

Owing to the fact that five new sections of ambulances have recently been sent to the front, the waiting list of the past eighteen months has been depleted, and accordingly a limited number of

Volunteer Ambulance Drivers are Wanted

New men are also needed from time to time to fill the places of those who return to America on leave, or who are unable to re-enlist at the expiration of their six months in the field.

REQUISITE QUALIFICATIONS

American Citizenship — Good Health — Clean Record — Ability to drive Automobiles (superficial knowledge of repair work an advantage) — No salary, but living expenses paid

For further details and terms of service apply to

WILLIAM R. HEREFORD
Headquarters American Ambulance,
14 Wall Street, New York

or to

HENRY D. SLEEPER
c/o Lee, Higginson & Co.,
State Street, Boston

Fund raising leaflet for the American Ambulance Field Service Fund. Also illustrated is a recruiting promotion.

E
UNITED STATES NAVY

Proficiency Medals

U.S. Navy Expert Pistol Shot Medal

The U.S. Navy Expert Pistol Shot Medal was established in 1920 as incentive to recognize outstanding marksmanship. It is awarded to members of the Navy or Naval Reserve who qualify as Expert with their issue pistol firing a prescribed qualification course.

The service ribbon of the Pistol Shot medal is awarded to Naval personnel who qualify marksman or sharpshooter. When awarded for marksman qualification only the ribbon is awarded. When awarded for sharpshooter qualification the ribbon is awarded with a Silver "S". Those who qualify expert receive the medal and the accompanying service ribbon with a Silver "E".

U.S. Navy Expert Rifleman Medal

The U.S. Navy Expert Rifleman Medal was established in 1920 as incentive to recognize outstanding rifle marksmanship. It is awarded to members of the Navy or Naval Reserve who qualify as Expert with their issue rifle firing a prescribed qualification course.

The service ribbon of the Rifleman medal is awarded to Naval personnel who qualify marksman or sharpshooter. When awarded for marksman qualification only the ribbon is awarded. When awarded for sharpshooter qualification the ribbon is awarded with a Silver "S". Those who qualify expert receive the medal and the accompanying service ribbon with a Silver "E".

U.S. Coast Guard Expert Pistol Shot Medal

The U.S. Coast Guard Expert Pistol Shot Medal was established as incentive to recognize outstanding marksmanship. It is awarded to all personnel of the Coast Guard or Coast Guard Reserve who qualify as Expert with their issue pistol firing a prescribed qualification course.

The service ribbon of the Pistol Shot medal is awarded to Coast Guard personnel who qualify marksman or sharpshooter. When awarded for marksman qualification only the ribbon is awarded. When awarded for sharpshooter qualification the ribbon is awarded with a Silver "S". Those who qualify expert receive the medal and the accompanying service ribbon with a Silver "E".

U.S. Coast Guard Expert Rifleman Medal

The U.S. Coast Guard Expert Rifleman Medal was established as incentive to recognize outstanding rifle marksmanship. It is awarded to members of the Coast Guard and Coast Guard Reserve who qualify as Expert with their issue rifle firing a prescribed course established by the Commandant, U.S. Coast Guard.

The service ribbon of the Rifleman medal is awarded to Coast Guard personnel who qualify marksman or sharpshooter. When awarded for marksman qualification only the ribbon is awarded. When awarded for sharpshooter qualification the ribbon is awarded with a Silver "S". Those who qualify expert receive the medal and the accompanying service ribbon with a Silver "E".

U.S. Naval Academy Short Range Battle Practice Medal

The Short Range Battle Practice Medal (SRBPM) was approved by the Secretary of the Navy on 11 January 1934. The main purpose of the SRBPM was to recognize First Class and Third Class Midshipmen from the Naval Academy who had been members of gun turrets which had been awarded the Navy "E" when their ships fired in annual competition.

Naval regulations did not authorize Officers to wear the "E" and so these young Midshipmen, who often held key positions such as gun pointer or gun captain, during their summer cruises, received no recognition for their achievements.

J. Voigt

In order to foster an increased interest in Naval gunnery and to recognize the achievements of the individual Midshipmen in gunnery, the Superintendent of the Naval Academy suggested to the Navy Department that a suitable award be authorized for those Midshipmen who had qualified on their summer cruise.

The first awards of the Short Range Battle Practice Medal were presented on 1 May 1935. The final awards were presented to the Third Classmen of the Class of 1943 for the summer cruise of 1940. Award of the SRBPM was discontinued in 1944.

It has been estimated that between 500 and 600 medals were issued during the seven years the medal was awarded. The Short Range Battle Practice Medal was authorized for wear only while the recipient was attending the Naval Academy. The Short Range Battle Practice Medal is also known as the Excellence with Great Guns Medal and the Great Guns Medal.

The design of the SRBPM was based on the Navy Expert Rifleman Medal and depicts a Battleship firing its main guns and the words "UNITED STATES NAVY" below. The reverse is most often encountered blank. The ribbon for the SRBPM is Navy Blue with five equally spaced narrow yellow, or gold, stripes.

Navy Marksmanship Badge

The Navy Marksmanship badge was introduced in approximately 1904 to promote proficiency in both pistol and rifle marksmanship among officers and enlisted personnel of the Navy and the Marine Corps. The Marksmanship Badge was discontinued in approximately 1914.

The basic badge consisted of a top bar with the word "Sharpshooter" in raised letters, a Requalification Bar with three silver oval slugs, and the pendant. When the badge was awarded, the pendant was engraved in two lines with the recipient's name on one line and "USN" or "USMC" on the second line. If the recipient was an officer the second line had the recipient's rank preceding the "USN" or "USMC."

Upon qualification one of the silver oval slugs was removed from the Requalification Bar and a date oval bearing the year of qualification was inserted. If the recipient qualified as an expert, a bar was added to the badge with the word "Expert" in raised letters and the year of qualification engraved on the front of the bar. The reverse of the expert bar was engraved with the recipient's name. Bars also existed for "Expert Pistol Shot."

J. Voigt

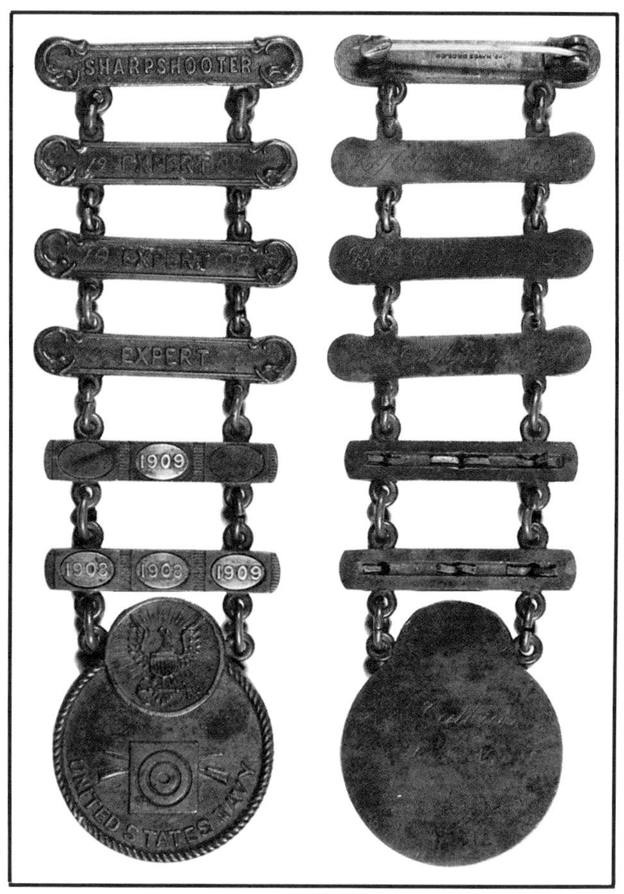

Original style Navy Marksmanship badge with multiple bars.

J. Voigt

The Marksmanship Badge exists in two varieties, distinguished by the size of the target and rifles on the pendant. The badge is believed to have been discontinued about 1914 as that is the latest date observed on any Requalification Bar or Expert Bar. In 1920 the Navy introduced the Expert Marksman and Expert Pistol Shot medals, which presented a more harmonious appearance when worn with other medals, to continue to recognize proficiency with small arms. These medals borrowed their basic pendant design from the Navy Marksmanship Badge.

Revenue Cutter Service Marksmanship Badge

The Revenue Cutter Service Marksmanship badge was introduced in approximately 1904 to promote proficiency in both pistol and rifle marksmanship among officers and enlisted personnel of the United States Revenue Cutter Service. The Marksmanship Badge was discontinued in approximately 1914.

The basic badge consisted of a top bar with the word "Sharpshooter" in raised letters, a Requalification Bar with three silver oval slugs, and the pendant. When the badge was awarded the pendant was engraved in two lines with the recipient's name on one line and "USRCS" on the second line. If the recipient was an officer the second line had the recipient's rank preceding the "USRCS."

Upon qualification, one of the silver oval slugs was removed from the Requalification Bar and a date oval bearing the year of qualification was inserted. If the recipient qualified as an expert, a bar was added to the badge with the word "Expert" in raised letters and the year of qualification engraved on the front of the bar. The reverse of the expert bar was engraved with the recipient's name. Bars also existed for "Expert Pistol Shot."

The Marksmanship Badge is believed to have been discontinued about 1914 as that is the latest date observed on any Requalification Bar or Expert Bar. In 1920 the Coast Guard introduced the Expert Marksman and Expert Pistol Shot medals, which presented a more harmonious appearance when worn with other medals, to continue to recognize proficiency with small arms. These medals borrowed their basic pendant design from the Revenue Cutter Service Marksmanship Badge.

Top bar with "The Hayes Bros. Co." marking.

Greg Gritsch

Revenue Cutter Service Marksmanship Badge.

BAKER

Commendation and Service Ribbons

While service ribbons, or ribbon bars as they are also called, serve to represent the actual medal a servicemember has received, many awards exist only as ribbons with no accompanying medal.

Prior to the Korean War, service ribbons for wear by Army and Air Force personnel differed in size from those worn by Navy and Marine Corps personnel. Navy and Marine Corps service ribbons before the Korean War were 1/2 inch wide by 1 3/8th inches long. Following the Korean War service ribbons were standardized for all branches of the Armed Forces and the Navy and Marine Corps adopted the smaller style 3/8th inch wide by 1 3/8th inch long service ribbons used by Army and Air Force personnel.

Brigadier General Floyd W. Baker, Commanding General, Brooke Army Medical Center, August 1974

Combat Action Ribbon (Navy and Marine Corps)

The Combat Action Ribbon was authorized by the Secretary of the Navy on 17 February 1969. The award is made retroactive to 1 March 1961 to members of the Navy, Marine Corps, and Coast Guard, (when units of the Coast Guard are under control of the Navy) in the grade of colonel/ captain and below, who actively participate in ground or surface combat. The main criteria for eligibility is that the individual must have demonstrated satisfactory participation in a bona fide ground or surface combat fire fight or action during which he was under enemy fire.

Personnel serving aboard ship are eligible for the Combat Action Ribbon if the ship and the crew were engaged by enemy shore, surface, air or submarine attack.

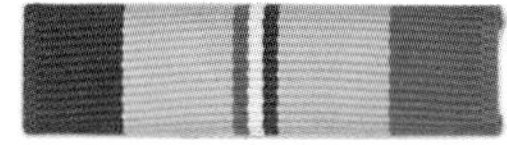

Coast Guard Commandant's Letter of Commendation Ribbon

One of the Coast Guard's oldest awards is the Commandant's Letter of Commendation. On 17 March 1979 the Commandant of the U.S. Coast Guard authorized the wear of a ribbon by any member of the Armed Forces of the United States who, while serving in any capacity with the U.S. Coast Guard, is awarded the Commandant's Letter of Commendation.

The service for which the Coast Guard Commandant's Letter of Commendation Ribbon is awarded is of a degree less than that required for award of the Coast Guard Achievement Medal.

Presidential Unit Citation (Air Force and Army)

The Presidential Unit Citation (PUC) was established by Executive Order 9075 on 26 February 1942 as the Distinguished Unit Badge. The PUC is awarded to Army and Air Force units that display the same degree of heroism in combat as would warrant the Distinguished Service Cross or Air Force Cross to an individual. The name was changed from Distinguished Unit Badge to Presidential Unit Citation on 3 November 1966.

Presidential Unit Citation (Navy and Marine Corps)

The Presidential Unit Citation for Navy and Marine Corps units was established by Executive Order on 10 January 1957. To justfy the award, the unit must have clearly distinguished itself by action of a character comparable to that which would merit the award of a Navy Cross to an individual.

Valorous Unit Award (Army)

The Valorous Unit Award is awarded to units of brigade or battalion size which exhibit a degree of gallantry, determination and esprit de corps in combat of a lesser degree than that which is required for award of the Presidential Unit Citation, but which nevertheless sets it apart from similar units participating in the same conflict.

Joint Meritorious Unit Award

This award was established by the Secretary of Defense on 22 July 1982. The JMUA is intended to recognize units which distinguish themselves by exceptionally meritorious achievement while participating in joint activities of the US Armed Forces. Award of the Joint Meritorious Unit Award is retroactive to 23 January 1979.

Army Superior Unit Award

The Army Superior Unit Award was established 8 April 1985 for award to battalion and smaller sized units which distinguish themselves by outstanding meritorious performance during peacetime of a difficult and challenging mission under extraordinary circumstances.

Navy Unit Commendation

The Navy Unit Commendation ribbon was authorized on 18 December 1944. Awarded by the Secretary of the Navy to any qualifying unit of the Navy or Marine Corps, the Navy Unit Commendation ribbon is awarded to any unit which distinguishes itself by outstanding heroism in combat against a hostile foreign force.

Coast Guard Unit Commendation

The Coast Guard Unit Commendation ribbon was established on 1 January 1963. The ribbon is awarded by the Commandant of the Coast Guard to any ship, aircraft, or any other Coast Guard unit which distinguishes itself by valorous or extremely meritorious service of a noncombat nature. The degree of valour or meritorious service must be comparable to that which would be required for award of the Coast Guard Commendation Medal to individual personnel.

Coast Guard Bicentennial Unit Commendation Ribbon

The Commandant of the Coast Guard, Admiral P.A. Yost, authorized the award of the Bicentennial Unit Commendation (BUC) on 2 January 1990. Eligibility for award of the BUC Ribbon was extended to all members of the Coast Guard and Coast Guard Reserve for service from 1 March 1989 through 1 October 1989. Personnel need have only one day of qualifying service to be eligible for the award.

Air Force Outstanding Unit Award

The Air Force Outstanding Unit Award (AFOUA) was established by the Secretary of the Air Force on 6 January 1954. The AFOUA is awarded to Air Force units for outstanding achievement or exceptionally meritorious service. When awarded for combat heroism a bronze "V" is worn on the ribbon. If awarded for exceptionally meritorious service, the exceptionally meritorious service must cover a period of at least one year but not more than two years

Air Force Organizational Excellence Award

The Air Force Organizational Excellence Award was established by the Secretary of the Air Force on 26 August 1966. This ribbon is awarded to unnumbered organizations such as MAJCOM headquarters, DRUs, centers, etc. for service of a similar nature to that required for award of the Air Force Outstanding Unit Award.

Meritorious Unit Commendation (Army)

This unit commendation is given for exceptionally meritorious service for a period of at least six months during operations against an armed enemy on or after 1 January 1944. Units need not be in direct combat with the enemy to be eligible for award of the Meritorious Unit Commendation ribbon. However, their actions must be directly related to the combat effort and the unit must be deployed within the geographic area of combat operations.

The Meritorious Unit Commendation is intended to recognize the achievements of battalion size and smaller units. The degree of meritorious service is comparable to that which would be required for award of the Legion of Merit for an individual.

Meritorious Unit Commendation (Navy and Marine Corps)

The Meritorious Unit Commendation ribbon was established by the Secretary of the Navy on 17 July 1967. The Meritorious Unit Commendation is awarded to units of the Navy or Marine Corps for valorous or meritorious service either in a combat or noncombat situation. Unit service which would warrant award of the Bronze Star or Meritorious Service Medal to an individual is considered the standard for award of the Meritorious Unit Commendation.

Coast Guard Meritorious Unit Commendation

The Coast Guard Meritorious Unit Commendation ribbon was authorized 13 November 1973. The ribbon is awarded to any unit of the U.S. Coast Guard or Coast Guard Reserve which distinguishes itself by either valorous or meritorious achievement or service of a noncombat nature.

Navy "E" Award Ribbon

The Navy "E" Award ribbon was established in June 1976 to replace the Battle Efficiency Award (a letter "E") which was worn sewn on the sleeve of the uniform. The ribbon is authorized for wear by all personnel who seved as crew members of ships and aviation squadrons winning the Battle Efficiency Award. Subsequent awards of the ribbon are denoted by additional "E"s on the sevice ribbon. Four or more awards are designated by an "E" surrounded by a wreath.

Reserve Special Commendation Ribbon (Navy and Marine Corps)

The Reserve Special Commendation Ribbon was established by the Secretary of the Navy on 16 April 1946. The ribbon was awarded to those officers of the Organized Reserve who had officially commanded at the battalion, squadron, or seperate division level in a meritorious manner for a period of 4 years between 1 January 1930 and 7 Dec. 1941.

The period of command need not have been continuous, but the officer must have been regularly assigned to command such units for a total of four years within a ten year period of time.

This award, obsolete the day it was authorized, is relatively unheard of and often overlooked. However, the officers who received this award formed the backbone of the Navy and Marine Corps as America entered the Second World War. Mostly junior officers during World War I, these men continued to develop their military skills in the Reserves and became the first to lead the fight in our Navy's battles at the Coral Sea and Midway.

Outstanding Airman of the Year Ribbon

This ribbon was established by the Secretary of the Air Force on 21 February 1968. The ribbon is awarded to airman nominated by by the MAJCOMs, SOAs, and DRUs for competition in the 12 Outstanding Airman of the Year competition sponsored by the Air Force Association.

Sea Service Deployment Ribbon

The Sea Service Deployment Ribbon was approved by the Secretary of the Navy on 22 May 1980. The ribbon is awarded retroactively to 15 August 1974 to officers and enlisted personnel of the Navy and Marine Corps for 12 months accumulative sea duty or duty with the Fleet Marine Force which includes at least one 90 day deployment.

Subsequent awards of the Sea Service Deployment Ribbon are recognized by the addition of 3/16th inch bronze stars to the ribbon.

Coast Guard Special Operations Service Ribbon

The Coast Guard Special Operations Service Ribbon was authorized by the Commandant of the Coast Guard on 1 July 1987. The ribbon may be awarded to any member of the Armed Forces serving in any capacity with the Coast Guard who participate in a Coast Guard special operation, not involving combat. To qualify for award of the Special Operations Service Ribbon, participation in the operation must not also qualify for any other service award, such as the Humanitarian Service Medal

Personnel participating in a qualifying operation must be attached or assigned to a unit engaged in direct support of the operation for a minimum of 21 consecutive days, or for the entire operation if it lasts less than 21 days.

Coast Guard Sea Service Ribbon

The Coast Guard Sea Service Ribbon was instituted 3 March 1984 by the Commandant of the U.S. Coast Guard. The ribbon is awarded to Coast Guard personnel who complete a total of two years sea duty on a Coast Guard cutter of 65 feet or more in length in an active status. Bronze service stars are used to denote completion of each additional five years of qualifying service.

Coast Guard Restricted Duty Ribbon

This ribbon is awarded to Coast Guard Personnel who complete a permanent change of station tour of duty at a shore station where accompanying dependents are not authorized. Established by the Commandment of the Coast Guard on 3 March 1984, the ribbon was created to recognize the unique demands of unaccompanied duty. Subsequent awards of the Restricted Duty Ribbon are recognized by the addition of bronze service stars.

Navy Arctic Service Ribbon

The Navy Arctic Service Ribbon was athorized by Secretary of the Navy John Lehman on 8 May 1986. However, it was not until 3 June 1987 that the Chief of Naval Operations published the criteria for awarding the ribbon.

The Navy Arctic Service Ribbon is awarded retroactively to 1 January 1982 to officers and enlisted personnel of the US Navy or civilian citizens who participate inoperations in support of the Arctic Warfare Program. To be eligible for award, a qualified individual must serve 28 consecutive or non-consecutive days north of or within 50 nautical miles of the Marginal Ice Zone (MIZ)

The MIZ is defined as that area which has a greater than 10% ice concentration and may differ from one operation to the next. There are no provisions for subsequent awards of the Navy Arctic Service Ribbon.

Naval Reserve Sea Service Ribbon

The Naval Reserve Sea Service Ribbon was established on 15 August 1974. This ribbon is awarded to any officer or enlisted member of the US Navy and US Naval Reserve who satisfactorily completes a cumulative total of 36 months of service aboard a Naval Reserve ship or as a member of its Reserve unit or embarked active or Reserve staff. A 3/16th inch Bronze Star is authorized for each subsequent award of the Naval Reserve Sea Service Ribbon.

Marine Corps Reserve Ribbon

The Marine Corps Reserve Ribbon was authorized by the Secretary of the Navy on 17 December 1945. This ribbon was awarded to any member of the Marine Corps Reserve who completed ten cumulative years of satisfactory service in any class of the Marine Corps Reserve. The Marine Corps Reserve Ribbon was discontinued after 17 December 1965, at which time it was superseded by the Armed Forces Reserve Medal.

Air Force Recognition Ribbon

The Air Force Recognition Ribbon was established 12 October 1980 to recognize Air Force personnel who have been individually awarded Air Force - level trophies and awards. The ribbon is not authorized when the individual is a member of a unit which receives a special trophy or award. A bronze oak leaf cluster is worn on the ribbon to denote each subsequent award.

NCO Professional Developement Ribbon (Army)

The NCO Professional Development Ribbon was established by the Secretary of the Army on 10 April 1981. This Ribbon is awarded to NCOs upon completion of a designated NCO professional development course. Completion of the Primary level course is recognized by award of the ribbon bar and Arabic numerals are attached to the ribbon to signify completion of the following courses:

Numeral	Course Level
2	Basic Level
3	Advanced Level
4	Senior Level

Courses completed prior to 1976 for active duty personnel or 1980 for Reserve Component personnel are credited for the Primary level only. First Sergeants Courses completed after 1 January 1987 are no longer credited for award of a numeral.

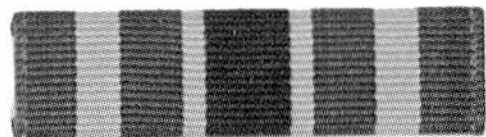

Army Service Ribbon

The Army Service Ribbon (ASR) was established on 10 April 1981 for award to all personnel who successfully complete initial entry training. This award is available retroactively to all personnel who completed initial entry training prior to 1 August 1981 provided they have an active status after that date with the US Army, Army National Guard or Army Reserve.

Officer personnel are awarded the ASR after completion of their Officer Basic Course. Only one award of the Army Service Ribbon is authorized regardless of whether an individual completes both officer and enlisted initial entry training.

Air Force Overseas Ribbon - Short Tour

This ribbon was authorized on 12 October 1980 for all Air Force and Air Force Reserve personnel who complete short overseas tours. All short overseas tours during an individuals career are creditable for award regardless of when such tours took place.

Multiple awards are represented by oak leaf clusters worn on the ribbon. A silver oak leaf cluster is worn in lieu of five bronze clusters. When both the Short Tour and Long Tour ribbons are worn the Short Tour ribbon takes precedence over the Long Tour Ribbon.

Air Force Overseas Ribbon - Long Tour

This ribbon was authorized on 12 October 1980 for all Air Force and Air Force Reserve personnel who complete long overseas tours. All long overseas tours during an individuals career are creditable for award regardless of when such tours took place.

Multiple awards are represented by oak leaf clusters worn on the ribbon. A silver oak leaf cluster is worn in lieu of five bronze clusters. When both the Short Tour and Long Tour ribbons are worn the Short Tour ribbon takes precedence over the Long Tour Ribbon.

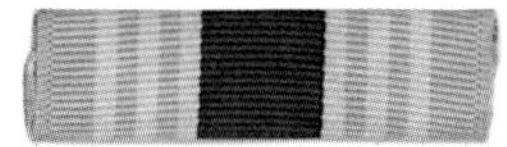

Air Force Longevity Service Award Ribbon

The Air Force Longevity Service Award Ribbon (AFLSA) was authorized on 25 November 1957. The AFLSA ribbon is designed to recognize an aggregate of 4 years of honorable active service by Air Force or Air Force Reserve personnel with any branch of the Armed Forces or Reserve Components. Unlike the Air Reserve Forces Meritorious Service medal which is awarded only for service in the Air Force Reserve or Air National Guard, service in other branches is creditable towards award of the the AFLSA ribbon.

Overseas Service Ribbon (Army)

The Overseas Service Ribbon (OSR) was established on 10 April 1981 and is awarded to active duty personnel who complete an overseas tour for which no other service medal is authorized. Overseas tours completed prior to 1 August 1981 will be credited for award of the OSR provided the individual is still in an active status with the US Army, Army National Guard or Army Reserve after that date.

Subsequent qualifying overseas tours are recognized by Arabic numerals of the same type as used for the NCO Professional Development Ribbon and Air Medal.

Navy and Marine Corps Overseas Service Ribbon

The Navy and Marine Corps Overseas Service Ribbon (NMCOSR) was established 1 January 1979. Active duty officer andnlisted personnel who serve 12 months at an overseas duty station qualify for award of the NMCOSR. Inactive reservists who serve 30 consecutive or 45 nonconsecutive days duty at on overseas duty station are also qualified for this award.

The award of the Navy and Marine Corps Overseas Service Ribbon is retroactive to 15 August 1974. Qualifying service between 15 August 1974 and 1 January 1979 is counted towards only the first award. Subsequent awards of the NMCOSR are recognized by the addition of 3/16th inch bronze stars to the ribbon.

Navy Recruiting Service Ribbon

The Navy Recruiting Service Ribbon (NRSR) was approved by the Secretary of the Navy on 2 February 1989 to recognize the unique and demanding nature of recruiting duty. Eligibility for the NRSR was made retroactive to 1 January 1980 and includes officers and enlisted personnel.

The Navy Recruiting Service Ribbon is awarded to Career Recruiting Force (CRF) personnel upon completion of three consecutive years of recruiting duty. Non CRF personnel become eligible for the NRSR upon completion of a successful tour of duty in recruiting and at the recommendation of their commanding officer.

The NRSR is worn after the Overseas Service Ribbon and before the Armed Forces Reserve Medal. Second and subsequent awards are denoted by the addition of 3/16 inch bronze stars.

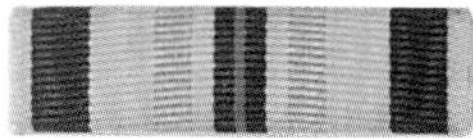

Navy Fleet Marine Force Ribbon

The Navy Fleet Marine Force Ribbon was authorized by the Secretary of the Navy on 1 September 1984 to recognize the service of officers and enlisted personnel of the U.S. Navy who serve with the Fleet Marine Force.

Navy personnel who serve a period of 12 months duty with the FMF and successfully complete the Marine Corps Physical Fitness Test as well as the Essential Subjects Test qualify for award of the Navy Fleet Marine Force Ribbon.

NCO Professional Military Education Graduate Ribbon (Air Force)

Instituted on 28 August 1962, this ribbon is awarded for successful graduation from a resident NCO professional military education school. Graduation from more than one PME school is recognized by the addition of an oak leaf cluster to the ribbon for each USAF NCO Academy course completed.

USAF Basic Military Training Honor Graduate Ribbon

This ribbon was established on 3 April 1976 for award to those BMT airmen who are recommended as honor graduates by military training instructors and school commanders. No more than the top ten percent of each squadron are designated as honor graduates. This ribbon is not awarded retroactively for those designated honor graduates who graduated from Basic Military Training prior to 30 July 1976.

Coast Guard Basic Training Honor Graduate Ribbon

This ribbon was authorized on 3 March 1984 for award effective 1 April 1984. U.S. Coast Guard personnel who graduate in the top three percent of each U.S. Coast Guard recruit training graduating class.

Coast Guard Reserve Meritorious Service Ribbon

The Coast Guard Reserve Meritorious Service Ribbon (CGRMSR) was authorized to recognize four consecutive years of qualifying service by enlisted personnel. The CGRMSR was discontinued in 1963 when the Commandant of the Coast Guard authorized the Coast Guard Reserve Good Conduct Medal.

Army Reserve Components Overseas Training Ribbon

This ribbon was established by the Secretary of the Army on 11 July 1984. The ARCOTR is awarded to members of the Army National Guard or Army Reserve who complete at least ten consecutive days of duty in a foreign country. Training duty completed prior to 11 July 1984 is creditable provided the individual is still active in either the US Army, Army National Guard or Army Reserve after that date.

The Army Reserve Components Overseas Training Ribbon is intended to recognize completion of training duty overseas and does not conflict with service medals or decorations.

Subsequent awards of the ARCOTR are recognized by the addition of bronze numerals to the ribbon.

Small Arms Expert Marksmanship Ribbon (Air Force)

This ribbon was established on 28 August 1962 for award to any member of the Air Force , including Reserve Component members, who qualify "Expert" with either the M-16 Rifle or their issue handgun. The ribbon is awarded only one time regardless of the number of times an individual may qualify. Personnel who qualify as "Expert" with both the rifle and handgun are authorized to wear a bronze star on the ribbon.

Distinguished Marksman Distinguished Pistol Shot Ribbon (Navy)

This award is intended to recognize individuals who have won three medals in either or both National Rifle/Pistol Matches, or who have won two medals in National Rifle Matches and a place medal in either Force or Fleet Rifle Matches.

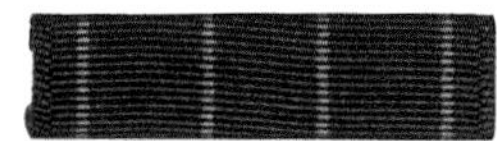

Distinguished Marksman Distinguished Pistol Shot Ribbon (USCG)

Awarded to members of the United States Coast Guard who have won three medals in either or both National Rifle Matches, or who have won two medals in National Rifle Matches and a place medal in either a Force or Fleet Rifle Match.

Distinguished Marksman Ribbon (Navy)

Awarded for similar accomplishments to the Distinguished Marksman, Pistol Shot Ribbon. It is believed that the Distinguished Marksman Ribbon was subsequently replaced by that ribbon.

Distinguished Pistol Shot Ribbon (Navy)

Awarded for similar accomplishments to the Distinguished Marksman, Pistol Shot Ribbon. It is believed that the Distinguished Pistol Shot Ribbon was subsequently replaced by that ribbon.

Air Force Training Ribbon

The Air Force Training Ribbon was established 12 October 1980 for award to all Air Force personnel upon completion of any accession training program such as Basic Military Training or Officer Training School. Unlike the Army Service Ribbon which is its counterpart, the Air Force Training Ribbon can be awarded more than one time. Subsequent awards are represented by the addition of an oak leaf cluster to the ribbon.

Appurtenances

Appurtenances are devices attached to service or suspension ribbons. They are used to denote subsequent awards of the same medal, participation in specific events, or other distinguished characteristics of an award or decoration. The first such appurtenance was a 3/16th inch silver star called the Citation Star, authorized by Congress on 9 July 1918. The Citation Star was awarded for gallantry in action and was affixed to the suspension and service ribbons of the appropriate campaign medal for the action in which the recipient was cited. This Citation Star was later elevated in importance and became the Silver Star medal.

While some devices are common to all branches of the service, such as the 3/16th inch bronze star and the "V" device, their specific use among branches of the Armed Forces may vary. In addition, some branches have developed their own unique devices, such as the Operational Distinguishing Device (Silver O) of the Coast Guard, for use on their own awards.

The collector should be aware that the use of some devices on specific medals has not remained consistent over time. For example, the Army originally denoted subsequent awards of the National Defense Service Medal with a bronze oakleaf cluster. However, in 1987 this practice was changed and the Army now uses the 3/16th inch bronze star for subsequent awards of the NDSM.

Captain Eddie Rickenbacker wears nine Oak Leaf Branches on his DSC.

Oak Leaf Cluster

Oak Leaf Clusters are used by the Army and Air Force to denote subsequent awards of the same decoration. The device itself is a bronze or silver twig of four oak leaves with three acorns on the stem. The Oak Leaf Cluster is used to denote the second and succeeding awards of decorations (with the exception of the Air Medal) and the ARCAM. The silver Oak Leaf Cluster, used in lieu of five bronze clusters, was instituted in 1947.

The Oak Leaf Cluster was first authorized by the Army in Special Regulations 41 dated 8 February 1919. As originally prescribed the cluster was 7/8th of an inch long. The size was later reduced to the present 13/32nd inch long for wear on the suspension ribbon and 5/16th inch long when worn on the service ribbon in 1932, by the change announced on War Department Circular 46, dated 3 September 1932.

Note: Originally an oak branch, and later a cluster.

First style oak leaf cluster.

Current style oak leaf cluster.

Bronze Numerals

Bronze Arabic numerals 3/16th inch high are used to denote subsequent awards of the Air Medal, Army Reserve Components Overseas Training Ribbon, and the Overseas Service Ribbon. Numerals are also used to denote completion of higher level NCO courses on the NCO Professional Development Ribbon. When used by the Navy and Marine Corps on the Air Medal this appurtenance is known as the Strike/Flight Device.

2

Gold Numerals

Gold Aribic numerals 3/16th inch high are used by the Navy, and Marine Corps to indicate individual awards of the Air Medal for meritorious achievement.

"V" Device

The "V" device, also called the Combat Distinguishing Device by the Navy, is a bronze block letter "V" 1/4 inch high with serifs at the top of the members. It is worn to denote participation in acts of heroism involving conflict with an armed enemy. Originally authorized in December 1945 and used only on the service and suspension ribbons of the Bronze Star, the use of the "V" device was expanded on 29 February 1964. Current regulations authorize the "V" device for issue on the following awards:

ARMY -
Bronze Star, Air Medal, ARCOM

NAVY/MARINE CORPS -
Bronze Star, Legion of Merit, DFC, Air Medal, NCOM, NAM

COAST GUARD -
Bronze Star, Legion of Merit, CGCOM, CGAM

AIR FORCE -
Bronze Star, Air Medal, AFCOM, Outstanding Unit Award, Organizational Excellence Award

Service Stars

Service stars are used by all branches of the service for wear on the service and suspension ribbons of campaign and service medals. The Service Star is a 3/16th inch five pointed star in bronze or silver. When used with campaign medals, the addition of service stars denote participation in recognized campaigns associated with the campaign for which the medal was issued. Service stars are also used to denote subsequent awards of the Good Conduct Medals for the Navy and Marine Corps, Armed Forces Expeditionary Medal and National Defense Service Medal.

Brown

This 1987 photograph of CDR Brown provides an excellent example of the proper wear of ribbons and their appurtenances on Navy and Marine Corps uniforms. CDR Brown's awards are: Bronze Star with "V" device and gold star (note how members of the Navy and Marine Corps center the "V" device whereas Army and Air Force personnel always wear the "V" to the viewer's right of any other appurtenances), Purple Heart, Navy Commendation Medal, Navy Achievement Medal with "V" device and gold star, Combat Action Ribbon, Navy Unit Commendation Ribbon with three bronze stars, Meritorious Unit Commendation Ribbon with one bronze star, Good Conduct Medal with bronze star for 2nd award, National Defense Service Medal, Vietnam Service Medal with Fleet Marine Force Combat Operations insigne and bronze and silver stars, Humanitarian Service Medal with bronze Arabic numberal "2", Republic of Vietnam Gallantry Cross Unit Citation, Republic of Vietnam Civil Actions Unit Citation, Republic of Vietnam Campaign Medal, Navy Expert Rifleman Medal (silver "E" denotes expert qualification), Navy Expert Pistol Shot Medal (silver "E" denotes expert). CDR Brown's final ribbon is from the Association of Military Surgeons of the United States (AMSUS).

Arrowhead

First authorized 23 December 1944, the Arrowhead is a bronze replica of an indian arrowhead 1/4 inch high. The arrowhead denotes participation by Army personnel in a combat parachute jump, helicopter assault landing, combat glider landing, or amphibious assault landing, while assigned or attached as a member of an organized force carrying out an assigned tactical mission. The device is worn on both the service and suspension ribbons of the Asiatic-Pacific Campaign Medal, E-A-M E Campaign Medal, Korean Service Medal, Vietnam Service Medal and the Armed Forces Expeditionary Medal. Only one arrowhead is worn on any one service ribbon. When worn the point of the arrowhead is oriented up and the device is worn to the right of any service or campaign stars.

Berlin Airlift Device

The Berlin Airlift device is a gold colored 3/8th inch replica of a C-54 aircraft. The device is awarded for wear on the Army of Occupation Medal for 92 consecutive days of service with a unit credited with participation in the Berlin airlift. Qualifying service must have occurred between 26 June 1948 and 30 September 1949. Award of the Berlin Airlift device does not automatically entitle the individual to award of the Medal for Humane Action as that medal required 120 days of qualifying service.

Ten - Year Device

The Ten-Year device is a bronze hourglass with the roman numeral "X" superimposed. The device is 5/16th inches in height and is worn on the service and suspension ribbons of the Armed Forces Reserve Medal to denote subsequent awards of the medal.

Antarctic Wintering Over Device

Personnel who are awarded the Antarctic Service Medal and meet the requirements for wintering over on the continent are awarded a bronze disk 5/16th inches in diameter inscribed with the outline of the Antarctic continent for wear on the service ribbon. Subsequent awards of the wintering over device are in gold for the second award and silver for the third award. The device is worn with the peninsula pointing up.

Clasps

Clasps are authorized for wear on a variety of campaign and service medals. The clasps may differ in both design and style as well as be in bronze, silver or gold. However, all clasps except the Good Conduct Medal clasps for the Army, are only worn on the suspension ribbon of the medal.

Good Conduct Medal (Army)

The clasp for the Army Good Conduct Medal is a bar 1/8th inch by 1 3/8th inches upon which is a stylized rope with a loop for each award. The bar is in bronze for the second through fifth award, silver for the sixth through tenth award, and gold for the eleventh through fifteenth award.

World War I Victory Medal

The clasps for the World War I victory medal come in two types; one for the Army and one for the Navy or Marine Corps. Clasps for Army personnel are a bronze bar with rounded ends measuring 1/8th inch by 1 1/2 inches with the name of a battle, country or "Defensive Sector". Battle clasps also have a star at each end while service clasps with country names do not. Clasps for Navy and Marine Corps personnel are rectangular bronze bars with stylized rope borders measuring 1/4th inch by 1 1/2 inches. Clasps for Navy and Marine Corps personnel are inscribed with duty stations or countries.

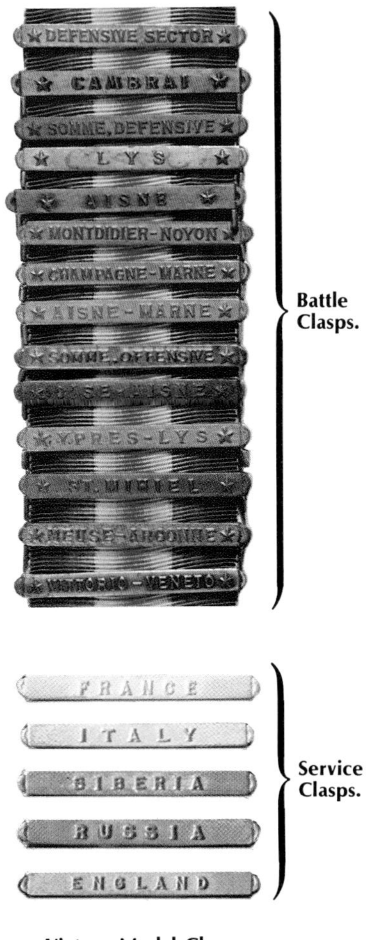

Victory Medal Clasps
(Army)

Victory Medal Clasps
(Navy and Marine Corps)

American Defense Service Medal

Clasps for the ADSM are similiar in style to the clasps used for the WW I Victory Medal. The Army clasp is inscribed with the words "Foreign Service". Two clasps are issued for wear by authorized Navy and Marine Corps personnel; "Fleet" and "Base". Personnel of the Coast Guard were authorized a "Sea" clasp of the same Design as the Navy clasps.

(Army - Air Force)

(Navy - Marine Corps - Coast Guard)

Occupation Medal

Clasps for the Army of Occupation Medal are similar to those used for Army personnel on the WW I Victory medal and are inscribed either "Germany" or "Japan". Clasps for the Navy Occupation Service Medal are the same as those used for Navy and Marine Corps personnel on the WW I Victory Medal and are inscribed either "Europe" or "Asia".

(Army - Air Force)

(Navy - Marine Corps - Coast Guard)

Antarctic Service Medal

Clasps for the Antarctic Service Medal are awarded in bronze for the first winter, gold for the second winter and silver for the third winter. The clasp is a rectangle with the words "Wintered Over" inscribed within a narrow raised border. The clasp measures 1/4 inch by 1 1/2 inches.

Navy and Marine Corps Expeditionary Medals

The only clasp authorized for wear on these medals is the "Wake Island" clasp which was awarded to Navy and Marine Corps personnel for defense of Wake Island during World War II.

D. Boyce

Bronze Maltese Cross

The Bronze Maltese Cross device is worn centered on the World War I Victory Medal by members of the Marine Corps, Medical Corps, and Navy who served with the A.E.F. in France between 6 April 1917 and 11 November 1918. To qualify for the device personnel must not qualify for any battle clasps as issued by the Army

Silver W

The Silver W device is a 1/4th inch high block "W" without serifs on its members. The device is worn on the service ribbon of the Navy and Marine Corps Expeditionary Medals by personnel who participated in the defense of Wake Island.

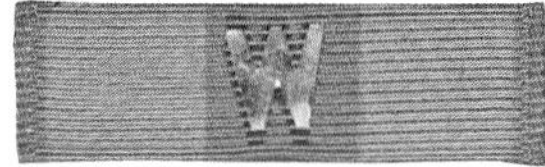

Bronze A

The Bronze A device is a 1/4th inch block letter "A" authorized for wear by personnel serving on board specific ships with the Atlantic Fleet between 22 June 1941 and 7 December 1941. The device is worn on both the service and suspension ribbons of the American Defense Service Medal. When authorized, other service stars or clasps are not authorized for wear on the ribbon.

Variant A

Gold Star and Silver Star

The gold star and silver star device is used to denote subsequent awards of all decorations for Navy, Marine Corps and Coast Guard personnel. The star measures 5/16th inches and is worn on both the suspension and service ribbons of all Navy and Marine Corps decorations. The silver 5/16th inch star is worn in lieu of five gold stars.

Silver E

The Silver E is a block letter "E" 1/4th inch high with serifs at the ends of the upper and lower arms. The device is authorized for wear on Navy and Coast Guard marksmanship ribbons to denote expert qualification. Because award of the marksmanship medals are reserved for those who qualify expert, the Silver E is worn only on the service ribbon and not authorized for wear on the suspension ribbon of the medals.

Navy "E" Device

The Navy "E" Device is a silver block letter E without serifs and is used on the Navy "E" Ribbon to denote the first through third awards of that ribbon. The device is 3/16th inches high. For the fourth award, the device incorporates a smaller "E" which is surrounded by a laurel wreath.

Silver S

The Silver S device is a 1/4th inch block letter "S" worn on the Navy and Coast Guard marksmanship ribbons to denote sharpshooter qualification.

Fleet Marine Force Combat Operations Insigna

The Fleet Marine Force Combat Operations Insigna is a bronze replica of the Marine Corps Insigna 5/16th inches high. The device is worn on the service ribbon of the American Campaign Medal, E-A-M E Campaign Medal, Asiatic-Pacific Campaign Medal, Korean Service Medal, Vietnam Service Medal or Armed Forces Expeditionary Medal by Navy personnel attached to Fleet Marine Force units participating in combat operations. The device is worn centered on the service ribbon and campaign stars are placed alternately on either side of the device, the first star to the right.

Operational Distinguishing Device (Coast Guard)

This devise is a silver "O" in block letter form 1/4th inches high. The device is intended to be worn on the following Coast Guard awards:

Unit Commendation ribbon
Coast Guard Meritorious Unit Comendation
Coast Guard Commendation Medal
Coast Guard Achievement Medal
Coast Guard Commandant's Letter of Commendation Ribbon

This device is intended to denote distinguished operational performance.

Gold N

The Gold N device is a 1/4th inch block letter "N" without serifs at the end of its members. The device is worn on the Navy Presidential Unit Citation ribbon by personnel who were serving on board the U.S.S. Nautilus when it was awarded the Presidential Unit Citation.

Bronze Globe

The Bronze Globe device is worn on the Navy Presidential Unit Citation ribbon by Navy personnel who were serving on board the U.S.S. Triton when it was cited.

Silver Sea Horse

The Silver Sea Horse device is used by the Merchant Marine on the Gallant Ship Unit Citation Bar to denote the first, and all subsequent awards.

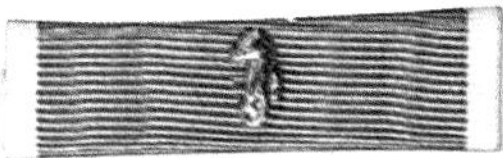

Planet

A winged planet symbol is authorized for wear on the suspension ribbon and service ribbon of the NASA Distinguished Service Medal to denote subsequent awards of that medal. Award of the NASA DSM to members of the Armed Forces is extremely rare and this device is included for reference purposes only.

(illustration unavailable)

Lifesaving Medals

An Award bar for the Gold and Silver Lifesaving Medals is attached to the suspension ribbon to recognize subsequent awards of the same medal. The obverse of the bar is engraved with the number of the award and the reverse is engraved with the recipient's name, date of the award, and citation details.

D.S.C.

Presentation Cases and Issue Boxes

The practice of issuing medals to U.S. service personnel in presentation cases or protective boxes began well before the federal government began issuing medals. Many Mexican War veterans received state and regimental awards for war service in plush velvet lined and custom fitted cases. The Civil War, with the corresponding issue of the Medal of Honor, saw the beginning of the practice of issuing medals in cases at the federal level.

The boxes for the first issue of Army Medals of Honor were supplied by the Philadelphia company of William Wilson and Son. These presentation cases measured 2 3/4th inches by 4 1/2 inches and had a design impressed into both the top and bottom of the black leather case. The designs on these cases are not all identical. The lining of the lid is white with the William Wilson company logo printed in black. The bottom of the case is fitted precisely for the Army Medal of Honor and is covered in dark blue.

During the early 1870's, Wilson changed the size of the case to 2 9/16th inches by 4 1/2 inches. The color of the bottom lining was also changed to purple and a white silk ribbon was attached to the left side to prevent the lid from being opened past 90 degrees and breaking the hinges. The change in the style of presentation cases should help distinguish Civil War issue Medals of Honor from those awarded for heroism during the Indian Wars.

When the Army approved the 1896 style Medal of Honor it also changed the supplier for the presentation case, contracting with Tiffany and Company of New York to supply the cases. These maroon leather cases have a dark red silk lining in the lid and a maroon velvet bottom section with a tab to hold the brooch pin and a slot for the rosette. These cases are quite scarce owing to the fact that when the Army adopted the 1904 style Medal of Honor the cases had to be redesigned.

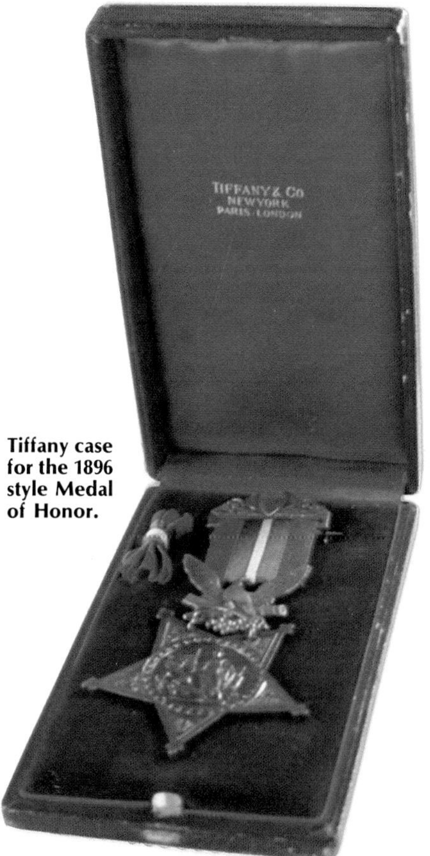

Tiffany case for the 1896 style Medal of Honor.

The 1904 Army Medal of Honor rests in an untitled maroon leather presentation case lined with white silk and measuring 2 1/4th inches by 4 7/8th inches. Following WW I and the introduction of the Distinguished Service Medal and the Distinguished Service Cross, Tiffany and Company supplied a similiar maroon leather case for the new awards. Cases for the DSM and DSC were 2 5/8th inches by 4 5/8th inches and were stamped "D.S.M." or "D.S.C." in 5/8th inch gold letters.

Navy presentation cases for the Navy Cross were supplied by Bailey, Banks and Biddle. These cases measured 2 3/8th inches by 4 5/8th inches and were covered in blue leather. The interior of the bottom was covered by a plush blue pad and the lid lined in white cloth. Unlike the Army DSC case, the case for the Navy Cross is untitled.

Between World War I and the beginning of World War II the number of awards available to Navy and Marine Corps personnel greatly increased and new presentation cases began to appear. Beginning in the early 1940's Navy cases were 2 1/2 inches by 4 3/4th inches and unusually high. The Purple Heart box is 1 1/4th inches high and the Silver Star box is 1 1/16th inches high. Each of the various boxes had a different color scheme. The Purple Heart box was purple with a plush purple bottom pad and a white silk upper lining. The box for the Silver Star was dark red with a

Bailey, Banks & Biddle Purple Heart. Note 2-12-32 date and matching numbers of case and medal.

Navy and Marine Corps issue.

Navy issue Silver Star.

D. Boyce

matching bottom pad and white lining. The case for the Navy DSM was dark blue with a matching pad and white lining. The Navy and Marine Corps Medal was issued in the same size box as the Purple Heart but the box itself was red with a red bottom pad.

While the Navy was producing a rainbow of colored boxes, the Army was standardizing the presentation cases for its awards. The new cases which debuted in the early 1940's were 3 1/2 inches by 6 1/2 inches in size and covered in a black leather. The cases were titled in gold colored letters with a simple gold border composed of two wavy lines with a design at each corner of the inner line. The lid is lined with a yellow-gold silk and the bottom pad is of a plush matching color with a divider between the slotted pad for the lapel pin and the tab which secured the medal brooch.

Bronze Star case of the WWII variety.

Later inWorld War II the Navy adopted this style of case for its gallantry awards, although in a slightly different size. Navy cases of this period measured 3 1/4th inches by 5 3/4th inches.

D. Boyce

Purple Heart case of the WWII period.

D. Boyce

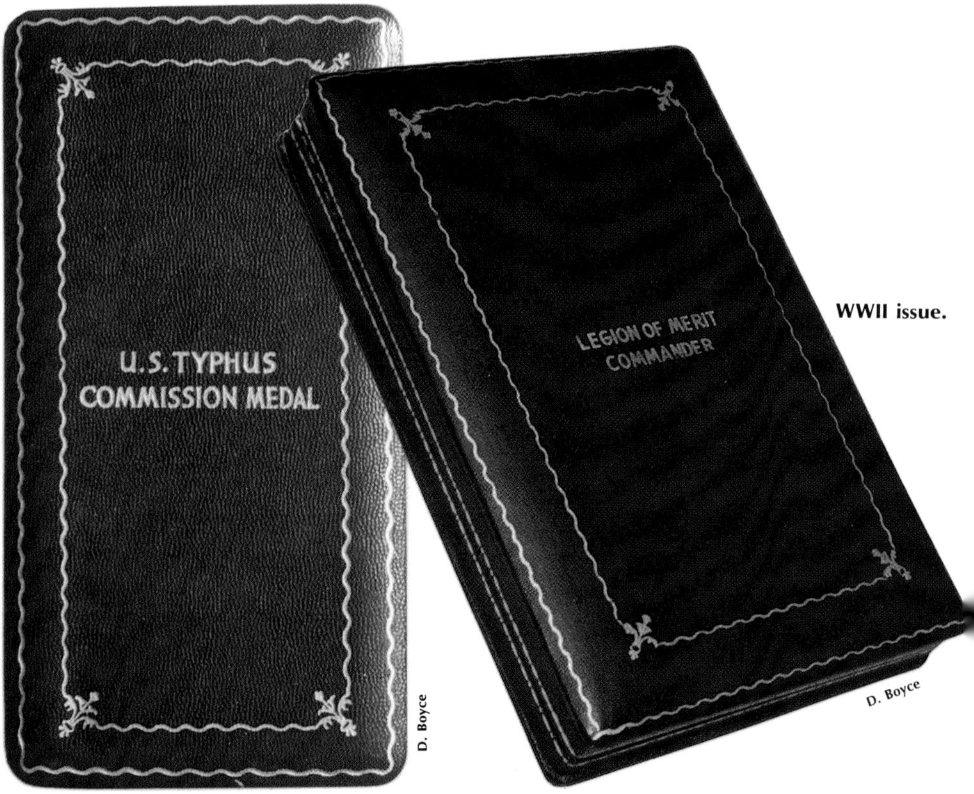

WWII issue.

D. Boyce

D. Boyce

During the late 1950's award cases for all branches of the service were standardized. The new presentation case was 3 1/4th inches by 6 1/2 inches. The bottom half of the new case was dark blue plastic, lined with a plush dark blue pad. The pad featured metal clips which secured the lapel pin, service ribbon, and the brooch pin for the suspension ribbon of the medal. The lid was clear plastic with a gold colored border which allowed the medal to be viewed in the case. The case also featured a notch cut out of the back to allow it to be displayed on the wall.

This plastic case was replaced in the 1970's with a metal case covered in dark blue imitation leather. These presentation cases measure 4 1/4th inches by 7 inches and are seen either titled or untitled. Whether titled or untitled, this style of presentation case is embossed with the words "United States of America" in gold on the lower right corner of the lid. This presentation

1960's era case with clear plastic lid.

punched which secure the service ribbon, lapel pin and the brooch. In addition the pad features a pouch into which the planchet can be slipped to protect the medal during shipping and handling.

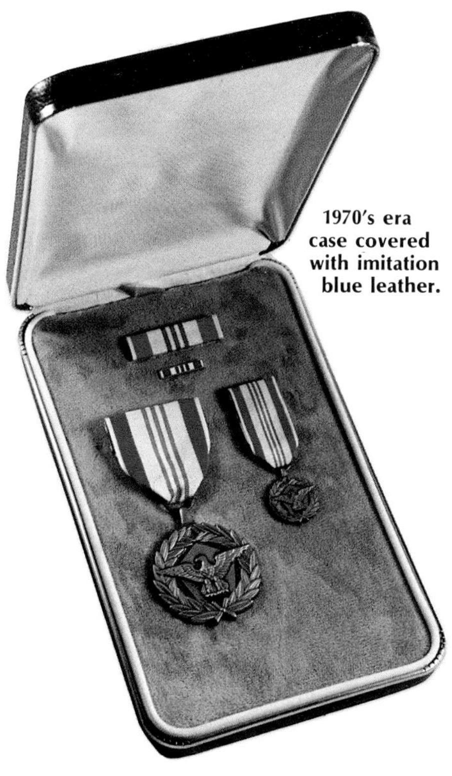

1970's era case covered with imitation blue leather.

Current dark blue, plastic presentation case.

case is also incountered with two different styles of bottom pads. Both pads are covered with a soft grey velvet-like material and are pre-punched for the service ribbon and lapel pin. However, one style pad features tabs which hold both the full size medal and a miniature medal side-by-side. The second style pad has only one tab, centered below the lapel pin, for the brooch pin of the full size medal.

Even these relatively inexpensive cases have proved to be too expensive for the large numbers of commendation and achievement medals awarded by the various branches of the service. Beginning in the early 1980's commendation and achievement medals began appearing in an inexpensive dark blue plastic presentation case. This case features a heavy paper lining covered in white cloth inserted in the lid and a removable soft plastic pad, flocked with a dark gray material, inserted in the bottom of the case. The pad has holes pre-

So far this discussion has been limited to gallantry awards, however boxes also exist for the various campaign medals. The majority of campaign medals issued by the Army, Navy, Marine Corps and Air Force come in small cardboard boxes. These boxes all have a label affixed to one end which includes the manufacturer's name, the title of the medal and the rim-number of the medal. Following WW I this label also included the contract number and date. Rim-number information was of course omitted when this practice was discontinued.

Early boxes for Army campaign medals were generally black (used by the Mint), tan or cardboard colored and varied slightly from one commercial manufacturer to another. Most of these pre-World War I campaign medal boxes had the name of the medal either imprinted on the lid or a label affixed to the lid with the name of the medal printed on it. Many of these labels also bore the manufacturer's name and address.

T. Wheatley

T. Wheatley

T. Wheatley

T. Wheatley

T. Wheatley

T. Wheatley

T. Wheatley

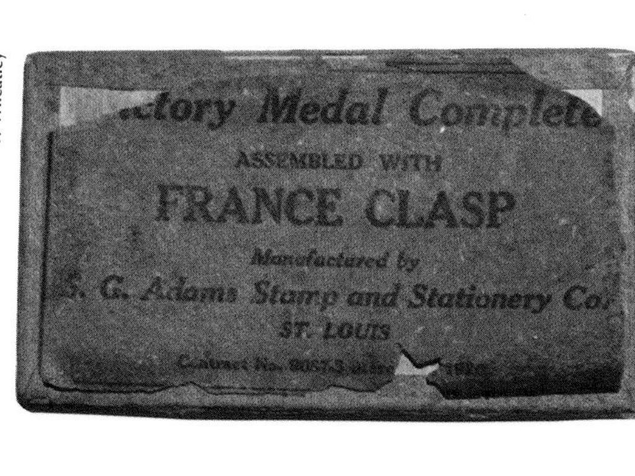

T. Wheatley

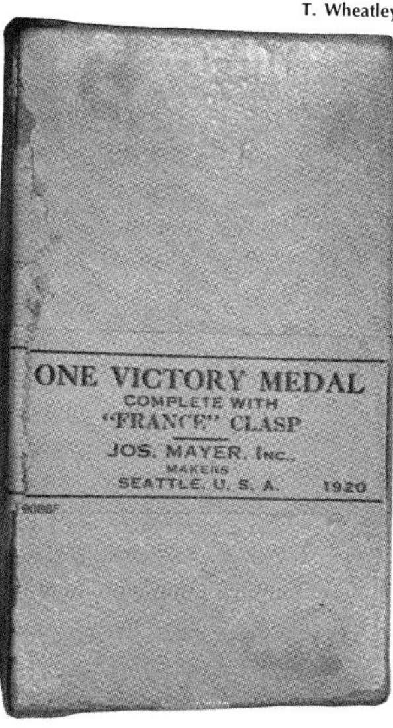

D. Boyce

While the boxes for Army campaign medals were all basically the same, the Navy used the rainbow idea for color coding its early campaign medal boxes. Pre-World War II Navy boxes were also titled and imprinted with a serial number corresponding to the rim number on the medal. For example, the Second Nicaraguan Campaign Medal was issued in a light blue box with gold lettering, the Yangtze Service Medal came in a yellow box with blue lettering , and the China Service Medal was issued in a red box with gold lettering.

D. Boyce

D. Boyce

Jon Jensen

With the issuing of the various World War II campaign medals both the Army and Navy adopted boxes which were either black or various shades of blue. The only distinguishing feature on these current boxes is the manufacturer's label which is affixed to the end of the box.

Although most campaign medals came in one variety or another of cardboard box, both the Sampson and Dewey medals were issued in plush, custom fitted cases. The case for the Dewey Medal is tan leather, measuring 2 7/8th inches by 3 3/4th inches, with a soft leather interior. Sampson Medals were issued in a black leather case measuring 2 3/16th inches by 3 1/2 inches. The interior of the case was specially fitted and lined with deep purple velvet.

Dewey Medal in its fitted, tan case.

Sampson Medal in its fitted case.

Unique case for the Merchant Marine Distinguished Service Medal.

Although they are difficult to display, presentation cases and issue boxes can add to the value of a medal; provided they are original to the medal or correct for the time period.

Order of Precedence of US Awards and Decorations

There is currently no order of precedence which is uniform among all the various branches of the U.S. Armed Forces. Instead, each branch has established its own order of precedence, and while they all follow the same general guidelines, there are almost as many differences as there are similarities.

The differences are accentuated by the fact that the Army is the only branch of the service which requires that all unit awards, including those of the Navy, Air Force and foreign governments, be worn on the right breast. Therefore the Army, unlike the other services does not include unit awards in its order of precedence. As a result, the Army maintains a separate order of precedence for unit awards.

This discrepancy is due to the fact that Army unit awards are viewed in two distinct ways. First, unit awards (such as the Valorous Unit Award) are awarded individually to each member assigned to the unit at the time it received the award and are part of that person's permanent awards. In this respect the Army policy is similar to those of its sister services. Second, unit awards may be worn by any individual serving in a unit authorized a unit award for as long as that person is assigned to that specific unit. Awards worn under the second circumstance are not part of an individual's permanent awards and may not be worn

:ear Admiral J.B. ·ockdale, Com- ·ander Anti- ·ubmarine War- ·re Wing, U.S. ·acific Fleet, ·ebruary 1974.

once the individual is no longer assigned to that unit.

Equating one branch's order of precedence to another is further complicated by the fact that some decorations such as the Air Force's Combat Readiness Medal have no counterpart in the other branches of the service.

The order of precedence for each branch of the service is laid out in the following pages. These lists represent only those decorations and service awards which are most likely to be seen on the uniforms for each branch of the service. Interservice orders of precedence are simply too complicated for the sane collector to attempt to decifer. Thus, the order of precedence for the Army does not include Navy awards and so on, although an individual soldier may be awarded them.

Each branch of the service also catagorizes awards. The order of precedence for award catagorigies is shown below:

Army

US Military Decorations
US Nonmilitary Decorations
Good Conduct Medals
US Service Medals and Ribbons
US Merchant Marine Awards
Foreign Military Decorations
Foreign Service Awards

Navy / USMC / USCG

US Military Decorations
US Unit Awards
US Nonmilitary Decorations
US Merchant Marine Decorations
Good Conduct Medals
US Service Medals and Ribbons
US Reserve Service Awards
US Merchant Marine Service
Medals and Ribbons
Foreign Military Decorations
Foreign Unit Awards
Foreign Service Awards
Marksmanship Awards

Air Force

US Military Decorations
US Unit Awards
US Nonmilitary Awards
US Merchant Marine Decorations
Combat Readiness Medal
Good Conduct Medals
Outstanding Airman of the Year Ribbon
Air Force Recognition Ribbon
US Service Medals and Ribbons
US Reserve Service Medals and Ribbons
NCO Professional Military Education
Graduate Ribbon
Basic Military Training Honor Graduate Ribbon
Marksmanship Awards
Air Force Training Ribbon
Philippine Service Awards
US Merchant Marine Service Awards
Foreign Military Decorations
Foreign Unit Awards
UN Service Awards
Foreign Service Awards

Order of Precedence - United States Army

MEDAL OF HONOR
DISTINGUISHED SERVICE CROSS
DEFENSE DISTINGUISHED SERVICE MEDAL
DISTINGUISHED SERVICE MEDAL
CERTIFICATE OF MERIT
SILVER STAR
DEFENSE SUPERIOR SERVICE MEDAL
LEGION OF MERIT
DISTINGUISHED FLYING CROSS
SOLDIER'S MEDAL
BRONZE STAR
PURPLE HEART
DEFENSE MERITORIOUS SERVICE MEDAL
MERITORIOUS SERVICE MEDAL
AIR MEDAL
JOINT SERVICE COMMENDATION MEDAL
ARMY COMMENDATION MEDAL
JOINT SERVICE ACHIEVEMENT MEDAL
ARMY ACHIEVEMENT MEDAL
POW MEDAL
GOOD CONDUCT MEDAL
ARMY RESERVE COMPONENTS ACHIEVEMENT MEDAL
CIVIL WAR CAMPAIGN MEDAL
INDIAN CAMPAIGN MEDAL
SPANISH CAMPAIGN MEDAL
SPANISH WAR SERVICE MEDAL
ARMY OF CUBAN OCCUPATION MEDAL
ARMY OF PUERTO RICAN OCCUPATION MEDAL
PHILIPPINE CAMPAIGN MEDAL
PHILIPPINE CONGRESSIONAL MEDAL
CHINA CAMPAIGN MEDAL
ARMY OF CUBAN PACIFICATION MEDAL
MEXICAN SERVICE MEDAL
MEXICAN BORDER SERVICE MEDAL
WORLD WAR I VICTORY MEDAL
TEXAS CAVALRY CONGRESSIONAL MEDAL
ARMY OF OCCUPATION OR GERMANY MEDAL
AMERICAN DEFENSE SERVICE MEDAL
WOMAN'S ARMY CORPS SERVICE MEDAL
AMERICAN CAMPAIGN MEDAL
ASIATIC-PACIFIC CAMPAIGN MEDAL
E-A-ME CAMPAIGN MEDAL
WORLD WAR II VICTORY MEDAL
ARMY OF OCCUPATION MEDAL
MEDAL FOR HUMANE ACTION
NATIONAL DEFENSE SERVICE MEDAL
KOREAN SERVICE MEDAL
ANTARCTICA SERVICE MEDAL
ARMED FORCES EXPEDITIONARY MEDAL
VIETNAM SERVICE MEDAL
SOUTHWEST ASIA SERVICE MEDAL
HUMANITARIAN SERVICE MEDAL
ARMED FORCES RESERVE MEDAL
NCO PROFESSIONAL DEVELOPMENT RIBBON
ARMY SERVICE RIBBON
OVERSEAS SERVICE RIBBON
ARMY RESERVE COMPONENTS OVERSEAS TRAINING RIBBON

Order of Precedence - Army (Unit Awards)

PRESIDENTIAL UNIT CITATION
JOINT MERITORIOUS UNIT AWARD
VALOROUS UNIT AWARD
MERITORIOUS UNIT COMMENDATION
ARMY SUPERIOR UNIT AWARD

Order of Precedence - Army (Non military decorations)

PRESIDENTIAL MEDAL OF FREEDOM
GOLD LIFESAVING MEDAL
MEDAL FOR MERIT
SILVER LIFESAVING MEDAL
NATIONAL SECURITY MEDAL
MEDAL OF FREEDOM
DISTINGUISHED CIVILIAN SERVICE MEDAL
OUTSTANDING CIVILIAN SERVICE MEDAL
SELECTIVE SERVICE DISTINGUISHED SERVICE MEDAL
SELECTIVE SERVICE EXCEPTIONAL SERVICE MEDAL
SELECTIVE SERVICE MERITORIOUS SERVICE MEDAL
CIVILIAN SERVICE IN VIETNAM MEDAL

Order of Precedence - United States Navy

MEDAL OF HONOR
NAVY CROSS
DEFENSE DISTINGUISHED SERVICE MEDAL
DISTINGUISHED SERVICE MEDAL
SILVER STAR
DEFENSE SUPERIOR SERVICE MEDAL
LEGION OF MERIT
DISTINGUISHED FLYING CROSS
NAVY AND MARINE CORPS MEDAL
BRONZE STAR
PURPLE HEART
DEFENSE MERITORIOUS SERVICE MEDAL
MERITORIOUS SERVICE MEDAL
AIR MEDAL
JOINT SERVICE COMMENDATION MEDAL
NAVY COMMENDATION MEDAL
JOINT SERVICE ACHIEVEMENT MEDAL
NAVY ACHIEVEMENT MEDAL
SPECIALLY MERITORIOUS MEDAL
COMBAT ACTION RIBBON
PRESIDENTIAL UNIT CITATION
JOINT MERITORIOUS UNIT AWARD
NAVY UNIT COMMENDATION
MERITORIOUS UNIT COMMENDATION
NAVY "E" RIBBON
POW MEDAL
GOOD CONDUCT MEDAL
NAVAL RESERVE MERITORIOUS SERVICE MEDAL
FLEET MARINE FORCE RIBBON
MANILA BAY MEDAL (DEWEY MEDAL)
WEST INDIES NAVAL CAMPAIGN MEDAL (SAMPSON MEDAL)
PEARY POLAR EXPEDITION MEDAL
NC-4 MEDAL
1st BYRD ANTARCTIC EXPEDITION MEDAL
2nd BYRD ANTARCTIC EXPEDITIONARY MEDAL
UNITED STATES ANTARCTIC EXPEDITION MEDAL
CIVIL WAR CAMPAIGN MEDAL
NAVY EXPEDITIONARY MEDAL
WEST INDIES CAMPAIGN MEDAL
SPANISH CAMPAIGN MEDAL
PHILIPPINE CAMPAIGN MEDAL
CHINA RELIEF EXPEDITION MEDAL
NICARAGUAN CAMPAIGN MEDAL (1912)
MEXICAN SERVICE MEDAL
HAITIAN CAMPAIGN MEDAL (1915)
DOMINICAN CAMPAIGN MEDAL
WORLD WAR I VICTORY MEDAL
HAITIAN CAMPAIGN MEDAL (1919-1920)
2nd NICARAGUAN CAMPAIGN MEDAL
YANGTZE SERVICE MEDAL
CHINA SERVICE
AMERICAN DEFENSE SERVICE MEDAL
AMERICAN CAMPAIGN MEDAL
ASIATIC-PACIFIC CAMPAIGN MEDAL
E-A-ME CAMPAIGN MEDAL
WORLD WAR II VICTORY MEDAL
NAVY OCCUPATION SERVICE MEDAL
MEDAL FOR HUMANE ACTION
NATIONAL DEFENSE SERVICE MEDAL
KOREAN SERVICE MEDAL
ANTARCTICA SERVICE MEDAL
ARMED FORCES EXPEDITIONARY MEDAL
VIETNAM SERVICE MEDAL
SOUTHWEST ASIA SERVICE MEDAL
HUMANITARIAN SERVICE MEDAL
SEA SERVICE DEPLOYMENT RIBBON
NAVY ARCTIC SERVICE RIBBON
NAVAL RESERVE SEA SERVICE DEPLOYMENT RIBBON
NAVY AND MARINE CORPS OVERSEAS SERVICE RIBBON
NAVY RECRUITING SERVICE RIBBON
ARMED FORCES RESERVE MEDAL
NAVAL RESERVE MEDAL
EXPERT RIFLEMAN MEDAL
EXPERT PISTOL SHOT MEDAL

Order of Precedence - United States Marine Corps

MEDAL OF HONOR
BREVET MEDAL
NAVY CROSS
DEFENSE DISTINGUISHED SERVICE MEDAL
DISTINGUISHED SERVICE MEDAL
SILVER STAR
DEFENSE SUPERIOR SERVICE MEDAL
LEGION OF MERIT
DISTINGUISHED FLYING CROSS
NAVY AND MARINE CORPS MEDAL
BRONZE STAR
PURPLE HEART
DEFENSE MERITORIOUS SERVICE MEDAL
MERITORIOUS SERVICE MEDAL
AIR MEDAL
JOINT SERVICE COMMENDATION MEDAL
NAVY COMMENDATION MEDAL
JOINT SERVICE ACHIEVEMENT MEDAL
NAVY ACHIEVEMENT MEDAL
SPECIALLY MERITORIOUS MEDAL
COMBAT ACTION RIBBON
PRESIDENTIAL UNIT CITATION
JOINT MERITORIOUS UNIT AWARD
NAVY UNIT COMMENDATION
MERITORIOUS UNIT COMMENDATION
NAVY "E" RIBBON
POW MEDAL
GOOD CONDUCT MEDAL
SELECTED MARINE CORPS RESERVE MEDAL
MANILA BAY MEDAL (DEWEY MEDAL)
WEST INDIES NAVAL CAMPAIGN MEDAL (SAMPSON MEDAL)
PEARY POLAR EXPEDITION MEDAL
NC-4 MEDAL
1st BYRD ANTARCTIC EXPEDITION MEDAL
2nd BYRD ANTARCTIC EXPEDITIONARY MEDAL
UNITED STATES ANTARCTIC EXPEDITION MEDAL
CIVIL WAR CAMPAIGN MEDAL
MARINE CORPS EXPEDITIONARY MEDAL
WEST INDIES CAMPAIGN MEDAL
SPANISH CAMPAIGN MEDAL
PHILIPPINE CAMPAIGN MEDAL
CHINA RELIEF EXPEDITION MEDAL
NICARAGUAN CAMPAIGN MEDAL (1912)
MEXICAN SERVICE MEDAL
HAITIAN CAMPAIGN MEDAL (1915)
DOMINICAN CAMPAIGN MEDAL
WORLD WAR I VICTORY MEDAL
HAITIAN CAMPAIGN MEDAL (1919-1920)
2nd NICARAGUAN CAMPAIGN MEDAL
YANGTZE SERVICE MEDAL
CHINA SERVICE
AMERICAN DEFENSE SERVICE MEDAL
AMERICAN CAMPAIGN MEDAL
ASIATIC-PACIFIC CAMPAIGN MEDAL
E-A-ME CAMPAIGN MEDAL
WORLD WAR II VICTORY MEDAL
CHINA SERVICE MEDAL
NAVY OCCUPATION SERVICE MEDAL
MEDAL FOR HUMANE ACTION
NATIONAL DEFENSE SERVICE MEDAL
KOREAN SERVICE MEDAL
ANTARCTICA SERVICE MEDAL
ARMED FORCES EXPEDITIONARY MEDAL
VIETNAM SERVICE MEDAL
SOUTHWEST ASIA SERVICE MEDAL
HUMANITARIAN SERVICE MEDAL
SEA SERVICE DEPLOYMENT RIBBON
NAVY ARCTIC SERVICE RIBBON
NAVY AND MARINE CORPS OVERSEAS SERVICE RIBBON
ARMED FORCES RESERVE MEDAL

Order of Precedence - United States Coast Guard

MEDAL OF HONOR
NAVY CROSS
DEFENSE DISTINGUISHED SERVICE MEDAL
DISTINGUISHED SERVICE MEDAL
DEPARTMENT OF TRANSPORTATION DISTINGUISHED SERVICE MEDAL
SILVER STAR
DEPARTMENT OF TRANSPORTATION GOLD MEDAL
DEFENSE SUPERIOR SERVICE MEDAL
LEGION OF MERIT
DISTINGUISHED FLYING CROSS
COAST GUARD MEDAL
GOLD LIFESAVING MEDAL
BRONZE STAR
PURPLE HEART
DEFENSE MERITORIOUS SERVICE MEDAL
MERITORIOUS SERVICE MEDAL
AIR MEDAL
SILVER LIFESAVING MEDAL
DEPARTMENT OF TRANSPORTATION SILVER MEDAL
JOINT SERVICE COMMENDATION MEDAL
COAST GUARD COMMENDATION MEDAL
JOINT SERVICE ACHIEVEMENT MEDAL
DEPARTMENT OF TRANSPORTATION BRONZE MEDAL
COAST GUARD ACHIEVEMENT MEDAL
COMMANDANT'S LETTER OF COMMENDATION RIBBON
COMBAT ACTION RIBBON
PRESIDENTIAL UNIT CITATION
JOINT MERITORIOUS UNIT AWARD
COAST GUARD UNIT COMMENDATION
COAST GUARD MERITORIOUS UNIT COMMENDATION
COAST GUARD BICENTENNIAL UNIT COMMENDATION
NAVY "E" RIBBON
POW MEDAL
GOOD CONDUCT MEDAL
COAST GUARD RESERVE GOOD CONDUCT MEDAL
NAVAL RESERVE MERITORIOUS SERVICE MEDAL
NAVY EXPEDITIONARY MEDAL
CHINA SERVICE
AMERICANDEFENSE SERVICE MEDAL
AMERICAN CAMPAIGN MEDAL
ASIATIC-PACIFIC CAMPAIGN MEDAL
E-A-ME CAMPAIGN MEDAL
WORLD WAR II VICTORY MEDAL
UNITED STATES ANTARCTIC EXPEDITION MEDAL
NAVY OCCUPATION SERVICE MEDAL
MEDAL FOR HUMANE ACTION
NATIONAL DEFENSE SERVICE MEDAL
KOREAN SERVICE MEDAL
ANTARCTICA SERVICE MEDAL
COAST GUARD ARCTIC SERVICE MEDAL
ARMED FORCES EXPEDITIONARY MEDAL
VIETNAM SERVICE MEDAL
SOUTHWEST ASIA SERVICE
HUMANITARIAN SERVICE MEDAL
COAST GUARD SPECIAL OPERATIONS SERVICE RIBBON
COAST GUARD SEA SERVICE RIBBON
COAST GUARD RESTRICTED DUTY RIBBON
COAST GUARD BASIC TRAINING HONOR GRADUATE RIBBON
ARMED FORCES RESERVE MEDAL
NAVAL RESERVE MEDAL
COAST GUARD RESERVE MERITORIOUS SERVICE RIBBON

Order of Precedence - United States Air Force

MEDAL OF HONOR
AIR FORCE CROSS
DEFENSE DISTINGUISHED SERVICE MEDAL
DISTINGUISHED SERVICE MEDAL
SILVER STAR
DEFENSE SUPERIOR SERVICE MEDAL
LEGION OF MERIT
DISTINGUISHED FLYING CROSS
AIRMAN'S MEDAL
BRONZE STAR
PURPLE HEART
DEFENSE MERITORIOUS SERVICE MEDAL
MERITORIOUS SERVICE MEDAL
AIR MEDAL
AERIAL ACHIEVEMENT MEDAL
JOINT SERVICE COMMENDATION MEDAL
AIR FORCE COMMENDATION MEDAL
JOINT SERVICE ACHIEVEMENT MEDAL
AIR FORCE ACHIEVEMENT MEDAL
PRESIDENTIAL UNIT CITATION
JOINT MERITORIOUS UNIT AWARD
AIR FORCE OUTSTANDING UNIT AWARD
AIR FORCE ORGANIZATIONAL EXCELLENCE AWARD
POW MEDAL
COMBAT READINESS MEDAL
AIR FORCE GOOD CONDUCT MEDAL
GOOD CONDUCT MEDAL
AIR RESERVE FORCES MERITORIOUS SERVICE MEDAL
OUTSTANDING AIRMAN OF THE YEAR RIBBON
AIR FORCE RECOGNITION RIBBON
MEXICAN SERVICE MEDAL
MEXICAN BORDER SERVICE MEDAL
WORLD WAR I VICTORY MEDAL
ARMY OF OCCUPATION OF GERNANY MEDAL
AMERICAN DEFENSE SERVICE MEDAL
WOMAN'S ARMY CORPS SERVICE MEDAL
AMERICAN CAMPAIGN MEDAL
ASIATIC-PACIFIC CAMPAIGN MEDAL
E-A-ME CAMPAIGN MEDAL
WORLD WAR II VICTORY MEDAL
ARMY OF OCCUPATION MEDAL
MEDAL FOR HUMANE ACTION
NATIONAL DEFENSE SERVICE MEDAL
KOREAN SERVICE MEDAL
ANTARCTICA SERVICE MEDAL
ARMED FORCES EXPEDITIONARY MEDAL
VIETNAM SERVICE MEDAL
SOUTHWEST ASIA SERVICE MEDAL
HUMANITARIAN SERVICE MEDAL
AIR FORCE OVERSEAS RIBBON - SHORT TOUR
AIR FORCE OVERSEAS RIBBON - LONG TOUR
AIR FORCE LONGEVITY SERVICE AWARD RIBBON
ARMED FORCES RESERVE MEDAL
AIR FORCE NCO PROFESSIONAL MILITARY EDUCATION GRADUATE RIBBON
BASIC MILITARY TRAINING HONOR GRADUATE
SMALL ARMS EXPERT MARKSMANSHIP RIBBON
AIR FORCE TRAINING RIBBON

United States Merchant Marine

The Shipping Act of 1916 created the United States Shipping Board which built and purchased ships, and regulated shipping. In 1936, the Merchant Marine Act replaced the Shipping Board with the U.S. Maritime Commission. The Maritime Commission had increased powers to enlarge the merchant fleet.

In order to insure a competent, professional commissioned officer corps to meet the needs of the fleet, the Maritime Commission established the United States Merchant Marine Cadet Corps in 1938. Its academy, founded in 1942, became a permanent, government-sponsored school in 1956, and received equal status with the academies of the armed forces. The academy, located on 65 acres along the north shore of Long Island, at Kings Point N.Y., is currently operated by the Maritime Administration of the United States Department of Transportation.

From America's entry into World War II through Operation Desert Shield/Desert Storm, the men and ships of the Merchant Marine have made significant contributions to America's military efforts. However, because the Merchant Marine is a governmental agency and not a uniformed branch of service, members of the Merchant Marine are considered civilians, and as such

Louis George Finch of Lowell, Massachusetts, receives the Merchant Marine Distinguished Service Medal.

have been ineligible for many military awards, decorations and service medals.

To rectify this situation, the Maritime Commission and its successor organizations instituted a system of decorations, service medals, and ribbons to recognize the service and achievements of merchant seamen.

J. Mull

Merchant Marine Distinguished Service Medal

The outbreak of World War II brought the American Merchant Marine into direct combat with German submarine Wolf Packs, surface raiders and the Luftwaffe. As a result of its combat experiences and increased role in supplying the war effort, numerous awards and service ribbons were developed specifically for members of the Merchant Marine.

The Merchant Marine Distinguished Service Medal (MMDSM) was established as the highest award for members of the Merchant Marine by Joint Resolution of Congress on 11 April 1943. During WW II the MMDSM was awarded 145 times, 30 awards were posthumous. The MMDSM is awarded by the U. S. Maritime Administration.

National Archives

Captain G. Sledman presents Commander Peter J. Sigona with the Merchant Marine Distinguished Service Medal.

Merchant Marine Meritorious Service Medal

The Merchant Marine Meritorious Service Medal (MMMSM) was authorized on 29 August 1944, and amended 24 July 1956. The MMMSM was instituted to recognize any member of the Merchant Marine, regardless of grade or rate, who distinguishes himself by outstanding meritorious service or achievement.

To justify this award, the accomplishment or performance of duty must be sufficient to distinguish the individual from those performing similar duties. During WW II the MMMSM was awarded 242 times, 16 of those awards were posthumous.

Subsequent awards of the MMMSM are signified by the addition of a 5/16th inch gold star to both the service and supension ribbons of the medal.

Mariner's Medal

The Merchant Marine played a large role in the convoy operations in the Atlantic during the Second World War. Officers and men of the Merchant Service fought, and in many cases sacrificed their lives, along side their comrades in the armed forces, yet the Purple Heart was not available to these heroes. To solve this dilemma the Mariner's Medal was established by an Act of Congress on 10 May 1943.

Awarded only to members of the Merchant Marine, the Mariner's Medal recognizes seamen who are killed or wounded as a direct result of conflict against an opposing armed force. 6,635 Mariner's Medals were awarded for service in World War II. All further awards of the Mariner's Medal were suspended on 26 March 1954.

Designed by Paul Manship, subsequent awards of the medal are represented by 5/16th inch gold stars affixed to both the suspension ribbon and ribbon bar.

Note that on original Mariner's Medals a small triangle separates "United" and "States." Reproductions have a small dot. Also on originals the designer's initials, "P.M." (Paul Manship), are below the wreath, to either side of the cuff.

Merchant Marine World War II Victory Medal

The Merchant Marine World War II Victory Medal was established on 8 August 1946 and awarded for at least 30 days service on any vessel, flying the U.S. flag, between 7 December 1941 and 3 September 1945.

Merchant Marine Expeditionary Medal

The Merchant Marine Expeditionary Medal (MMEM) was created under the authority of the Merchant Marine Decorations and Medals act of 30 May 1988. The MMEM is intended to recognize participation in military operations as designated by the Maritime Administrator.

The first awards of the Merchant Marine Expeditionary Medal will go to mariners who served aboard US flag vessels operating in support of Operation Desert Shield/ Desert Storm. Service must have been after 2 August 1990 in waters of the Persian Gulf, Red Sea, Gulf of Aden and the portion of the Arabian Sea north of 10 degrees north latitude and west of 68 degrees east longitude. The Department of Transportation's Maritime Administrator is also considering earlier expeditions for qualification.

Gallant Ship Unit Citation Bar - Merchant Marine

The Gallant Ship Unit Citation Plaque and the Gallant Ship Unit Citation Bar were established by Executive Order 9472, 29 August 1944. The original order was amended by Public Law 759 on 24 July 1956.

The Gallant Ship Unit Citation is awarded as a unit citation to a ship which subsequent to 8 September 1938 serves in a gallant manner in marine disasters and other emergencies or in an outstanding manner against enemy attack.

The plaque is a circular copper disk 1/8th inch thick, approximately 18 inches in diameter, showing in relief a merchant ship under full steam below which is spelled out in a design simulating rope, the words "Gallant Ship". This disk is mounted on an oak plaque measuring approximately 24 x 34 inches and 1 inch thick. The citation discribing the action for which the award is made is in bronze, measuring 9 x 18 inches and 1/2 inch thick.

Above: Gallant Ship Award Plaque.
Below: Gallant Ship Unit Citation Bar.

The Gallant Ship Unit Citation Bar is awarded to each member of the ship's crew along with a copy of the citation. A silver Sea Horse device is affixed to the center of the ribbon bar.

As of 1984 there were 40 awards of the Gallant Ship Unit Citation, four of which went to foreign ships.

Merchant Marine Combat Bar

The Merchant Marine Combat Bar was established by Public Law 52 on 10 May 1943. The ribbon is awarded to any person who serves on a vessel in the American Merchant Marine which is attacked or damaged by direct or indirect enemy action. A silver star is attached to the bar to represent each time the recipient was forced to abandon ship. Award of the Merchant Marine Combat Bar was suspended on 26 March 1954.

During World War II there were 114,145 awards of the Merchant Marine Combat Action Bar.

WAR SHIPPING ADMINISTRATION

This is to certify that

Edward Adamson

HAS BEEN AWARDED

The Merchant Marine Combat Bar

confirming active service with THE UNITED STATES MERCHANT MARINE *in a ship which was engaged in direct enemy action*

ADMINISTRATOR

10—35373-1

Merchant Marine Combat Bar wallet card with original 2" ribbon. Card measures 2½ by 3½ inches.

Note:
The Merchant Marine Decorations and Medals Act of 30 May 1988 authorized the creation of medals to correspond to the following Merchant Marine ribbon bars: Defense Bar, Atlantic War Zone Bar, Pacific War Zone Bar, Mediterranean-Middle East War Zone Bar, Korean Service Bar, and Vietnam Service Bar.

Merchant Marine Defense Bar

The Merchant Marine Defense Bar was established by Executive Order 9472 on 29 August 1944. The ribbon is awarded to any member of the Merchant Marine who served at any time during the period 8 September 1939 and 6 December 1941.

There were a total of 17,091 awards of the Merchant Marine Defense Bar for qualifying service. The Merchant Marine Decorations and Medals Act of 30 May 1988 authorized the creation of a medal to correspond to the Defense Bar.

WAR SHIPPING ADMINISTRATION

This is to certify that

Edward Adamson

HAS BEEN AWARDED

The Merchant Marine Defense Bar

indicating active service in THE UNITED STATES MERCHANT MARINE *during the National Emergency—September 8, 1939 to December 7, 1941.*

16—42130-1

ADMINISTRATOR

Atlantic War Zone Bar

Public Law 52 on 10 May 1943 established the Atlantic War Zone Bar for service by any member of the Merchant Marine in the area prescribed as the Atlantic War Zone between 7 December 1941 and 8 November 1946. This Zone included the North and South Atlantic, Gulf of Mexico, Caribbean Sea, Barents Sea, and the Greenland Sea.

A total of 235,298 Atlantic War Zone Bars were issued for qualifying service. The Merchant Marine Decorations and Medals Act of 30 May 1988 authorized the creation of a medal to correspond to the Atlantic War Zone Bar.

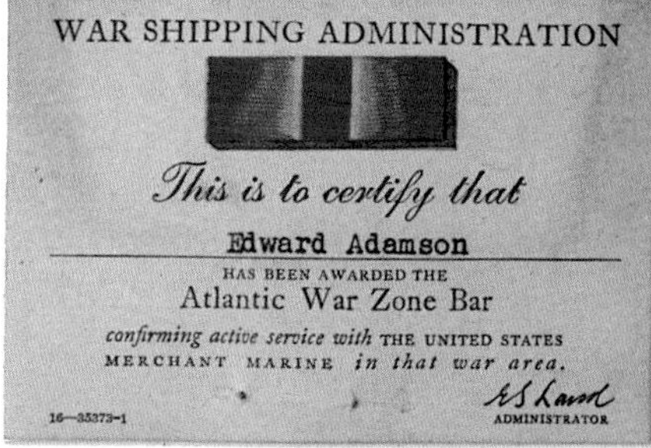

WAR SHIPPING ADMINISTRATION

This is to certify that

Edward Adamson

HAS BEEN AWARDED THE

Atlantic War Zone Bar

confirming active service with THE UNITED STATES MERCHANT MARINE *in that war area.*

16—35373-1

ADMINISTRATOR

Merchant Marine Defense (top) and Atlantic War Zone ribbon (bottom). The ribbon alone is of WWII manufacture. The suspension ribbon with medal is of current manufacture. Note difference in the variegation of the ribbon colors from original WWII to the current.

Mediterranean Middle East War Zone Bar

Established at the same time as the other Merchant Marine war zone bars, the Mediterranean Middle East War Zone Bar was issued for service in the area which included the Mediterranean Sea, the Red Sea, the Arabian Sea, and the Indian Ocean west of 80 degrees east longitude.

A total of 150,184 awards of the Mediterranean Middle East War Zone Bar were made to merchant seamen and officers for qualifying service between 7 December 1941 and 8 November 1945. The Merchant Marine Decorations and Medals Act of 30 May 1988 authorized the creation of a medal to correspond to the Mediterranean Middle East War Zone Bar.

WAR SHIPPING ADMINISTRATION

This is to certify that

Edward Adamson

HAS BEEN AWARDED THE

Mediterranean Middle East War Zone Bar

confirming active service with THE UNITED STATES MERCHANT MARINE *in that war area.*

16—35373-1

ADMINISTRATOR

Pacific War Zone Bar

Establish by Public Law 52 on 10 May 1943, the Pacific War Zone Bar recognized service by any member of the Merchant Marine in the Zone which included the North and South Pacific and the Indian Ocean east of 80 degrees east longitude.

A total of 177,926 officers and enlisted personnel qualified for award of the Pacific War Zone Bar for service between 7 December 1941 and 8 November 1945. The Merchant Marine Decorations and Medals Act of 30 May 1988 authorized the creation of a medal to correspond to the Pacific War Zone Bar.

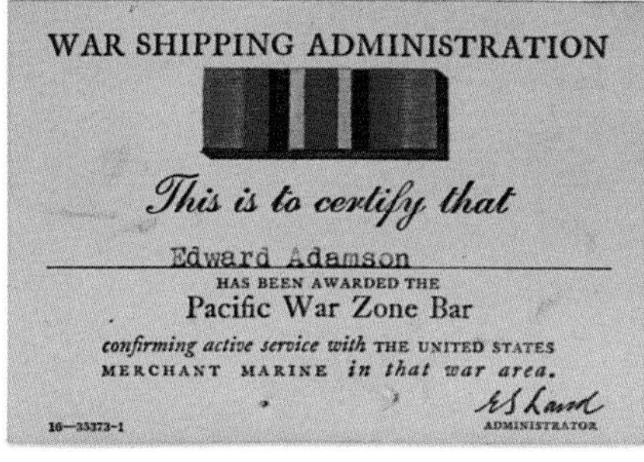

WAR SHIPPING ADMINISTRATION

This is to certify that

Edward Adamson

HAS BEEN AWARDED THE

Pacific War Zone Bar

confirming active service with THE UNITED STATES MERCHANT MARINE *in that war area.*

ADMINISTRATOR

16—35373-1

The Korean Service Bar

Designed to recognize service by officers and crew member of ships of the United States Merchant Marine operating in Korean waters between 30 June 1950 and 30 September 1953. The Korean Service Bar was established by Public Law 759 on 24 July 1956.

The exact number of Korean Service Bars issued is not known. However, over 900 are known to have been awarded. The Merchant Marine Decorations and Medals Act of 30 May 1988 authorized the creation of a medal to correspond to the Korean Service Bar.

The Vietnam Service Bar

Established by Public Law 822 on 8 July 1965, the Vietnam Service Bar is intended to recognize service by officers and crews of United States Merchant Marine vessels which operated in Vietnamese waters between 4 July 1965 and 15 August 1973.

The Merchant Marine Decorations and Medals Act of 30 May 1988 authorized the creation of a medal to correspond to the Vietnam Service Bar.

United States Public Health Service

Many of us who collect American awards and decorations tend to think of the uniformed services in terms of the Army, Navy, Air Force, Marine Corps and Coast Guard. However, there are two more uniformed services; the United States Public Health Service, and the National Oceanic and Atmospheric Administration.

The roots of the U.S. Public Health Service are closely tied to those of the maritime services of the United States. As early as the first session of Congress in 1788 the matter of providing for the care of sick and disabled seamen was of great concern to the government. Ten years later, on 16 July 1798, Congress passed an Act directing the establishment of an organization to provide "temporary relief and maintenance of sick or disabled seamen".

Thus was born the Marine Hospital Fund. Originally, operating funds were provided by dues collected from each sailor and merchant seaman. In the years that followed, the Marine Hospital Fund functioned as a bureau of the Treasury Department, staffed with only one clerk. This staffing shortage, combined with a lack of central direction from the Treasury Department, placed the Marine Hospital Fund at the mercy of the political climate of each port city in which it constructed a hospital. Despite these problems, the development of a centrally administered hospital program would not begin until after the Civil War.

During World War II PHS officers served with both the army and the navy. This PHS officer wears the army uniform and rank with his PHS insignia.

By 1869 complaints about care in the Marine Hospitals were flooding the Treasury Department, as were allegations of graft, corruption and misuse of funds. These complaints prompted Treasury Secretary George Boutwell to commission Dr. W.D. Stewart of his staff, and the Army's expert on hospitals, Dr. John Billings, to travel the country inspecting and reporting on the Marine Hospitals. Based upon their findings, the position of Supervising Surgeon General was established in 1871, and Dr. John Woodworth was appointed to the position.

Dr. Woodworth's service during the Civil War as General Sherman's chief medical officer provided the basis upon which he transformed the Marine Hospital Fund into the Marine Hospital Service. Under his guidance uniforms were designed for the cadre of physicians he had assembled. Additionally, Dr. Woodworth placed the doctors under the central control of the Surgeon General, not the individual Marine Hospitals. These doctors formed the nucleus of what would soon become a competent, mobile, professional, career service medical organization.

Dr. John Hamilton succeeded Dr. Woodworth as Surgeon General of the Marine Hospital Service in 1879. It was Hamilton who convinced President Cleveland of the need to establish a corps of Commissioned Officers within the MHS to provide the long term stability the Service needed. On 4 January 1889 President Grover Cleveland signed into law an Act which established the Commissioned Corps of the Marine Hospital Service.

Throughout the next one hundred years the Marine Hospital Service steadily expanded its professional health care role. By the turn of the century, with programs touching nearly every aspect of American life, a name change seemed inevitable. In 1912 the U.S. Public Health and Marine Hospital Service became the United States Public Health Service (PHS). Positioning itself as a major force in combating disease in America, the PHS undertook a five-fold mission; health care, biomedical research, disease control, health protection, and health education.

As the possibility of American involvement in World War II increased, the programs of the PHS began to emphasize military preparedness. One of the chief problems facing the nation was an acute shortage of nurses. Congress addressed the issue by allocating $65 million for the U.S. Cadet Nurse Corps, which was created by the Nurse Training Act of 1943. Under the direction of Lucile Petry Leone, head of the PHS Division of Nurse Education, the U.S. Cadet Nurse Corps graduated 124,000 nurses from schools throughout the country during the period from 1943 through 1949.

The war years had an enormous impact on the PHS and established the profession of nursing as a strong and permanent part of the PHS. The promotion of Lucile Petry Leone to the rank of Assistant Surgeon General (the equivalent of Rear Admiral) in 1949 made her the first woman in the uniformed services of the United States to achieve flag rank.

As a result of their dedication and professionalism, Public Health Service physicians and scientists have contributed immeasurably to medical victories over polio, venereal disease, tuberculosis, malaria, influenza, and even the bubonic plague. Today the PHS is at the forefront of AIDS research and AIDS education. In addition, officers of the Commissioned Corps have served in every major conflict from World War I through Desert Storm.

The Commissioned Corps of the Public Health Service grew from just 107 Commissioned Officers in 1900 to 6,146 in 1991. Yet, despite its humanitarian and public service mission, the Commissioned Corps suffered serious morale set-backs from 1965 to 1985. First, the uniform, resembling that of the Navy, drew negative attention during the Vietnam War years and gradually its wear all but disappeared. Then, a series of budget cuts slashed the size of the Corps from 7,300 in 1980 to just 5,800 in 1983 and the overall strength of the PHS from 56,000 to 48,000.

With criticism coming from all quarters of government, even from the Health and Human Services itself, and with the future of the Commissioned Corps in jeopardy, Dr. C. Everett Koop, Surgeon General from 1981 to 1989, decided to personnally intervene to insure the future of the Commissioned Corps. In late 1987 Koop set about a major revitalization of the Commissioned Corps.

Assuming formal command authority over the officers in April 1987, Dr. Koop began his revitalization efforts by requiring increased wear of the uniform, invigorating the system of mobility in assignments, and promoting recruitment activities directed at attracting more women and minorities. Dr. Koop also appointed his chief of staff to coordinate PHS activities and programs with the Department of Defense and other federal agencies.

Dr. Koop's efforts to boost the image of the Commissioned Corps were tremendously successful. Today, a revitalized Commissioned Corps of the PHS provides medical care to federal inmates with more than 170 Commissioned Officers on duty in 55 federal prisons. PHS officers also provide medical care to native Americans through the Indian Health Service, and service the medical needs of immigrants in the custody of the Immigration and Naturalization Service.

In addition, PHS officers continue to serve as medical officers in the Coast Guard, a relationship almost as old as the PHS itself. Currently more than 160 PHS officers are on assignment with the Coast Guard, including a senior physician who serves as the Chief Medical Officer of the Coast Guard and who holds the rank of Assistant Surgeon General.

Despite its long history, it was not until 1961 that the Commissioned Corps of the United States Public Health Service undertook to establish an Awards Program to recognize the service and achievements of its Commissioned Officers.

On 8 September 1976 the Assistant Secretary for Health, Theodore Cooper, expanded the Commissioned Officers' Awards Program by authorizing the establishment of medals and ribbons as part of the program. Initially only three medals were established; the Distinguished Service Medal, Meritorious Service Medal, and the Commendation Medal. However, the program has been expanded several times throughout the years and now consists of fifteen individual awards and two unit awards.

U.S. Public Health Service Distinguished Service Medal

The Distinguished Service Medal (DSM) is awarded to any officer of the Public Health Service who has made outstanding contributions to the mission of the PHS. The achievement or service may range from the management of a major health program, to initiative resulting in a major impact on the health of the nation. The DSM may also be awarded for a one-time heroic act resulting in a great saving of life, health, or property.

The planchets of all PHS decorations are identical, only the finishes differ. The obverse of the planchet features the Commissioned Officer's insignia surrounded by the inscription "Public Health Service" in a

Type I reverse.

curved line above, and "United States of America" in a curved line below the insignia. The reverse of early examples of the DSM are inscribed in two curved lines "Department of Health/ Education and Welfare", whereas current issue decorations have a blank reverse. The Distinguished Service Medal planchet is gold finished.

When awarded for a heroic act at the risk of the officer's life, a bronze "V" device is worn centered on both the suspension and service ribbon of the medal.

A gold 5/16th inch star is worn on the suspension and service ribbons of this, and all other PHS decorations, to denote subsequent awards of the same decoration. A silver 5/16th inch star is worn in lieu of five gold stars.

U.S. Public Health Service Meritorious Service Medal

The Meritorious Service Medal (MSM) is presented to PHS officers by the Assistant Secretary for Health for high level achievement. The medal represents meritorious service on the basis of a single particularly important achievement, a career notable for accomplishments in technical or professional fields, or high quality and initiative in leadership.

The levels of performance meriting this award include a highly significant achievement in research, program direction, or program administration; a series of significant contributions; a continuing period of meritorious service; or exhibition of great courage in dangerous work or in an emergency.

When awarded for a heroic act at the risk of the officer's life, a bronze "V" device is worn centered on both the suspension and service ribbon of the Meritorious Service Medal.

The planchet of the PHS MSM is finished in silver. Like the Distinguished Service Medal, the reverse of early issue planchets is engraved "Department of Health/ Education and Welfare" in two curved lines, while current issue medals have blank reverses.

Surgeon General's Medallion

The Surgeon General's Medallion (SGM) is awarded at the sole discretion of the Surgeon General to an officer of any of the uniformed services or a civilian for the highest level of contributions to initiatives of the Office of the Surgeon General.

The SGM consists of a medallion, identical to the Surgeon General's Exemplary Service Medal planchet, suspended from a neck ribbon of the same design as the SGESM suspension ribbon.

The SGM also exists in the form of a table-top medallion, 2 1/2 inches in diameter. The obverse of the medallion is identical to that of the planchet of the Surgeon General's Exemplary Service Medal. However, the reverse is blank. It is believed that this table-top medallion is intended for civilian recipients of the SGM.

SGM table-top medallion, obverse.

Obverse.

Reverse.

Surgeon General's Exemplary Service Medal

This award, established by Dr. C. Everett Koop, who served as Surgeon General of the U.S. Public Health Service from 1981 to 1989, is awarded solely at the discretion of the Surgeon General.

The Surgeon General's Exemplary Service Medal (SGESM) is intended to recognize officers who have demonstrated exemplary service or who have performed a single accomplishment which has had a major impact on the mission of the PHS. The SGESM can also be awarded to officers of other uniformed services or civilians for exemplary contributions to the Office of the Surgeon General.

The obverse of the planchet features a Commissioned Officer and a PHS Nurse at the bedside of a patient. Behind them is a scene which recalls the maritime heritage of the PHS; to the right is a lighthouse with its light shining on a sailing ship which appears on the left of the scene. The reverse of the SGESM is identical to the obverse of the PHS service medals and features the PHS seal surrounded by the inscription "U.S. Public Health Service".

U.S. Public Health Service Outstanding Service Medal

The Outstanding Service Medal (OSM) is awarded to officers who have demonstrated continuous outstanding leadership in carrying out the mission of the PHS, or who have performed a single accomplishment which has had a major impact on the health of the nation. The OSM is also awarded for acts of heroism resulting in the preservation of health or property.

When awarded for a heroic act at the risk of the officer's life, a bronze "V" device is worn centered on both the suspension and service ribbon of the Outstanding Service Medal.

The planchet of the OSM is finished in rhodium. No examples of the OSM have been encountered with engraved reverses similar to those found on the DSM and MSM.

U.S. Public Health Service Commendation Medal

The Commendation Medal is awarded to any officer who has exhibited a level of proficiency and dedication distinctly greater than that normally expected and which clearly sets the officer apart from his or her peers.

The Commendation Medal is designed to recognize sustained high quality work in scientific, administrative, or other professional fields; the application of a unique skill or creative imagination to the approach or solution to problems; or noteworthy technical and professional contributions that are significant but in a limited area.

Type I reverse.

The Commendation Medal is not authorized to recognize acts of bravery or heroism. The planchet of the Commendation medal is bronze. Early examples of the Commendation Medal feature engraved reverses identical to the DSM and MSM.

U.S. Public Health Service Achievement Medal

The Achievement Medal is presented to an officer in the grade of Lieutenant Commander (04) or below in recognition of significant contributions toward the attainment of program directives; sustained above-average performance of duty; and superior performance of duty over a relatively short period of time, such as a short tour of duty of 120 days or less.

The Achievement Medal is not awarded for acts of heroism. The planchet has a copper-bronze finish. Like the OSM, the Achievement Medal is only encountered with a blank reverse.

U.S Public Health Service Citation

The PHS Citation is a ribbon bar which is awarded to recognize noteworthy performance of duty which does not warrant an award of the Achievement Medal but nevertheless is of a commendable nature. A handsome oak and brass plaque as well as a certificate accompany award of the PHS Citation ribbon.

U.S. Public Health Service Outstanding Unit Citation

The Outstanding Unit Citation (OUC) is presented to Commissioned Officers in a PHS unit when that unit has exhibited superior service toward achieving the goals and objectives of the PHS. The award requires the performance of exceptional service of national or international significance. The period recognized must be marked by a definite beginning and ending date and will normally be of short duration.

A bronze 3/16th inch star is worn on all Public Health Service unit awards to denote subsequent awards of the same ribbon. A silver 3/16th inch star is worn in lieu of five bronze stars.

U.S. Public Health Unit Commendation

The Unit Commendation is made under the same circumstances as the Outstanding Unit Citation, but for a lesser level of performance. However, while the level of performance is less than that required for award of the OUC, it must nevertheless be well above that normally expected of similar units.

U.S. Public Health Service National Emergency Preparedness Award

In keeping with its increasing role of assisting with the medical relief efforts associated with natural disasters and other public emergencies, the PHS instituted the National Emergency Preparedness Award (NEPA) in 1988.

This medal was developed for award to officers of the Commissioned Corp who actively participate in emergency relief efforts of the Public Health Service. To qualify for award of the NEPA an officer must serve a minimum of four continuous years in an emergency preparedness activity of the PHS or other Federal Agencies or Departments.

Approved units for the NEPA include:

1. National Disaster Medical System (NDMS): Rockville Clearing and Staging Unit.
2. National Disaster Medical System (NDMS): Bethesda Clearing and Staging Unit.
3. Office of Foreign Disaster Assistance.

The obverse of the planchet on the NEPA medal features the PHS seal encircled by six lightening bolts pointing in a counter-clockwise direction. The reverse of the planchet features two entwined branches, each with five leaves; and the words "National Emergency/Preparedness/Award" in modified block letters.

U.S. Public Health Service Foreign Duty Award

When initially created, the Foreign Duty Award (FDA) was simply a ribbon with no accompanying medal. After more than a decade of use, a review of the Commissioned Officer's Award Program recommended that this and the other existing PHS service awards be "upgraded" by the addition of a corresponding medal. This recommendation was approved in 1988, however, these PHS service awards are still presented only as ribbons and the recipient must purchase the full size and miniature medals if they desire them.

The Foreign Duty Award is presented to any officer who has served at least 30 consecutive or 90 nonconsecutive days in a post outside the United States. As defined in Title 42 of the U.S. Code 201, the term "state" includes the 50 states, Washington D.C. , Puerto Rico, the Northern Mariana Islands, the Virgin Islands, American Samoa, and all other areas formerly encompassed in the Trust Territories of the Pacific Islands.

The obverse of the planchet on all PHS service awards depicts the Public Health Service seal. The reverse of each award is inscribed with the name of the award, in large block letters, on three lines; in this case FOREIGN/SERVICE/AWARD.

U.S. Public Health Service Hazardous Duty Award

Originally The Hazardous Duty Service Award (HDA) was known as the Hazardous Duty Service Award Ribbon. However, a corresponding medal was authorized in the late 1980's.

The Hazardous Duty Service Award is authorized for any officer who has served a minimum of 180 days in a position which required frequent risk to his or her safety. The appropriateness of the medal for specific assignments is determined by the Public Health Service and generally includes service which requires frequent flights on unscheduled airlines to remote areas, working with dangerous substances, or assignment to hostile areas. Assignments where the professional knowledge of the officer should significantly reduce or eliminate the risk do not qualify an officer for this award.

Specific assignments that are eligible for the HDA include:

1. Frequent unscheduled aircraft flights in Alaska. To qualify under this assignment an officer must complete 18 round trips, or flights to 36 duty destinations, using charter service flights within a 12-month period.

2. Assignment for a minimum of 180 days to a billet requiring contact with inmates in any Bureau of Prisons Federal Corrections Facility.
3. Assignment for a minimum of 180 days to a billet requiring contact with patients in the Forensic Hospital portion of St. Elizabeths.
4. Assignment for a minimum of 180 days to a billet requiring direct contact with detained aliens in an Immigration and Naturalization Service facility or aircraft.
5. Completion of 20Q exposure hours while conducting mine site surveys within a 6-month period.

The reverse of the HDA is engraved; HAZARDOUS/DUTY/AWARD.

U.S. Public Health Service Isolated Hardship Award

Initially introduced as the Isolated Hardship Service Ribbon, this award is presented to any officer who has served a minimum of 180 consecutive days in any of the 91 areas designated by the Public Health Service as being isolated, remote, or a hardship duty assignment. Officers in the ready reserve are eligible for the Isolated Hardship Award if they serve an aggregate of 180 days within a 3-year period.

A bronze 3/16th inch star is worn on both the suspension and service ribbons of this, and all other PHS service medals, to denote subsequent awards of the same medal. A silver 3/16th inch star is worn in lieu of five bronze stars.

The reverse of the Isolated Hardship Award is engraved; ISOLATED/HARDSHIP/AWARD.

U.S. Public Health Service Special Assignment Award

The Special Assignment Award (SAA) is presented to any officer who has been detailed a minimum of 30 days to a special program initiatives of other Federal or State agencies or to other organizations as specified by the Assistant Secretary of Health.

The reverse of the SAA is engraved; SPECIAL/ASSIGNMENT/AWARD.

U.S. Public Health Service Smallpox Eradication Campaign Ribbon

Unlike the other Service Awards, the Small Pox Eradication Campaign Ribbon (SPEC) exists only in the form of a ribbon.

The SPEC ribbon is presented to any officer who served a minimum of 90 days cumulative service, between 1 January 1966 and 26 October 1977, in the Centers for Disease Control's Bureau of Smallpox Eradication or Smallpox Labratory, in the World Health Organization's Smallpox Eradication Program, or in a temporary duty assignment in a smallpox effort abroad.

Between 1962 and 1977 more than 300 PHS personnel from the Centers for Disease Control actively took part in the World Health Organization's efforts which resulted in the worldwide eradication of smallpox.

The ribbon of the SPEC Ribbon was unavailable for photographing at the time of publication; it consists of verticle stripes: 1/16" maroon, 5/32" white, 3/32" navy blue, 3/32" maroon, 3/32" navy blue, 5/32" white, 1/16" maroon, 5/32" white, 3/32" navy blue, 3/32" maroon, 3/32" navy blue, 5/32" white, and 1/16" maroon.

Regular Corps Ribbon

The Regular Corps Ribbon is worn by all officers of the USPHS Commissioned Corps who hold a Regular Corps commission.

Like the other services, a PHS officer may hold either a regular commission or a reserve commission, and may serve on active duty with either type of commission. In addition to the two types of commissions, the PHS has four categories of officer service; active duty, active reserve, inactive reserve, and retired.

Of those four catagories only those officers with Regular Corps commissions, about 40% of the active force and 15% of the total force, are eligible for the Regular Corps Ribbon.

Officers selected for assimilation into the Regular Corps must meet strict service and educational requirements, which include a minimum of four years continuous PHS service in their current tour of duty and a supervisory recommendation.

National Oceanic and Atmospheric Administration

The National Oceanic and Atmospheric Association (NOAA) is perhaps the least known of all the uniformed services of the United States. Most collectors tend to think of the uniformed services only in terms of the Army, Navy, Marine Corps, Air Force, and Coast Guard. However, the uniformed services also include the Public Health Service, Merchant Marine and NOAA. NOAA's current uniform and rank structure are patterned after the Navy, although the NOAA Corps is composed only of commissioned Officers.

The National Oceanic and Atmospheric Administration was formed on 3 October 1970 by Reorganization Plan No. 4 of 1970. However, the roots of NOAA date back to February 1807, when Congress authorized a survey of the coast of the United States. At President Jefferson's suggestion a bureau of Coast Survey was established under the Treasury Department. In March of 1871 an Act of Congress enlarged the work of the bureau to include earth measurements, or geodetic surveying.

The name of the bureau was changed in June of 1878 to Coast and Geodetic Survey to reflect its increased mission. The Coast and Geodetic Survey was transferred to the Department of Commerce and Labor in 1903 and in 1913 to the Department of Commerce.

Today NOAA remains under the Department of Commerce. During time of war, personnel in the C & GS were transferred to control of either the Army or Navy. During World War I, 109 G & GS officers served in the Army and 131 served in the Navy.

Throughout the years the mission of the C & GS continued to expand; adding seismology, aeronautical charting, and measuring the earth's magnetic field. Today the primary mission of NOAA is to explore, map, and chart the ocean and its living resources and to mange, use, and conserve those resources; to describe, monitor and predict conditions in the atmosphere, ocean and space environment; to issue warnings against impending destructive natural events; to assess the impact of inadvertent environmental changes; and to manage and disseminate environmental information.

To accomplish its mission, NOAA is organized into five Line Organizations; the National Ocean Service (the original Coast and Geodetic Survey); National Weather Service; National Marine Fisheries Service; National Environmental Satellite, Data, and Information Service; and Office of Oceanic and Atmospheric Research. To provide leadership and professionalism, the NOAA Corps provides a nucleus of officer-scientists for all major NOAA organizations.

Despite its long history, and close association with the military services, the Coast and Geodetic Survey did not institute any awards or decorations to recognize the service or achievements of its personnel until 1945. The awards that were created in that year by Executive Order 9590, resemble those of the Merchant Marine in both scope and name. Although some Coast and Geodetic Survey awards were titled "Medal," due to budget restrictions no pendant designs were initially approved to accompany the ribbons. It was not until 1988, following the adoption of the Merchant Marine Decoration and Medals Act, and the subsequent approval of medal designs to accompany the Merchant Marine War Zone Bars, that NOAA revived the original C & GS awards. The medal designs were quickly approved and became available for survivors who were eligible for the World War II Coast and Geodetic Survey awards.

After its creation NOAA also began to develop a system of medals and ribbons to recognize the achievements and service of its officers. Today NOAA's pyramid of honor consists of four medals, one achievement ribbon, one unit citation, four service ribbons, and two marksmanship ribbons.

NOAA Administrator's Award Medal

The NOAA Administrator's Award Medal was established on 1 October 1985 for award to any employee of NOAA. However, only members of the NOAA commissioned Corps receive the medal and ribbon bar. The Administrator's Award Medal is intended to recognize exceptional achievement, service, leadership, or professional achievement. The medal may also be awarded for heroic acts or service which reflect the preservation of life or property.

To merit award of the NOAA Administrator's Award Medal the service or achievement must be significantly superior to that usually expected of an individual commensurate with his or her grade. The achievement should also constitute a significant contribution to the government, the Department of Commerce, NOAA or the NOAA Corps.

NOAA Corps Commendation Medal

The NOAA Corps Commendation Medal was established on 1 October 1985 to recognize meritorious or outstanding service, achievement or leadership which does not warrant award of the NOAA Administrator's Award Medal. Any member of the NOAA Commissioned Corps, or a member of another uniformed service who is detailed, assigned or attached to NOAA is eligible for award of the NOAA Corps Commendation Medal.

To merit this award, the service or achievement must be accomplished in an exemplary manner above that normally expected and must be sufficient to distinguish the individual from his or her peers. The NOAA Corps Commendation Medal may also be given for heroic acts which reflect the preservation of life or property, for professional achievement that merits special recognition, or for sustained leadership which reflects creditably on the efforts of the individual towards accomplishment of the unit mission.

NOAA Special Achievement Award

The NOAA Special Achievement Award was established on 1 October 1985 to recognize meritorious or superior service, achievement or leadership which does not warrant award of the NOAA Corps Commendation Medal.

Any employee of NOAA, or a member of another uniformed service who is detailed, assigned or attached to NOAA is eligible for award of the NOAA Special Achievement Award. Only members of the NOAA Commissioned Corp or members of other uniformed services are awarded the medal and ribbon bar, however the honor is the same.

To merit this award, the service or achievement must be accomplished in a superior manner and must be sufficient to set the individual apart from his or her peers. The NOAA Special Achievement Award may also be awarded for professional achievement that merits special recognition, or for sustained leadership which reflect creditably on the efforts of the individual towards accomplishment of the unit mission.

NOAA Corps Director's Ribbon

The NOAA Corps Director's Ribbon was established on 1 October 1985 for award to any member of the NOAA Commissioned Corps, or a member of another uniformed service who is detailed, assigned or attached to NOAA, in recognition of noteworthy accomplishments in the performance of duty. Such accomplishments must be unusual or substantial yet less than that required for the NOAA Special Achievement Award.

Qualifying accomplishments could include special acts or service which contribute to the attainment of program objectives, or sustained superior performance of duty. In either case the act or service must be substantially above what is or was expected as the ordinary, routine or customary for personnel of similar grade and experience.

NOAA Unit Citation Ribbon

The NOAA Unit Citation Ribbon is awarded to any employee of NOAA or to a member of another uniformed service who is detailed, assigned or attached to a NOAA unit during a time period for which that unit is recognized by award of the NOAA Unit Citation Ribbon. While all NOAA employees assigned to a unit which is recognized are awarded this honor, only NOAA Officers and members of other uniformed services so recognized are authorized to wear the ribbon.

To merit this award, the unit recognized must have provided exceptional service of national or international significance. The period recognized will usually be short and marked by a definite beginning and ending date.

NOAA ACO Awards Medal

The NOAA Association of Commissioned Officers Awards Medal is presented to those NOAA Commissioned Corps personnel selected by the ACO to receive recognition in three areas; Junior Officer of the Year (Lieutenant Commander or below), Scientific Achievement, and Engineering Achievement.

Recipients for ACO awards are selected by a board composed of selected ACO members. When awarded for Scientific Achievement, the NOAA ACO Awards Medal is worn with a "Silver S" on the service and suspension ribbons. When awarded for Engineering Achievement the medal is worn with a "Silver E." Both the "Silver S" and the "Silver E" are block letters with serifs at the end of their members, identical to those worn on the Navy and Coast Guard marksmanship ribbons.

NOAA Corps Atlantic Service Ribbon

The NOAA Corps Atlantic Service Ribbon was established on 1 June 1986 for award to members of the NOAA Commissioned Officer Corps, or members of another uniformed service who are detailed, assigned or attached to NOAA who meet certain eligibility requirements.

Eligibility was made retroactive to 1 January 1946, and includes any qualifying officer who completes a sea duty assignment of at least 180 consecutive days aboard a NOAA vessel operating in the waters of the Atlantic Ocean, Gulf of Mexico, Great Lakes or adjacent waters. Minimum time requirement may be waived by the Director of the NOAA Corps.

Personnel who qualify for subsequent awards of the NOAA Corps Atlantic Service Ribbon are authorized one 3/16th inch bronze star for each subsequent qualification. A 3/16th inch silver star is worn in lieu of five bronze stars.

NOAA Corps Pacific Service Ribbon

The NOAA Corps Pacific Service Ribbon was established on 1 June 1986 for award to members of the NOAA Commissioned Officer Corps, or members of another uniformed service who are detailed, assigned or attached to NOAA who meet certain eligibility requirements.

Eligibility was made retroactive to 1 January 1946, and includes any qualifying officer who completes a sea duty assignment of at least 180 consecutive days aboard a NOAA vessel operating in the waters of the Pacific Ocean, Indian Ocean, Bering Sea, or adjacent waters. The minimum time requirement may be waived by the Director of the NOAA Corps.

Personnel who qualify for subsequent awards of the NOAA Corps Pacific Service Ribbon are authorized one 3/16th inch bronze star for each subsequent qualification. A 3/16th inch silver star is worn in lieu of five bronze stars.

NOAA Corps Mobile Duty Service Ribbon

The NOAA Corps Mobile Duty Service Ribbon was established on 1 June 1986 for award to members of the NOAA Commissioned Officer Corps, or members of another uniformed service who are detailed, assigned or attached to NOAA who meet certain eligibility requirements.

Eligibility was made retroactive to 1 January 1946, and includes any qualifying officer who completes a mobile duty assignment of at least 180 consecutive days in the United States, its possessions or territories. The minimum time requirement may be waived by the Director of the NOAA Corps.

Personnel who qualify for subsequent awards of the NOAA Corps Mobile Duty Service Ribbon are authorized one 3/16th inch bronze star for each subsequent qualification. A 3/16th inch silver star is worn in lieu of five bronze stars.

NOAA Corps International Service Ribbon

The NOAA Corps International Service Ribbon was established on 1 June 1986 for award to members of the NOAA Commissioned Officer Corps, or members of another uniformed service who are detailed, assigned or attached to NOAA who meet certain eligibility requirements.

Eligibility was made retroactive to 1 January 1946, and includes any qualifying officer who completes a duty assignment of at least 21 consecutive days aboard a United States vessel operating in foreign or international waters, with at least one foreign port call, and participating in a foreign or international project as part of the deployment. The minimum time requirement may be waived by the Director of the NOAA Corps.

Personnel who qualify for subsequent awards of the NOAA Corps International Service Ribbon are authorized one 3/16th inch bronze star for each subsequent qualification. A 3/16th inch silver star is worn in lieu of five bronze stars.

NOAA Corps Rifle Ribbon

The Director of the NOAA Commissioned Corps established the NOAA Corps Rifle Ribbon on 17 April 1990 for award to any member of the NOAA Commissioned Corps who successfully completes training as specified in OMO Instruction 8370 or any other service-approved qualification course.

No device is authorized for wear on the NOAA Corps Rifle Ribbon to denote a specific level of qualification. Rather the ribbon is intended to denote qualification only.

NOAA Corps Pistol Ribbon

The Director of the NOAA Commissioned Corps established the NOAA Corps Pistol Ribbon on 17 April 1990 for award to any member of the NOAA Commissioned Corps who successfully completes training as specified in OMO Instruction 8370 or any other service-approved qualification course.

No device is authorized for wear on the NOAA Corps Pistol Ribbon to denote a specific level of qualification. Rather the ribbon is intended to denote qualification only.

C & GS Distinguished Service Medal

The Coast and Geodetic Survey Distinguished Service Medal was authorized 31 July 1945 by Executive Order 9590. The award existed in ribbon form only until amended by NOAA Corps Bulletin 880401 which authorized and approved a medal for all recipients of the Distinguished Service Ribbon.

The Distinguished Service Medal was authorized for issue to Commissioned Officers, Ship's Officers and Crew Members of the Coast and Geodetic Survey (C & GS) for distinguished service or extraordinary achievement which had a significant impact on the mission of the C & GS. The period of eligibility extended from 8 September 1939 to 28 April 1952.

When worn with other military decorations by C & GS Commissioned Officers, the C & GS Distinguished Service medal takes precedence immediately following the Distinguished Service Medal of any branch of the Armed Forces.

As NOAA's predecessor, the Coast and Geodetic Survey had been authorized a limited series of awards under Executive Order 9590, dated 31 July 1945. The six awards authorized by this executive order were initially in ribbon form only. The Executive Order did authorize the Secretary of Commerce "to provide and issue an appropriate 'medal,' with suitable appurtenances, to the recipient of any ribbon at such time as he may determine, and when necessary funds are available therefore." Despite this authorization, it was not until the passage of the Merchant Marine Decorations and Medals Act in 1988 that medal designs were approved and made available to qualified veterans.

C & GS Meritorious Service Medal

The Coast and Geodetic Survey Meritorious Service Medal was authorized 31 July 1945 by Executive Order 9590. The award existed in ribbon form only until amended by NOAA Corps Bulletin 880401 which authorized and approved a medal for all recipients of the Meritorious Service Ribbon.

The Meritorious Service Medal was authorized for issue to Commissioned Officers, Ship's Officers and Crew Members of the Coast and Geodetic Survey (C & GS) for highly significant achievement or meritorious service which had a major impact on the mission of the Coast and Geodetic Survey. The period of eligibility extended from 8 September 1938 to 28 April 1952.

When worn with other military decorations by C & GS Commissioned Officers, the C & GS Meritorious Service medal takes precedence immediately before the Legion of Merit.

C & GS Good Conduct Medal

The Coast and Geodetic Survey Good Conduct Medal was authorized 31 July 1945 by Executive Order 9590. The Award existed in ribbon form only until amended by NOAA Corps Bulletin 880401 which authorized and approved a medal for all recipients of the Good Conduct Ribbon.

The Good Conduct Medal was authorized for issue to Commissioned Officers, Ship's Officers and Crew Members of the Coast and Geodetic Survey (C & GS) for service between 8 September 1939 and 28 April 1952.

C & GS Defense Service Medal

Following the end of World War I, the Commissioned Officers of the Coast and Geodetic Survey returned to the control of the Department of Commerce. With the United States' declaration of war against the Axis Powers in December 1941, a Joint Resolution of the Secretaries of War, Navy and Commerce on 20 January 1942 again placed the Commissioned Officers of the Coast and Geodetic Survey under the operational control of the Army and Navy for the duration of hostilities.

To recognize the service of C & GS Commissioned Officers during the time of limited national emergency, the Coast and Geodetic Survey Defense Service Medal was authorized 31 July 1945 by Executive Order 9590. The award existed in ribbon form only until amended by NOAA Corps Bulletin 880401 which authorized and approved a medal for all recipients of the Defense Service Ribbon.

The Defense Service Medal was authorized for issue to Commissioned Officers, Ship's Officers and Crew Members of the Coast and Geodetic Survey (C & GS) for service during the period from 8 August 1939 to 6 December 1941.

C & GS Atlantic War Zone Medal

The Coast and Geodetic Survey Atlantic War Zone Medal was authorized 31 July 1945 by Executive Order 9590. The award existed in ribbon form only until amended by NOAA Corps Bulletin 880401 which authorized and approved a medal for all recipients of the Atlantic War Zone Ribbon.

The Atlantic War Zone Medal was authorized for issue to Commissioned Officers, Ship's Officers and Crew Members of the Coast and Geodetic Survey (C & GS) for service in the Atlantic War Zone during the period from 7 December 1941 to 8 November 1945.

C & GS Pacific War Zone Medal

The Coast and Geodetic Survey Pacific War Zone Medal was authorized 31 July 1945 by Executive Order 9590. The award existed in ribbon form only until amended by NOAA Corps Bulletin 880401 which authorized and approved a medal for all recipients of the Pacific War Zone Ribbon.

The Pacific War Zone Medal was authorized for issue to Commissioned Officers, Ship's Officers and Crew Members of the Coast and Geodetic Survey (C & GS) for service in the Pacific War Zone during the period from 7 December 1941 to 8 November 1945.

THE NATIONAL AERONAUTICS AND SPACE ADMINISTRATION

Awards to

Alan B. Shepard, Jr.

the

NASA

DISTINGUISHED SERVICE MEDAL

For Outstanding Contributions to Space Technology

His flight as the first United States astronaut was an outstanding contribution to the advancement of human knowledge of space technology and a demonstration of man's capabilities in suborbital space flight.

Signed and sealed at Washington, D.C.
this fifth day of May
Nineteen Hundred and Sixty One

James E. Webb
ADMINISTRATOR, NASA

Hugh L. Dryden
DEPUTY ADMINISTRATOR, NASA

National Aeronautics and Space Administration

America's dedication to aeronautics and flight research began in 1915 with the creation of the National Advisory Committee for Aeronautics (NACA). The NACA was created by a rider to the Naval Appropriations Act of 1915, with a budget of $5,000. In the four decades following the inception of the NACA, advancements in aeronautics, rocketry, and other scientific fields lead to the proliferation of societies, panels, and committees dedicated to aeronautics and space research.

On 18 January 1958 the NACA recommended to President Eisenhower that a national space program be implemented through the cooperation of the DoD, NACA, National Academy of Science, National Science Foundation, universities, research institutions, and industrial companies.

The President quickly recognized the pitfalls of a decentralized national space program, and on 6 February 1958 he recommended a different approach to Congress. The President's proposal called for the establishment of a National Aeronautics and Space Administration (NASA) into which the NACA and several other research societies would be absorbed. The Bureau of the Budget approved the creation of NASA and on 29 July 1958, President Eisenhower signed the National Aeronautics and Space Act which formally created the agency.

It took less than 90 days for NASA to be organized and prepared to discharge its duties, and on 1 October 1958 NASA officially took its place as the country's sole agency for civilian space research and development. The primary mission of NASA remains to conduct and coordinate United States nonmilitary research into the problems associated with flight, both within and beyond the earth's atmosphere. Currently NASA employs more than 15,000 personnel; mostly scientists, engineers, and technicians.

Until Congress passed the Government Employee Incentive Award Act in 1954, employees of the National Advisory Committee for Aeronautics did not have any unique awards to recognize their service or achievements. The sole sources of recognition for members of the NACA were military awards or awards from private foundations and organizations.

The board of directors for the NACA was quick to recognize the value of instituting their own system of awards. On 30 November 1954, the NACA established two honors awards, a Distinguished Service Medal and an Exceptional Service Medal. When NASA officially replaced the NACA it inherited these two awards and there was little or no break in the honor awards program.

The final award presentation of the NACA and the first honor award presentation of NASA, both Distinguished Service Medals, were less than one year apart. The NACA presentation was during the Committee's final meeting on 21 August 1958, to its first employee and Executive Secretary, John F. Victory. The NASA presentation to John B. Crowley Jr., a national leader in aeronautical science and NASA's first Director of Aeronautical and Space Research, occurred on 30 June 1959 on the occasion of his retirement.NASA initially instituted only three awards; the Distinguished Service Medal (DSM), the Outstanding Service Medal (OSM), and the Exceptional Service Medal (ESM). Both the DSM and the OSM were similar in design and intent to the original two awards of the NACA. However, by mid 1961, with only three DSM awards and two OSM awards, and with only a draft proposal for criteria for the ESM in existance, NASA decided to redesign and expand its honor award system.

In July of 1961 the NASA Incentive Awards Board, under pressure from the Commission of Fine Arts to redesign the DSM and OSM, enlisted the services of the United States Army Institute of Herladry to assist in developing a series of awards. The results of this collaboration produced four initial awards: a redesigned Distinguished Service Medal and three new awards of equal rank to replace the Exceptional Service Medal. The new medals were the Outstanding Leadership Medal, Exceptional Scientific Achievement Medal, and the Exceptional Bravery Medal. The Outstanding Service Medal was discontinued. Over the years NASA has continued to expanded its awards program. Currently the honor awards program includes 11 individual medals which reflect NASA's unique, and often dangerous mission.

Unlike the military services, which have a decentralized awards system, the NASA awards system is administered by a central Incentives Award Board (IAB) which is chaired by the Associate Deputy Administrator. Once each year the IAB calls for nominations from each installation, reviews the nominations, and either approves or disapproves the award nomination. Currently each installation is limited to a maximum of 25 nominations. In addition to its system for approving and awarding medals, the pyramid of honor for the NASA awards also reflects the unique nature of NASA and its mission. Unlike the various branches of the Armed Forces, most NASA awards are considered to be of equal precedence. The order of precedence for NASA awards is as follows:

1. Congressional Space Medal of Honor
2. Distinguished Service Medal
   Distinguished Public Service Medal
3. Outstanding Service Medal (obsolete)
4. Outstanding Leadership Medal
   Exceptional Scientific Achievement Medal
   Exceptional Engineering Achievement Medal
   Exceptional Bravery Medal
   Exceptional Service Medal
   Public Service Medal
   Exceptional Achievement Medal
   Space Flight Medal
   Equal Employment Opportunity Medal

Congressional Space Medal of Honor

The Congressional Space Medal of Honor is not part of NASA's pyramid of honor. However, it represents the highest award an astronaut may receive. Authorized by Public Law 91-76 on 29 September 1969, the Congressional Space Medal of Honor is awarded in the name of the President of the United States to any astronaut who distinguishes himself or herself by exceptionally meritorious service and contributions to the welfare of the United States and of mankind.

To date only eight astronauts have received this prestigious award. The first six were presented by President Jimmy Carter on 1 October 1979 to Neil Armstrong, Frank Borman, Charles Conrad Jr., John Glenn, Alan Shepard Jr., and Virgil "Guss" Grissom (posthumous). The seventh award was presented by President Ronald Regan to John Young in April 1981. The eighth award was presented by President Bush to Lt. Gen. Thomas P. Stafford on November 4, 1992.

The original government contract called for twelve medals to be produced by the Medallic Art company of New York at a cost of ten thousand dollars. The diamond in the center of the Congressional Space Medal of Honor is the only gemstone set in an American decoration or medal.

President Reagan poses with Atronauts John Young, Robert Crippen, and NASA Administrator Dr. Alan Lovelace following an awards ceremony. Young wears the Congressional Space Medal of Honor with neck ribbon which is proper. The breast ribbon shown at right was changed to the neck ribbon prior to the date of the first awards.

NASA Distinguished Service Medal

The Distinguished Service Medal (DSM) was one of two awards inherited by NASA when it absorbed the NACA, and is the highest honor that NASA confers. The DSM is intended for award to any individual serving in any capacity with the National Aeronautics and Space Administration, or any other Federal agency, who distinguishes him or herself by service, ability, or courage, and has personally made a significant contribution to the NASA mission or the interests of the United States.

The Distinguished Service Medal exists in two types. The first design, a gold circular planchet bearing the NASA seal, was awarded from 1959 to 1961. This first design is obsolete and has been superseded by the current design. Only three individuals received the first style NASA DSM, they were; J.W. Crowley, Alan B. Sheppard Jr., and Virgil I. "Guss" Grissom.

NASA has been very conservative in awarding the DSM. Between 1958 and 1989 only 364 Distinguished Service Medals were awarded.

Below: The first seven Mercury astronauts at Patrick Air Force Base, Florida, March 1961. Left to right: M. Scott Carpenter, L. Gordon Cooper, Jr., John H. Glenn, Jr., Virgil I. Grissom, Walter M. Schirra, Jr., Alan B. Shepard, Jr., and Donald K. Slayton.

Original design.

J. Mull

Current design.

NASA Photo

NASA Distinguished Public Service Medal

The NASA Distinguished Public Service Medal (DPSM) was authorized in 1963 and first awarded in 1966. The DPSM is awarded to individuals whose contributions measurably improved, expedited, or clarified administrative procedures, scientific progress, work methods, manufacturing techniques, personnel procedures, public information services and other efforts relating to the accomplishment of the missions of NASA.

The DPSM is specifically designed to parallel the DSM and recognizes the contributions of citizens of the United States who are not employed by the National Aeronautics and Space Administration or other Federal Government agencies.

NASA has been very conservative in awarding the DPSM. As of December 1988, only 140 Distinguished Public Service Medals had been awarded.

NASA Outstanding Service Medal

The Outstanding Service Medal (OSM) was established in 1959 for award to any individual serving in any capacity with the National Aeronautics and Space Administration who distinguishes him or herself by service, ability, or courage and who has made a significant contribution to the NASA mission or the interests of the United States. The OSM was identical in design to the first style DSM, however, the planchet was in silver rather than gold. In many respects, the NASA OSM was similiar in design and intent to the NACA ESM. NASA intended the newly titled Outstanding Service Medal to recognize service or achievement which, although significant, was of a lesser degree than that which would warrant award of the Distinguished Service Medal.

Bowing to pressure from the Commission of Fine Arts, which had formally objected to the design of both the Distinguished Service Medal and the Outstanding Service Medal, the OSM was discontinued under a revised awards system introduced by NASA in September 1961. The only recipients of the OSM were Dr. Edward R. Sharp and Dr. H.J.E. Reid.

McDowell

NASA Exceptional Service Medal

The NASA Exceptional Service Medal (ESM) was originally inherited from the NACA along with the DSM. Originally the ESM was authorized by NACA FPM Supplement, 1 May 1957 for significant scientific achievement, significant leadership in aeronautical science, significant contribution to public administration, and unusual courage or competence in an emergency.

NASA never decided on a final design for its version of the ESM before it decided to mothball the award. In 1961, amid pressure from the Commission for Fine Arts to develop awards which more suitably represented the achievements for which they were awarded, the NASA Incentive Awards Board decided to replace the ESM with three new awards; the Outstanding Leadership Medal, Exceptional Scientific Achievement Medal, and the Exceptional Bravery Medal.

After a three year absence, NASA reinstituted the ESM in 1964. Under the most recent guidelines, the ESM is intended for award to any individual serving in any capacity with the National Aeronautics and Space Administration who distinguishes him or herself by significant achievement or service characterized by unusual initiative or creative ability that clearly demonstrates substantial improvement in engineering, aeronautics, space flight or space related endeavors which contribute to the programs of NASA.

No awards of the NASA ESM occurred before it was discontinued in 1961. Between its reinstatement in 1964, and 1989, NASA awarded 3,181 Exceptional Service Medals.

NASA Outstanding Leadership Medal

The NASA Outstanding Leadership Medal (OLM) was established on 19 May 1961 and is awarded for single accomplishments or sustained contributions which have a profound impact on the technical or administrative programs of NASA.

The Outstanding Leadership Medal is given for an individual act of leadership or for sustained contributions based on an individual's effectiveness or demonstrated ability to develop the administrative or technical talents of other NASA employees.

The OLM is generally recognized as being equal in precedence to the ESM. However because of its more specific award criteria, only 417 Outstanding Leadership Medals were awarded between 1961 and 1989.

NASA Exceptional Scientific Achievement Medal

The Exceptional Scientific Achievement Medal (ESAM) was established on 15 September 1961, when the original ESM was divided into three seperate awards.

Under the current guidelines, the ESAM is awarded for unusually significant scientific contribution toward achievement of aeronautical or space exploration goals. This award may be given for individual efforts which have resulted in a contribution of fundamental importance in this field or have significantly enhanced understanding of this field.

NASA awarded 595 Exceptional Scientific Achievement Medals between 1961 and 1989.

NASA Exceptional Bravery Medal

The NASA Exceptional Bravery Medal (EBM) was established on 15 September 1961. This decoration is awarded for exemplary and courageous handling of an emergency in NASA program activities or for exemplary and courageous service in the performance of an official task of importance to the NASA mission.

To qualify for award of the EBM, the act must be voluntary and undertaken without regard to personal danger. In addition, the act for which the award is made may involve either lifesaving or the safeguarding of human life or government property.

Since the intent of the Exceptional Bravery Medal is to recognize heroic action taken during an emergency, the EBM is among the rarest NASA decorations currently in use. Only 21 EBMs were awarded between 1961 and 1989.

NASA Exceptional Engineering Achievement Medal

The Exceptional Engineering Achievement Medal (EEAM) was established in 1981 to recognize unusually significant engineering contributions towards achievement of aeronautical or space exploration goals.

While NASA does not officially rank the EEAM on an equal level with the ESAM, with the exception of the word, "engineering", the award criteria for both medals are identical.

As of December 1988, NASA had awarded 225 Exceptional Engineering Achievement Medals, an average of about 25 per year.

NASA Public Service Medal

The NASA Public Service Medal (PSM) was established in 1963 as the Public Service Award. Initially presented in the form of a certificate, the award was 'upgraded' to a medal in 1977.

The PSM is awarded to any individual who is not an employee of the Federal Government and whose contributions to the engineering design and development or management coordination of programs has had a significant impact on the accomplishment of the NASA mission. As of December 1988 a total of 735 PSA/PSMs had been awarded by NASA.

NASA Exceptional Achievement Medal

The Exceptional Achievement Medal (EAM) is NASA's newest decoration. Established in 1991, the EAM ranks equally with the OLM, ESM, ESAM, EEAM, and the Exceptional Bravery Medal.

The EAM recognizes significant, specific accomplishments or contributions which are characterized by a substantial and significant improvement in operations, efficiency, service, financial savings, science, or technology which contribute to the mission of NASA.

NASA Equal Employment Opportunity Medal

The NASA Equal Employment Opportunity Medal (EEOM) was initially established as the Equal Employment Opportunity Award in 1969 and "upgraded" to a medal in 1977. The EEOM is awarded for outstanding achievement and significant contributions to the goal of the Equal Employment Opportunity programs of either the Federal Government, civilian employeers, or community organizations.

Due to the narrow focus of the award, as of December 1988 only 78 EEOA/EEOMs had been awarded.

Original NASA Equal Opportunity Award which later became the Equal Opportunity Medal.

NASA Space Flight Medal

The NASA Space Flight Medal (SFM) embodies what most Americans consider the primary mission of NASA, space exploration. The award, established in 1981, is presented only to crew members of Space Transportation System flights which perform orbital missions in outer space. The SFM is considered equal in precedence to the Exceptional Service Medal.

Due to the requirement that crew members must have actually flown in outer space, the SFM was not awarded to members of the Space Shuttle Challenger, which exploded shortly after take-off on 28 January 1986, with the loss of the entire crew.

NACA Distinguished Service Medal

The National Advisory Committee for Aeronautics (NACA) was established in March 1915 to advance all aspects of aeronautical research. The NACA was abolished on 1 October 1958 and many of its activities were absorbed by NASA.

The NACA established the Distinguished Service Medal (DSM) on 30 November 1954, following the enactment of the Government Employees Incentive Awards Act.

The NACA Distinguished Service medal was awarded for distinguished service to the NACA or significant contributions to the United States Space Research Program. The first award was presented in January 1956 to Richard T. Whitcomb for discovery and experimental verification of the Area Rule making supersonic flight possible. There were a total of only seven DSMs awarded. Recipients of the NACA DSM were:

Richard T. Whitcomb,	19 January 1956
Charles W. Littleton,	19 April 1956
John W. Moise,	19 April 1956
Jerome C. Hunsaker,	21 March 1957
H. Julian Allen,	18 April 1957
I. Irving Pinkel,	18 April 1957
John F. Victory,	21 August 1958

McDowell

NACA Exceptional Service Medal

The NACA Exceptional Service Medal (ESM) was awarded for exceptional service to the NACA or significant contributions to the United States Space Research Program which were of a lesser degree than that required for the NACA Distinguished Service medal.

Of identical design to the NACA's DSM, the planchet of the ESM was silver rather than gold. Established in 1954, only seven ESMs were awarded prior to 1 October 1958, when NASA officially replaced the NACA. The first three ESMs were presented for bravery during the test flight accident involving the X-lA in August 1955, the remaining ESMs were presented for significant scientific achievement. Recipients of the NACA ESM were:

Stanley P. Butchart,	5 April 1956
Joseph A. Walker,	5 April 1956
Richard G. Payne,	5 April 1956
Seymour Lieblein,	20 August 1957
Robert G. Deissler,	20 August 1957
John B. Parkinson,	4 October 1957
Anshal I. Neilhouse,	4 October 1957

McDowell

APPENDICES

Appendix A

Navy Campaign Medals Eligibility

Philippine Campaign Medal

Vessel	Dates of Service
Albany	22 Nov - 26 Dec 1900
	29 Feb - 3 Jul 1901
Albay	21 May 1899 - 5 Mar 1900
	12 Sep - 6 Oct 1900
	19 Nov 1901 - 4 Jul 1902
	17 Sep - 20 Nov 1902
	31 Jan - 30 Jun 1903
Annapolis	24 Apr 1900 - 1 Aug 1902
	10 Feb - 20 Feb 1903
	22 Mar - 11 Apr 1903
Arayat	10 Aug 1900 - 4 Jul 1902
Arethust	5 Dec 1900 - 4 Jul 1902
Baltimore	4 Feb 1899 - 5 Apr 1900
Barry	6 May - 11 May 1905
Basco	2 Jun 1899 - 4 Jul 1902
Bennington	22 Feb - 5 Jul 1899
	15 Jul 1899 - 5 Apr 1900
	27 May 1900 - 3 Jan 1901
Boston	4 Feb - 8 Jun 1899
Brooklyn	16 Dec 1899 - 28 Mar 1900
	28 May 1900 - 26 Jun 1900
	3 Nov 1900 - 31 Jan 1901
	27 Feb 1901 - 10 Apr 1901
	7 Aug 1901 - 26 Sep 1901
	13 Feb - 28 Feb 1902
Buffalo	4 Feb - 23 Mar 1899
	14 Aug - 21 Aug 1900
	26 Feb - 8 Mar 1901
	25 Mar - 4 Apr 1901
Calamianes	4 Aug 1899 - 1 Mar 1900
	23 Apr - 10 Aug 1900
	6 Oct 1900 - 6 Jun 1901
	27 Jan - 4 Jul 1902
Callao	4 Feb 1899 - 21 Feb 1901
Castine	21 Apr 1899 - 18 Jan 1900
	19 Sep 1900 - 23 Jun 1901
Celtic	30 Mar - 20 May 1899
	8 Sep - 20 Nov 1899
	22 Feb - 8 May 1900
	9 Jul - 10 Dec 1900
	3 Apr - 4 Jun 1901
	1 Sep - 5 Oct 1901
	11 Jan - 18 Feb 1902
	18 Jun - 4 Jul 1902
Charleston	4 Feb - 2 Nov 1899
Chauncey	6 May - 11 May 1905
Concord	4 Feb 1899 - 17 Mar 1900
	27 May 1900 - 18 Feb 1901
Culgoa	4 Feb 1899 - 13 Jan 1900
	22 Apr - 16 Jun 1900
	1 Nov 1900 - 9 Feb 1901
	20 May - 23 Jul 1901
Don Juan de Austria	28 Nov 1900 - 25 Jul 1901
	3 Sep 1901 - 22 May 1902
	22 Aug - 16 Sep 1902
	8 Feb - 12 Apr 1903
Frolic	24 Apr 1901 - 4 Jul 1902
	31 Jan - 15 Jul 1903
	9 Oct - 12 Nov 1905
Gardoqui	2 Jun 1899 - 23 Apr 1900
	26 Sep - 3 Oct 1900
	30 Nov 1900 - 15 Feb 1902
	1 Oct - 31 Dec 1904
General Alava	9 Mar 1900 - 4 Jul 1902
Glacier	15 Jul - 4 Aug 1899

	4 Sep 1899 - 2 Mar 1900
	27 May - 12 Aug 1900
	6 Jan - 16 Apr 1901
	12 Jul - 12 Aug 1901
	7 Nov - 2 Dec 1901
	30 Mar - 8 May 1902
Helena	19 Feb 1899 - 9 Oct 1900
Iris	18 Mar - 16 Nov 1899
	14 Dec 1899 - 16 Jan 1900
	31 May - 21 Jun 1900
	1 Aug 1900 - 27 Apr 1901
	18 Jul 1901 - 4 Jul 1902
Isla de Cuba	19 May 1900 - 11 Mar 1902
	23 Jun - 4 Jul 1902
	21 Jul - 3 Aug 1902
	2 Sep - 17 Oct 1902
	21 Apr - 9 May 1903
	20 Jun - 15 Jul 1903
Isla de Luzon	31 Mar 1900 - 12 Jan 1901
	25 May 1901 - 4 Jul 1902
Kentucky	3 Feb - 9 Feb 1901
	9 Apr - 29 May 1901
	28 Jun - 29 Aug 1901
	10 Mar - 8 Apr 1902
Leyte	19 Mar - 12 Sep 1900
	29 Sep 1900 - 27 Jan 1902
Manila	4 Feb 1899 - 15 Apr 1902
Manileno	26 May 1899 - 31 Oct 1900
Marietta	3 Jan - 22 Sep 1900
	20 Nov 1900 - 3 Jun 1901
Mariveles	17 Jun 1899 - 14 Mar 1900
	16 Aug - 22 Aug 1900
	1 May 1901 - 4 Jul 1902
Mindoro	11 Jun 1899 - 23 Apr 1900
	31 Oct 1900 - 26 Sep 1901
	31 Aug - 31 Dec 1904
Monadnock	4 Feb 1899 - 1 Jan 1900
	3 Apr - 27 Oct 1900
Monterey	4 Feb 1899 - 6 Apr 1900
Nanshan	4 Feb 1899 - 8 Aug 1900
	11 Sep 1900 - 27 Jan 1901
	28 Mar - 8 Jul 1901
	8 Oct 1901 - 4 Feb 1902
Nashville	31 Dec 1899 - 8 Jun 1900
	2 Feb - 22 Jun 1901
Newark	25 Nov 1899 - 20 Mar 1900
	3 Apr - 7 Apr 1900
	18 Aug - 30 Nov 1900
	22 Dec 1900 - 2 Mar 1901
New Orleans	21 Dec 1899 - 19 Feb 1900
	22 May - 15 Aug 1900
New York	20 May - 25 Jun 1901
	27 Aug 1901 - 13 Mar 1902
Olympia	4 Feb - 20 May 1899
Oregon	18 Mar - 7 Oct 1899
	8 Nov 1899 - 13 Feb 1900
Pampanga	8 Jun 1899 - 29 Sep 1900
	15 Dec 1900 - 18 Jun 1902
	11 Mar - 12 Apr 1904
	4 May - 11 May 1904
	30 May - 9 Jul 1904
	30 Jul - 4 Dec 1904
	2 Mar - 10 Mar 1906
	16 Aug - 15 Sep 1906
Panay	2 Jun 1899 - 4 Jul 1902
Paragua	22 May 1899 - 4 Jul 1902
	2 Nov - 29 Nov 1904
	15 Mar - 2 Apr 1905
	23 Apr - 30 May 1905
Petrel	4 Feb - 17 Aug 1899
	13 Jan 1900 - 12 Jun 1901
Piscataqua	24 Apr 1901 - 4 Jul 1902
Princeton	16 Apr - 8 Aug 1899
	15 Oct 1899 - 26 Jun 1900
	4 Dec 1900 - 26 Oct 1901
	13 Dec 1901 - 20 Jul 1902
	9 Feb - 5 Apr 1903
Quiros	14 Mar 1900 - 2 Aug 1902
	31 Aug - 25 Nov 1902
	30 Jan - 3 May 1903
	29 Jun - 15 Jul 1903
Rainbow	3 Apr - 4 Jul 1902
	28 Nov - 4 Dec 1904
Samar	26 May 1899 - 10 Oct 1901
	19 Jun - 29 Nov 1902
	31 Jan 1903 - 8 Feb 1904
	22 Mar - 5 Aug 1904
Solace	11 Dec - 22 Dec 1900
	15 Jan - 24 Jan 1901
	27 May - 12 Jun 1901
	19 Jul - 28 Jul 1901
	20 Dec - 31 Dec 1901
	18 Jan - 25 Jan 1902
Urdaneta	22 Jun 1899 - 17 Sep 1900
	12 May - 26 Sep 1900
	3 Oct 1900 - 4 Jul 1902
Vicksburg	2 Feb - 13 Nov 1901
	2 Jun - 4 Jul 1902
Villalobos	5 Mar 1900 - 4 Jul 1902
Wheeling	14 Apr 1899 - 13 Jan 1900
	10 Mar - 21 Mar 1900
Wilmington	20 Jan - 10 May 1901
Wompatuck	24 Apr 1901 - 4 Jul 1902
Yorktown	23 Feb - 12 Jul 1899
	3 Aug 1899 - 9 Apr 1900
	17 Sep 1900 - 23 May 1901
	11 Sep - 28 Sep 1901
	17 Nov 1901 - 15 Apr 1902
Yosemite	18 Jul - 1 Aug 1899
	14 Jun - 30 Jun 1900
	7 Aug - 12 Aug 1900
Zafiro	4 Feb - 10 Jun 1899
	6 Jul - 4 Aug 1899
	20 Aug - 13 Oct 1899
	3 Nov - 10 Nov 1899
	27 Nov 1899 - 21 Mar 1900
	3 Jun - 21 Jun 1900
	20 Oct 1900 - 27 Aug 1901
	11 Oct 1901 - 15 Feb 1902

Officers and men on duty at:

Cavite, P.I	4 Feb 1899 - 4 Jul 1902
Olongapo, P.I	4 Feb 1899 - 4 Jul 1902
Polloc, P.I	4 Feb 1899 - 3 Jun 1904
Isabella de Basilan, P.I.	4 Feb1899 - 15 Jul 1903

China Relief Expedition Medal

Vessel	Dates of service
Brooklyn	7 Jul - 12 Oct 1900
Buffalo	3 Aug - 6 Aug 1900
Iris	29 Jun - 24 Jul 1900
Monocacy	14 Jun - 27 May 1900
Nashville	18 Jun - 7 Sep 1900
New Orleans	14 Sep - 27 May 1901
Newark	27 May - 22 Jul 1900
Solace	18 Jun - 29 Jul 1900
Wheeling	5 Apr - 1 May 1900
Yorktown	15 Jun - 10 Sep 1900
Zafiro	10 Jul - 11 Oct 1900

Cuban Pacification Medal

Vessel	Dates of service
Alabama	11 Feb - 16 Feb 1907
Brooklyn	7 Oct - 1 Nov 1906
Celtic	28 Sep 1906 - 15 Jan 1907
Cleveland	21 Sep 1906 - 13 Jan 1907
Columbia	20 Oct 1906 - 17 Apr 1907
Denver	12 Sep - 2 Oct 1906
Des Moines	15 Sep 1906 - 25 Jan 1907
Dixie	12 Sep - 21 Sep 1907
	7 Jan - 18 Aug 1906
Dubuque	18 May - 19 May 1906
Eagle	4 Dec 1906 - 1 Jun 1906
Illinois	11 Feb - 16 Feb 1906
Indiana	30 Sep - 8 Oct 1907
	11 Feb - 16 Feb 1907
Iowa	11 Feb - 16 Feb 1907
Kentucky	30 Sep - 9 Oct 1906
Louisiana	21 Sep - 13 Oct 1906
	25 Dec - 29 Dec 1906
Marietta	14 Sep - 9 Oct 1906
	18 Jan - 21 Jan 1907
	7 Feb 1907 - 7 Feb 1908
	18 Mar - 25 Mar 1908
	15 Apr - 16 Apr 1908
	27 May - 9 Jun 1908
	30 Jun - 11 Jul 1908
Minneapolis	22 Sep - 22 Oct 1906
Newark	22 Sep - 9 Nov 1906
New Jersey	21 Sep - 13 Oct 1906
Paducah	12 Sep 1906 - 1 Apr 1909
Prairie	6 Oct - 21 Nov 1906
	29 Jan - 16 May 1907
	25 Dec - 31 Dec 1908
	17 Jan - 23 Jan 1909
Tacoma	21 Sep 1906 - 26 Feb 1907
Texas	9 Oct - 30 Oct 1906
Virginia	21 Sep - 13 Oct 1906

Nicaraguan Campaign Medal

Vessel	Dates of service
Annapolis	29 Jul - 14 Nov 1912
California	29 Jul - 14 Nov 1912
Cleveland	29 Jul - 14 Nov 1912
Colorado	29 Jul - 14 Nov 1912
Denver	29 Jul - 14 Nov 1912
Glacier	29 Jul - 14 Nov 1912
Maryland	29 Jul - 14 Nov 1912
Tacoma	29 Jul - 14 Nov 1912

Mexican Service Medal

Vessel	Dates of service
Albany	22 Apr - 23 Nov 1914
	4 Jul - 23 Jul 1916
	25 Nov - 2 Dec 1916
Ammem	22 Apr - 5 May 1914
	9 May - 27 May 1914
Annapolis	21 Apr - 3 Oct 1914
	4 Jul - 18 Sep 1916
	11 Nov - 15 Nov 1916
	19 Nov 1916- 7 Feb 1917
Arethusa	30 Apr - 2 May 1914
	2 Jun - 7 Jun 1914
Arkansas	22 Apr - 30 Sep 1914
	25 May - 1 Jun 1916
Balch	28 Apr - 3 May 1914
Beale	22 Apr - 27 May 1914
Birmingham	22 Apr - 27 May 1914
Brutus	13 Jun - 3 Aug 1914
	6 Jul - 17 Aug 1916
Buffalo	14 Nov - 26 Nov 1914
	28 Mar - 29 Mar 1916
	22 Jun - 30 Jun 1916
	31 Aug 1916 - 7 Feb 1917
Burrows	22 Apr - 15 May 1914
	20 May - 27 May 1914
California	21 Apr - 24 Jun 1914
	16 Jul - 18 Aug 1914
Cassin	29 Apr - 14 Jun 1914
Chattanogga	21 Apr - 8 Jun 1914
	6 Jul - 26 Nov 1914
	14 Mar - 13 Apr 1916
	30 Apr - 31 Aug 1916
	11 Dec - 16 Dec 1916
Celtic	25 Apr - 5 May 1914
	5 Jul - 13 Jul 1914
	4 Sep - 12 Oct 1914
Chester	21 Apr - 8 Jun 1914
Cheyenne	15 May - 16 May 1914
Cleveland	1 May - 27 Oct 1914
	18 Mar - 20 Nov 1916

Colorado	24 Jun - 14 Aug 1914
Connecticut	21 Apr - 2 Jul 1914
Culgoa	13 May - 28 May 1914
	19 Jul - 13 Aug 1914
Cummings	29 Apr - 18 May 1914
	9 Jun - 12 Jun 1914
Cyclops	6 Jun - 4 Aug 1914
Delaware	8 Jul - 9 Oct 1914
Denver	7 Jul - 8 Jul 1914
	13 Aug - 24 Aug 1914
	4 Apr - 29 Jun 1916
	15 Jul - 14 Sep 1916
	16 Dec 1916 - 7 Feb 1917
Des Moines	14 May - 19 Jun 1914
	19 Jul - 21 Aug 1914
	27 Aug - 15 Oct 1914
Dixie	23 Apr - 24 Apr 1914
	2 May - 27 May 1914
	25 Jun - 27 Jun 1916
	13 Jul - 28 Aug 1916
Dolphin	21 Apr - 20 Jun 1914
	2 Jul - 8 Jul 1916
Drayton	22 Apr - 4 May 1914
Eagle	3 May - 15 Aug 1914
Fanning	22 Apr - 27 May 1914
Florida	21 Apr - 13 Jul 1914
Flusser	28 Apr - 29 Apr 1914
	2 Jul - 9 Jul 1916
Georgia	1 May - 1 Aug 1914
Glacier	21 Apr - 25 Apr 1914
	10 Jul - 6 Aug 1914
	27 Aug - 28 Sep 1914
	29 Mar - 12 Apr 1916
	16 Jun - 30 Jun 1916
	1 Jul - 7 Jul 1916
	1 Aug - 17 Aug 1916
	2 Oct - 30 Oct 1916
	12 Dec - 20 Dec 1916
Hancock	21 Apr - 14 Jul 1914
	15 Apr - 25 Jun 1916
	30 Jun - 30 Sep 1916
Henley	22 Apr - 2 May 1914
	8 May - 22 May 1914
Hopkins	6 May - 20 Jun 1914
	6 Jul - 27 Aug 1914
	20 Jun - 24 Jun 1916
	3 Jul - 22 Aug 1916
Hull	2 May - 11 Aug 1914
	24 Jun - 21 Jul 1916
Illinois	13 Oct 1916 - 7 Feb 1917
Iris	29 Apr - 20 May 1914
Jarvis	4 Jun - 12 Jun 1914
	22 Apr - 20 May 1914
	4 Jun - 12 Jun 1914
Jenkins	22 Apr - 10 May 1914
	14 May - 14 Jun1914
Jouett	22 Apr - 25 May 1914
	31 May - 12 Jun 1914
Jupiter	27 Apr - 9 Jul 1914
	6 Apr - 23 Apr 1916
Kansas	14 Jul - 29 Oct1914
Kentucky	23 Mar - 2 Jun 1916
Lamson	2 Jul - 9 Jul 1916
Lawrence	2 May - 27 Aug 1914
Lebanon	25 Apr - 1 Sep 1914
Louisiana	22 Apr - 29 May 1914
Machias	15 May - 14 Jun 1914
	14 Mar - 28 Jun 1916
Marietta	14 Mar - 27 Jun 1916
Maryland	28 Apr - 19 Sep 1914
	28 Jun - 28 Nov 1916
Michigan	22 Apr - 29 May 1914
Milwaulkie	25 Jun - 22 Aug 1916
Minnesota	12 Apr - 2 May 1914
	29 Jul - 7 Aug 1914
	11 Oct - 26 Nov 1914
Mississippi	24 Apr - 12 Jun 1914
Monaghan	26 Apr - 28 Apr 1914
Montana	28 Apr - 3 May 1914
Morro Castle	29 Apr - 10 May 1914
Nanshan	8 Aug - 6 Sep 1914
	1 Oct - 24 Oct 1914
	1 Jul - 11 Jul 1916
	2 Oct - 19 Oct 1916
	11 Dec - 13 Dec 1916
Nashville	23 Apr - 16 Jul 1914
	18 Jul 1916 - 7 Feb 1917
Nebraska	1 May - 21 Jun 1914
	1 Jun - 13 Oct 1916
Neptune	25 Aug - 3 Sep 1916
	25 Oct - 1 Nov 1916
Nereus	29 Apr - 13 May 1914
	30 May - 8 Jun 1914
	21 Oct - 30 Nov 1914
	29 Oct - 20 Oct 1916
	6 Feb - 7 Feb 1917
Nero	19 May - 20 Jun 1914
	16 Jul - 7 Aug 1914
	29 Oct - 26 Nov 1914
	14 Jul - 20 Jul 1916
	15 Jan - 20 Jan 1917
New Hampshire	21 Apr - 21 Jun 1914
New Jersey	22 Apr - 13 Aug 1914
New Orleans	21 Apr - 9 Sep 1914
	26 Nov - 6 Dec 1914
	25 Nov - 15 Dec 1916
	27 Dec 1916 - 7 Feb 1917
New York	4 May - 5 Sep 1914
	14 Sep - 17 Sep 1914
North Dakota	26 Apr - 8 Oct 1914
	4 Jul - 10 Aug 1916
Ontario	22 Apr - 5 Jul 1914
	11 Jul - 26 Jul 1914
Orion	22 Apr - 4 Jul 1914
	29 Jul - 2 Sep 1914
Ozark	15 May - 25 May 1914
Paducah	14 May - 17 Jun 1914
Patapsco	22 Apr - 8 Sep 1914
Patterson	22 Apr - 26 May 1914
Patuxent	23 Apr - 8 Oct 1914
Paulding	22 Apr - 27 May 1914
Paul Jones	25 Apr - 28 Apr 1914

	18 Jul - 22 Aug 1916
	1 Dec 1916 - 29 Jan 1917
Perry	25 Apr - 16 Aug 1914
Petrel	10 Oct - 14 Nov 1914
	18 Nov - 26 Nov 1914
Pittsburgh	23 Jun - 4 Oct 1916
Prairie	21 Apr - 26 May 1914
	18 Jun - 2 Jun 1914
Preble	2 May - 16 Aug 1914
	19 Apr - 20 Apr 1916
	18 Jul - 22 Aug 1916
Proteus	20 Jun - 1 Jul 1914
Raleigh	21 Apr - 2 Jun 1914
	11 Jul - 10 Aug 1914
	23 Oct - 26 Nov 1914
	27 Mar - 29 Mar 1916
	2 Aug - 21 Oct 1916
Reid	28 Apr - 30 Apr 1914
	26 Jun - 28 Jun 1914
Rhode Island	8 Oct - 26 Nov 1914
Sacramento	20 May - 13 Jul 1914
	16 Dec 1916 - 7 Feb 1917
Salem	5 May - 19 Sep 1914
	25 Jun - 30 Aug 1916
San Diego	10 Jul - 19 Sep 1914
	24 Nov - 26 Nov 1916
	22 Jun - 18 Jul 1916
	6 Aug - 19 Aug 1916
San Francisco	21 Apr - 13 Jun 1914
	6 Jul - 17 Jul 1914
Saturn	23 Apr - 20 May 1914
	7 Jun - 15 Jun 1914
	22 Jul - 8 Aug 1914
	23 Sep - 26 Nov 1914
	12 Oct - 14 Dec 1916
	13 Jan - 16 Jan 1917
Solace	26 Apr - 5 May 1914
	24 Jun - 30 Oct 1914
Sonoma	22 Apr- 5 Sep1914
South Carolina	21 Apr - 31 May 1914
South Dakota	1 Jul - 2 Jul 1914
	29 May - 1 Aug 1916
Sterrett	29 Apr- 30 Apr 1914
Stewart	25 Apr - 16 Aug 1914
	30 Jun - 22 Aug 1914
Tacoma	4 May - 27 Jul 1914
	11 Jan - 7 Feb 1917
Terry	28 Apr - 30 Apr 1914
Texas	26 May - 8 Aug1914
	9 Oct - 4 Nov 1914
Trippe	22 Apr - 25 May 1914
Truxton	25 Apr - 13 Jul 1914
	24 Jun - 27 Aug 1916
Utah	21 Apr - 15 Jun 1914
Vermont	21 Apr - 22 Oct 1914
Vestal	2 May - 20 Sep 1914
Vicksburg	15 May - 16 May 1914
Virginia	1 May - 13 Aug 1914
	7 Sep - 11 Oct 1914
Vulcan	22 Apr - 9 Jun 1914
	7 Jul - 28 Jul 1914
Walke	26 Apr - 28 Apr 1914
Warrington	22 Apr - 2 May 1914
	14 May - 27 May 1914
Washington	14 Jun - 27 Jun 1914
West Virginia	9 May - 3 Jul 1914
	9 Sep - 26 Nov 1914
	9 Oct - 8 Nov 1916
Wheeling	25 Apr - 30 Jun 1914
	27 Mar - 29 Jun 1916
	1 Jul - 16 Dec 1916
Whipple	25 Apr - 13 Jul 1914
	17 Mar - 24 Apr 1916
	26 Jun - 31 Jul 1916
	14 Aug - 21 Aug 1916
Wyoming	18 May - 7 Sep 1914
Yankton	25 Apr - 1 May 1914
	9 May - 7 Sep 1914
Yorktown	21 Apr - 16 Jun 1914
	9 Sep - 26 Nov 1914
	14 Mar - 21 Nov 1916
	18 Jan - 20 Jan 1917

Haitian Campaign Medal (1915)

Vessel	Dates of Service
Castine	4 Aug - 6 Dec 1915
Celtic	28 Oct - 9 Nov 1915
	28 Nov - 6 Dec 1915
Connecticut	4 Aug - 2 Dec 1915
Culgoa	6 Sep - 8 Oct 1915
Eagle	9 Jul - 2 Nov 1915
Marietta	31 Aug - 19 Sep 1915
	2 Dec - 6 Dec 1915
Nashville	9 Jul - 6 Dec 1915
Osceola	8 Aug - 2 Nov 1915
Patuxent	1 Nov - 6 Dec 1915
Prairie	7 Nov - 6 Dec 1915
Sacramento	9 Sep - 6 Dec 1915
Solace	9 Aug - 24 Sep 1915
Tennessee	15 Aug - 18 Aug 1915
	31 Aug - 3 Sep 1915
Washington	9 Jul - 6 Dec 1915

Haitian Campaign Medal (1919-1920)

Vessel	Dates of Service
Beaufort	3 Apr - 1 May 1920
Delaware	12 Dec - 16 Dec 1919
Dolphin	4 Feb - 5 Feb 1920
	17 Apr 1920
	26 Apr - 27 Apr 1920
Gulfport	22 Jun - 5 Jul 1919

	23 Aug - 8 Sep 1919
	23 Oct 1919
	29 Oct - 13 Nov 1919
	30 Dec 1919 - 19 Jan 1920
Hancock	18 Apr 1919
	21 Jun 1919
	21 Aug - 25 Aug 1919
Henderson	26 Jan - 1 Feb 1920
	7 Mar - 19 Mar 1920
	21 Mar - 25 Mar 1920
	14 Apr - 26 Apr 1920
Kittery	6 Apr - 8 Apr 1919
	29 Apr - 30 Apr 1919
	7 May - 8 May 1919
	27 May - 8 Jun 1919
	30 Jun 1919
	6 Jul - 8 Jul 1919
	31 Aug - 9 Sep 1919
	1 Oct - 9 Oct 1919
	26 Oct - 5 Nov 1919
	28 Nov 1919
	30 Nov - 8 Dec 1919
	3 May - 12 May 1920
	28 May - 1 Jun 1920
Kwasind	1 Apr - 13 Apr 1919
	19 Apr - 9 Jun 1919
Lake Bridge	7 Apr - 15 Apr 1919
Lake Worth	18 Jun - 2 Jul 1919
Long Beach	8 Mar - 14 Mar 1920
May	23 May - 27 Jul 1919
Mercy	29 May - 1 Jun 1920
Mohave	18 May - 4 Jun 1919
	8 Jun - 30 Jul 1919
	7 Nov - 11 Nov 1919
Osceola	12 Apr - 13 Apr 1919
	15 May 1920
Pensacola	22 May - 27 May 1919
Peoria	6 Oct - 5 Nov 1919
Potomac	1 Apr - 9 Apr 1919
	25 Jan 1920
	20 Apr - 1 Jun 1920
Prometheus	9 Dec - 11 Dec 1919
	11 Feb - 15 Feb 1920
Rowan	1 Apr 1919
Sandpiper	2 Feb - 12 Feb 1920
Shubrick	31 Oct 1919
Sub chaser	
No. 135	1 Apr - 5 Nov 1919
No. 136	1 Apr - 5 Nov 1919
No. 165	1 Aug - 15 Jun 1920
No. 180	14 Aug 1919 - 15 Jun 1920
No. 21O	1 Apr - 19 Sep 1919
No. 211	1 Apr - 19 Sep 1919
No. 212	1 Apr - 4 Aug 1919
No. 213	1 Apr - 4 Aug 1919
No. 214	6 Sep - 21 Dec 1919
	5 Jan - 11 Jun 1920
No. 223	10 Sep 1919
No. 251	1 Apr - 14 May 1919
	16 May - 15 Jul 1919
No. 253	10 Sep - 15 Oct 1919
	30 Oct 1919 - 1 Jun 1920
No. 443	15 Oct 1919 - 1 Jun 1920
No. 444	15 Oct 1919 - 1 Jun 1920
Winslow	1 Apr 1919

Dominican Campaign Medal

Vessel	Dates of Service
Celtic	6 Jul 1916
	23 Jul 1916
	18 Aug 1916
	1 Sep - 2 Sep 1916
Castine	5 May - 27 Jun 1916
	15 Jul - 5 Aug 1916
	17 Aug - 22 Aug 1916
	26 Aug 1916
	28 Aug - 9 Sep 1916
	12 Sep - 19 Sep 1916
	25 Sep - 10 Oct 1916
	12 Oct - 15 Oct 1916
	17 Oct - 26 Oct 1916
Culgoa	10 May - 28 May 1916
	7 Jun - 9Jun 1916
	8 Oct 1916
	23 Oct 1916
Dixie	6 Sep - 8 Sep 1916
	16 Sep - 18 Sep 1916
Dolphin	12 May - 22 May 1916
Eagle	25 Nov - 28 Nov 1916
	2 Dec - 5 Dec 1916
Flusser	8 May - 17 Jun 1916
Hancock	18 Jun - 19 Jun 1916
	12 Sep - 30 Sep 1916
	7 Nov - 22 Nov 1916
Hector	9 May - 3 Jun 1916
Kentucky	11 Jun - 12 Jun 1916
Lamson	9 May - 13 May 1916
	16 May - 29 May 1916
	10 Jun - 17 Jun 1916
Memphis	27 May - 16 Jul 1916
	24 Jul - 25 Jul 1916
	31 Jul 1916
	18 Aug - 29 Aug 1916
Machias	24 Nov - 25 Nov 1916
Neptune	15 Jun - 25 Jun 1916
	2 Jul - 3 Jul 1916
	9 Jul - 11 Jul 1916
	14 Oct 1916
Olympia	20 Nov - 4 Dec 1916
Panther	22 May - 25 May 1916
Potomac	28 Aug - 1 Sep 1916
	26 Sep 1916
Prairie	5 May - 27 May 1916
	1 Sep - 10 Sep 1916
	12 Sep - 17 Oct 1916
	26 Oct - 8 Nov 1916
Preston	20 May - 22 Nov 1916
Reid	9 May - 17 Jun 1916

Sacramento	4 May - 4 Dec 1916
Salem	7 Sep - 8 Sep 1916
	29 Sep - 30 Sep 1916
Solace	27 Aug 1916
	1 Sep - 2 Sep 1916
Sterrett	8 May - 18 Jun 1916
Terry	15 May - 8 Jul 1916
Walke	11 May - 17 Jun 1916

Second Nicaraguan Campaign Medal

Vessel	Dates of Service
Ashville	5 Aug - 12 Aug 1929
	26 Dec 1929
	7 Feb - 9 Feb 1930
	31 Jan - 3 Mar 1931
	13 May - 17 Jun 1931
Bainbridge	26 Apr - 4 Jun 1927
Barker	10 Jan 1927
	13 Jan - 31 Jan 1927
Barry	19 Dec - 30 Dec 1926
	2 Jan - 9 Jan 1927
Borie	9 Jan - 18 Jan 1927
	24 Jan - 15 Mar 1927
Brooks	18 Dec - 21 Dec 1926
Cincinnati	11 Jan 1927
	14 Jan - 27 Jan 1927
Cleveland	12 Dec 1926 - 17 Jan 1927
	21 Jan - 22 Mar 1927
	28 Mar - 24 May 1927
	20 May - 7 Jun 1927
	18 Jun - 21 Jul 1927
	4 Aug - 24 Aug 1927
	16 Sep - 19 Sep 1927
	23 Sep - 1 Oct 1927
	11 Oct - 14 Oct 1927
	28 Oct - 20 Nov 1927
Cleveland	24 Mar - 24 Apr 1928
	29 Apr 1928
	15 May - 14 Jun 1928
	11 Jul 1928
	23 Jul - 26 Jul 1928
	31 Jul - 8 Aug 1928
	25 Aug - 22 Sep 1928
	4 Oct - 15 Oct 1928
	20 Oct 1928
	3 Nov - 8 Nov 1928
	19 May - 21 May 1929
	27 Jun - 2 Aug 1929
Coghlan	18 Feb - 21 Mar 1927
Denver	18 Sep 1926
	25 Sep - 16 Nov 1926
	27 Nov 1926 - 13 Jan 1927
	17 Jan - 20 Mar 1927
	26 Mar - 30 May 1927
	2 Jun - 29 Jun 1927
	15 Jul - 13 Aug 1927
	24 Aug - 6 Sep 1927
	29 Dec 1927 - 12 Jan 1928
	21 Jan - 22 Jan 1928
	29 Jan - 19 Feb 1928
	5 Mar - 28 Mar 1928
	9 Apr - 15 May 1928
	17 Jun - 22 Jul 1928
	8 Aug - 12 Aug 1928
	25 Aug - 28 Aug 1928
	6 Dec - 14 Dec 1928
	1 Jan - 4 Jan 1929
	16 Jan - 21 Jan 1929
	11 Apr - 14 Apr 1929
	9 Aug 1929
	16 Aug - 30 Sep 1929
	27 Nov - 28 Nov 1929
	29 Mar - 31 May 1930
	22 Apr - 7 May 1930
	5 Sep - 10 Oct 1930
Detroit	23 Mar - 17 Apr 1927
Edwards, J.D	9 Jan 1927
	17 Jan - 27 Jan 1917
	31 Jan - 3 Feb 1927
	7 Feb - 13 Feb 1927
Flusser	24 Apr - 19 May 1927
	23 May - 12 Jun 1927
Galveston	27 Aug - 1 Nov 1926
	13 Nov -7 Dec 1926
	10 Dec - 27 Dec 1926
	5 Jan - 22 Feb 1927
	4 Mar - 20 Apr 1927
	30 Apr - 18 Jun 1927
	26 Sep - 13 Oct 1927
	6 Nov - 20 Nov 1927
	2 Dec - 30 Dec 1927
	8 Jan - 23 Jan 1928
	26 Feb - 31 Mar 1928
	4 Apr - 11 Apr 1928
	30 Apr 1928
	15 May - 18 Jun 1928
	26 Sep - 19 Oct 1928
	2 Nov - 15 Nov 1928
	18 Feb - 19 Feb 1929
	18 Apr - 19 Apr 1929
	2 Jun - 27 Jun 1929
	2 Aug - 4 Aug 1929
	5 Apr - 22 Apr 1930
Gilmore	25 Sep - 7 Oct 1926
	11 Oct - 30 Oct 1926
Goff	15 Jan - 11 Feb 1927
Hatfield	13 Feb - 27 Feb 1927
	3 Mar - 21 Mar 1927
Henderson	7 Mar - 26 Mar 1927
Humphreys	21 Nov - 22 Nov 1926
Kane	19 Mar - 4 Apr 1927
	24 Apr 1927
Kidder	13 Jun - 27 Jun 1927
King	26 Apr - 3 May 1927
	7 May - 9 Jun 1927
La Vallette	13 Jun - 23 Jun 1927
Lawrence	13 Feb - 11 Mar 1927

Vessel	Dates of Service
	14 Mar - 21 Mar 1927
Litchfield	23 Jun - 10 Jul 1927
	31 Jul 1927
Marblehead	11 Jan - 29 Jan 1928
Marcus	11 Aug - 13 Aug 1927
McFarland	19 Mar - 8 Apr 1927
	12 Apr - 24 Apr 1927
Melvin	25 Jun - 18 Jul 1927
Memphis	26 Oct - 8 Nov 1932
Mervine	26 Jun 1927
	9 Jul - 20 Jul 1927
Milwaukie	29 Jan - 8 Feb 1927
	11 Feb - 15 Feb 1927
	19 Feb - 2 May 1927
	2 Jun - 4 Jun 1927
	9 Jun - 13 Jun 1927
Mullany	30 Jul - 13 Aug 1927
Osborne	11 Jan - 16 Jan 1927
Overton	30 Aug - 13 Sep 1932
Paulding, J.K	1 Nov - 13 Nov 1926
	16 Nov - 19 Nov 1926
	19 Mar - 29 Mar 1927
	3 Apr - 24 Apr 1927
Philip	31 Jan - 9 Feb 1932
	8 Apr - 11 Apr 1932
	30 Apr 1932
Preston	29 Apr - 10 May 1927
	15 May - 3 Jun 1927
	7 Jun - 13 Jun 1927
Quail	27 Dec - 31 Jan 1927
	9 Feb - 12 Feb 1927
Raleigh	5 Feb - 23 Mar 1927
Reid	24 Apr - 22 May 1927
	26 May - 12 Jun 1927
Reuben James	21 Jan - 15 Mar 1927
Robert Smith	12 Jun - 25 Jun 1927
	16 Jul - 9 Aug 1927
Rochester	31 Aug - 6 Oct 1926
	15 Oct - 9 Dec 1926
	22 Dec 1926 - 20 Jan 1927
	27 Jan - 1 Feb 1927
	21 Jul - 24 Jul 1927
	2 Aug - 5 Aug 1927
	10 Oct - 11 Oct 1927
	6 Nov - 7 Nov 1927
	7 Jan - 1 Feb 1928
	16 Feb - 15 Mar 1928
	24 Mar - 7 Apr 1928
	28 May - 31 May 1928
	27 Jun - 30 Jun 1928
	8 Jul - 18 Jul 1928
	21 Jul - 25 Aug 1928
	22 Sep - 27 Sep 1928
	19 Oct - 27 Nov 1928
	31 Dec 1928 - 7 Jan 1929
	4 Feb - 11 Feb 1929
	13 Jul - 18 Jul 1929
	25 Nov - 19 Dec 1929
	9 Oct - 16 Nov 1930
	3 Apr - 14 Apr 1931
Sacramento	16 Mar - 27 Mar 1929
	2 Jun - 4 Jun 1929
	22 Sep - 24 Sep 1929
	14 Mar - 24 Mar 1930
	3 Jan - 31 Jan 1931
	17 Apr - 13 May 1931
	14 Aug - 11 Sep 1931
Selfridge	18 Jun - 17 Jul 1927
	23 Jul - 26 Jul 1927
Shirk	2 Jul - 23 Jul 1927
Sloat	25 Jun - 9 Jul 1927
	22 Jul - 8 Aug 1927
Smith Thompson	25 Sep - 30 Sep 1926
	3 Oct - 1 Nov 1926
	11 Jan - 16 Jan 1927
Sturteveant	19 Sep - 4 Oct 1932
Tracy	22 Nov - 18 Dec 1926
	15 Mar - 26 Apr 1927
Trenton	17 Apr - 16 May 1927
Tulsa	29 Aug - 28 Sep 1926
	7 Oct - 8 Oct 1926
	12 Oct - 16 Oct 1926
	1 Nov - 14 Dec 1926
	3 Mar - 30 Apr 1926
	7 May - 19 Jul 1927
	13 Aug - 24 Sep 1927
	14 Oct - 7 Nov 1927
	30 Nov - 20 Dec 1927
	6 Jan - 16 Feb 1928
	10 Mar 1928
	14 Jun - 2 Jul 1928
	7 Jul - 11 Jul 1928
	21 Jul - 25 Jul 1928
	7 Aug - 21 Aug 1928
	31 Aug - 16 Sep 1928
	28 Sep - 4 Oct 1928
	18 Nov - 9 Dec 1928
Whipple	22 Nov 1926
	5 Dec - 7 Dec 1926
	9 Dec - 19 Dec 1926
	15 Mar - 27 Apr 1927
Wickes	30 Jan - 9 Feb 1932
Willamson	15 Jan - 29 Jan 1927
	2 Feb - 18 Feb 1927
Wood	27 Jun - 16 Jul 1927
Yarborough	12 Jun - 18 Jun 1927
	8 Jul - 5 Aug 1927

Yangtze Service Medal

Vessel	Dates of Service
Alva, General	20 Sep - 6 Nov 1926
	14 Apr - 14 May 1927
	7 Jun - 30 Jun 1927
	24 Aug - 21 Oct 1927
Asheville	3 Nov 1926 - 2 Apr 1927
	13 May - 18 May 1927
	2 Aug - 23 Aug 1927
	18 Mar - 23 Mar 1932
	27 Jun - 9 Oct 1932

Avocet	23 Apr - 7 May 1931
	9 Oct - 22 Oct 1931
Barker	28 Nov 1930 - 12 Jan 1931
	8 Jul - 21 Aug 1931
	18 Oct - 2 Nov 1931
	5 Feb - 27 Mar 1932
	4 Oct - 25 Oct 1932
Beaver	25 May - 2 Jun 1931
	9 Oct - 10 Oct 1931
Bittern	7 Feb - 9 Mar 1932
	27 May - 3 Jun 1932
	6 Oct - 9 Oct 1932
Black Hawk	21 Oct - 28 Oct 1926
	24 Apr - 6 Jun 1927
	21 Apr - 3 May 1931
	15 Sep - 17 Sep 1931
	23 Sep - 24 Sep 1931
	20 Oct - 2 Nov 1931
	9 Feb - 23 May 1932
	5 Oct - 25 Oct 1932
Borie	19 May - 16 Jul 1930
	29 Jan - 10 Mar 1932
Bulmer	7 Jan - 3 Mar 1927
	23 May - 28 Jun 1927
	21 Aug - 21 Oct 1927
	1 Feb - 28 Feb 1930
	4 Aug - 1 Oct 1930
	2 May - 11 May 1931
Bulmer	27 Aug - 29 Aug 1931
	24 Oct - 2 Nav 1931
	2 Feb - 6 Feb 1932
	8 Feb - 19 Feb 1932
	21 Feb 1932
	15 Apr - 2 May 1932
	6 May - 9 May 1932
	13 May - 16 May 1932
	19 May - 23 May 1932
	5 Aug - 7 Aug 1932
Canopus	16 May - 30 Jun 1930
	8 May - 16 May 1932
Cincinnati	4 Apr - 9 Sep 1927
	27 Sep - 15 Oct 1927
Edsall	16 Jan - 2 Mar 1927
	18 Apr - 2 Jul 1927
	21 Aug - 22 Aug 1927
	1 Oct - 21 Oct 1927
	1 Feb - 28 Feb 1930
	16 Jul - 26 Sep 1930
	15 Apr - 22 Apr 1931
	27 Aug - 1 Sep 1931
	2 Feb 1932
	4 Feb - 25 Mar 1932
	27 Mar - 2 May 1932
	6 May - 9 May 1932
	13 May - 16 May 1932
	19 May - 23 May 1932
	4 Oct - 25 Oct 1932
Edwards, John D	22 May - 16 Jul 1930
	7 Jul - 8 Jul 1931
	21 Aug - 2 Sep 1931
	19 Oct - 2 Nov 1931
	5 Feb - 13 Mar 1932
	15 Mar - 16 Mar 1932
	10 May - 23 May 1932
	4 Oct - 25 Oct 1932
Elcano	3 Sep - 21 Oct 1927
Finch	7 Feb - 5 Apr 1932
	8 Apr - 11 Apr 1932
	15 Apr - 24 May 1932
Ford, John D	11 Sep 1926 - 18 Jan 1927
	28 Mar - 7 Jul 1927
	2 May - 17 Jun 1931
	6 Jul - 31 Jul 1931
	5 Oct 1931
	4 Feb - 10 Mar 1932
	25 Apr - 23 May 1932
	4 Oct - 11 Oct 1932
Guam	1 Mar 1930 - 31 Dec 1932
Hart	12 Oct - 1 Dec 1926
	19 Dec 1926 - 9 Jan 1927
Hart	25 May - 4 Aug 1927
	11 Oct - 17 Oct 1927
Henderson	2 May - 2 Jun 1927
	23 Jun - 29 Jun 1927
Heron	23 Apr - 7 May 1931
	18 Oct - 22 Oct 1931
	23 Sep - 6 Oct 1932
Houston	15 Apr - 8 Jun 1931
	22 Aug - 5 Sep 1931
	24 Sep - 16 Nov 1931
	3 Feb - 5 May 1932
	31 May - 7 Jun 1932
	24 Sep 1932
	27 Sep - 12 Oct 1932
	14 Oct - 10 Nov 1932
Hulbert	20 Oct - 28 Oct 1926
	24 Feb - 11 May 1927
	27 Jun - 23 Aug 1927
Huron	20 Sep - 6 Nov 1926
Isabel	3 Sep - 1926 - 21 Oct 1927
	5 Apr - 5 Jun 1931
	21 Aug - 20 Sep 1931
	23 Sep - 25 Sep 1931
	27 Sep - 16 Nov 1931
	6 Feb - 25 Feb 1932
	3 May - 7 Jun 1932
	20 Sep - 24 Sep 1932
	27 Sep - 1 Oct 1932
	3 Oct - 8 Oct 1932
	10 Oct - 10 Nov 1932
Jason	23 Apr - 7 May 1931
	16 Sep - 28 Sep 1931
Jones, Paul	20 Oct - 28 Oct 1926
	11 Mar - 1 Jun 1927
	7 Sep - 15 Sep 1927
	14 Apr - 30 Jun 1930
	22 Apr - 3 May 1931
	19 Jun - 3 Jul 1931
	19 Oct - 2 Nov 1931
	2 Feb - 22 Mar 1932
	24 May - 23 May 1932
	13 Aug - 14 Aug 1932

	13 Oct - 27 Oct 1932
Luson	1 Mar 1930 - 31 Dec 1932
MacLeish	7 Jan - 10 Mar 1927
	20 Apr - 19 Jun 1927
	21 Aug - 22 Aug 1927
	29 Jan - 22 Apr 1931
	28 Aug - 2 Nov 1931
Marblehead	3 Apr - 10 Jun 1927
	9 Aug - 27 Aug 1927
	6 Sep - 18 Oct 1927
McCormick	7 Jan - 2 Mar 1927
	18 Apr - 19 Jun 1927
	21 Aug - 21 Oct 1927
	1 Feb - 28 Feb 1930
	13 Apr - 20 Apr 1931
Monocacy	3 Sep - 21 Oct 1927
	1 Jul - 13 Feb 1931
	23 Apr 1931 - 31 Dec 1932
Noa	31 Jan - 2 Feb 1927
	24 Feb - 1 Jun 1927
	4 Jul - 27 Aug 1927
Oahu	1 May 1930 - 31 Dec 1932
Palos	3 Sep 1926 - 21 Oct 1927
	1 Jul 1930 - 13 Feb 1931
	23 Apr 1931 - 31 Dec 1932
Panay	1 Mar 1930 - 31 Dec 1932
Parrett	7 Jan - 20 Jan 1927
	22 Feb - 2 Mar 1927
	18 Apr - 9 Jun 1927
	13 Jun - 28 Jun 1927
	21 Aug - 21 Oct 1927
	16 Jul - 22 Aug 1930
	1 Feb - 11 May 1931
	25 Aug - 2 Sep 1931
	2 Feb - 6 Feb 1932
	8 Feb - 2 May 1932
	6 May - 9 May 1932
	13 May - 16 May 1932
	19 May - 23 May 1932
	5 Aug - 6 Aug 1932
	5 Oct 25 Oct 1932
Peary	15 Sep - 18 Jan 1927
	28 Mar - 2 Jul 1927
	13 Jul - 22 Jul 1927
	15 Oct - 21 Oct 1927
	20 Sep - 28 Nov 1930
	4 Jun - 15 Jul 1931
	19 Oct - 11 Dec 1931
	4 Feb - 10 Mar 1932
	4 Oct - 25 Oct 1932
Pecos	16 Jul - 24 Jul 1931
	29 Aug - 30 Aug 1931
Penguin	3 Sep 1926 - 21 Oct 1927
Pigeon	3 Sep 1926 - 21 Oct 1927
	16 May - 28 May 1931
	22 Jun - 23 Jun 1931
	6 Jun - 13 Jun 1932
Pillsbury	11 Sep 1926 - 16 Jan 1927
	28 Mar - 1 Apr 1927
	6 May - 19 Jul 1927
	15 Oct - 21 Oct 1927
	1 Mar - 14 Apr 1930
	2 Jun - 3 Jun 1931
	19 Oct - 21 Oct 1931
	16 May - 23 May 1932
	5 Oct - 25 Oct 1932
Pittsburgh	13 Jan - 30 Jun 1927
	24 Aug - 21 Oct 1927
Pope	3 Sep - 20 Sep 1926
	3 Oct 1926 - 17 Mar 1927
	3 May - 16 Jul 1927
	15 Oct - 21 Oct 1927
	1 Mar - 14 Apr 1930
	1 May - 8 May 1931
	17 May - 25 May 1931
	14 Jul - 15 Jul 1931
	19 Oct - 17 Oec 1931
	5 Feb - 9 Mar 1932
	6 May - 23 May 1932
	4 Oct - 8 Oct 1932
Preble	20 Oct - 28 Oct 1926
	24 Feb - 30 May 1927
	26 Jun - 4 Aug 1927
Preston, William B.	20 Oct - 28 Oct 1926
	2 Mar - 29 Mar 1927
	29 May - 1 Jun 1927
	26 Jun - 27 Aug 1927
Pruitt	20 Oct - 28 Oct 1926
	2 Mar - 2 Jun 1927
	27 Jun - 28 Jun 1927
	12 Aug - 15 Aug 1927
Richmond	3 Apr - 2 Jun 1927
	22 Jun - 29 Jul 1927
	3 Aug - 19 Sep 1927
Rizal	26 Oct 1926 - 9 Jan 1927
	5 Jun - 19 Aug 1927
	11 Oct - 17 Oct 1927
	18 Sep - 20 Oct 1930
Rochester	29 Apr - 31 Dec 1932
S-30	25 May - 2 Jun 1931
S-31	25 May - 2 Jun 1931
	22 Jun - 30 Jun 1931
	12 Aug - 27 Aug 1931
S-34	25 May - 2 Jun 1931
S-35	25 May - 2 Jun 1931
S-36	15 May - 28 May 1931
	8 May - 16 May 1932
S-37	15 May - 28 May 1931
	8 May - 16 May 1932
S-38	15 May - 28 May 1931
	10 Oct - 16 Oct 1931
	28 May - 2 Jun 1932
S-39	15 May - 28 May 1931
	8 May - 16 May 1932
	23 Sep - 3 Oct 1932
S-40	15 May - 28 May 1931
	6 Jun - 13 Jun 1932
S-41	15 May - 28 May 1931
	8 May - 16 May 1932
Sacramento	1 Nov 1926 - 20 Apr 1927
	28 Aug - 26 Sep 1927

	13 Apr - 2 May 1932
	5 May - 11 Jun 1932
	2 Sep - 19 Sep 1932
Sicard	20 Oct - 26 Oct 1926
	2 Mar - 2 May 1927
	8 Jun - 10 Jun 1927
	4 Jul - 22 Aug 1927
Simpson	7 Jan - 3 Mar 1927
	18 Apr - 20 Jun 1927
	21 Aug - 21 Sep 1927
	16 Jul - 1 Oct 1930
	11 Dec 1931 - 18 Feb 1932
Stewert	3 Sep - 18 Sep 1926
	31 Jan - 2 Feb 1927
	11 Mar - 13 Jul 1927
	20 Sep - 21 Oct 1927
	17 Sep - 28 Nov 1930
	2 May - 15 Jul 1931
	15 Oct 1931
	26 Feb - 2 May 1932
	6 May - 9 May 1932
	13 May - 16 May 1932
	19 May - 23 May 1932
	11 Oct - 25 Oct 1932
Thompson, Smith	1 Jul - 16 Jul 1930
	20 Nov 1930 - 4 Feb 1931
	12 Jul - 13 Jul 1931
	15 Jul - 31 Jul 1931
	29 Aug - 1 Sep 1931
	19 Oct - 2 Nov 1931
	5 Feb - 29 Mar 1932
	4 Oct - 25 Oct 1932
Tracy	14 Apr - 24 May 1930
Truxtun	15 Sep - 17 Mar 1927
	16 May - 22 Jul 1927
	15 Oct - 21 Oct 1927
	1 Mar - 14 Apr 1930
	21 Jan - 1 Apr 1932
Tulsa	15 Oct - 7 Nov 1932
	10 Nov - 31 Dec 1932
Tutuila	1 Mar 1930 - 31 Dec 1932
Villalobos	3 Sep 1926 - 21 Oct 1927
Whipple	14 Apr - 19 May 1930
	28 Nov 1930 - 4 Feb 1931
	19 Jul - 23 Feb 1931
	19 Oct - 2 Nov 1931
	5 Feb - 26 Feb 1932
	27 Feb - 23 Apr 1932
	4 Oct - 25 Oct 1932

Personnel from the landing parties of the following ships

Vessel	Dates of Service
Chaumont	23 Dec 1926 - 1 Jan 1927
	24 Feb - 5 May 1927
	20 May - 30 May 1927
	13 Jun - 25 Jun 1927
	2 Jul - 7 Jul 1927
	16 Oct - 20 Oct 1927
Pecos	9 Feb - 23 Apr 1927
	18 Jun - 21 Jun 1927
	16 Jul - 18 Jul 1927

Also Qualifying:

6th Regt. USMC aboard the USS Henderson	2 May - 2 Jun 1927
Expeditionary Detachment, Aircraft Squadrons, and 3rd Bd. USCM aboard the USS Henderson	23 Jun - 27 Jun 1927

China Service Medal - 1st Period

Vessel	Dates of Service
Alden	7 Jul - 24 Jul 1937
	3 Aug - 18 Nov 1937
	18 Jul - 37 Sep 1938
	30 Jan - 27 Feb 1939
Asheville	6 Jun - 8 Aug 1938
	7 Jul - 28 Dec 1938
	6 Apr - 17 Jul 1939
Augusta	7 Jul - 24 Jul 1937
	3 Aug 1937 - 6 Jan 1938
	20 Jan - 22 Jan 1938
	8 Apr - 28 Dec 1938
	22 Apr - 7 Sep 1939
Barker	Jul - 24 Jul 1937
	3 Aug - 18 Nov 1937
	9 Feb - 28 Feb 1938
	18 Jul - 27 Sep 1938
	26 Feb - 3 Apr 1939
	6 Jun - 14 Aug 1939
Bittern	7 Jul - 4 Oct 1937
	6 May - 15 May 1939
	8 Jun - 7 Sep 1939
Blackhawk	7 Jul - 18 Nov 1937
	4 Apr - 6 Apr 1938
	18 Jul - 28 Sep 1938
	5 Jun - 7 Sep 1939
Bridge	8 Nov 1937 - 9 Mar 1938
Bulmer	7 Jul - 10 Nov 1937
	26 Nov - 18 Dec 1937
	8 Apr - 6 Aug 1938
	3 Apr - 4 Sep 1939
Canopus	7 Jul - 21 Sep 1937
	3 Oct 6 Oct 1937
	19 Oct - 25 Oct 1937
	13 Oct - 29 Oct 1938
	11 May - 12 Aug 1939

Chaumont	7 Jul - 19 Jul 1937
	18 Sep - 4 Oct 1937
	17 Oct - 23 Oct 1937
	6 Nov - 13 Nov 1937
	11 Feb - 18 Feb 1938
	29 Oct - 19 Nov 1938
	15 May - 6 Jun 1939
	22 Aug - 7 Sep 1939
Edsall	7 Jul - 28 Oct 1937
	10 Nov - 18 Dec 1937
	24 Mar - 12 Jul 1938
	3 Apr - 4 Sep 1939
Edwards, John D.	7 Jul - 18 Nov 1937
	18 Jul - 27 Sep 1938
	30 Jan - 26 Feb 1939
	6 Jun - 7 Sep 1939
Finch	7 Jul - 4 Dec 1937
	10 Jul - 6 Sep 1938
	6 May - 15 May 1939
	18 Jun - 7 Sep 1939
Ford, John D.	7 Jul - 19 Nov 1937
	15 Jan - 3 Feb 1938]
	17 Feb - 24 Feb 1938
	15 Jul - 15 Sep 1938
	2 Nov - 15 Dec 1938
	5 Jun - 7 Sep 1939
Gold Star	26 Aug - 7 Sep 1937
	22 Sep - 28 Sep 1937
	27 Nov - 1 Dec 1937
	11 Feb - 14 Feb 1938
	26 Sep - 11 Oct 1938
	25 Nov - 29 Nov 1938
	10 Feb - 27 Feb 1939
	5 May - 19 May 1939
	18 Jul - 1 Aug 1939
Guam	7 Jul 1937 - 7 Sep 1939
Henderson	24 Oct - 14 Nov 1937
	2 May - 23 May 1938
	30 Dec 1938 - 20 Jan 1939
	2 Jul - 25 Jul 1939
Heron	7 Jul - 4 Oct 1937
	15 Sep - 22 Sep 1938
	27 Jul - 3 Aug 1939
Isabel	7 Jul - 29 Oct 1937
	5 Jan 1938 - 7 Sep 1938
Jones, Paul	7 Jul - 24 Jul 1937
	26 Sep - 19 Nov 1937
	12 Aug - 27 Sep 1938
	5 Jun - 7 Sep 1939
Luson	7 Jul 1937 - 7 Sep 1939
Marblehead	19 Sep 1937 - 16 Feb 1938
	14 May - 7 Aug 1938
Mindanao	7 Jul 1937 - 7 Sep 1939
Monocacy	7 Jul 1937 - 31 Jan 1939
Oahu	7 Jul 1937 - 7 Sep 1939
Pennay	7 Jul - 12 Dec 1937
Parrott	7 Jul - 18 Dec 1937
	12 Mar - 25 Mar 1938
	14 Sep - 28 Sep 1938
	3 Jun - 4 Sep 1939
Peary	16 Aug - 17 Nov 1937
	15 Dec - 24 Dec 1937
	6 Jan - 25 Jan 1938
	8 Feb - 27 Feb 1938
	15 Jul - 14 Oct 1938
	5 Jun - 7 Sep 1939
Pecos	19 Aug - 4 Oct 1937
	16 Jul - 31 Jul 1938
	23 Aug - 28 Sep 1938
	31 May - 7 Sep 1939
Pigeon	7 Jul - 19 Sep 1937
	13 Oct - 29 Oct 1938
	2 May - 11 May 1939
	30 Jul - 7 Sep 1939
Pillsbury	7 Jul - 17 Nov 1937
	31 Dec 1937 - 6 Jan 1938
	20 Jan - 2 Feb 1938
	16 Jul - 11 Nov 1938
	5 Jun - 7 Sep 1939
Pope	7 Jul - 17 Nov 1937
	15 Dec 1937 - 17 Jan 1938
	31 Jan - 1 Mar 1938
	15 Jul - 20 Sep 1938
	15 Nov - 16 Dec 1938
	5 Jun - 7 Sep 1939
Ramapo	1 Aug - 15 Aug 1937
	21 Oct - 25 Oct 1947
	28 Mar - 5 Apr 1939
	3 Jul - 14 Jul 1939
S-36	7 Jul - 19 Sep 1937
	13 Oct - 29 Oct 1938
	25 Mar - 7 Sep 1939
S-37	7 Jul - 25 Aug 1937
	13 Oct - 29 Oct 1938
	19 Jul - 7 Sep 1939
S-38	7 Jul - 21 Jul 1937
	13 Oct - 29 Oct 1938
	2 May - 7 Sep 1939
S-39	7 Jul - 21 Jul 1938
	13 Oct - 29 Oct 1938
	4 Jul - 7 Sep 1939
S-40	7 Jul - 21 Jul 1937
	13 Oct - 29 Oct 1938
	25 May - 7 Sep 1939
S-41	7 Jul - 25 Aug 1937
	13 Oct - 29 Oct 1938
	4 Jul - 7 Sep 1939
Sacramento	7 Jul - 26 Sep 1937
	5 Oct 1937 - 27 Mar 1938
	3 Jun 1938 - 2 Jan 1939
Stewart	7 Jul - 17 Oct 1937
	30 Oct - 18 Dec 1937
	24 Feb - 7 Apr 1938
	3 Jun - 4 Sep 1939
Trinity	28 Aug - 7 Sep 1939
Tulsa	7 Jul 1937 - 13 Jul 1938
	17 Sep 1938 - 4 Feb 1939
	6 Apr - 7 Sep 1939
Tutuila	7 Jul 1937 - 7 Sep 1939
Whipple	7 Jul - 24 Jul 1937
	3 Aug - 18 Nov 1937
	18 Jul - 27 Sep 1938

26 Feb - 3 Apr 1939
6 Jun - 7 Sep 1939

The "USS Parrott" in Chinese waters.

Appendix B

Army and Navy Clasps authorized for the World War I Victory Medal.

Army

Clasp Eligibility Dates

Cambrai, 12 May 1917 - 4 Dec 1918
Somme Defensive, 21 Mar 1918 - 6 Apr 1918
Lys, 9 Apr 1918 - 27 Apr 1918
Asine, 27 May 1918 - 5 June 1918 (see note)
Montdidier-Noyon, 9 - 13 June 1918
Champaigne-Marne, 15 - 18 July 1918
Aisne-Marne, 18 July 1918 - 6 Aug 1918 (see note)
Somme Offensive, 8 Aug 1918 - 11 Nov 1918
Oise-Aisne, 18 Aug 1918 - 11 Nov 1918
Ypres-Lys, 19 Aug 1918 - 11 Nov 1918 (see note)
St. Mihiel, 12 - 16 Sep 1918 (see note)
Meuse-Argonne, 26 Sep 1918 - 11 Nov 1918 (see note)
Vittorio-Veneto, 24 Oct 1918 - 4 Nov 1918
Defensive Sector (see note)
England, 6 Apr 1917 - 11 Nov 1918 (see note)
France, 6 Apr 1917 - 11 Nov 1918 (see note)
Italy, 6 Apr 1917 - 11 Nov 1918 (see note)
Russia, 11 Nov 1918 - 5 Aug 1919 (see note)
Siberia, 12 Nov 1918 - 1 Apr 1920 (see note)
Note: Navy and Marine Corps personnel also eligible for this Army style clasp.

Navy

Naval personnel serving on board specific ships during dates specified in N.D. G.O. No. 482 were eligible for the following Service Clasps. In many cases naval personnel could have been eligible for more than one clasp, however regulations limited award of Service Clasps to one per service member.

Clasp Eligibility Dates

Overseas - On shore in Europe 6 Apr 1916 - 11 Nov 1918
Armed Guard - Regularly attached to vessel for one voyage across the North Atlantic from 6 Apr 1916 - 11 Nov 1918.
Atlantic Fleet - For such duty from 25 May 1918 - 11 Nov 1918
Aviation- For such duty east of the 37th meridian and north of the Equator from 6 Apr 1918 - 11 Nov 1918 or on the high seas of the Atlantic Ocean between 25 May 1918 and 11 Nov 1918.
Destroyer - Same as for Aviation
Escort - Same as for Armed Guard
Grand Fleet - Regularly attached to any vessel of the Grand Fleet between 9 Dec 1917 and 11 Nov 1918.
Mine Laying - For such duty from 26 May 1918 to 11 Nov 1918
Mine Sweeping - For such duty from 6 Apr 1917 until operations were completed.

Mobile Base - For duty on tenders and repair vessels east of the 37th meridian and north of the Equator from 6 April 1917 to 11 Nov 1918.
Naval Battery - For such duty from 10 July 1918 to 11 Nov 1918
Subchaser - Same as for Patrol
Salvage - For such duty 6 April 1917 to 11 Nov 1918.
Transport - Same as for Armed Guard.

Submarine - Same as for Aviation.
Patrol - Same as for Armed Guard.
West Indies - For service in Haiti, Santo Domingo, Cuba or the Vergin Islands between 6 Apr 1917 and 11 Nov 1918.
White Sea - For service on any vessel which made a Russian port between 6 April 1917 and 11 Nov 1918 or any combat ship operating in the White Sea not less than 10 days between 12 Nov 1918 and 31 July 1919.
Asiatic - For service on any vessel which made a Siberian port between 6 April 1917 and 11 Nov 1918 or on any combat vessel in Siberian waters not less than 10 days from 12 Nov 1918 to 30 March 1920.

Appendix C

The list below contains an alphabetical list of operations which qualify for the Marine Corps Expeditionary Medal:

Abyssinia, 21 Nov. 1903 - 18 Jan. 1904
Alexandria, Egypt, 10 June - 29 Aug. 1882
American Legation Guard, Seoul, Korea, 5 Jan. 1904 - 11 Nov. 1905
Apia, Samoa, 13 Nov. 1888 - 20 March 1889
Apia, Samoa, March - May 1899
Armed Guards, SS Mei Lu and SS I'Ping, China, 22 April - 15 May 1928
Beirut, Syria, 8-13 Sept. and 10-17 Oct. 1903
Bluefields, Nicaragua, 6 July - 6 Aug. 1894
Bluefields, Nicaragua, 7 May - 4 June 1926
Bluefields, Nicaragua, 20 Dec. 1909 - 15 March 1910
Bluefields, Nicaragua, 24-28 Feb. 1899
Boca Del Toro, Colombia, 17-19 April 1902
Boca del Toro, Colombia, 8-9 March 1895
Buenos Aires, Argentina, 30 July 1890
Canton, China, December 1927
Chefoo, China, 1-18 March 1895
Corinto, Nicaragua, 7-8 Feb. 1898
Corinto, Nicaragua, 30 May 1910 - 4 Sept. 1910
Cuba, 3 Jan. 1961 - 23 Oct. 1962
Dominican Republic and Haiti, 15 Aug. - 17 Dec. 1914
Dominican Republic, 5 Dec. 1916 - 5 April 1917 and 12 Nov. 1918 - September 1924
Embassy Guard, St. Petersburg, Russia, December 1905 - 1 Jan. 1907
Guantanamo Bay, Cuba, 28 May - 5 Aug. 1912
Haiti, 4 Dec. 1929 - 5 Aug. 1931
Haiti, 7 Dec. 1915 - 5 April 1917
Haiti, 12 Nov. 1918 - 31 March 1919
Haiti, 16 June 1920 - 24 Nov. 1924
Honolulu, Hawaii, 12-20 Feb. 1874
Honolulu, Hawaii, 16 Jan. - 1 April 1893
Honolulu, Hawaii, 30-31 July 1889
Iran, Yemen, Indian Ocean Area, 8 Dec. 1978 - 6 June 1979, and 21 Nov. 1979 - 1 Oct. 1981
Ismir, Turkey, 28 June - 3 July 1921
Isthmus of Panama, 18-22 Sept. 1902
La Ceiva, Puerto Cortez, Tela, and Tegucigalpa, Honduras, 28 Feb. - 13 March 1924, and 18 March - 30 April 1924
Laguna and Choloma, Honduras, 28 April - 8 June 1907
Lebanon, 20 August 1982 - 31 May 1983
Legation Guard, Managua, Nicaragua, 15 Nov. 1912 - 5 April 1917 and 12 Nov. 1918 - 3 Aug. 1925
Legation Guard, Peking, China, 9 Sept. 1924 - 1 March 1925
Legation Guard, Peking, China, 10 Oct. 1911 - 19 Jan. 1914
Libya, 20 Jan. 1986 - 27 June 1986
Navassa Island, Haiti, 2 May - 20 June 1891
Panama and Colon, 23 Sept. - 18 Nov. 1902
Peking and Shanghai, China, 10 Oct. 1911 - 19 Jan. 1914
Peking and Tientsin, China, 4 Nov. 1898 - 15 March 1899
Persian Gulf, 1 Feb. 1987 - to be announced
Port-au-Prince, Gonaives, and Cape Haitien, Haiti, 26 Jan. - 7 Nov. 1914
Republic of Panama, 4 Nov. 1903 - 26 Feb. 1904
Russian Island, Siberia, 31 March 1920 - 19 Nov. 1922
San Juan del Sur, Nicaragua, 7-8 Feb. 1898
Santo Domingo City and San Pedro de Marcoris, Dominican Republic, January - 27 Feb. 1904
Santo Domingo City, Dominican Republic, 1-19 April 1903
Seoul, Korea, 19-30 June 1888
Seoul, Korea, 24 July 1894 - 3 April 1896
Shanghai, China, 9-24 Sept. 1934
Shanghai, China, 15 Jan. - 31 Aug. 1925
Smvrna, Turkey, 7 Sept. - 18 Oct. 1922
State of Panama, 11 Nov. - 4 Dec. 1901
State of Panama, 31 March - 22 May 1885
Thailand, 16 May - 10 August 1962
Tientsin, China, is Dec. 1894 - 16 May 1895
Trujillo, La Ceiba, and Puerto Cortex, Honduras, 21 March - 16 April 1903.
Valparaiso, Chile, 28-30 Aug. 1891
Wake Island, 7-22 Dec. 1941
Wuchow, China, 3 April 1926

Note: The bars illustrated at left are BB&B produced, which are quite uncommon in comparison to other existing bars.

Appendix C continued:

The list below contains a chronological list of operations which qualify for the Marine Corps Expeditionary Medal:

1. Honolulu, Hawaii, 12-20 Feb. 1874
2. Alexandria, Egypt, 10 June - 29 Aug. 1882
3. State of Panama, 31 March - 22 May 1885
4. Seoul, Korea, 19-30 June 1888
5. Apia, Samoa, 13 Nov. 1888 - 20 March 1889
6. Honolulu, Hawaii, 30-31 July 1889
7. Buenos Aires, Argentina, 30 July 1890
8. Navassa Island, Haiti, 2 May - 20 June 1891
9. Valparaiso, Chile, 28-30 Aug. 1891
10. Honolulu, Hawaii, 16 Jan. - 1 April 1893
11. Bluefields, Nicaragua, 6 July - 6 Aug. 1894
12. Seoul, Korea, 24 July 1894 - 3 April 1896
13. Tientsin, China, is Dec. 1894 - 16 May 1895
14. Chefoo, China, 1-18 March 1895
15. Boca del Toro, Colombia, 8-9 March 1895
16. Corinto, Nicaragua, 7-8 Feb. 1898
17. San Juan del Sur, Nicaragua, 7-8 Feb. 1898
18. Peking and Tientsin, China, 4 Nov. 1898 - 15 March 1899
19. Bluefields, Nicaragua, 24-28 Feb. 1899
20. Apia, Samoa, March - May 1899
21. State of Panama, 11 Nov. - 4 Dec. 1901
22. Boca Del Toro, Colombia, 17-19 April 1902
23. Isthmus of Panama, 18-22 Sept. 1902
24. Panama and Colon, 23 Sept. - 18 Nov. 1902
25. Trujillo, La Ceiba, and Puerto Cortex, Honduras, 21 March - 16 April 1903.
26. Santo Domingo City, Dominican Republic, 1-19 April 1903
27. Beirut, Syria, 8-13 Sept. and 10-17 Oct. 1903
28. Republic of Panama, 4 Nov. 1903 - 26 Feb. 1904
29. Abyssinia, 21 Nov. 1903 - 18 Jan. 1904
30. Santo Domingo City and San Pedro de Marcoris, Dominican Republic, January - 27 Feb. 1904
31. American Legation Guard, Seoul, Korea, 5 Jan. 1904 - 11 Nov. 1905
32. Embassy Guard, St. Petersburg, Russia, December 1905 - 1 Jan. 1907
33. Laguna and Choloma, Honduras, 28 April - 8 June 1907
34. Corinto, Nicaragua, 30 May 1910 - 4 Sept. 1910
35. Bluefields, Nicaragua, 20 Dec. 1909 - 15 March 1910
36. Legation Guard, Peking, China, 10 Oct. 1911 - 19 Jan. 1914
37. Peking and Shanghai, China, 10 Oct. 1911 - 19 Jan. 1914
38. Guantanamo Bay, Cuba, 28 May - 5 Aug. 1912
39. Legation Guard, Managua, Nicaragua, 15 Nov. 1912 - 5 April 1917 and 12 Nov. 1918 - 3 Aug. 1925
40. Port-au-Prince, Gonaives, and Cape Haitien, Haiti, 26 Jan. - 7 Nov. 1914
41. Dominican Republic and Haiti, 15 Aug. - 17 Dec. 1914
42. Haiti, 7 Dec. 1915 - 5 April 1917
43. Dominican Republic, 5 Dec. 1916 - 5 April 1917 and 12 Nov. 1918 - September 1924
44. Haiti, 12 Nov. 1918 - 31 March 1919
45. Russian Island, Siberia, 31 March 1920 - 19 Nov. 1922
46. Ismir, Turkey, 28 June - 3 July 1921
48. Haiti, 16 June 1920 - 24 Nov. 1924
49. Smvrna, Turkey, 7 Sept. - 18 Oct. 1922
50. La Ceiva, Puerto Cortez, Tela, and Tegucigalpa, Honduras, 28 Feb. - 13 March 1924, and 18 March - 30 April 1924
51. Legation Guard, Peking, China, 9 Sept. 1924 - 1 March 1925
52. Shanghai, China, 15 Jan. - 31 Aug. 1925
53. Wuchow, China, 3 April 1926
54. Bluefields, Nicaragua, 7 May - 4 June 1926
55. Canton, China, December 1927
56. Armed Guards, SS Mei Lu and SS I'Ping, China, 22 April - 15 May 1928
57. Haiti, 4 Dec. 1929 - 5 Aug. 1931
56. Shanghai, China, 9-24 Sept. 1934
57. Wake Island, 7-22 Dec. 1941
58. Cuba, 3 Jan. 1961 - 23 Oct. 1962
59. Thailand, 16 May - 10 August 1962
60. Iran, Yemen, Indian Ocean Area, 8 Dec. 1978 - 6 June 1979, and 21 Nov. 1979 - 1 Oct. 1981
61. Lebanon, 20 August 1982 - 31 May 1983
62. Libya, 20 Jan. 1986 - 27 June 1986
63. Persian Gulf, 1 Feb. 1987 - to be announced

Appendix D

US Army campaign designations for World War II campaign medals used to determine eligibility for service stars.

American Campaign Medal

Campaign and Inclusive dates

Antisubmarine 7 Dec 1941 - 2 Sept 1945
Ground Combat 7 Dec 1941 - 2 Sept 1945
Air Combat 7 Dec 1941 - 2 Sept 1945

Asiatic - Pacific Campaign Medal

Campaign and Inclusive dates

Philippine Islands, 7 Dec 1941 - 10 May 1942
Burma, 1942, 7 Dec 1941 - 26 May 1942
Central Pacific, 7 Dec 1941 - 6 Dec 1943
East Indies, 1 Jan 1942 - 22 July 1942
India - Burma, 2 April 1942 - 28 Jan 1945
Air Offensive, Japan ,17 April 1942 - 2 Sep 1945
Aleutian Islands, 3 June 1942 - 24 Aug 1943
China Defensive, 4 July 1942 - 4 May 1945
Papua, 23 July 1942 - 23 Jan 1943
Guadalcanal, 7 Aug 1942 - 21 Feb 1943
New Guinea, 24 Jan 1943 - 31 Dec 1944
Northern Solomons, 22 Feb 1943 - 21 Nov 1944
Eastern Mandates (Air),
 7 Dec 1943 - 16 April 1944
Eastern Mandates (Ground),
 31 Jan 1944 - 14 June 1944
Bismark Archipelago, 15 Dec 1943 - 27 Nov 1944
Western Pacific (Air), 17 April 1944 - 2 Sep 1945
Western Pacific (Ground),
 15 June 1944 - 2 Sep 1945
Leyte, 17 Oct 1944 - 1 July 1945
Luzon, 15 Dec 1944 - 4 July 1945
Central Burma, 29 Jan 1945 - 15 July 1945
Southern Philippines, 27 Feb 1945 - 4 July 1945
Ryukyus, 26 Mar 1945 - 2 July 1945
China Offensive, 5 May 1945 - 2 Sep 1945
Antisubmarine, 7 Dec 1941 - 2 Sep 1945
Ground Combat, 7 Dec 1941 - 2 Sep 1945
Air Combat, 7 Dec 1941 - 2 Sep 1945

European - African - Middle Eastern Campaign Medal

Campaign and Inclusive dates

Egypt - Libya, 11 June 1942 - 12 Feb 1943
Air Offensive, Europe,4 July 1942 - 5 June 1944
Algeria - French Morocco,
 8 Nov 1942 - 11 Nov 1942
Tunisa (Air), 12 Nov 1942 - 13 May 1943
Tunisa (Ground), 17 Nov 1942 - 13 May 1943
Sicily (Air), 14 May 1943 - 17 Aug 1943
Sicily (Ground), 9 July 1943 - 17 Aug 1943
Naples - Foggia (Air), 18 Aug 1943 - 21 Jan 1944
Naples - Foggia (Ground),
 9 Sep 1943 - 21 Jan 1944
Anzio, 22 Jan 1944 - 9 Sep 1944
Rome - Arno, 22 Jan 1944 - 9 Sep 1944
Normandy, 6 June 1944 - 24 July 1944
Northern France, 25 July 1944 - 14 Sep 1944
Southern France, 15 Aug 1944 - 14 Sep 1944
Northern Apennines, 10 Sep 1944 - 4 April 1944
Rhineland, 15 Sep 1944 - 21 Mar 1945
Ardennes - Alsace, 16 Dec 1944 - 25 Jan 1945
Central Europe, 22 Mar 1945 - 11 May 1945
Po Valley, 5 April 1945 - 8 May 1945
Antisubmarine, 7 Dec 1941 - 2 Sep 1945
Ground Combat, 7 Dec 1941 - 2 Sep 1945
Air Combat, 7 Dec 1941 - 2 Sep 1945

Appendix E

US Navy, Marine Corps and Coast Guard campaign designations for the World War II campaign medals service stars.

European - African - Middle Eastern Campaign Medal

Campaign and Inclusive dates

North African Occupation: 8 Nov 1942 - 9 Jul 1943

one star only for any of the following

Algeria-Morocco Landings, 8 - Il Nov 1942
Action off Casablanca, 8 Nov 1942
Tunisian Operations, 8 Nov 1942 - 9 Jul 1943
Sicilian Occupation, 9 - 15 Jul 1943, and 28 Jul - 17 Aug 1943
Salerno Landings, 9 - 21 Sep 1943
West Coast of Italy operations 1944: 22 Jan - 17 Jun 1944

one star only for any of the following

Anzio-Nettuno advanced landings, 22 Jan - 1 Mar 1944
Bombardments Formia-Anzio area, 12 May - 4 Jun 1944
Elba and Pianosa landings, 17 Jun 1944
Invasion of Normandy (including the 6 - 25 Jun 1944 bombardment of Cherbourg)

Northeast Greenland operation: 10 Jul - 17 Nov 1944

Invasion of Southern France, 15 Aug - 25 Sep 1944
Reinforcement of Malta, 14 - 21 Apr, 3 - 16 May 42

Escort, antisubmarine, armed guard and special operations:

one star only for each of the following

Russian convoy operations, 16 Dec 41 - 27 Feb 1943
Convoy ON-166. 20 - 25 Feb 1943
Convoy UC-1, 22 - 24 Feb 1943
Convoy SC-121, 3 - 10 Mar 1943
Convoy UGS-6, 12 - 18 Mar 1943
Convoy HX-233 16 - 18 Apr 1943
Task Group 21.12, 20 Apr - 20 Jun 1943
Task Group 21.11, 13 Jun - 4 Aug 1943
Task Group 21.12, 27 Jun - 31 Jul 1943
Convoy MKS-21, 13 Aug 1943
Task Group 21.14, 25 Sep - 9 Nov 1943
Convoy KMF-25A, 6 Nov 1943
Task Group 21.13, 11 Nov - 29 Dec 1943
Task Group 21.14, 2 Dec 1943 - 1 Jan 1944
Task Group 21.12, 7 Mar - 26 Apr 1944
Task Group 21.16, 16 Feb - 31 Mar 1944
Convoy UGS-36, 1 Apr 1944
Convoy UGS-37, 11 -12 Apr 1944
Convoy UGS-38, 20, Apr 1944
Task Group 21.11, 22 Apr - 29 May 1944
Convoy UGS-40, 11 May 1944
Task Group 22.3, 13 May - 19 Jun 1944
Norway Raid, 2 - 6 Oct 1943
Task Group 22.5, 3 Jun - 22 July 1944
Convoy HX-229, 16 - 18 Mar 1943
Minesweeping operations in the Bay of Cagliri, Oct - Nov 1943
Convoy KMS-31, 11 Nov 1943
U.S.S. Buck (DD 420), 8 - 9 Oct 1943
U.S.S. Swerve (AM 121), 9 Jul 1944

Asiatic - Pacific Campaign Medal

Campaign and Inclusive Dates

Pearl Harbor - Midway, 7 December 1941
Wake Island, 8 - 23 December 1941
Philippine Island Operation, 8 Dec 1941 - 6 May 1942
Netherlands East Indies Engagements:

one star only for any of the following

Makassar Strait, 23 - 24 Jan 1942
Badoeng Strait, 19 - 20 Feb 1942
Java Sea, 27 Feb 1942

Pacific Raids - 1942:

one star only for any of the following

Marshall - Gilbert Raids, 1 Feb 1942
Air Action off Bougainville, 20 Feb 1942
Wake Island Raid, 24 Feb 1942
Marcus Island Raid, 4 Mar 1942
Salamaua - Lae Raid, 10 March 1942
Coral Sea, 4 - 8 May 1942
Midway, 3 - 6 Jun 1942
Guadalcanal - Tulagi Landings, 7 - 9 Aug 1942
Capture and Defense of Guadalcanal, 10 Aug 1942 - 8 Feb 1943
Makin Raid, 17 - 18 Aug 1942
Eastern Solomons (Stewart Island), 23 - 25 Aug 1942
Buin - Faisi - Tonolai Raid, 5 Oct 1942
Cape Esperance (Second Savo), 11 - 12 Oct 1942
Santa Cruz Islands, 26 Oct 1942
Guadalcanal (Third Savo), 12 - 15 Nov 1942
Tassafaronga (Forth Savo), 30 Nov - 1 Dec 1942

Eastern New Guinea Operation:

one star only for any of the following

Torpedo boat operations, 17 Dec 1942 - 24 Jul 1944
Lae occupation, 4 - 22 Sep 1943
Finschhafen occupation, 22 Sep 1943 - 17 Feb 1944
Saidor occupation, 2 Jan - 1 Mar 1944
Wewak-Aitape operations, 14 - 24 Jul 1944
Woodlark Island occupation, 30 Jun - 7 Dec 1942
Rennell Island, 29 - 30 Jan 1943

Consolidation of Solomon Islands:
one star only for any of the following
Consolidation of southern Solomons, 8 Feb - 20 Jun 1943
Consolidation of northern Solomons, 27 Oct 1943 - 15 Mar 1945

Aleutians Operation:
one star only for any of the following
Komandorski Islands, 26 Mar 1943
Attu Islands, 11 May - 2 Jun 1943

New Georgia Group Operation:
one star only for any of the following
New Georgia-Rendova-Vangunu Occ., 20 Jun - 16 Oct 1943
Kula Gulf Action, 5 - 6 Jul 1943
Kolombangara Action, 12 - 13 Jul 1943
Vella Gulf Action, 6 - 7 August 1943
Vella Lavella Occupation, 15 Aug - 16 Oct 1943
Action off Vella Lavella, 6 - 7 October 1943

Bismark Archipelago Operation:
one star only for any of the following
Torpedo boat operations, 25 Jun 1943 - 1 May 1944
Supporting air operations, 25 Jun 1943 - 1 May 1944
Arawe, New Britain, 26 Dec 1943 - 1 Mar 1944
Kavieng strike, 1 Jan 1944
Kavieng strike, 4 Jan 1944
Green Islands landing, 15 - 9 Feb 1944
Bombardment of Kavieng and Rabaul, 18 Feb 1944
Antishipping sweeps and bombardment of Kavieng, 21 - 25 Feb 1944
Antishipping sweeps and bombardment of Kavieng and New Ireland, 24 Feb - 1 Mar 1944
Admiralty Island landings, 29 Feb - 17 Apr 1944
Supporting operations designated by Commander 7th Fleet, 25 Jun 1943 - 1 May 1944

Pacific Raids - 1943:
one star only for any of the following
Marcus Island Raid 31 August 1943
Tarawa Island Raid 18 September 1943
Wake Island Raid 5 - 6 October 1943

Treasury - Bougainville Operation:
one star only for any of the following
Supporting air actions, 27 Oct - 15 Dec 1943
Treasury Island landings, 27 Oct - 6 Nov 1943
Choiseul Island diversion, 28 Oct - 4 Nov 1943
Occ. and Def. of Cape Torokina, 1 Nov - 15 Dec 1943
Bombardment of Buka-Bonis, 31 Oct - 1 Nov 1943
Buka-Bonis strike, 1 - 2 Nov 1943
Bombardment of Shortland area, 1 Nov 1943
Battle of Empress Augusta Bay, 8 - 9 Nov 1943
Rabaul strike, 5 Nov 1943
Action off Empress Augusta Bay, 8 -9 Nov 1943
Rabaul strike, 11 Nov 1943
Battle off Cape St. George, 24 -25 Nov 1943
Gilbert Islands operation, 13 Nov - 8 Dec 1943

Marshall Islands Operations:
one star only for any of the following
Designated air attacks, 26 Nov 1943 - 2 Mar 1944
Occupation of Kwajalein and Majuro Atolls, 29 Jan - 8 Feb 1944
Occupation of Eniwetok Atoll, 17 Feb - 2 Mar 1944
Attack on Jaluit Atoll, 17 Feb - 2 Mar 1944
Mille Atoll, 18 Mar 1944

Asiatic-Pacific Raids — 1944:
one star only for any of the following
Truk attack, 16 - 17 Feb 1944
Marianas attack, 21 - 22 Feb 1944
Palau, Yap, Ulithi, Woleai raid, 30 Mar - 1 Apr 1944
Sabang raid, 19 Apr 1944
Truk, Satawan, Ponape raid, 29 Apr - 1 May 1944
Soerabaja raid, 17 May 1944
Bombardment of Marcus Island, 9 Oct 1944

Western New Guinea Operation:
one star only for any of the following
Torpedo boat operations, 21 Apr - 15 Nov 1944
Toem-Wakde-Sarmi area operation, 17 May - 21 Jun 1944
Biak Island operation, 27 May - 21 Jun 1944
Noemfoor Island operation, 2 Jul - 23 Jul 1944
Cape Sansapor operation, 30 Jul - 31 Aug 1944
Supporting operations designated by Commander 7th Fleet, 21 Apr - 15 Nov 1944
Moretai Landings, 11 Sep 1944 - 9 Jan 1945

Marianas Operation:
one star only for any of the following
Neutralization of Japanese bases in the Bonins, Marianas, and western Pacific,

10 Jun - 27 Aug 1944
Capture and Occupation of Saipan, 11 Jun - 10 Aug 1944
First Bonins raid, 15 - 16 Jun 1944
Battle of the Philippine Sea, 19 - 20 Jun 1944
2nd Bonins raid, 24 Jun 1944
3rd Bonins raid, 3 - 4 Jul 1944
Capture and Occupation of Guam, 12 Jul - 15 Aug 1944
Palaul Yap, Ulithi raid, 25 - 27 Jul 1944
4th Bonins raid, 4 - 5 Aug 1944

Western Caroline Islands Operation:
one star only for any of the following
Raids on Volcano-Bonin Islands and Yap Island, 31 Aug - 8 Sep 1944
Capture and occupation of southern Palau Islands, 6 Sep - 14 Oct 1944
Assault on the Philippines Islands 9 -24 Sep 1944

Leyte Operation:
one star only for any of the following
Leyte landings, 10 Oct - 29 Nov 1944
Battle of Surigao Strait, 24 - 26 Oct 1943
3rd Fleet support of Okinawa attack, 10 Oct 1944
Northern Luzon and Formosa attacks 11 - 14 Oct 1944
Luzon attacks, 15, 17 - 19 Oct 1944, 13 - 14, 19 - 25 Nov 1944, 14 -16 Dec 1944
Visayas attacks, 20 - 21 Oct 1944, 11 Nov 1944
Ormoc Bay landings, 7 - 13 Dec 1944
Battle of Samar, 24 - 26 Oct 1944
Battle of Cape Engano, 24 - 26 Oct 1944
Submarine participation, 12, Dec 1944, - 1 Apr 1945

Luzon Operation:
one star only for any of the following
Mindoro landings, 12 - 18 Dec 1944
Lingayen Gulf landing, 4 - 18 Jan 1945
3rd Fleet supporting operations:
Luson attacks, 6 - 7 Jan 1945
Formosa attacks, 3 - 5,9,15,21 Jan 1945
China Coast attacks, 12,16 Jan 1945
Nansei attacks, 22 Jan 1945

Iwo Jima Operation:
one star only for any of the following
Assault and occ. of Iwo Jima, 11 Nov 1944 - 24 Jan 1945
5th Fleet raids against Honshu and Nansei Shoto, 15 Feb - 16 Mar 1945
Bombardments of Iwo Jima, 11 Nov 1944 - 24 Jan 1945

Okinawa Gunto Operation:
one star only for any of the following
Assault and occupation of Okinawa Gunto, 24 Mar - 30 Jun 1945
5th and 3rd Fleet raids in support of Okinawa Gunto opperation, 15 Feb - 16 Mar 1945
3rd Fleet operations against Japan, 10 Jul - 15 Aug 1945

Kurile Islands Operation:
one star only for any of the following
Massashi-Wan-Kurabu-Zaki, 4 Feb 1944
Matsuwa, 13 Jun 1944
Kurabu Zaki, 26 Jun 1944
Matsuwa, 21 Nov 1944
Suribachi Wan 5 Jan 1945
Kurbu Zaki, 18 Feb 1945
Matsuwa, 16 Mar 1945
Search in Okhotsk Sea and bombardment of Suribachi, 19 May 1945
Matsuwa, 11 - 12 Jun 1945
Attack on enemy convoy west of Kurile Islands, 25 Jun 1945
Search in Okhotsk Sea and bombardment of Suribachi Wan, 17 - 19,22 Jul 1945
Antishipping sweeps and bombardment of Matsuwa-Kurabu Zaki and Suribachi, 11 Aug 1945

Borneo Operations:
one star only for any of the following
Tarakan Island operation, 27 Apr - 29 May 1945
Brunei Bay operation, 7 Jun - 15 Jul 1945
Balikpapan operation, 15 Jun - 20 Jul 1945
Tinian capture and occupation, 24 Jul - 1 Aug 1944
Consolidation of the Southern Philippines, 28 Feb - 20 Jul 1945
Palawan Island landings, 28 Feb - 10 Mar 1945
Visayan Island landings, 1 Mar - 20 Apr 1945
Mindanao Island landings, 8 Mar - 20 Jul 1945
Zulu Archipelago landings, 2 - 20 Apr 1945
Mine sweeping operations, 1 Mar - 15 May 1945
Hollandia operation, 21 Apr - 4 Jun 1944

Manila Bay - Bicol Operations:
one star only for any of the following
Zambales - Subic Bay, 29 - 31 Jan 1945
Nasugbu, 31 Jan - 10 Feb 1945
Mariveles - Corregidor, 14 - 28 Feb 1945
Minesweeping of Manila Bay, 24 Feb - 15 Apr 1945
El Fraile, (Ft. Drum) Manila Bay, 13 Apr 1945
Carabao Island, Manila Bay, 16 Apr 1945

Escort, antisubmarinem armed guard and special operations:
one star only for any of the following
U.S.S. Navajo, Salvage operations, 8 Aug 1942 - 3 Feb 1943
Action off Vanikoro, 17 - 21 Jul 1943
Naval Group China (6 months duty), 19 Feb 1943 - 4 May 1945
Task Group 30.4, 22 May - 15 Jun 1945
Task Group 12.2, 5 Jul - 9 Aug 1944

Minesweeping operations Pacific:
one star only for any of the following

Tsugaru Straits, 7 Sep - 18 Oct 1945
Tokoyo Bay, 28 Aug - 3 Sep 1945
Nagoya, 28 Sep - 26 Aug 1945
Sendai-Choshi, 10 - 15 Sep 1945
Wakanoura-Kii, 11 Sep - 2 Oct 1945
Kochi-Shikoku, 8 Sep - 8 Nov 1945
Bungo-Suido, 22 Sep - 31 Oct 1945
Omai-Saki, 11 - 31 Dec 1945
Kobe, 28 Nov 1945 - 9 Mar 1946
Kure-Hiroshima, 27 Oct 1945 - 26 Feb 1946
Kagoshima, 1 - 8 Sep 1945
Nagasaki, 10 - 16 Sep 1945
Sasebo, 9 Sep - 17 Oct 1945
Arcadia, 1 - 7 Sep 1945
Van Dieman Straits, 15 Sep - 1 Dec 1945
Kadoura, 24 Oct - 29 Nov 1945
Tsushima Straits, 12 Oct 1945 - 14 Apr 1946
Fukuoka, 13 Oct 1945 - 11 Jan 1946
Tachibana Wan, 15 Dec 1945 - 26 Jan 19456
Fusan, 28 Sep 1945 - 29 Jan 1946
"Rickshaw", 19 Oct - 1 Dec 1945
"Klondike", 27 Oct - 7 Nov 1945
"Skagway", 14 Aug - 9 Nov 1945
"Reno", 2 - 28 Nov 1945
Yrnlinkan Bay Area, 15 Feb - 2 Mar 1946
East Hainan Area, 1 - 2 Mar 1946
Yangtse River Approaches, 22 Feb - 2 Mar 1946
Submarine War Patrols Pacific (one star for each war patrol), 7 Dec 1941 - 2 Sep 1945

American Campaign Medal

Campaign and Inclusive Dates

Escort, antisubmarine, armed guard and special operations:

one star for each of the following

Convoy ON-67, 21-26 Feb 1942
Convoy SC-107, 3 - 8 Nov 1942
Task Group 21.12, 12 Jul - 23 Aug 1942
Task Group 21.14, 27 Jul - 10 Sep 1943
Task Group 21.15, 24 Mar - 11 May 1944
Convoy TAG 18, 1 - 6 Nov 1942
U.S.S. Frederick C. Davis, 24 Apr 1945
U.S.S. Atik, 27 Mar 1942
U.S.S. Asterion, 22 Mar 1942 - 31 Jan 1943

Appendix F

Operations qualifying for of the Armed Forces Expeditionary Medal.

U.S. Military Operations

Lebanon, 1 Jul 1958 - 1 Nov 1958
Quemoy and Matsu Islands, 23 Aug 1958 - 1 Jun 1963
Taiwan Straits, 23 Aug 1958 - 1 Jan 1959
Berlin, 14 Aug 1961 - 1 Jun 1963
Cuba, 24 Oct 1962 - 1 Jun 1963
Congo, 23 - 27 Nov 1964
Dominican Republic, 28 Apr 1965 - 28 Sep 1966
Korea, 1 Oct 1966 - 30 Jun 1974
Cambodia (operation EAGLE PULL), 11 - 13 Apr 1975
Vietnam (operation FREQUENT WIND), 29 - 30 Apr 1975
Mayaguez Operation, 15 May 1975
Grenada (operation URGENT FURY), 23 Oct 1983 - 21 Nov 1983
Libya (operation ELDORADO CANYON), 12 - 17 Apr 1986
Panama (operation JUST CAUSE), 20 Dec 1989 - 31 Jan 1990

U.S. Operations in Direct Support of the U.N.

Congo, 14 Jul 1960 - 1 Sep 1962
Somalia (Operation Restore Hope), 5 Dec 1992 - TBA

U.S. Operations of Assistance for Friendly Foreign Nations

Laos, 19 Apr 1961 - 7 Oct 1962
Vietnam (including Thailand), 1 Jul 1958- 3 Jul 1963
Cambodia, 29 Mar 1973 - 15 Aug 1973
Thailand, 29 Mar 1973 - 15 Aug 1973
Lebanon, 1 Jun 1983 - TBA

Appendix G

Army, Navy and Marine Corps Campaign designations for the Vietnam Service Medal.

Vietnam Advisory Campaign,
15 Mar 1962 - 7 Mar 1965
Vietnam Defense Campaign,
8 Mar 1965 - 24 Dec 1965
Vietnamese Counteroffensive,
25 Dec 1965 - 30 Jun 1966
Vietnamese Counteroffensive Phase II,
1 Jul 1966 - 31 May 1967
Vietnamese Counteroffensive Phase III,
1 Jun 1967 - 29 Jan 1968
Tet Counteroffensive,
30 Jan 1968 - 1 Apr 1968
Vietnamese Counteroffensive Phase IV,
2 Apr 1968 - 30 Jun 1968
Vietnamese Counteroffensive Phase V,
1 Jul 1968 - 1 Nov 1968
Vietnam Counteroffensive Phase VI,
2 Nov 1968 - 22 Feb 1969
TET 69 / Counteroffensive,
23 Feb 1969 - 8 Jun 1969
Vietnam Summer - Fall 1969,
9 Jun 1969 - 31, Oct 1969
Vietnam Winter - Spring 1970,
1 Nov 1969 - 30 Apr 1970
Sanctuary Counteroffensive,
1 May 1970 - 30 Jun 1970
Vietnam Counteroffensive Phase VII,
1 Jul 1970 - 30 Jun 1971
Consolidation I,
1 Jul 1971 - 30 Nov 1971
Consolidation II,
1 Dec 1971 - 29 Mar 1972
Vietnam Ceasefire Campaign,
20 Mar 1972 - 28 Jan 1973

Air Force campaign designations for the Vietnam Service Medal

Vietnam Advisory Campaign,
15 Nov 1961 - 1 Mar 1965
Vietnam Defense Campaign,
2 Mar 1965 - 30 Jan 1966
Vietnam Air Campaign,
31 Jan 1966 - 28 Jun 1966
Vietnam Air Offensive Campaign Phase I,
29 Jun 1966 - 8 Mar 1967
Vietnam Air Offensive Campaign Phase II,
9 Mar 1967 - 31 Mar 1968
Vietnam Air/Ground Campaign
22 Jan 1968 - 7 Jun 1968
Vietnam Air Offensive Campaign Phase III,
1 Apr 1968 - 31 Oct 1968
Vietnam Air Offensive Campaign Phase II,
1 Nov 1968 - 22 Feb 1969
TET 69/ Counteroffensive Campaign,
23 Feb 1969 - 8 Jun 1969
Vietnam Summer-Fall 1969 Campaign,
9 Jun 1969 - 31 Oct 1969
Vietnam Winter-Spring 1979 Campaign ,
1 Nov 1969 - 30 Apr 1970
Sanctuary Counteroffensive Campaign,
1 May 1970 - 30 Jun 1970
Southwest Monsoon Campaign,
1 Jul 1970 - 30 Nov 1970
Commando Hunt V, 1 Dec 1970 - 14 May 1971
Commando Hunt VI, 15 May 1971 31 Oct 1971
Commando Hunt VII, 1 Nov 1971 - 29 Mar 1972
Vietnam Ceasefire Campaign, 30 Mar 1972 - 28 Jan 1973

Appendix H

The following is a list of operations qualifying for award of the Humanitarian Service Medal.

Operation and Operation Dates

1. Evacuation of Laos, 1 April - 15 Aug 1975
2. New Life/New Arrivals, 1 April - 20 Dec 1975
3a. Baby Lift (Vietnam), 4 April - 9 May 1975
3b. Baby Lift (Ft. Lewis, WA.), 29 April - 7 May 1975
4. Eagle Pull, 12 April 1975
5. Frequent Wind, 29-30 April 1975
6. Guatemala Earthquake, 4 Feb - 30 June 1976
7. Lion Assist, 7 May - 4 June 1976
8. Teton Dam Disaster Relief, 5 - 19 June 1976
9. Big Thompson Flood Disaster, 31 July - 3 Aug 1976
10. Bolivia Commercial Air Disaster, 13 - 21 Oct 1976
11. Turkey Earthquake Disaster, 24 Nov 1976 - 22 Jan 1977
12. Enewetak Radiological Cleanup, 24 Jan 1977 - 15 Apr 1980
13. SnowGo, 30 Jan - 8 Feb 1977
14. Port-au-Prince Disaster Relief, 22 March - 1 June 1977
15a. Canary Islands Air Disaster, 28 - 30 March 1977
15b. C.I. Air Disaster (Dover AFB), 28 March - 22 Apr 1977
16. Appalachia Flood Relief, 6 April - 30 June 1977
17. Johnstown Flood Relief, 22 July - 16 Aug 1977
18. North Carolina Flood Relief, 6 Nov - 21 Dec 1977
19. Washington State Flood Relief, 2 Dec 1977 - 30 Jan 1978
20. Snow Blow/Snow Blow II, 26 Jan - 18 February 1978
21. Texas Flood Relief, 3 -15 August 1978
22. Jonestown, Guyana Disaster Relief, 20 Nov - 20 Dec 1978
23. Sri Lanka Disaster Relief, 27 Nov - 31 Dec 1978
24. Louisiana Tornado Disaster Relief, 3 - 31 Dec 1978
25. Iran Rescue and Evacuation, 8 Dec 1978 - 20 Feb 1979
26. Illinois Snow Removal, 19 - 25 Jan 1979
27. Jackson, Miss. Tornado Relief, 8 April - 9 July 1979
28. Wichita Falls/Vernon, Tx. Flood, 10 - 21 April 1979
29. Red River of the North Flood (Minn), 17 Apr - 2 May 1979
    Red River of the North Flood (N.D.), 20 - 30 April 1979
30. Nicaraguan Noncombatants Evac., 11 June - 31 July 1979
31. Cheyenne, Wyoming Tornado Relief, 16 - 29 July 1979
32. Operation Boat People, 21 July 1979 - TBA
33. Graves Registration Effort, 10 Aug - 15 Sept 1979
34. Dominica Disaster Relief, 31 Aug - 30 Nov 1979
35. Dominican Rep. Disaster Relief, 1 Sep - 26 Oct 1979
36. Hurricane Frederick Relief, 12 Sep 1979 - 23 Feb 1980
37. Gallup Indian Med. Center Relief 3 Oct 1979 - 15 Apr 1980
38. Indochinese Refugee Rel. (Thailand), 26 Oct 1979 - 30 Apr 1980
39. Majuro Atoll Disaster Relief, 27 Nov 1979 - 8 Jan 1980
40. Tumaco, Col. Earthquake Relief, 13 - 30 Dec 197941.
41. Nicaragua Disaster Relief, 17 Dec 1979 - 10 Mar 1980
42. Azores Earthquake Relief, 1 - 15 Jan 1980
43. San Bernardina Flood Relief, 8 Feb - 15 Mar 1980
44. Liberia Coup D'Etat, 12 Apr - 22 May 1980
45. Cuban Refugee Reset. (Costa Rica), 21 - 27 Apr 1980
    Cuban Refugee Reset. (other areas), 27 Apr 1980 - 1 July 1985
46. Iran Hostage Rescue, 24 - 25 April 1980
47. Mt. St. Helens Volcano Relief, 18 May 1980 - 1 July 1985
48. Grand Island, Nb. Tornado Relief, 3 -18 June 1980
49. Haiti Hurricane Relief, 6 - 21 Aug 1980
50. Haiti Refugee Resettlement, 23 Sept 1980 - TBA
51. Algeria Earthquake Relief, 12 - 21 Oct 1980
52. Italy Earthquake Relief, 26 Nov - 7 Dec 1980
53. FAA Air Traffic Control Support, 3 Aug 1981 - TBA
54. San Francisco Area Flood Relief, 4 Jan - 12 Mar 1982
55. Air Florida Crash Recovery, 13 Jan - 27 Jan 1982
56. Fort Wayne, In. Flood Relief, 19 - 21 March 1982
57. Paris, Tx. Tornado Relief, 25 - 29 April 1982
58. Chiriqui River Bridge Disaster, 21 May - 2 July 1982
59. Tunisia Flood Relief, 2 Nov 1982 - 22 Apr 1983
60. Hurricane Iwa Relief (Hawaii), 25 - 29 Nov 1982

61. Mississippi River Flood, 2 Dec 1982 - 30 Jun 1983
62. New Baden, Ill. Tornado Relief, 2 - 12 Dec 1982
63. Southeast Missouri Flood Relief, 3 - 10 / 21 - 22 Dec 1982
64. Yemen Earthquake Disaster Relief, 17 - 29 Dec 1982
65. California Flood Relief, 24 Jan - 15 July 1983
66. Medical Support to Cent. America, 9 Feb 1983 - 25 May 1984
67. Viti Levu, Fiji Cyclone Relief, 9 - 26 March 1983
68. Popayan, Col. Earthquake, 31 Mar - 8 Apr 1983
69. Utah Flood Relief, 30 Apr 1983 - 1 July 1984
70. Coalinga Earthquake Relief (Cal.), 2 May - 18 May 1983
71. Piura, Peru Flood Relief, 26 June - 1 July 1983
72. San Isdro de General Earthquake, 5 - 13 July 1983
73. Truk Islands Cholera Epidemic, 7 Sep - 12 Dec 1983
74. Turkey Earthquake Relief, 31 Oct - 14 Nov 1983
75. Emergency Animal Disease Eradication Relief, 10 Nov 1983 - 12 Mar 1984
76. Agalega Is. , Mauritius Cyclone, 13 December 1983
77. Beirut, Lebanon (Civilian Evac.), 10 - 12 Feb 1984
78. North Carolina Tornado Relief, 28 Mar - 19 Apr 1984
79. Barnveld, Wis. Tornado Relief, 8 June 1984
80. Operation Intense Look, 8 Aug - 1 Oct 1984
81. N.C. Hurricane Diana Relief Op., 10 Sep - 8 Oct 1984
82. South Korea Flood Relief, 29 - 30 Sep 1984
83. Mali Raft Famine Relief, 23 May - 31 Oct 1985
84. Cheyenne, Wy. Flood Relief, 1 - 5 Aug 1985
85. Hurricane Elena Relief Op., 29 Aug - 8 Sep 1985
86. Mexico City Earthquake, 19 Sep - 4 Oct 1985
87. Puerto Rico Flood Relief, 6 - 21 Oct 1985
88. West Virginia Flood Relief, 5 - 28 Nov 1985
89. Colimbia Disaster Relief, 16 Nov - 20 Dec 1985
90. Lake Nyos, Camaroon Disaster, 25 Aug - 26 Sep 1986
91. US Mil Gp El Salvador Earthquake, 10 - 20 Oct 1986
92. Typhoon Kim Relief Operation, 3 - 23 Dec 1986
93. Typhoon Tusi Relief Operation, 24 Jan - 8 Mar 1987
94. Ecuador Earthquake Relief, 5 Mar - 5 Apr 1987
95. Operation Firebreak, 5-15 Sep 1987
96. Costa Rica Flood Relief, 31 Jan - 5 Feb 1988
97. Operation Firebreak 1988, 19 Aug - 6 Oct 1988
98. Grosse Tete Tornado Relief, 8 - 16 June 1989
99. Operation Firebreak 1989, 28 July - 25 Aug 1989
100. Ethiopian Search and Rescue, 9 - 23 Aug 1989
101. Evacuation of U.S. Embassy, Beirut, 6 September 1989
102. Hurricane Hugo, 18 Sep - 31 Oct 1989
103. California Earthquake Relief, 17 Oct - 13 Dec 1989
104. Hurricane Andrew Relief in Florida, 5 Apr - 14 June 1991

Appendix I

Navy World War I Medal Clasps Eligibility Roster

Name	Operating—		Clasp
	From—	To—	
Abarenda	15 Apr 18	20 Apr 18	Asiatic.
Do	13 Jun 18	13 Jun 18	Do.
Absaroka	22 Oct 18	11 Nov 18	Transport.
Do	26 Mar 18	22 Oct 18	Armed guard.
Absecon	12 Oct 18	5 Nov 18	Patrol.
Achilles	5 Jul 18	11 Nov 18	Armed guard.
Acteaon	15 Jun 17	25 Nov 17	Do.
Acushnet	15 May 18	16 Jul 18	Patrol.
Do	17 Jul 18	11 Nov 18	Salvage.
Adelheid	27 Apr 18	do	Armed guard.
Advance	28 Sept 18	do	Do.
Aeolus	10 Dec 17	do	Transport.
Agamemnon	12 Nov 17	do	Do.
Agawam	8 Oct 18	do	Armed guard.
Alabama	25 May 18	27 Oct 18	Atlantic Fleet.
Alamance	27 Mar 17	5 Feb 18	Armed guard.
Alamo	6 Apr 17	11 Nov 18	Do.
Alaskan	2 May 18	do	Transport.
Albany	14 Jul 17	4 Nov 18	Escort.
Do	19 Jun 19	26 Jul 19	Asiatic.
Do	19 Dec 19	30 Mar 20	Do.
Albatross	9 Jun 18	25 Oct 18	Atlantic Fleet.
Alcédo	12 Aug 17	5 Nov 17	Patrol.
Alert	25 May 18	11 Nov 18	Do.
Algonquin	14 Oct 17	do	Escort.
Allen	28 Jun 17	do	Destroyer.
Allianca	20 Sept 18	do	Armed guard.
Alloway	12 Sept 18	do	Transport.
Amabala	17 Sept 18	do	Do.
America	12 Nov 17	do	Do.
American	17 Jun 18	do	Do.
Ammen	24 Jun 17	do	Destroyer.
Ampetco	6 May 18	do	Armed guard.
Amphion	8 Sept 17	do	Do.
Amphitrite	25 May 18	do	Patrol.
Andalusia	2 Apr 18	do	Armed guard.
Anderton	6 Sept 17	28 Apr 19	Mine sweeper.
Androscoggin	25 May 18	11 Nov 18	Patrol.
Aniwa	12 Oct 18	do	Transport.
Anna	22 Jun 17	22 Dec 17	Armed guard.
Do	22 Dec 17	11 Nov 18	Transport.
Annapolis	3 Jul 18	1 Oct 18	Atlantic Fleet.
Anniston	2 Nov 18	11 Nov 18	Escort.
Antigone	27 Dec 17	do	Transport.
Antilla	5 Aug 18	28 Oct 18	Do.
Antilles	26 Jun 17	17 Oct 17	Armed guard.
Apache	4 Jun 18	11 Nov 18	Patrol.
Apelles	12 Oct 17	do	Armed guard.
Aphrodite	27 Jun 17	11 Nov 18	Patrol.
Arakan	1 Oct 18	do	Armed guard.
Aramis	5 Nov 17	do	Patrol.
Arapho	26 May 18	25 Jul 18	Escort.
Do	25 Jul 18	10 Nov 18	Patrol.
Arcadia	19 May 17	11 Nov 18	Armed guard.
Archbold, J. D	28 Apr 17	16 Jun 17	Do.
Arctic	25 May 18	11 Nov 18	Patrol.
Arcturus	7 Dec 17	do	Do.
Arethusa	27 Apr 18	do	Transport.
Argonne	4 Feb 18	19 Oct 18	Armed guard.
Arizona	25 May 18	11 Nov 18	Atlantic Fleet.
Arizonan	2 Nov 17	17 Sept 18	Armed guard.
Do	17 Sept 18	24 Oct 18	Transport.
Arkansas	21 May 18	25 Jul 18	Atlantic Fleet.
Do	25 Jul 18	11 Nov 18	Grand Fleet.
Armenia	4 Apr 17	27 Mar 18	Armed guard.
Do	27 Mar 18	11 Nov 18	Transport.
Aroostook	29 Jun 18	do	Mine layer.
Artemis	6 Apr 17	do	Armed guard.
Ascutney	do	do	Do.
Ashton, William	26 May 19	5 Aug 19	Mine sweeper.
Astoria	18 Feb 18	11 Nov 18	Transport.
Atlantic II	25 May 18	do	Atlantic Fleet.
Atlantic Sun	4 Apr 17	18 Mar 18	Armed guard.
Auk	29 Apr 19	30 Sept 19	Mine sweeper.
Ausable	7 Oct 18	11 Nov 18	Transport.

Name	Operating—		Clasp
	From—	To—	
ocet	15 Jul 19	30 Sept 19	Mine sweeper.
ondale	6 Apr 17	11 Nov 18	Armed guard.
win	11 Jan 18	do	Destroyer.
c	25 May 18	do	Patrol.
he	5 May 18	11 Nov 18	Do.
ey	25 May 18	do	Do.
nbridge	9 Aug 17	18 Aug 18	Destroyer.
ch	8 Nov 17	11 Nov 18	Do.
i	13 May 18	24 Oct 18	Transport.
timore	17 Mar 18	28 Sept 18	Mine layer.
atu	6 Apr 17	11 Nov 18	Armed guard.
negat	23 Jan 18	do	Patrol.
nes, George W	6 Apr 17	do	Armed guard.
ney	2 Oct 18	do	Patrol.
ry	9 Aug 17	15 Sept 18	Destroyer.
stow, F. Q	6 Apr 17	11 Nov 18	Armed guard.
h	26 Aug 18	do	Transport.
jan	12 Jul 18	22 Oct 18	Do.
iman, P. K	6 Sept 17	12 Jan 18	Mine sweeper.
aria	23 Mar 18	15 Apr 18	Transport.
le	19 Jan 18	11 Nov 18	Destroyer.
r	17 Jul 17	1 Nov 18	Asiatic.
trice	6 Apr 17	11 Nov 18	Armed guard.
ufort	19 Nov 17	do	Transport.
ford, A. C	6, Apr 17	11 Nov 18	Armed guard.
	12 Aug 18	do	Destroyer.
ham	24 May 17	do	Do.
wind	3 Aug 17	3 Aug 18	Armed guard.
wyn	2 Nov 18	16 Nov 18	Transport.
oeki	1 May 18	11 Nov 18	Do.
kelskijk	26 Aug 18	do	Do.
mingham	27 Jun 17	do	Escort.
ck Arrow	6 Jul 17	do	Armed guard.
ckhorn, Thomas	26 May 19	1 Oct 19	Mine sweeper.
ck Hawk	29 Jun 18	11 Nov 18	Mobile base.
keley	25 May 18	do	Patrol.
oolink	20 Apr 19	30 Sept 19	Mine sweeper.
inquen	13 Jun 17	11 Nov 18	Armed guard.
twick	6 Apr 17	do	Do.
bant	do	do	Do.
ley, Charles	do	do	Do.
mell Point	do	do	Do.
zos	do	do	Do.
akwater (S. P. 681)	3 Jul 18	do	Patrol.
ese	3 Nov 18	do	Destroyer.
merton	6 Apr 17	do	Armed guard.
lge	1 Oct 17	do	Transport.
dgeport	27 Apr 18	14 May 18	Mobile base.
Do	20 Jul 18	11 Nov 18	Do.
ndilla	6 Apr 17	do	Armed guard.
ad Arrow	6 May 18	do	Transport.
oklyn	23 Nov 17	11 Dec 17	Asiatic.
Do	1 Mar 18	9 Oct 18	Do.
Do	23 Dec 18	2 Apr 19	Do.
Do	28 Oct 19	8 Dec 19	Do.
k, Frank H	11 Mar 18	11 Nov 18	Transport.
kley, Thomas	28 May 19	3 Oct 19	Mine sweeper.
na Ventura	23 Aug 18	16 Sept 18	Transport.
falo	3 Jun 17	15 Jul 17	Asiatic.
Do	20 Jul 18	11 Nov 18	Mobile base.
tenzorg	21 Apr 18	do	Transport.
keley, Richard	31 May 19	12 Jul 19	Mine sweeper.
rows	27 Jun 17	11 Nov 18	Destroyer.
ton, George	26 May 19	6 Aug 19	Mine sweeper.
ton, W. M	6 Apr 17	11 Nov 18	Armed guard.
hnell	24 Dec 17	do	Patrol.
ayl	6 Apr 17	do	Armed guard.
	25 May 18	do	Submarine.
	do	do	Do.
	do	do	Do.
	do	do	Do.
	do	do	Do.
sar	30 Jul 17	27 Oct 18	Mobile base.
ique	11 Jun 18	17 Sept 18	Armed guard.
Do	17 Sept 18	24 Oct 18	Transport.
sar	30 Jul 17	27 Oct 18	Mobile base.
arty, Pat	26 May 19	16 Aug 19	Mine sweeper.
ill	6 Sept 17	8 Sept 19	Do.
amares	22 Sept 17	28 Apr 18	Armed guard.
Do	28 Apr 18	11 Nov 18	Transport.
dwell	28 Feb 18	do	Destroyer.
dwell, William	31 May 19	28 Sept 19	Mine sweeper.
ifornia	6 Oct 17	9 Feb 18	Armed guard.
ifornian	7 Jun 18	23 Jun 18	Transport.
oria	6 Apr 17	11 Nov 18	Armed guard.
nden	15 Sept 17	11 Apr 18	Transport.
npana	4 Jun 17	6 Aug 17	Armed guard.
nandaigua	26 May 18	11 Nov 18	Mine layer.
nfield, C. A	5 Sept 18	do	Armed guard.
nibas	13 Oct 18	30 Oct 18	Transport.
noga	24 Oct 18	11 Nov 18	Armed guard.
nonicus	26 May 18	do	Mine layer.
nton	11 Aug 18	do	Transport.
pe Henry	23 Jul 18	14 Oct 18	Armed guard.
pe Lookout	30 Aug 18	11 Nov 18	Transport.
pe May	8 Nov 18	24 Nov 18	Do.
pe Romaine	6 Nov 18	11 Nov 18	Do.
dinal	31 Aug 18	1 Dec 18	Mine sweeper.

Name	Operating—		Clasp
	From—	To—	
Carib	4 Jun 17	21 May 18	Armed guard.
Do	21 May 18	12 Oct 18	Transport.
Carola IV	29 Aug 17	11 Nov 18	Overseas.
Carolinian	21 Mar 17	5 Oct 18	Armed guard.
Do	5 Oct 18	11 Nov 18	Transport.
Carolyn	28 Jun 17	do	Armed guard.
Carillo	18 Oct 18	24 Oct 18	Transport.
Casco	24 Feb 18	11 Nov 18	Do.
S. S. Caserta (Italian)	8 May 18	do	Do.
Cassin	21 May 17	do	Destroyer.
Castine	16 Aug 16	do	Patrol.
Catina	6 Apr 17	do	Armed guard.
Cauto	13 Oct 17	11 Aug 18	Do.
Do	11 Aug 18	11 Nov 18	Transport.
Celebes	18 May 18	do	Do.
Celtic	30 Aug 18	do	Do.
Chalmette	26 Sept 18	do	Armed guard.
Charles	21 Jul 18	do	Transport.
Charleston	6 Jun 17	19 Jul 17	Escort.
Do	25 May 18	11 Nov 18	Atlantic Fleet.
Charlton Hall	9 Jul 18	do	Transport.
Chatham	18 Apr 18	28 Oct 18	Do.
Chattanooga	16 Mar 18	6 Nov 18	Escort.
Chauncey	9 Aug 17	19 Nov 17	Destroyer.
Chebaulip	6 Nov 18	11 Nov 18	Transport.
Chemung	25 May 18	do	Atlantic Fleet.
Chesapeake	1 May 19	30 Sept 19	Mine sweeper.
Chester	2 Sept 17	11 Nov 18	Escort.
Chester Sun	5 Nov 17	do	Armed guard.
Chestnut Hill	22 Apr 18	27 Apr 18	Transport.
Do	3 Oct 18	18 Oct 18	Do.
Chewink	5 Jun 19	30 Sept 19	Mine sweeper.
Cheyenne	15 Nov 17	11 Nov 18	
Chicago	27 Sept 17	26 Mar 18	Escort.
Do	25 May 18	11 Nov 18	Do.
Chinanpa	15 Nov 17	1 Nov 18	Armed guard.
Do	1 Nov 18	11 Nov 18	Transport.
Chincha	8 Jun 17	do	Armed guard.
Choctaw	26 May 18	do	Transport.
Cincinnati	1 Apr 18	do	Patrol.
City of Atlanta	6 Jun 18	14 Aug 18	Armed guard.
City of Lewes	6 Sept 17	8 Sept 19	Mine sweeper.
City of Savannah	2 Jul 17	28 Aug 18	Armed guard.
City of Wilmington	5 Jul 17	19 Apr 18	Do.
Clara	22 Jun 17	11 Nov 18	Do.
Clare	1 Mar 18	13 Oct 18	Do.
Do	13 Oct 18	11 Nov 18	Transport.
Clark, George	27 May 19	5 Aug 19	Mine sweeper.
Clay, John	26 May 19	7 Aug 19	Do.
Cleveland	22 Jul 17	11 Nov 18	Escort.
Coamo	28 Jun 18	do	Armed guard.
Cochrane, George	31 May 19	5 Aug 19	Mine sweeper.
Colhoun	23 Jun 18	11 Nov 18	Destroyer.
Collins, John	28 May 19	6 Aug 19	Mine sweeper.
Colon	7 Sept 18	11 Nov 18	Armed guard.
Columbia	11 Nov 17	do	Atlantic Fleet.
Comfort	21 Oct 18	4 Nov 18	Transport.
Concord	23 Jan 18	25 Oct 18	Mine sweeper.
Conestoga	20 Dec 17	22 Dec 17	Escort.
Do	27 Apr 18	6 May 18	Do.
Connecticut	25 May 18	31 Aug 18	Atlantic Fleet.
Connelly, John M	18 Apr 18	6 Jun 18	Armed guard.
Do	6 Jun 18	11 Oct 18	Transport.
Connor	21 May 18	11 Nov 18	Destroyer.
Constantia	1 Jun 18	27 Jun 18	Transport.
Conynham	4 May 17	11 Nov 18	Destroyer.
Cormorant	22 Aug 19	30 Sept 19	Mine sweeper.
Corning	6 Mar 18	11 Nov 18	Armed guard.
Corona	19 Aug 17	do	Patrol.
Coronado	22 May 18	do	Armed guard.
Corozal	9 May 18	do	Transport.
Corsair	27 Jun 17	do	Escort.
Courtney	6 Sept 17	27 Apr 19	Mine sweeper.
Covington	31 Oct 17	1 Jul 18	Transport.
Craster Hall	1 Jul 18	15 Oct 18	Do.
Cristabel	26 Jun 17	11 Nov 18	Patrol.
Crowell, Peter H	21 Mar 18	24 Oct 18	Transport.
Cubore	8 Jun 18	15 Aug 18	Armed guard.
Cudahy, Joseph	23 Jun 17	17 Aug 18	Do.
Culgoa	19 Feb. 18	11 Nov 18	Transport.
Cummings	24 May 17	do	Destroyer.
Cummunipaw	6 Apr 17	do	Armed guard.
Curlew	20 Apr 19	30 Sept 19	Mine sweeper.
Cushing	24 May 17	11 Nov 18	Destroyer.
Cuyama	18 Jan 18	5 Oct 18	Transport.
Cyclops	24 Jun 17	18 Jul 17	Do.
Cythera	6 Dec. 17	11 Nov 18	Patrol.
D-1	10 Jun 18	11 Jun 18	Submarine.
D-2	6 Apr 17	11 Nov 18	Do.
D-3	30 Sept 18	2 Oct 18	Do.
Dakotan	17 Jun 17	11 Nov 18	Armed guard.
Dale	9 Aug 17	do	Destroyer.
Danziger, J. M	7 Oct 18	do	Armed guard.
Darnold, William	2 Jun 19	6 Aug 19	Mine sweeper.
Davis	4 May 17	11 Nov 18	Destroyer.
Dayton	29 Jun 17	do	Armed guard.
Decatur	9 Aug 17	do	Destroyer.
Deep Water	24 Aug 17	do	Armed guard.

Name	Operating—		Clasp
	From—	To—	
Defiance	25 Oct 18	14 Nov 18	Transport.
Dekalb	14 Jun 17	11 Nov 18	Do.
Delaware	7 Dec 17	30 Jul 18	Grand Fleet.
De Long	25 May 18	11 Nov 18	Destroyer.
Democracy	5 Nov 17	25 Oct 18	Armed guard.
Do	25 Oct 18	11 Nov 18	Transport.
Dent	10 Sept 18	8 Nov 18	Destroyer.
Denver	22 Aug 17	3 Nov 18	Escort.
Des Moines	28 Jul 17	24 Oct 18	Do.
Do	13 May 19	31 Jul 19	White Sea.
De Soto	30 Apr 18	11 Nov 18	Armed guard.
Dixie	13 Jun 17	do	Mobile base.
Dochra	18 Jul 17	16 Dec 17	Armed guard.
Do	16 Dec 17	11 Nov 18	Transport.
Doheny, Edward L	20 Dec 17	do	Armed guard.
Doheny, Edward L., Jr	18 Sept 18	do	Do.
Dolphin	17 Jun 18	do	Patrol.
Don Juan de Austria	3 Jul 18	do	Do.
Donnell, J. C	6 Apr 17	do	Armed guard.
Dora	15 Jun 17	4 Sept 18	Do.
Dorothea	6 Jun 18	29 Jul 18	Atlantic Fleet.
Dorsey	20 Sept 18	11 Nov 18	Destroyer.
Douglas	6 Sept 17	27 Apr 19	Mine sweeper.
Downes	8 Nov 17	11 Nov 18	Destroyer.
Drake, Col. E. L	13 Jun 17	do	Armed guard.
Drayton	1 Jul 17	do	Destroyer.
Dreadnaught	26 May 18	29 Jul 19	Mine sweeper.
Drechterland	13 Jun 18	11 Nov 18	Transport.
Druid	6 Dec 17	do	Patrol.
Dubuque	25 May 18	4 Nov 18	Do.
Duca D'Aosta	10 May 18	11 Nov 18	Transport.
Duffey, Siam	28 May 19	1 Oct 19	Mine sweeper.
Duncan	15 Nov 17	11 Nov 18	Destroyer.
Dunkin, John	2 Jun 19	7 Aug 19	Mine sweeper.
Durham	28 Sept 18	15 Oct 18	Transport.
Dyer	7 Jul 18	11 Nov 18	Destroyer.
E-1	12 Jan 18	do	Submarine.
E-2	25 May 18	22 Oct 18	Do.
Eagle	do	23 Jun 18	Atlantic Fleet.
Eagle No. 1	22 May 19	13 Jul 19	White Sea.
Eagle No. 2	do	do	Do.
Eagle No. 3	do	31 Jul 19	Do.
Eaglet (S. P. 900)	do	26 Sept 18	Patrol.
Eastern Chief	8 Nov 18	11 Nov 18	Transport
Eastern Sun	14 Aug 18	do	Armed guard.
East Hampton	20 Jul 18	do	Patrol.
Edith	14 Mar 18	29 Oct 18	Armed guard.
Do	29 Oct 18	11 Nov 18	Transport.
Edwards, Wilbert A	25 May 18	do	Atlantic Fleet.
Eider	20 Apr 19	30 Sept 19	Mine sweeper.
El Capitan	16 Apr 18	8 Nov 18	Transport.
Elinor	do	30 Aug 18	Do.
El Occidente	29 Apr 17	5 Oct 18	Armed guard.
Do	5 Oct 18	22 Oct 18	Transport.
El Oriente	8 Sept 18	28 Aug 18	Armed guard.
Do	28 Aug 18	9 Sept 18	Transport.
El Sol	12 Sept 17	19 Sept 18	Armed guard.
Do	19 Sept 18	11 Nov 18	Transport.
Emeline	19 Aug 17	do	Patrol.
Ericsson	21 May 17	do	Destroyer.
Erny	2 Jun 17	do	Armed guard.
Esperanza	19 Oct 18	do	Do.
Euphane, Helen	23 May 18	30 May 18	Mine sweeper.
Eurana	17 May 17	20 Oct 18	Armed guard.
Do	20 Oct 18	11 Nov 18	Transport.
Evansville (ex-Lake Tahoe).	21 Mar 18	do	Do.
Evelyn	31 Jan 18	do	Armed guard.
Fairfax	2 Jun 18	do	Destroyer.
Fairmont	28 Mar 18	do	Transport.
Falcon	21 Aug. 19	30 Sept 19	Mine sweeper.
Fanning	26 Jun 17	11 Nov 18	Destroyer.
Favorite	20 Jul 18	do	Salvage.
Feltore	3 May 18	do	Armed guard.
Finch	21 Aug 19	30 Sept 19	Mine sweeper.
Finland	26 May 17	12 May 18	Armed guard.
Do	12 May 18	11 Nov 18	Transport.
Fish Hawk	28 Aug 18	do	Patrol.
Firmore	12 Jul 18	do	Armed guard.
Fitzgerald, John	2 Jun 19	7 Aug. 19	Mine sweeper.
Flagler, H. M	3 Jul 18	11 Nov 18	Armed guard.
Flamingo	5 Jul 19	30 Sept 19	Mine sweeper.
Florence, H	21 Mar 18	17 Apr 18	Armed guard.
Florida	7 Dec 17	11 Nov 18	Grand Fleet.
Floridian	21 Sept 17	do	Armed guard.
Flusser	12 Aug 17	do	Destroyer.
Foam	18 Jun 18	31 Dec 18	Mine sweeper.
Folger, H. C	28 May 17	do	Armed guard.
Franklin	27 Feb 18	do	Do.
Frasch, Herman	1 Oct 18	4 Oct 18	Transport.
Frederick	10 Jun 17	10 Jun 17	Patrol.
Do	1 Feb 18	11 Nov 18	Escort.
Freedom	26 Jun 17	do	Armed guard.
Freeman	18 Oct 18	do	Do.
Fresno	27 Aug 18	14 Sept 18	Transport.
Frieda	6 Nov 18	11 Nov 18	Do.
Froelich	3 Mar 18	do	Mine sweeper.
Fulton	18 May 18	do	Atlantic Fleet.
G-1	25 May 18	18 Jun 18	Submarine.
G-2	5 Jun 18	3 Oct. 18	Do.
G-3	28 Jun 18	21 Oct 18	Do.
G-4	6 Jun 18	24 Jul 18	Do.
Galatea	22 Jan 18	11 Nov 18	Patrol.
Galveston	24 Feb 18	3 Nov 18	Escort.
Gargoyle	21 Mar 18	21 Apr 18	Transport.
Do	20 Oct 18	8 Nov 18	Do.
Garibaldi	2 Oct 18	11 Nov 18	Armed guar
Genesee	12 Jan 18	do	Patrol.
Georgia	25 May 18	19 Sept 18	Atlantic Fle
Do	19 Sept 18	11 Nov 18	Escort.
Glacier	17 Jun 18	do	Transport.
Glen White	26 Aug 18	8 Nov 18	Do.
Gloucester	25 May 18	11 Nov 18	Patrol.
Glynn	16 Mar 17	14 Aug 18	Armed guar
Gold Shell	2 Apr 17	14 Sept 17	Do.
Do	14 Sept 17	30 Sept 18	Transport.
Goliah	6 Jun 18	11 Nov 18	Patrol.
Gorgas, Gen. W. C	10 Oct 18	do	Armed guar
Gorgona	26 Aug 18	7 Nov 18	Atlantic Fle
Gorontalo	1 Jun 18	11 Oct 18	Transport.
Grace	3 May 17	12 July 17	Armed guar
Graham, John	31 May 19	8 Aug 19	Mine sweep
Graham, Thomas	28 May 19	7 Aug 19	Do.
Great Northern	13 Mar 18	11 Nov 18	Transport.
Grebe	10 Jul 19	30 Sept 19	Mine sweep
Gregory	11 Jun 18	11 Nov 18	Destroyer.
Gresham	25 May 18	do	Patrol.
Guantanamo	17 Jun 18	do	Transport.
Guffy, J. M	14 Oct 18	do	Do.
Guinevere	19 Aug 17	25 Jan 18	Patrol.
Gulf Light	22 May 18	11 Nov 18	Armed guar
Gulf Maid	13 Jun 18	do	Do.
Gulfport	18 Jan 18	do	Transport.
Gypsum Queen	24 Jan 18	do	Patrol.
H-1	25 May 18	27 Oct 18	Submarine.
H-2	do	do	Do.
Hackett	do	30 Oct. 18	Atlantic Fle
Hancock	17 Jun 17	11 Nov 18	Transport.
Hannibal	7 Dec 17	do	Escort.
Harkness, S. V	29 Oct 18	do	Armed guar
Harrisburg	20 Jun 18	11 Nov 18	Transport.
Harvard	26 Jun 17	do	Patrol.
Harwood, Charles E	27 Jul 17	do	Armed guar
Harwood, Paul H	2 Aug 18	do	Do.
Hatteras	28 Apr. 18	30 Sept 18	Transport.
Hauoli	25 May 18	11 Nov 18	Patrol.
Havana	26 May 17	12 Jul 17	Armed guar
Havannah	6 Apr 17	11 Nov 18	Do.
Hawaiian	12 Nov 17	10 Aug 18	Do.
Do	4 Sept 18	11 Nov 18	Transport.
Helen	26 Sept 18	11 Nov 18	Armed guar
Helenita	25 May 18	do	Atlantic Fle
Henderson	13 Jun 17	do	Transport.
Henley	29 May 18	7 Nov 18	Destroyer.
Henrix, Thomas	2 Jun 19	6 Aug 19	Mine sweep
Henry, George G	1 Oct 17	15 Sept 18	Armed guar
Do	15 Sept 18	11 Nov 18	Transport.
Heredia	14 Jun 18	do	Armed guar
Heron	29 Apr 19	30 Sept 19	Mine sweep
Hewitt	24 Oct 17	11 Nov 18	Armed guar
Hilton	6 Nov 18	do	Overseas.
Hinton	6 Sept 17	8 Sept 19	Mine sweep
Hisko	12 Feb 18	11 Nov 18	Transport.
Hodges, Gen. H. L	6 Apr 17	do	Armed guar
Honolulu	20 Nov 17	do	Do.
Hopkins	27 May 18	4 Nov 18	Destroyer.
Housatonic	26 May 18	11 Nov 18	Mine layer.
Houston	27 Aug 17	31 Oct 18	Transport.
Howick Hall	22 Sept 17	27 Sept 18	Armed guar
Do	27 Sept 18	22 Oct 18	Transport.
Hubbard	17 Oct 17	8 Sept 19	Mine sweep
Hull	2 Jul 18	11 Nov 18	Destroyer.
Huntington	7 Sept 17	do	Escort.
Huron	20 Sept 17	do	Transport.
Hwah Jah	19 Apr 18	do	Armed guar
Hwah Yih	1 Nov 18	do	Do.
Ice King	2 Aug 18	24 Oct 18	Transport.
Ida	15 Jun 17	11 Nov 18	Armed guar
Illinois	25 May 18	9 Nov 18	Atlantic Fle
Indiana	30 May 18	11 Nov 18	Do.
Iowa	31 May 18	do	Do.
Iowan	1 Mar 18	8 Oct 18	Transport.
Irish, W. M	12 Aug 18	11 Nov 18	Armed guar
Iroquois	26 May 18	do	Patrol.
Isabel	20 Feb 18	do	Destroyer.
Isabella	13 May 18	22 Sept 18	Transport.
Isanti	3 Nov 18	11 Nov 18	Do.
Isis	14 Oct 18	30 Oct 18	Atlantic Fle
Islo de Luzon	16 Sept 18	30 Sept 18	Patrol.
Isom, William	8 Nov 17	1 May 18	Armed guar
Do	1 May 18	11 Nov 18	Transport.
Isonomia	28 Apr 17	do	Armed guar
Itasca	2 Jun 18	do	Patrol.
Israel	21 Sept 18	do	Destroyer.
Jacob Jones	21 May 17	6 Dec 17	Do.
James, W. T	6 Sept 17	28 Apr 19	Mine sweep

Name	Operating—		Clasp
	From—	To—	
rvis	8 Jun 17	11 Nov 18	Destroyer.
son	10 July 18	do	Armed guard.
Do	26 May 18	22 Jun 18	Transport.
an	22 Sept 17	29 Aug 18	Armed guard.
Do	30 Aug 18	3 Nov 18	Transport.
bson, William	24 Apr 18	11 Nov 18	Armed guard.
nkins	1 Jun 17	do	Destroyer.
nnings, O. B	30 Oct 17	24 Mar 18	Armed guard.
hnson, William	31 May 19	3 Oct 19	Mine sweeper.
nancy	24 Jun 18	11 Nov 18	Armed guard.
nes, Paul	26 May 18	27 Oct 18	Destroyer.
nes, Steven R	5 Jun 18	24 Oct 18	Transport.
siah, Macy	6 Apr 17	11 Nov 18	Armed guard.
uett	25 May 18	4 Oct 18	Destroyer.
piter	23 May 17	26 Jun 17	Transport.
-1	27 Oct 17	11 Nov 18	Submarine.
-2	do	20 Oct 18	Do.
-3	25 May 18	29 Aug 18	Do.
-4	do	do	Do.
-5	27 Oct 17	18 Apr 18	Do.
-6	do	11 Nov 18	Do.
-7	do	25 Aug 18	Do.
-8	do	4 Sept 18	Do.
anawha	17 Jun 17	22 Oct 18	Transport.
ansas	10 Sept 17	11 Nov 18	Escort.
earsarge	25 May 18	8 Nov 18	Atlantic Fleet.
entucky	do	do	Do.
entuckian	13 Oct 17	do	Armed guard.
eresan	21 Oct 18	do	Transport.
eresaspa	17 Aug 18	31 Oct 18	Armed guard.
erkenna	28 Sept 18	11 Nov 18	Transport.
ermanshah	31 Jan 18	4 Sept 18	Armed guard.
Do	4 Sept 18	10 Nov 18	Transport.
ermoor	1 Nov 18	11 Nov 18	Do.
erowlee	17 Oct 18	11 Nov 18	Transport.
erwood	19 Apr 18	4 Nov 18	Armed guard.
Do	5 Nov 18	11 Nov 18	Transport.
imberly	27 May 18	do	Destroyer.
ingfisher	16 Aug 18	15 Jan 19	Mine sweeper.
Do	20 Apr 19	30 Sept 19	Do.
iowa	20 May 18	21 Oct 18	Transport.
ittery	5 May 18	11 Nov 18	Do.
oningen der Nederlanden.	25 Aug 18	do	Do.
roonland	14 Mar 17	12 May 18	Armed guard.
Do	12 May 18	11 Nov 18	Transport.
wasind	25 May 18	do	Patrol.
-1	20 Dec 17	do	Submarine.
-2	do	do	Do.
-3	13 Jan 18	do	Do.
-4	11 Feb 18	do	Do.
-5	25 May 18	do	Do.
-6	do	do	Do.
-7	do	do	Do.
-8	do	do	Do.
-9	11 Feb 18	do	Do.
-10	20 Dec 17	do	Do.
-11	21 Dec 17	do	Do.
ake Arthur	1 Jun 18	17 Sept 18	Armed guard.
Do	17 Sept 18	11 Nov 18	Transport.
ake Benbow	19 Sept 18	do	Do.
ake Berdan	23 Oct 18	do	Do.
ake Blanchester	2 Sept 18	do	Do.
ake Bloomington	21 Oct 18	do	Do.
ake Borgne	5 Oct 18	19 Oct 18	Do.
ake Bridge	14 Jun 18	11 Nov 18	Do.
ake Capens	4 Jun 18	16 Oct 18	Armed guard.
Do	16 Oct 18	11 Nov 18	Transport.
ake Catherine	8 Nov 18	do	Do.
ake Champlain	1 Apr 18	do	Do.
ake Charlotte	18 Jul 18	17 Oct 18	Armed guard.
Do	17 Oct 18	11 Nov 18	Transport.
ake Clear	19 May 18	17 Jul 18	Armed guard.
ake Crescent	11 May 18	19 Oct 18	Do.
Do	19 Oct 18	11 Nov 18	Transport.
ake Damito	4 Sept 18	do	Do.
ake Dancey	6 Nov 18	25 Nov 18	Do.
ake Daraga	4 Sept 18	11 Nov 18	Do.
ake Dymer	21 Oct 18	do	Do.
ake Eckhart	19 Sept 18	do	Do.
ake Edon	1 Jul 18	21 Aug 18	Armed guard.
ake Eliko	5 Oct 18	11 Nov 18	Transport.
ake Elizabeth	27 May 18	26 Sept 18	Armed guard.
Do	26 Sept 18	11 Nov 18	Transport.
ake Elsinore	21 Oct 18	do	Do.
ake Erie	28 Apr 18	30 Oct 18	Do.
ake Ewow	6 Apr 18	11 Nov 18	Armed guard.
ake Fernwood	8 Jul 18	23 Sept 18	Do.
Do	23 Sept 18	11 Nov 18	Transport.
ake Forrest	6 Jun 18	do	Do.
ake Frances	28 Aug 18	do	Do.
ake Gakona	19 Sept 18	do	Do.
ake Garza	4 Nov 18	21 Nov 18	Do.
ake Gaspar	5 Nov 18	11 Nov 18	Do.
ake Gedney	8 Oct 18	do	Do.
ake Geneva	5 Nov 18	do	Do.
ake Harney	18 Aug 18	do	Do.
ake Harris	6 Sept 18	do	Do.

Name	Operating—		Clasp
	From—	To—	
Lake Helen	6 Nov 18	11 Nov 18	Transport.
Lake Huron	12 Mar 18	do	Do.
Lake Lasang	5 Jul 18	10 Sept 18	Armed guard.
Do	10 Sept 18	11 Nov 18	Transport.
Lake Lemando	27 May 18	17 Jul 18	Armed guard.
Lake Lillian	2 Oct 18	11 Nov 18	Transport.
Lake Michigan	27 Mar 18	do	Do.
Lake Moor	24 Mar 18	11 Apr 18	Do.
Lake Ontario	18 Apr 18	11 Nov 18	Do.
Lake Osweya	10 Nov 18	24 Nov 18	Do.
Lake Otisco	19 Aug 18	5 Oct 18	Armed guard.
Do	5 Oct 18	11 Nov 18	Transport.
Lake Owens	9 Jun 18	3 Sept 18	Armed guard.
Lake Pepin	23 Oct 18	11 Nov 18	Transport.
Lake Pewaukee	31 May 18	7 Sept 18	Armed guard.
Do	7 Sept 18	11 Nov 18	Transport.
Lake Placid	12 Apr 18	3 Nov 18	Do.
Lake Pleasant	5 Oct 18	11 Nov 18	Do.
Lake Port	28 May 18	9 Nov 18	Do.
Lake Portage	8 Jul 18	3 Aug 18	Armed guard.
Lake Shore	29 Mar 18	12 Oct 18	Transport.
Lake Side	13 Jun 18	11 Nov 18	Do.
Lake Silver	19 Sept 18	do	Do.
Lake St. Clair	14 Jun 18	31 Oct 18	Armed guard.
Do	31 Oct 18	11 Nov 18	Transport.
Lake St. Regis	19 May 18	17 Oct 18	Armed guard.
Do	17 Oct 18	11 Nov 18	Transport.
Lake Sunapee	28 May 18	17 Jul 18	Armed guard.
Lake Superior	do	8 Nov 18	Transport.
Lake Traverse	7 Jun 18	19 Oct 18	Armed guard.
Do	19 Oct 18	11 Nov 18	Transport.
Lake Tulare	15 May 18	19 Oct 18	Armed guard.
Do	19 Oct 18	11 Nov 18	Transport.
Lake View	21 Jun 18	27 Sept 18	Do.
Lake Weston	1 Jun 18	11 Nov 18	Armed guard.
Lake Wimico	4 Sept 18	do	Transport.
Lake Wood	18 Apr 18	do	Do.
Lake Worth	6 Jun 18	do	Do.
Lamberton	9 Sept 18	1 Nov 18	Escort.
Lamson	26 Jul 17	11 Nov 18	Destroyer.
Lancaster	21 Oct 18	do	Transport.
Lansdale	4 Nov 18	do	Destroyer.
Lapwing	1 Jul 18	do	Escort.
Do	1 May 19	30 Sept 19	Mine sweeper.
Lark	15 Jul 19	do	Do.
Laundry, Thomas	28 May 19	28 Sept 19	Do.
Lawrence	30 May 18	2 Nov 18	Destroyer.
Lea	5 Oct 18	6 Nov 18	Do.
Lebanon	25 May 18	11 Nov 18	Atlantic Fleet.
Lenape	14 Jun 17	10 Apr 18	Armed guard.
Do	23 May 18	11 Nov 18	Transport.
Leonidas	22 Apr 18	do	Patrol.
Leviathan	15 Dec 17	do	Transport.
Levisa	14 Sept 17	17 Jul 18	Armed guard.
Liberator	28 Aug 18	11 Nov 18	Transport.
Liberty	8 Nov 18	do	Do.
Little	27 May 18	do	Destroyer.
Long Beach	20 Dec 17	do	Transport.
Los Angeles	21 Sept 17	do	Do.
Long Island	20 Dec 17	do	Mine sweeper.
Louisiana	23 Sept 18	do	Escort.
Do	25 May 18	25 Sept 18	Atlantic Fleet.
Louisville	14 May 17	29 Apr 18	Armed guard.
Do	29 Apr 18	11 Nov 18	Transport.
Luce	19 Sept 18	do	Destroyer.
Lucia	21 Jun 17	18 Oct 18	Armed guard.
Luckenbach, Edw	17 Jun 17	2 Oct 18	Do.
Do	2 Oct 18	11 Nov 18	Transport.
Luckenbach, Edg. F	29 May 17	14 Aug 18	Armed guard.
Do	14 Aug 18	11 Nov 18	Transport.
Luckenbach, Florence	29 Jun 17	do	Armed guard.
Luckenbach, Fred	2 Oct 18	do	Transport.
Luckenbach, Frederick J	7 Dec 17	28 Feb 18	Armed guard.
Do	28 Feb 18	11 Nov 18	Transport.
Luckenbach, J. L	6 Apr 17	do	Armed guard.
Luckenbach, Julia	23 Sept 17	22 Sept 18	Do.
Do	22 Sept 18	28 Oct 18	Transport.
Luckenbach, Katrina	3 Jul 18	31 Jul 18	Do.
Luckenbach, K. I	4 Feb 18	28 Aug 18	Armed guard.
Do	28 Aug 18	11 Nov 18	Transport.
Luckenbach, Lewis	18 Aug 17	11 Oct 17	Armed guard.
Luckenbach, Walter A	30 Oct 18	11 Nov 18	Transport.
Luella	1 Oct 18	do	Do.
Lydonia	7 Dec 17	do	Patrol.
Lykens	27 Apr 18	do	Do.
M-1	25 May 18	15 Oct 18	Submarine.
Maartensdijk	13 May 18	28 Oct 18	Transport.
Machias	16 Aug 17	30 Sept 18	Patrol.
Macona	12 Apr 17	12 Sept 18	Armed guard.
Do	12 Sept 18	11 Nov 18	Transport.
Macy, Josiah	12 Aug 18	5 Dec 18	Armed guard.
Madawaska	26 Nov 17	11 Nov 18	Transport.
Mahan	2 Nov 18	do	Destroyer.
Maine	6 Oct 17	do	Armed guard.
Do	25 May 18	do	Atlantic Fleet.
Malang	13 May 18	do	Transport.
Malay	1 Jun 18	do	Patrol.
Mallard	22 Aug 19	30 Sept 19	Mine sweeper.

Name	Operating—		Clasp
	From—	To—	
Mallory, H. R	26 May 17	6 May 18	Armed guard.
Do	6 May 18	11 Nov 18	Transport.
Manchuria	14 Mar 17	12 May 18	Armed guard.
Do	12 May 18	11 Nov 18	Transport.
Mangore	17 Jun 18	do	Armed guard.
Manitowoc	27 Jul 18	do	Do.
Manley	26 Dec 17	do	Destroyer.
Manning	9 Sept 17	do	Escort.
Manta	31 Jul 18	30 Oct 18	Transport.
Marblehead	25 May 18	11 Nov 18	Atlantic Fleet.
Margaret	7 Dec 17	do	Patrol.
Mariana	14 Sept 17	20 Aug 18	Armed guard.
Do	20 Aug 18	11 Nov 18	Transport.
Marietta	24 Sept 17	do	Patrol.
Mariners Harbor	22 Oct 18	do	Armed guard.
Massachusetts	25 May 18	do	Atlantic Fleet.
Masuda	29 Oct 18	do	Armed guard.
Matanzas	21 Oct 18	do	Do.
Matsona	26 Mar 18	do	Transport.
Mauban	3 Oct 18	do	Do.
Do	6 Apr. 17	3 Oct 18	Armed guard.
Maui	28 Apr 18	11 Nov 18	Transport.
Maumee	13 Oct 18	31 Oct 18	Do.
Do	15 Sept 17	1 Nov 17	Do.
Maury	29 Sept 18	8 Nov 18	Destroyer.
May	6 Dec 17	11 Nov 18	Patrol.
Mayrant	29 Jun 18	do	Destroyer.
MacDonough	11 Feb 18	do	Do.
McCall	do	do	Do.
McClellan	9 May 17	15 Sept 17	Armed guard.
McCurdy, Robert H	25 Jul 18	11 Nov 18	Patrol.
McDougal	4 May 17	do	Do.
McGee, Jas	26 Sept 18	17 Dec 18	Armed guard.
McKee	do	11 Nov 18	Destroyer.
McKenney, William A	9 Jul 18	15 Oct 18	Transport.
McNeal, George H	15 Jun 17	11 Nov 18	Mine sweeper.
McNeal, Kenneth L	6 Sept 17	8 Sept 19	Do.
Medina	2 Jul 17	11 Nov 18	Armed guard.
Melrose	8 Oct. 18	do	Do.
Melville	24 May 17	do	Mobile base.
Meraukee	10 May 18	1 Nov 18	Transport.
Mercurious	13 Jun 18	30 Oct 18	Do.
Mercury	18 Jan 18	11 Nov 18	Do.
Mercy	6 Sept 18	4 Nov 18	Do.
Meridian	6 Apr 17	11 Nov 18	Armed guard.
Mexican	2 May 18	13 Nov 18	Transport.
Mexico	26 Sept 18	11 Nov 18	Armed guard.
Michigan	25 May 18	8 Nov 18	Atlantic Fleet.
Middlesex	30 Nov 17	18 Feb 18	Armed guard.
Do	18 Feb 18	25 Sept 18	Transport.
Mijdrecht	23 Jul 18	11 Nov 18	Armed guard.
Millenocket	27 Dec 17	30 Aug 18	Do.
Minneapolis	8 Mar 18	11 Nov 18	Escort.
Minnesota	6 Apr 17	do	Armed guard.
Do	25 May 18	29 Sept 18	Atlantic Fleet.
Minnesotan	14 Sept 17	20 Sept 18	Armed guard.
Do	20 Sept 18	21 Oct 18	Transport.
Mississippi	28 Jun 18	10 Nov 18	Atlantic Fleet.
Missouri	25 May 18	1 Sept 18	Do.
Moccasin	12 Oct 17	8 Apr 18	Armed guard.
Do	8 Apr 18	25 Oct 18	Transport.
Mohave	25 May 18	3 Nov 18	Atlantic Fleet.
Moldegaard	14 Sept 17	30 Oct 18	Armed guard.
Do	30 Oct 18	11 Nov 18	Transport.
Monaghan	14 Aug 17	do	Destroyer.
Mongolia	20 Mar 17	8 May 18	Armed guard.
Do	8 May 18	11 Nov 18	Transport.
Montana	1 Aug 17	do	Escort.
Montanan	17 Jun 17	15 Aug 18	Armed guard.
Montauk	5 Feb 18	11 Nov 18	Patrol.
Montclair	4 Nov 18	do	Transport.
Monterey	26 Sept 18	do	Armed guard.
Montgomery	1 Aug 18	do	Destroyer.
Monticello	13 Sept 17	do	Armed guard.
Montpelier	3 Oct 17	do	Do.
Moreni	11 Apr 17	12 Jun 17	Do.
Morrill	25 May 18	11 Nov 18	Patrol.
Morris	do	do	Patrol duty.
Morristown	27 Oct 18	15 Nov 18	Transport.
Morro Castle	8 Oct 18	11 Nov 18	Armed guard.
Motano	23 Jun 17	31 Jul 17	Do.
Mount Shasta	28 Oct 18	11 Nov 18	Transport.
Mount Vernon	12 Nov 17	do	Do.
Munaires	18 Feb 18	8 Oct 18	Do.
Munalbro	22 Sept 17	13 Oct 18	Armed guard.
Do	13 Oct 18	1 Nov 18	Transport.
Munamar	6 Apr 17	11 Nov 18	Armed guard.
Mundale	25 Sept 17	do	Do.
Mundelta	20 May 18	8 Oct 18	Transport.
Munindies	7 Dec 17	25 Jan 18	Armed guard.
Do	25 Jan 18	11 Nov 18	Transport.
Munplace	13 Oct 17	5 Oct 18	Armed guard.
Do	5 Oct 18	24 Oct 18	Transport.
Munsomo	27 Jun 17	25 Aug 18	Armed guard.
Do	25 Aug 18	11 Nov 18	Transport.
Munson, Walter D	10 May 18	22 Oct 18	Do.
Munwood	29 Sept 17	16 Oct 18	Armed guard.
Murray	28 Aug 18	11 Nov 18	Destroyer.

Name	Operating—		Clasp
	From—	To—	
Muscatine	14 Jun 18	11 Nov 18	Transport.
Muskogee	23 May 17	do	Armed guar
N-1	10 Jun 18	22 Oct 18	Submarine.
N-2	do	do	Do.
N-3	do	27 Oct 18	Do.
N-4	25 Jun 18	3 Nov 18	Do.
N-5	20 Jun 18	24 Oct 18	Do.
N-6	15 Jul 18	13 Oct 18	Do.
N-7	25 Jun 18	20 Oct 18	Do.
Nahant	24 Jan 18	11 Nov 18	Patrol.
Nahma	27 Aug 17	do	Do.
Nansemond (ex-Pennsylvania).	25 Jun 17	do	Armed guar
Nantasket	22 Oct 18	do	Do.
Nantucket	10 Jul 18	5 Oct 18	Patrol.
Narragansett	21 Jul 18	11 Nov 18	Transport.
Nashville	12 Aug 17	3 Aug 18	Patrol.
Navahoe	25 Jan 18	23 May 18	Armed guar
Navajo	15 Jun 17	4 Sept 17	Do.
Nebraska	25 May 18	5 Sept 18	Atlantic Fl
Do	5 Sept 18	11 Nov 18	Escort.
Neches	2 Jul 17	17 May 18	Armed guar
Neptune	25 May 17	8 Jul 17	Transport.
Do	25 May 18	11 Nov 18	Do.
Nereus	25 Jun 18	do	Do.
Nero	25 Sept 18	do	Do.
Neuse	15 Jun 17	do	Armed gua
Nevada	25 May 18	13 Aug 18	Atlantic Fl
Do	24 Aug 18	11 Nov 18	Grand Flee
New Hampshire	25 May 18	do	Escort.
New Jersey	do	20 Oct 18	Atlantic Fl
New Mexico	15 Aug 18	3 Nov 18	Do.
New Orleans	7 Sept 17	8 Oct 18	Escort.
Do	17 Jul 19	25 Sept 19	Asiatic.
Do	5 Oct 19	20 Dec 19	Do.
Newport News	27 Aug 17	15 Oct 18	Transport.
Newton	3 Sept 18	28 Sept 18	Do.
New York	7 Dec 17	11 Nov 18	Grand Flee
Niagara	25 May 18	13 Jun 18	Atlantic Fl
Do	13 Jun 18	24 Jul 18	Patrol.
Do	24 Jul 18	10 Sept 18	Escort.
Do	11 Sept 18	11 Nov 18	Atlantic Fl
Nicholson	24 May 17	do	Destroyer.
Nokomis	24 Jan 18	do	Patrol.
Nomo	26 Jun 17	do	Do.
Nopatin	5 Jul 18	do	Transport.
Do	25 Apr 17	18 Jun 18	Armed gua
Norlina	18 Jun 18	22 Sept 18	Transport.
Norman Bridge	30 Jun 17	11 Nov 18	Armed gua
North Carolina	24 Jun 17	do	Escort.
North Dakota	26 Oct 17	do	Do.
North Western	28 Jul 17	do	Armed guar
Northern Pacific	30 Mar 18	do	Transport.
Nyanza	16 Nov 17	do	Armed guar
O-3	26 Jun 18	do	Submarine.
O-4	13 Jun 18	do	Do.
O-5	25 Jul 18	do	Do.
O-6	29 Jun 18	do	Do.
O-7	15 Jul 18	do	Do.
O-8	12 Jul 18	do	Do.
O-9	5 Aug 18	do	Do.
O-10	30 Aug 18	do	Do.
O-11	29 Oct 18	do	Do.
O-12	16 Oct 18	do	Do.
O-16	29 Oct 18	do	Do.
Oakland	28 Aug 18	do	Transport.
O'Brien	24 May 17	do	Destroyer.
O'Brien, William	6 Apr 17	do	Armed guar
Oconee	5 Jul 17	9 Sept 18	Armed guar
Ohio	25 May 18	8 Nov 18	Atlantic Fl
Ohian	12 Nov 17	5 Aug 18	Armed guar
Do	28 Aug 18	13 Nov 18	Transport.
Oklahoma	25 May 18	13 Aug 18	Atlantic Fl
Do	25 Aug 18	11 Nov 18	Grand Flee
Old Colony	15 May 18	27 May 18	Transport.
Olean	19 May 17	22 Jul 18	Armed guar
Olivant	14 Jun 18	11 Nov 18	Do.
Olympia	12 Mar 18	do	White Sea.
Omask	6 Apr 17	do	Armed guar
Onega	1 Apr 17	23 May 17	Do.
Do	28 Feb 18	2 Jul 18	Do.
O'Neil, J. E	10 Sept 18	11 Nov 18	Do.
Ontario	6 Jun 18	19 Jul 19	Mine sweep
Oosterdijk	10 May 18	10 Jul 18	Transport.
Ophir	5 Jun 18	11 Nov 18	Do.
Oregonian	28 Sept 17	11 Sept 18	Armed gua
Do	11 Sept 18	11 Nov 18	Transport.
Oriole	20 Dec 18	7 Mar 19	Mine sweep
Do	29 Apr 19	30 Sept 19	Do.
Orion	1 June 17	11 Nov 18	Transport.
Orizaba	19 June 18	do	Do.
Orleans	3 June 17	1 July 17	Armed guar
Osage	27 Dec 17	11 Nov 18	Do.
Osceola	25 May 18	do	Patrol.
Osprey	20 Apr 19	30 Sept 19	Mine sweep
Ossineke	28 May 18	11 Nov 18	Armed guar
Ossippee	25 Aug 17	do	Escort.
Otsego	6 Apr 17	do	Armed guar

Name	Operating— From—	Operating— To—	Clasp
r Brook	26 Mar 18	do	Armed guard.
asco	18 June 17	10 Dec 17	Do.
ega	15 Nov 17	11 Nov 18	Do.
era	25 May 18	do	Patrol.
l	23 Jul 18	do	Mine sweeper.
ma	4 June 17	20 May 18	Armed guard.
Do	20 May 18	21 Oct 18	Transport.
rk	25 May 18	11 Nov 18	Atlantic Fleet.
ldleford, George E	18 Oct 18	do	Armed guard.
lucah	17 Oct 17	do	Patrol.
nama	30 Aug 18	do	Armed guard.
naman	11 Sept 17	7 Sept 18	Do.
Do	7 Sept 18	11 Nov 18	Transport.
ther	12 Aug 17	do	Mobile base.
uco	13 Oct 18	do	Transport.
ker	17 June 17	do	Destroyer.
sadena	24 Jul 18	1 Nov 18	Transport.
ssaic	10 Jul 18	2 Nov 18	Salvage.
stores	26 May 17	6 May 18	Armed guard.
Do	23 May 18	11 Nov 18	Transport.
apsco	26 May 18	30 Sept 19	Mine sweeper.
h Finder	3 Aug 17	11 Nov 18	Armed guard.
terson	1 June 17	10 Nov 18	Destroyer.
uxent	26 May 18	30 Sept 19	Mine sweeper.
ulding	1 June 17	11 Nov 18	Destroyer.
ulsboro	2 Oct 17	do	Armed guard.
wnee	15 June 17	do	Do.
arl Shell	9 Apr 17	11 Nov 18	Do.
ican	20 Apr 19	30 Sept 19	Mine sweeper.
nguin	5 June 19	do	Do.
nnsylvania	25 May 18	11 Nov 18	Atlantic Fleet.
nnsylvanian	21 Sept 17	13 Sept 18	Armed guard.
nobscot	24 Jan 18	11 Nov 18	Patroll.
nsacola	7 Dec 17	do	Transport.
quot	23 May 17	5 Nov 18	Armed guard.
Do	5 Nov 18	11 Nov 18	Transport.
kins	8 June 17	17 Nov 17	Destroyer.
ry	30 May 18	18 Sept 18	Do.
rel	8 June 18	16 Oct 18	Patrol.
rolite	13 Apr 17	11 June 17	Armed guard.
iladelphia	7 Apr 17	16 May 18	Do.
ilip	31 Aug 18	11 Nov 18	Destroyer.
ilippines	13 Oct 17	do	Armed guard.
oneer	25 Apr 17	do	Do.
qua	26 June 17	do	Patrol.
tsburgh	10 June 17	10 June 17	Do.
ttsburg	14 Mar 17	24 June 18	Armed guard.
Do	24 June 18	11 Nov 18	Transport.
tura	27 Mar 17	15 Sept 17	Armed guard.
iades	28 June 17	26 Sept 18	Do.
Do	26 Sept 18	16 Oct 18	Transport.
mouth	11 Sept 18	30 Sept 18	Transport.
Do	18 Aug 17	11 Sept 18	Armed guard.
cahontas	20 Sept 17	11 Nov 18	Transport.
int Bonita	7 Nov 17	do	Do.
larine	6 Apr 17	do	Armed guard.
lar Sea	6 Nov 18	23 Nov 18	Transport.
rter	4 May 17	11 Nov 18	Destroyer.
whatan	26 Nov 17	do	Transport.
airie	14 Oct 18	20 Oct 18	Escort.
att, Char	10 Oct 18	11 Nov 18	Armed guard.
att, Herbert L	5 Aug 18	do	Transport.
ble	10 May 18	9 Nov 18	Destroyer.
esident Grant	25 Oct 17	11 Nov 18	Transport.
esident Lincoln	31 Oct 17	1 June 18	Do.
eston	31 Jul 17	11 Nov 18	Destroyer.
ncess Matoika	23 May 18	do	Transport.
ometheus	11 Feb 18	do	Mobile base.
oteus	27 Jul 18	5 Sept 18	Transport.
eblo	10 Jun 17	10 Jun 17	Patrol.
Do	10 Feb 18	17 Apr 18	Escort.
Do	14 May 18	11 Nov 18	Do.
ail	15 Jul 19	30 Sept 19	Mine sweeper.
incy	21 Mar. 18	6 Sept 18	Transport.
innebaug	26 May 18	11 Nov 18	Mine layer.
ivilly	6 Apr 17	do	Transport.
1	6 Nov 18	do	Submarine.
15	13 Sept 18	do	Do.
16	30 Sept 18	do	Do.
17	29 Oct 18	do	Do.
18	do	do	Do.
dford	13 Oct 18	do	Destroyer.
dnor	15 Sept 18	4 Nov 18	Transport.
il	20 Apr 19	30 Sept 19	Mine sweeper.
inbow	6 Jun 18	11 Nov 18	Atlantic Fleet.
leigh	25 May 18	do	Patrol.
mbler	7 Dec 17	do	Do.
nger	13 Nov 17	20 Oct 18	Do.
ppahannock	11 Jan 18	11 Nov 18	Transport.
thburno	27 Jun 18	do	Destroyer.
dfern	21 Dec 18	25 Dec 18	Mine sweeper.
d Rose	do	do	Do.
hoboth	16 Aug 17	4 Oct 17	Patrol.
id	31 Jul 17	11 Nov 18	Destroyer.
mlik	19 Aug 17	do	Patrol.
poso	25 May 18	do	Do.
ode Island	do	9 Nov 18	Atlantic Fleet.
jndam	23 May 18	11 Nov 18	Transport.

Name	Operating— From—	Operating— To—	Clasp
Rijnland	25 May 18	11 Nov 18	Transport.
Roanoke	26 May 18	do	Mine layer.
Robin	27 Sept 18	7 Mar 19	Mine sweeper.
Do	20 Apr 19	30 Sept 19	Do.
Robinson	3 Nov 18	8 Nov 18	Destroyer.
Rochester	18 Jun 17	2 Nov 17	Armed guard.
Do	26 Dec 17	11 Nov 18	Escort.
Rockefeller, J. D	20 Sept 18	do	Armed guard.
Rockefeller, William	29 Nov 17	26 Aug 18	Transport.
Rockingham	2 Apr 17	1 May 17	Armed guard.
Rodgers	25 May 18	11 Nov 18	Patrol.
Roe	30 Sept 17	do	Destroyer.
Roepat	17 Jun 18	29 Sept 18	Transport.
Rogers, H. H	18 Sept 18	11 Nov 18	Armed guard.
Rondo	22 May 18	16 Aug 18	Transport.
Rowan	21 Nov 17	11 Nov 18	Destroyer.
Ruby	14 Oct 18	do	Armed guard.
Sabin Sun	18 Jun 18	do	Do.
Sachem	25 May 18	do	Patrol.
Sacramento	1 Aug 17	do	Do.
Do	22 May 19	13 Jul 19	White Sea.
Saetia	31 Mar 18	24 Oct 18	Transport.
Sagadahoc	18 Aug 18	11 Nov 18	Do.
Sagua	4 Sept 18	1 Nov 18	Do.
Saint Paul	23 Mar 17	17 Oct 18	Armed guard.
Salem	25 May 18	5 Nov 18	Atlantic Fleet.
Samarinda	24 Apr 18	30 Oct 18	Transport.
Sampson	24 May 17	11 Nov 18	Destroyer.
Sandlering	29 Apr 19	30 Sept 19	Mine sweeper.
San Diego	3 Oct 17	19 Jul 18	Escort.
San Francisco	26 May 18	11 Nov 18	Mine layer.
San Jacinto	14 Jun 17	do	Armed guard.
Santa Barbara	10 May 18	do	Transport.
Santa Cecilia	19 May 17	do	Armed guard.
Santa Clara	25 Oct 17	30 Oct 18	Armed guard.
Do	30 Oct 18	11 Nov 18	Transport.
Santa Luisa	11 Sept 18	do	Do.
Santa Maria	23 Mar 17	25 Feb 18	Armed guard.
Santa Olivia	5 Aug 18	11 Nov 18	Transport.
Santa Paula	8 Jun 18	15 Sept 18	Armed guard.
Do	15 Sept 18	12 Oct 18	Transport.
Santa Rita	16 Apr 17	11 Nov 18	Armed guard.
Santa Rosa	12 Sept 17	do	Do.
Santa Rosalia	9 Jul 18	do	Transport.
Santiago	4 Jul 18	do	Do.
Santore	8 Jun 18	do	Armed guard.
Saranac	29 Jun 18	do	Mine layer.
Sara Thompson	25 May 18	do	Atlantic Fleet.
Saratoga	26 May 17	2 Aug 17	Armed guard.
Satsuma	31 Mar 17	9 Nov 18	Do.
Do	9 Nov 18	11 Nov 18	Transport.
Saturn	30 Dec 18	12 Jan 19	Asiatic.
Savannah	1 Aug 18	do	Patrol.
Sayonara II	25 May 18	do	Do.
SC-1	20 Jul 18	do	Submarine chaser.
SC-2	18 Jun 18	30 Jun 18	Do.
SC-3	do	do	Do.
SC-4	do	26 Jun 18	Do.
SC-6	4 Jun 18	22 Sept 18	Do.
SC-17	11 Jun 18	11 Nov 18	Do.
SC-18	19 Jul 18	25 Aug 18	Do.
SC-19	3 Aug 18	11 Nov 18	Do.
SC-20	4 Aug 18	27 Oct 18	Do.
SC-21	1 Aug 18	11 Nov 18	Do.
SC-22	5 Aug 18	3 Sept 18	Do.
SC-23	2 Aug 18	11 Nov 18	Do.
SC-24	31 Aug 18	17 Oct 18	Do.
SC-25	27 Oct 18	11 Nov 18	Do.
SC-26	31 Jul 18	6 Aug 18	Do.
SC-27	28 Jul 18	14 Sept 18	Do.
SC-34	26 May 18	11 Nov 18	Do.
SC-35	do	do	Do.
SC-36	do	do	Do.
SC-37	do	do	Do.
Do	29 Apr 19	30 Sept 19	Mine sweeper.
SC-38	26 May 18	11 Nov 18	Submarine chaser.
Do	29 Apr 19	30 Sept 19	Mine sweeper.
SC-39	6 Jun 18	11 Nov 18	Submarine chaser.
SC-40	26 May 18	do	Do.
Do	29 Apr 19	30 Sept 19	Mine sweeper.
SC-41	26 May 18	11 Nov 19	Submarine chaser.
SC-42	4 Jun 18	5 Nov 18	Do.
SC-43	23 Jul 18	3 Oct 18	Do.
SC-44	20 Jul 18	11 Nov 18	Do.
Do	29 Apr 19	30 Sept 19	Mine sweeper.
SC-45	20 Jul 18	11 Nov 18	Submarine chaser.
Do	29 Apr 19	30 Sept 19	Mine sweeper.
SC-46	20 Jul 18	11 Nov 18	Submarine chaser.
Do	29 Apr 19	30 Sept 19	Mine sweeper.
SC-47	20 Jul 18	11 Nov 18	Submarine chaser.
Do	29 Apr 19	30 Sept 19	Mine sweeper.
SC-48	20 Jul 18	11 Nov 18	Submarine chaser.
Do	29 Apr 19	30 Sept 19	Mine sweeper.
SC-49	10 Jul 18	22 Jul 18	Submarine chaser.
SC-50	30 Jun 18	19 Sept 18	Do.
SC-52	do	10 Jul 18	Do.
SC-53	17 Jun 18	30 Jun 18	Do.
SC-54	10 Jul 18	22 Jul 18	Do.

Name	Operating—		Clasp
	From—	To—	
SC-55	17 Jun 18	29 Oct 18	Submarine chaser.
SC-56	do	do	Do.
SC-57	13 Aug 18	do	Do.
SC-58	10 Jul 18	22 Jul 18	Do.
SC-59	23 Jul 18	13 Aug 18	Do.
SC-60	24 Jul 18	12 Aug 18	Do.
SC-61	30 Sept 18	18 Oct 18	Do.
SC-62	8 Oct 18	do	Do.
SC-63	do	24 Oct 18	Do.
SC-64	do	do	Do.
SC-68	4 Jun 18	2 Aug 18	Do.
SC-69	do	30 Jun 18	Do.
SC-70	do	9 Aug 18	Do.
SC-71	5 Jul 18	29 Sept 18	Do.
SC-72	17 Oct 18	11 Nov 18	Do.
SC-73	5 Jul 18	29 Sept 18	Do.
SC-74	18 Jul 18	3 Aug 18	Do.
SC-77	27 Apr 18	11 Nov 18	Submarine chaser.
SC-78	do	do	Do.
SC-79	do	do	Do.
SC-80	do	do	Do.
SC-81	do	do	Do.
SC-82	26 May 18	do	Do.
SC-83	6 Jun 18	do	Do.
SC-84	do	do	Do.
SC-85	do	do	Do.
SC-86	do	do	Do.
SC-87	do	do	Do.
SC-88	25 May 18	do	Do.
SC-89	30 Jun 18	10 Jul 18	Do.
SC-90	22 Apr 18	11 Nov 18	Do.
SC-91	6 Jun 18	do	Do.
SC-92	27 Apr 18	do	Do.
SC-93	do	do	Do.
SC-94	22 Apr 18	do	Do.
SC-95	do	do	Do.
Do	18 Jun 19	9 Jul 19	Mine sweeper.
Do	28 Jul 19	25 Nov 19	Do.
SC-96	27 Apr 18	11 Nov 18	Submarine chaser.
SC-97	26 May 18	do	Do.
SC-98	do	do	Do.
SC-99	6 Jun 18	do	Do.
SC-100	do	do	Do.
SC-101	do	do	Do.
SC-102	4 Jun 18	24 Oct 18	Do.
SC-103	20 Jul 18	11 Nov 18	Do.
SC-104	18 Jun 18	8 Aug 18	Do.
SC-105	4 Jun 18	28 Oct 18	Do.
SC-107	3 Jun 18	11 Nov 18	Do.
SC-110	20 Jul 18	do	Do.
Do	29 Apr 19	30 Sept 19	Mine sweeper.
SC-111	17 Oct 18	11 Nov 18	Submarine chaser.
SC-112	26 May 18	11 Sept 18	Do.
SC-113	do	do	Do.
SC-114	13 Jun 18	13 Aug 18	Do.
SC-115	8 Jun 18	do	Do.
SC-116	11 Jun 18	4 Oct 18	Do.
SC-118	4 Aug 18	19 Oct 18	Do.
SC-119	25 Aug 18	5 Nov 18	Do.;
SC-120	27 Oct 18	28 Oct 18	Do.
SC-121	5 Aug 18	2 Nov 18	Do.
SC-122	18 Jul 18	5 Nov 18	Do.
SC-123	11 Jun 18	28 Sept 18	Do.
SC-124	27 Apr 18	11 Nov 18	Do.
SC-125	do	do	Do.
SC-126	17 Oct 18	do	Do.
SC-127	27 Apr 18	do	Do.
SC-128	do	do	Do.
SC-129	do	do	Do.
SC-130	26 May 18	do	Do.
SC-131	do	do	Do.
SC-132	4 Jun 18	5 Jun 18	Do.
SC-133	14 Jun 18	5 Nov 18	Do.
SC-134	4 Jun 18	24 Oct 18	Do.
SC-135	do	11 Nov 18	Do.
SC-136	17 Oct 18	do	Do.
SC-137	26 May 18	do	Do.
SC-138	31 July 18	28 Aug 18	Do.
SC-143	22 Apr 18	11 Nov 18	Do.
SC-144	18 July 18	3 Aug 18	Do.
SC-145	4 Jun 18	30 Jun 18	Do.
SC-147	22 Apr 18	11 Nov 18	Do.
SC-148	do	do	Do.
SC-150	8 Jun 18	4 Oct 18	Do.
SC-151	22 Apr 18	11 Nov 18	Submarine chaser.
SC-155	26 May 18	17 Jul 18	Do.
SC-158	8 Jun 18	11 Jun 18	Do.
SC-164	20 Jul 18	11 Nov 18	Do.
Do	29 Apr 19	30 Sept 19	Mine sweeper.
SC-165	18 May 18	11 Nov 18	Submarine chaser.
SC-166	25 May 18	do	Do.
SC-177	22 Apr 18	do	Do.
SC-178	20 Jul 18	do	Do.
Do	29 Apr 19	30 Sept 19	Mine sweeper.
SC-179	22 Apr 18	11 Nov 18	Submarine chaser.
SC-180	17 Oct 18	do	Do.
Do	29 Apr 19	30 Sept 19	Mine sweeper.
SC-181	20 Jul 18	10 Nov 18	Submarine chaser.

Name	Operating—		Clas
	From—	To—	
SC-181	29 Apr 19	30 Sept 19	Mine swee
SC-182	29 Apr 19	30 Sept 19	Mine swee
SC-184	19 Jun 18	10 Jul 18	Submarine
SC-185	3 Sept 18	24 Sept 18	Do.
SC-186	10 Jul 18	5 Oct 18	Do.
SC-187	do	3 Aug 18	Do.
SC-188	19 Jun 18	10 Nov 18	Do.
SC-189	4 Jun 18	30 Jun 18	Do.
SC-190	17 Oct 18	11 Nov 18	Do.
SC-191	4 Jun 18	do	Do.
SC-192	10 Jul 18	do	Do.
SC-193	6 Aug 18	3 Sept 18	Do.
SC-194	24 Sept 18	22 Oct 18	Do.
SC-195	6 Aug 18	3 Sept 18	Do.
SC-197	do	do	Do.
SC-198	27 Sept 18	22 Oct 18	Do.
SC-199	10 Jul 18	2 Nov 18	Do.
SC-200	19 Jun 18	10 Jul 18	Do.
SC-201	10 Jul 18	6 Sept 18	Do.
SC-202	do	22 Oct 18	Do.
SC-203	do	3 Nov 18	Do.
SC-204	11 Jun 18	24 Sept 18	Do.
SC-205	do	do	Do.
SC-206	20 Jul 18	11 Nov 18	Do.
Do	29 Apr 19	30 Sept 19	Mine swee
SC-207	20 Jul 18	11 Nov 18	Submarine
Do	29 Apr 19	30 Sept 19	Mine swee
SC-208	20 Jul 18	11 Nov 18	Submarine
Do	29 Apr 19	30 Sept 19	Mine swee
SC-209	16 Aug 18	23 Aug 18	Submarine
SC-210	17 Oct 18	11 Nov 18	Do.
SC-211	4 Jun 18	28 Oct 18	Do.
SC-212	17 Oct 18	11 Nov 18	Do.
SC-213	4 Jun 18	24 Oct 18	Do.
SC-214	17 Oct 18	11 Nov 18	Do.
SC-215	22 Apr 18	do	Do.
SC-216	26 May 18	do	Do.
SC-217	do	do	Do.
SC-218	25 May 18	do	Do.
SC-219	4 Jun 18	9 Oct 18	Do.
SC-220	6 Jun 18	11 Nov 18	Do.
SC-221	do	do	Do.
SC-222	do	do	Do.
SC-223	17 Oct 18	do	Do.
SC-224	22 Apr 18	do	Do.
SC-225	do	do	Do.
SC-226	do	do	Do.
SC-227	do	do	Do.
SC-228	28 May 18	27 Jul 18	Do.
SC-229	do	do	Do.
SC-230	23 Oct 18	29 Jul 18	Do.
SC-231	24 Jul 18	do	Do.
SC-232	2 Aug 18	4 Nov 18	Do.
SC-233	11 Jun 18	11 Nov 18	Do.
SC-234	5 Aug 18	do	Do.
SC-235	11 Jun 18	28 Oct 18	Do.
SC-236	do	11 Nov 18	Do.
SC-237	26 Sept 18	28 Sept 18	Do.
SC-238	11 Jun 18	26 Sept 18	Do.
SC-239	28 Jul 18	17 Sept 18	Do.
SC-241	25 May 18	11 Nov 18	Do.
SC-244	27 Apr 18	do	Do.
SC-245	2 Aug 18	10 Nov 18	Do.
SC-246	11 Jun 18	17 Oct 18	Do.
SC-248	6 May 18	11 Nov 18	Do.
SC-249	7 Jul 18	20 Jul 18	Do.
SC-250	30 Oct 18	5 Nov 18	Do.
SC-251	24 Oct 18	11 Nov 18	Do.
SC-252	6 Jun 18	do	Do.
SC-253	17 Oct 18	11 Nov 18	Do.
SC-254	20 July 18	do	Do.
Do	29 Apr 19	30 Sept 19	Mine swee
SC-255	[illegible] Apr 18	11 Nov 18	Submarine
SC-256	do	do	Do.
Do	28 Jul 19	30 Sept 19	Mine swee
Do	18 Jun 19	9 Jul 19	Do.
SC-257	6 Jun 18	11 Nov 18	Submarine
SC-258	26 May 18	do	Do.
SC-259	6 Jun 18	do	Do.
Do	29 Apr 19	30 Sept 19	Mine swee
SC-260	6 Jun 18	11 Nov 18	Submarine
SC-261	18 Jun 18	[illegible] Jul 18	Do.
SC-262	6 Jun 18	11 Nov 18	Submarine
SC-263	25 Sept 18	27 Oct 18	Do.
SC-264	10 Oct 18	11 Nov 18	Do.
SC-265	7 Aug 18	28 Aug 18	Do.
SC-266	31 Jul 18	11 Nov 18	Do.
SC-268	7 Aug 18	do	Do.
SC-269	31 Jul 18	5 Nov 18	Do.
SC-270	17 Oct 18	11 Nov 18	Do.
SC-271	20 Jul 18	do	Do.
SC-272	do	do	Do.
Do	20 Apr 19	30 Sept 19	Mine swee
SC-273	10 Jul 18	2 Nov 18	Submarine
SC-274	do	18 Jul 18	Do.
SC-275	do	11 Nov 18	Do.
SC-276	do	22 Aug 18	Do.
SC-277	do	11 Nov 18	Do.

Name	Operating—		Clasp
	From—	To—	
78	10 Jul 18	11 Nov 18	Submarine chaser.
79	24 Jun 18	30 Jun 18	Do.
88	11 Jul 18	11 Nov 18	Do.
89	do	do	Do.
90	do	do	Do.
91	30 Jun 18	do	Do.
2	do	5 Aug 18	Do.
3	10 Jul 18	26 Sept 18	Do.
94	do	1 Oct 18	Do.
95	do	27 Jul 18	Do.
96	do	do	Do.
97	do	11 Oct 18	Do.
98	1 Jul 18	2 Sept 18	Do.
99	10 Jul 18	do	Do.
00	1 Jul 18	do	Do.
1	7 Jul 18	11 Nov 18	Do.
02	10 Jul 18	28 Jul 18	Do.
1	16 Jul 18	2 Aug 18	Do.
2	23 Jul 18	do	Do.
3	15 May 18	5 Jun 18	Do.
20	18 Jun 18	8 Aug 18	Do.
21	26 May 18	11 Nov 18	Do.
22	6 Jun 18	do	Do.
23	do	do	Do.
24	27 Apr 18	do	Do.
25	6 Jun 18	do	Do.
26	28 May 18	2 Jun 18	Do.
27	27 Apr 18	11 Nov 18	Do.
28	30 Jun 18	10 Jul 18	Do.
29	20 Jul 18	11 Nov 18	Do.
o	29 Apr 19	30 Sept 19	Mine sweeper.
30	17 Oct 18	11 Nov 18	Submarine chaser.
31	do	do	Do.
32	do	do	Do.
33	8 Jun 18	10 Jun 18	Do.
34	23 May 18	22 Aug 18	Do.
37	22 Apr 18	11 Nov 18	Do.
38	do	do	Do.
39	4 Jun 18	9 Aug 18	Do.
40	do	1 Nov 18	Do.
41	do	24 Oct 18	Do.
42	20 Jul 18	11 Nov 18	Do.
43	do	do	Do.
44	do	do	Do.
45	do	do	Do.
46	do	do	Do.
49	27 Apr 18	do	Do.
51	22 Apr 18	do	Do.
52	6 Jun 18	do	Do.
53	17 Oct 18	do	Do.
54	6 Jun 18	do	Do.
o	18 Jun 19	9 Jul 19	Do.
o	28 Jul 19	30 Sept 19	Mine sweeper.
55	17 Oct 18	11 Nov 18	Submarine chaser.
56	20 Jul 18	do	Do.
o	29 Apr 19	30 Sept 19	Mine sweeper.
on, M. J	1 Nov 18	17 Nov 18	Transport.
y	20 Oct 18	9 Nov 18	Destroyer.
z	25 May 18	19 Jun 18	Atlantic Fleet.
ion	7 Apr 17	11 Nov 18	Overseas.
ton	15 Oct 18	3 Nov 18	Transport.
ll	10 Jul 19	30 Sept 19	Mine sweeper.
over	28 May 18	11 Nov 18	Patrol.
	1 Mar 18	9 Nov 18	Transport.
e	14 June 17	11 Nov 18	Escort.
le (see Western o).	3 Mar 18	do	Armed guard.
anca	3 May 18	19 Aug 18	Do.
nole	25 Mar 18	11 Nov 18	Patrol.
a	4 Sept 17	do	Escort.
ance	18 Sept 25	15 Oct 18	Transport.
	17 Jun 17	11 Nov 18	Destroyer.
mut	29 Jun 18	do	Mine layer.
one	6 Nov 17	do	Armed guard.
	25 May 18	31 Oct 18	Atlantic Fleet.
ey	6 May 18	11 Nov 18	Transport.
	21 July 18	do	Do.
rney	25 May 18	do	Destroyer.
Shell	26 Apr 17	do	Armed guard.
	30 Aug 18	12 Oct 18	Transport.
a	13 Oct 18	29 Oct 18	Do.
er, Francis L	[illegible] Oct 18	11 Nov 18	Armed guard.
er, Jeannette	[illegible] May 18	do	Transport.
	1 Aug 17	do	Destroyer.
omish	26 May 18	10 Nov 18	Patrol.
l	27 Jun 18	11 Nov 18	Armed guard.
dijk	2 Nov 18	16 Nov 18	Transport.
e	16 July 18	11 Nov 18	Atlantic Fleet.
rset	20 Apr. 18	do	Armed guard.
na	26 May 18	10 Jun 19	Mine sweeper.
Carolina	25 May 18	8 Nov 18	Atlantic Fleet.
Dakota	10 Jun 17	10 Jun 17	Patrol.
o	3 Jan 18	11 Nov 18	Escort.
o	12 Jan 20	11 Mar 20	Asiatic.
erland	6 Apr 17	11 Nov 18	Armed guard.
ery [1]			

[1] nserviceable during war.

Name	Operating—		Clasp
	From—	To—	
Spaulding, S. M	14 Aug 18	11 Nov 18	Armed guard.
Spray	18 Jun 18	31 Dec 18	Mine sweeper.
Standard	27 Aug 18	11 Nov 18	Armed Guard.
Standard Arrow	18 Dec 17	30 Oct 18	Transport.
Steed, W. L	18 Sept 18	11 Nov 18	Do.
Sterett	5 Jun 17	do	Destroyer.
Sterling	8 Feb 18	do	Transport.
Stevens	3 Jun 18	do	Do.
Stewart	4 Feb 18	do	Do.
St. Francis	19 Jun 18	30 Oct 18	Transport.
St. Louis	17 Jun 17	11 Nov 18	Escort.
Stockton	7 Feb 18	do	Destroyer.
Stribling	25 Aug 18	do	Do.
Stringham	8 Jul 18	do	Do.
Sudbury	8 Apr 18	7 Oct 18	Transport.
Suffolk	26 Nov 17	11 Nov 18	Armed guard.
Sultana	26 Jun 17	do	Patrol.
Sun	23 Mar 17	do	Armed guard.
Sun Oil	30 July 18	do	Do.
Suruga	6 Apr 17	do	Do.
Surveyor	5 Feb 18	do	Patrol.
Susana	3 Aug 17	do	Armed guard.
Susquehanna	20 Dec 17	do	Transport.
Suwannee	26 Sept 17	do	Armed guard.
Swallow	20 Apr 19	30 Sept 19	Mine sweeper.
Swan	do	do	Do.
Sylvan Arrow	15 Dec 17	13 Aug 18	Armed guard.
Do	13 Aug 18	11 Nov 18	Transport.
Tacoma	14 Aug 17	30 Oct 18	Escort.
Tallapoosa	25 May 18	11 Nov 18	Patrol.
Talbot	22 Jul 18	5 Nov 18	Destroyer.
Tampa	17 Oct 17	26 Sept 18	Escort.
Tanager	9 Jul 18	11 Nov 18	Patrol.
Do	1 May 19	30 Sept 19	Mine sweeper.
Tanamo	20 Oct 18	3 Nov 18	Transport.
Taussig, Felix	13 Oct 17	29 Aug 18	Armed guard.
Do	29 Aug 18	28 Oct 18	Transport.
Tavernilla	25 May 18	11 Nov 18	Atlantic Fleet.
Taylor	7 Aug 18	do	Destroyer.
Teagle, W. C	6 Aug 18	do	Armed guard.
Teal	20 Apr 19	30 Sept 19	Mine sweeper.
Tenadores	26 May 17	6 May 18	Armed guard.
Do	6 May 18	11 Nov 18	Transport.
Teresa	22 Jun 17	4 Mar 18	Armed guard.
Do	4 Mar 18	24 Oct 18	Transport.
Ternate	9 Jun 18	8 Oct 18	Do.
Terry	19 Jan 18	11 Nov 18	Destroyer.
Texaco	14 Dec 17	do	Armed guard.
Texan	1 Feb 18	24 Apr 18	Armed guard.
Do	24 Apr 18	9 Oct 18	Transport.
Texas	11 Feb 18	11 Nov 18	Grand Fleet.
Do	20 Aug 18	do	Armed guard.
Thompson, Robert M	19 Nov 17	23 Oct 18	Do.
Do	23 Oct 18	11 Nov 18	Transport.
Thornton	25 May 18	do	Patrol.
Thrush	5 Jun 19	30 Sept 19	Mine sweeper.
Ticonderoga	7 Mar 18	30 Sept 18	Transport.
Tide Water	23 Jun 17	11 Nov 18	Armed guard.
Tiger	1 Jan 18	do	Do.
Tilford, W. H	1 Feb 18	do	Do.
Tingey	25 May 18	24 Sept 18	Mine sweeper.
Tippecanoe	11 Dec 17	25 Jul 18	Armed guard.
Tivives	22 Oct 17	28 Jul 18	Mine sweeper.
Do	28 Jul 18	11 Nov 18	Transport.
Tjikembang	25 Aug 18	14 Sept 18	Do.
Tjisondari	19 Jul 18	17 Oct 18	Do.
Tonopah	11 Feb 18	11 Nov 18	Patrol.
Topila	19 Jan 18	5 Mar 18	Transport.
Do	26 Sept 18	11 Nov 18	Armed guard.
Truxton	17 Sept 17	do	Destroyer.
Trinadadian	18 Aug 17	do	Armed guard.
Trippe	1 Jun 17	do	Destroyer.
Tucker	21 May 17	do	Do.
Tunica	27 Mar 18	do	Armed guard.
Turkey	20 Apr 19	30 Sept 19	Mine sweeper.
Tuscarora	25 May 18	11 Nov 18	Transport.
Tyler	4 Jun 17	2 May 18	Armed guard.
Ulua	26 May 18	8 Jun 18	Transport.
Ulysses	26 Jun 18	11 Nov 18	Armed guard.
Uncas	25 May 18	do	Atlantic Fleet.
Undaunted	13 Nov 18	19 Jul 19	Mine sweeper.
Utah	21 May 18	11 Sept 18	Atlantic Fleet.
Do	11 Sept 18	11 Nov 18	Grand Fleet.
Utowana	6 Jan 18	do	Patrol.
Vacuum	23 Mar 17	28 Apr 17	Armed guard.
Van Dyke, J. W	31 Aug 18	11 Nov 18	Do.
Vedette	26 Jun 17	do	Patrol.
Veendijk	13 May 18	14 Oct 18	Transport.
Venetia	23 Jan 18	11 Nov 18	Patrol.
Vermont	25 May 18	5 Nov 18	Atlantic Fleet.
Vestal	do	11 Nov 18	Do.
Vigo	21 Apr 17	11 Sept 18	Armed guard.
Virginia	25 May 18	28 Aug 18	Atlantic Fleet.
Do	28 Aug 18	7 Nov 18	Escort.
Virginian	23 Oct 17	11 Nov 18	Armed guard.
Vittorio Emanuelle III	15 Oct 18	3 Nov 18	Transport.
Vixen	25 May 18	11 Nov 18	Patrol.
Von Steuben	31 Oct 17	do	Transport.

Name	Operating—		Clasp
	From—	To—	
Vulcan	25 May 18	11 Nov 18	Transport.
Wabash	16 May 18	4 Nov 18	Do.
Wachusetts	24 Feb 18	11 Nov 18	Do.
Wadena	27 Apr 18	do	Patrol.
Wadsworth	4 May 17	do	Destroyer.
Wainwright	do	do	Do.
Wakiva, 2d	6 Sept 17	22 May 18	Patrol.
Wakulla	29 Sept 18	9 Nov 18	Transport.
Walke	5 Jun 17	4 Oct 18	Destroyer.
Wampum	7 Oct 18	11 Nov 18	Armed guard.
Wando	25 May 18	do	Atlantic Fleet.
Wanderer	19 Aug 17	do	Patrol.
Warden, William G	29 Aug 18	do	Armed guard.
Waring, O. T	21 Sept 18	do	Do.
Warrington	1 Jun 17	do	Destroyer.
Washington, George	4 Dec 17	do	Transport.
Washington, Martha	24 Feb 18	do	Do.
Waters	10 Aug 18	do	Destroyer.
Watts, Albert	25 May 17	22 Jan 18	Armed guard.
Weller, Fred W	6 Aug 18	11 Nov 18	Do.
Wenonah	6 Dec 17	do	Patrol.
West Alsek	18 Aug 18	22 Sept 18	Transport.
West Apaum	1 Sept 18	11 Nov 18	Do.
West Arrow	8 Apr 18	do	Armed guard.
West Borough	14 Jun 18	do	Do.
West Bridge	22 Aug 18	15 Oct 18	Transport.
West Brook	9 May 18	11 Nov 18	Armed guard.
West Chester	23 May 18	15 Sept 18	Do.
Do	15 Sept 18	28 Oct 18	Transport.
West Cohas	28 Oct 18	11 Nov 18	Do.
West Durfee	27 Sept 18	do	Armed guard.
West Eagle	15 May 18	11 Nov 18	Armed guard.
West Ekonk	19 Sept 18	8 Oct 18	Transport.
Westerdijk	24 Apr 18	do	Do.
Western Chief	11 Sept 18	25 Oct 18	Do.
Western City	6 Apr 17	11 Nov 18	Armed guard.
Western Cross	18 Oct 18	do	Do.
Westerner	17 Aug 18	22 Sept 18	Transport.
Western Front	16 Mar 18	22 Jun 18	Armed guard.
Do	22 Jun 18	6 Oct 18	Transport.
Western Hero (see Seattle)	3 Mar 18	11 Nov 18	Armed guard.
Western King	6 Apr 17	do	Do.
Western Hope	28 Oct 18	7 Nov 18	Transport.
Western Light	4 Nov 18	19 Nov 18	Do.
Western Ocean	27 Sept 18	24 Oct 18	Do.
Western Maid	17 Aug 18	11 Nov 18	Do.
Western Queen	1 Jun 18	do	Armed guard.
Western Sea	19 Sept 18	29 Oct 18	Transport.
Western Spirit	8 Nov 18	11 Nov 18	Do.
West Field	4 Nov 18	do	Armed guard.
West Ford	24 Aug 18	11 Nov 18	Transport.
Westford	12 Aug 18	do	Do.
West Gambo	8 Oct 18	do	Do.
West Gate	22 Jul 18	24 Aug 18	Do.
West Grove	24 Jun 18	11 Nov 18	Armed guard.
West Hampton	25 Jun 18	do	Do.
West Havan	10 Jul 18	3 Nov 18	Transport.
West Lake	18 Apr 18	11 Nov 18	Armed guard.
West Land	do	do	Do.
West Lianga	11 Jun 18	11 Sept 18	Do.
Do	11 Sept 18	11 Nov 18	Transport.
West Mount	29 Jul 18	do	Do.
West Oil	4 Jun 17	23 Oct 18	Armed guard.
Westover	27 Jun 18	11 Jul 18	Transport.
West Point	8 Apr 18	5 Sept 18	Armed guard.
Do	5 Sept 18	8 Oct 18	Transport.
West Shore	24 May 18	12 Oct 18	Armed guard.
Do	12 Oct 18	6 Nov 18	Transport.
Westward Ho	17 Jun 18	19 Oct 18	Armed guard.
Do	19 Oct 18	11 Nov 18	Transport.
West Wego	21 Apr 17	do	Armed guard.
West Wind	20 June 18	do	Do.
Westwood	26 Apr 18	25 Aug 18	Do.
Do	25 Aug 18	22 Sept 18	Transport.
Wheeling	16 Sept 17	11 Nov 18	Patrol.
Whipple	17 Sept 17	do	Destroyer.
Whippoorwill	15 Jul 19	30 Sept 19	Mine sweeper.
Wickes	31 Jul 18	11 Nov 18	Destroyer.
Wico	25 Apr 17	do	Armed guard.
Widgeon	24 Aug 18	11 Feb 19	Mine sweeper.
Do	10 July 19	30 Sept 19	Do.
Wieldrecht	24 Jul 18	8 Oct 18	Transport.
Wieringen	1 Nov 18	11 Nov 18	Armed guard.
Wilhelmina	15 Feb 18	do	Transport.
Wilkes	26 Jun 17	do	Destroyer.
Wilmore	4 May 17	12 Sept 17	Armed guard.
Winding Gulf	19 Sept 18	8 Oct 18	Transport.
Winifred	16 Oct 17	21 Jun 18	Armed guard.
Do	21 Jun 18	11 Nov 18	Transport.
Winnebago	20 Apr 18	13 May 18	Do.
Winslow	21 May 17	11 Nov 18	Destroyer.
Wisconsin	3 Jun 18	do	Atlantic Fleet.
Woodcock	10 Jul 19	30 Sept 19	Mine sweeper.
Woolsey	6 Oct 18	5 Nov 18	Destroyer.
Woonsocket	7 Dec 17	11 Nov 18	Armed guard.
Worden	29 Feb 18	do	Destroyer.
Wyandotte	18 Jun 17	do	Armed guard.
Wylie, Herbert O	13 Jun 17	do	Do.
Wyoming	7 Dec 17	11 Nov 18	Grand Flee
Xarifa	25 May 18	do	Patrol.
Yacona	22 Apr 18	do	Do.
Yadkin	14 Jun 17	do	Armed gua
Yale	21 Jul 18	do	Transport.
Yamacraw	11 Sept 17	do	Escort.
Yankton	2 Sept 17	6 Sept 18	Do.
Do	8 Feb 19	9 Jul 19	White Sea.
Yellowstone	27 Oct 18	15 Nov 18	Transport.
Yorktown	29 Jun 18	9 Nov 18	Patrol.
Yosemite	21 Mar 18	11 Nov 18	Armed gua
Zaanland	3 May 18	13 May 18	Transport.
Zeelandia	30 May 18	11 Nov 18	Do.
Zuiderdijk	1 Jun 18	5 Oct 18	Do.

* Indicates engagement for which medal was given. This engagement is engraved on the reverse of the medal and not represented by an engagement bar.

' Indicates only selected personnel participating in a boat expedition or landing force are eligible.

Appendix J

Engagement Bars and dates for the West Indies Naval Campaign Medal (Sampson Medal)

Engagement and Date	
Baracoa,	July 15
Casilda,	June 22
Casilda,	June 23
Cape Muno,	June 29
Cabanas,	May 12
Cardenas,	May 11
Cardenas,	July 5
Cienfuegos,	April 29
Cienfuegos,	May 11
Caibarien,	August 14
Guantanamo,	June 11-13
Havana,	May 7
Havana,	May 14
Havana,	June 10
Havana,	August 12
Isle of Pines,	August 2
Isle of Pines,	August 4
Mariel,	May 13
Mariel,	June 21
Mariel,	July 4
Mariel,	July 5
Matanzas,	April 27
Matanzas,	May 6
Manzanillo,	June 30
Manzanillo,	July 1
Manzanillo,	July 18
Manzanillo,	August 12
Nipe Bay,	July 21
Naguerro,	July18
Punta Colorado,	April 29
Rio Hondo,	June 29
Santiago de Cuba,	May 1
Santiago de Cuba,	May 18
Santiago de Cuba,	May 31
Santiago de Cuba,	June 6
Santiago de Cuba,	June 13
Santiago de Cuba,	June 14
Santiago de Cuba,	June 14
Santiago de Cuba,	July 3
Santiago de Cuba,	July 4
Santiago de Cuba,	August 3
San Juan,	May 10
San Juan,	May 12
San Juan,	June 22
San Juan,	June 28
Sagua al Grande,	August 3
Tunas,	July 2

The "Sampson Medal" was initially issued with the bars attached to each other with rings at each end, the ribbon attached to the lowest bar, which was the ship's name, and the bars arranged in acending order with the latest engagement on top. The top bar served as the brooch.

In 1908 the arrangement of the bars was changed and the bar bearing the ship's name served as the brooch with the ribbon attached to it. The engagement bars were attached to the ribbon then arranged in descending order with the latest engagement on the bottom. This bottom bar also served as the means of attaching the planchet to the ribbon.

Roster of Ships Eligible for the Sampson Medal

Vessel	Engagement Bar	Date
Abarenda	*Guantanamo,	June 11-13
Alvarado	*Manzanillo,	August 12
Amphitrite	*San Juan, P.R.,	May 12
	'Cape San Juan,	Aug 8
Annapolis	*Baracoa,	July 15
Bancroft	'*Cortes Bay,	Aug 2
	'Isle of Pines,	Aug 4
	Nipe Bay,	July 21
Brooklyn	*Santiago,	July 3
	Santiago,	June 6
	Santiago,	June 16
	Santiago,	July 2
Cincinnati	*Matanzas,	April 27
Castine	*Mariel,	July 5
Detroit	*San Juan, P.R.,	May 12
Dixie	*Casilda,	June 22
Dolphin	*Santiago,	June 6
	Guantanamo,	June 13
Dupont	*Matanzas,	May 6
	Santiago,	July 2
Eagle	*Cienfuegos,	April 29
	Cape Muno,	June 29
	'Isle of Pines,	July 5
Ericsson	*Santiago,	July 3
Fern	*Santiago,	July 3
Gloucester	*Santiago,	July 3
	Santiago,	July 2
	'Guanica,	July 25
Hamilton	*Mariel,	June 21
Harvard	*Santiago,	July 3

Hawk	*Mariel,	July 5
Helena	*Tunas,	July 2
	Tunas,	July 3
	Manzanillo,	July 18
	Manzanillo,	July 26
Hist	*Santiago,	July 3
	Manzanillo,	June 30
	Manzanillo,	July 18
	Manzanillo,	August 12
Hornet	*Manzanillo,	June 30
	Manzanillo,	July 18
Indiana	*Santiago,	July 3
	San Juan, P.R.,	May 12
	Santiago,	June 22
	Santiago,	July 2
	Santiago,	July 4
Iowa	*Santiago,	July 3
	San Juan,	May 12
	Santiago,	May 31
	Santiago,	June 6
	Santiago,	June 16
	Santiago,	July 2
	Santiago,	July 4
Leyden	*Nipe Bay,	July 21
Machias	*Cardenas,	May 11
Mangrove	*Caibairien,	Aug 14
Manning	*Cabanas,	May 12
	Mariel,	May 13
	Naguerro,	July 18
Maple	*Isle of Pines,	Aug 4
Marblehead	*Cinfuegos,	May 11
	Cinfuegos,	April 29
	Santiago,	June 6
	Guantanamo,	June 11-13
	Guantanamo,	June 15
	Cabanas Bay,	June 17
Massachusetts	*Santiago,	May 31
	Santiago,	June 6
	Santiago,	June 16
	Santiago,	July 2
	Santiago,	July 4
	'Cabanas Bay,	June 17
Mayflower	*Havana,	May 14
McKee	*Sagua Ia Grande,	August 3
Montgomery	*San Juan, P.R.,	May 12
Morrill	*Havana,	May 7
Nashville	*Cienfuegos,	May 11
Newark	*Santiago,	July 2
	Manzanillo,	August 12
New Orleans	*Santiago,	May 31
	Santiago,	June 6
	Santiago,	June 14
	Santiago,	June 16
New York	Santiago,	July 3
	Matanzas,	April 27
	San Juan, P.R.,	May 12
	Santiago,	June 6
	Santiago,	June 16
	Santiago,	July 2
	Santiago,	July4
	'Santiago,	June 6
	'Cabanas Bay,	June 17
Oregon	*Santiago,	July 3
	Santiago,	June 6
	Santiago,	June 16
	Santiago,	July 2
	Santiago,	July 4
Osceola	* Manzanillo,	July 18
	Manzanillo,	August 12
	Tunas,	July 26
Panther	*Guantanamo,	June 11-13
Peoria	*Tunas,	July 2
Porter	*San Juan, P.R.,	May 12
	Santiago,	June 7
Prairie	*Mariel,	July 5
Puritan	*Matanzas,	April 27
Resolute	*Santiago,	July 3
	Manzanillo,	August 12
St. Louis	*Santiago,	May 18
St. Paul	*San Juan, P.R.,	June 22
Suwanee	*Santiago,	June 6
	Guantanamo,	June 15
	Manzanillo,	August 12
San Francisco	*Havana,	August 12
Scorpion	*Manzanillo,	July 1
	Manzanillo,	July 18
Terror	*San Juan, P.R.,	May 12
Texas	*Santiago,	July 3
	Santiago,	June 6
	Guantanamo,	June 12
	Guantanamo,	June 15
	Santiago,	June 16
	Santiago,	June 22
	Santiago,	July 2
	Santiago,	July 4
Topeka	Nipe Bay,	July 21
Vixen	*Santiago,	July 3
	Santiago,	June 6
	Santiago,	July 2
Vesuvius	*Santiago,	June 13
	Santiago,	July 4
Vicksburg	*Havana,	May 7
Wasp	*Cabanas,	May 12
	Mariel,	May 13
	Nipe Bay,	July 21
Wilmington	*Cardenas,	May 11
	Manzanillo,	July 18
Windom	*Cienfuegos,	May 11
Winslow	*Cardenas,	May 11
Wompatuck	*Santiago,	May 18
	Manzanillo,	June 30
	Manzanillo,	July 18
Yale	*San Juan, P.R.,	May 10
Yankton	*Cape Muno,	June 29
Yankee	*Santiago,	June 6
	Cienfuegos,	June 13
	Casilda,	June 20
Yosemite	*San Juan, P.R.,	June 28

Appendix K

Ships and Officers Eligible for the Manila Bay Medal (Dewey Medal)

U.S.S. Olympia

Protected Cruiser, 14 Guns, 5,870 Tons, 17,213 Horse Power

Charles V. Gridley	Captain
Corwin P. Rees	Lieutenant
Carlos G. Calkins	Lieutenant
Valentine S. Nelson	Lieutenant
Stokely Morgan	Lieutenant
Samuel M. Strite	Lieut. J.G.
Montgomery M. Taylor	Ensign
Frank B. Upham	Ensign
Arthur G. Kavanaugh	Ensign
Henry B. Butler, Jr	Ensign
Abel F. Price	Medical Inspector
John E. Page	Passed Assistant Surgeon
Charles Kindleberger	Assistant Surgeon
Daniel A. Smith	Pay Inspector
James Entwistle	Chief Engineer
Gustav Kaemmerling	Passed Assistant Engineer
Edwin H. DeLany	Assistant Engineer
John F. Marshall, Jr	Assistant Engineer
Edward H. Dunn	Assistant Engineer
John B. Frazier	Chaplain
William P. Biddle	Captain of Marines
Leonard Kuhlwein	Gunner
William M. Long	Pay Clerk
William J. Rightmire	Fleet Pay Clerk

U.S.S. Baltimore

Protected Cruiser, 10 Guns, 4,413 Tons, 10,064 Horse Power

Nehemiah M. Dyer,	Captain
John B. Briggs,	Lt. Commander
Frank H. Holmes,	Lieutenant
Frank W. Kellogg,	Lieutenant
John M. Ellicott,	Lieutenant J.G.
Charles S. Stanworth,	Lieutenant J.G.
George N. Hayward,	Ensign
Noble E. Irwin,	Ensign
Michael J. McCormack,	Ensign
John C. Wise,	Medical Inspector
Reginald K. Smith,	Assistant Surgeon
Edward Bellows,	Pay Inspector
John D. Ford,	Chief Engineer
Edward L. Beach,	Passed Assistant Engineer
Henry B. Price,	Assistant Engineer
Hutch I. Cone,	Assistant Engineer
Thaddeus S. K. Freeman,	Chaplain
Otway C. Berryman,	Captain of Marines
Dion Williams,	1LT of Marines
Harry R. Brayton,	Acting Boatswain
Louis J. Connelly,	Gunner
Levin J. Wallace,	Acting Gunner
Otto Barth,	Carpenter
William J. Corwin,	Pay Clerk

U.S.S. Raleigh

Protected Cruiser, 11 Guns, 3,213 Tons, 10,000 Horsepower

Joseph B. Coghlan,	Captain
Frederic Singer,	Lt. Commander
William Winder,	Lieutenant
Benjamin Tappan,	Lieutenant
Hugh Rodman,	Lieutenant
Casey B. Morgan,	Ensign
Frank L. Chadwick,	Ensign
Provoost Babin,	Ensign
Emlyn H. Marsteller,	Surgeon
Dudley N. Carpenter,	Assistant Surgeon
William W. Galt,	Paymaster
Frank H. Bailey,	Chief Engineer
Alexander S. Halstead,	Passed Assistant Engineer
John R. Bradey,	Assistant Engineer
Thomas C. Treadwell,	1LT of Marines
Edward J. Norcott,	Acting Boatswain
Gaston D. Johnstone,	Acting Gunner
Timothey E. Kiley,	Acting Carpenter
George A. White,	Pay Clerk

U.S.S. Petrel

Gunboat, 4 Guns, 892 Tons, 1,092 Horse Power

Edward P. Wood,	Commander
Edward M. Hughes,	Lieutenant

Bradley A. Fiske,	Lieutenant
Albert N. Wood,	Lieutenant
Charles P. Plunkett,	Lieutenant J.G.
George L. Fermier,	Ensign
William S. Montgomery,	Ensign
Carl D. Brownell,	Passed Assistant Surgeon
George G. Seibels,	Assistant Paymaster
Reynold T. Hall,	Chief Engineer
Robert S. Blakeman,	Assistant Surgeon
John R. Martin,	Paymaster
Richard Inch,	Chief Engineer
Leland F. James,	Assistant Engineer
Robert McM. Dutton,	1Lt. of Marines
Joel C. Evans,	Gunner
Osgood H. Hilton,	Carpenter
George H. Grendle,	Pay Clerk

U.S.S. Concord

Gunboat, 6 Guns, 1,700 Tons, 3,405 Horse Power

Asa Walker,	Commander
George P. Colvocoresses,	Lt. Commander
Thomas B. Howard,	Lieutenant
Patrick W. Hourigan,	Lieutenant
Charles M. McCormick,	Lieutenant J.G.
Louis A. Kaiser,	Ensign
William C. Davidson,	Ensign
Orlo S. Knepper,	Ensign
Richard G. Broderick,	Passed Assistant Surgeon
Eugene D. Ryan,	Passed Assistant Paymaster
George B. Ransom,	Chief Engineer
Horace W. Jones,	Passed Assistant Engineer
Frederick K. Hunt,	Pay Clerk

U.S.S. Boston

Protected Cruiser, 8 Guns, 3,000 Tons, 4,030 Horse Porwer

Frank Wildes,	Captain
John A. Norris,	Lt. Commander
Bernard O. Scott,	Lieutenant
John Gibson,	Lieutenant
William L. Howard,	Lieutenant J.G.
Samual S. Robison,	Ensign
Lay H. Everhart,	Ensign
John S. Doddridge,	Ensign
Millard H. Crawford,	Surgeon

U.S.S.R.C. McCulloch

Revenue Cutter, 1,280 Tons, 2,400 Horse Power

William P. Elliot,	Lieutenant, USN
Daniel B. Hodgsdon,	Captain, RCS
Daniel P. Foley,	1st Lieut. , RCS
Walker W. Joynes,	2nd Lieut., RCS
Randolph Ridgely Jr.,	3rd Lieut. , RCS
William E. AtLee,	3rd Lieut. , RCS
John Mel, 3rd Lieut. ,	RCS
Joseph B. Green,	Assistant Surgeon, Marine Hospital Service
William C. Meyers,	1st Assistant Engineer, RCS
William E. Maccoun,	1st Assistant Engineer, RCS
Henry F. Schoenborn,	2nd Assistant Engineer, RCS
George A. Loud,	Acting Paymaster

Nanshan

Collier

Ben W. Hodges,	Lieutenant, USN

Zafiro

Supply Vessel

Henry A. Pearson,	Ensign, USN

Appendix L

Recipients of the Specially Meritorious Service Medal for "rescuing crews from and in close proximity to burning ships after the battle of Santiago, Cuba, 3 July 1898."

USS Indiana

Ensign Percy N. Olmstead
Naval Cadet Frank P. Helm, Jr.
Assistant Surgeon George D. Costigan
Chaplain Percy G. Cassard
Captain Littleton W.T. Waller, USMC

USS Iowa

Ensign Nathan C. Twining
Naval Cadet Arthur J. Hepburn
John Clune, Coxwain
John W.M. Moseley, Coxwain
James Treinor, Coxwain
William Allen, Seaman
Daniel H. Murphy, Seaman
Stephen Nolan, Seaman
Emil Totterman, Seaman
John Casey, Ordinary Seaman
Robert Walsh, Apprentice 1st Class
Carl H. George, Apprentice 1st Class
Joseph M. Murphy, Apprentice 2nd Class

USS Gloucester

Lieutenant Thomas G. Wood
Lieutenant JG George H . Norman
Ensign John T. Edson
Assistant Engineer Andre M. Procter
William H. Sellers, Chief Yeoman
William G. Bee, Chief Gunner's Mate
John Bond, Chief Boatswain's Mate
George Chipman, Electrician 1st Class
George B. Evans, Quartermaster 1st Class
Patric Kay, Ship's Cook 1st Class
Peter Keller, Boatswain's Mate 1st Class
Hans Dahl, Coxwain
Adam Jaggi, Coxwain
Patrick Lynch, Coxwain
Neil H. Lykke, Seaman Gunner
Otto Brown, Seaman
Carl A. Collin, Seaman
Alvin D. Thompson, Seaman
Martin J. Tierney, Seaman
Frank Wirtane, Seaman
Oscar Halvorson, Ordinary Seaman
Samual Kastell, Ordinary Seaman
William M. Lawrence, Ordinary Seaman
John W. Lewis, Ordinary Seaman
Thomas Macklin, Ordinary Seaman
Griffith Roberts, Ordinary Seaman
Charles Rozzle, Ordinary Seaman
Michael Magee, Painter
John Cooksey, Landsman
Milo K. Davis, Landsman
Bernard Loehrs, Landsman
Louis Quentin, Landsman

USS Harvard

Lieutenant Joseph Beale
Lieutenant JG Archibald H. Davis
Naval Cadet John Halligan, Jr.
Paul D. Mills, Gunner's Mate 2nd Class
Max L. Scull, Gunner's Mate 3rd Class
James A. McGreger, Seaman
Arthur J. Amundsen, Ordinary Seaman
C. Earle Skeen, Ordinary Seaman

USS Hist

Lieutenant JG Felix H. Hunicke
Assistant Engineer Edward S. Kellogg
August H. Brown, Chief Yeoman
Edward J. Bourke, Chief Gunner's Mate
Joel E. Bean, Fireman 1st Class
Henry Wethley, Boatswain's Mate 1st Class
Clarence J. Webster, Electrician 2nd Class
Fred G. Simcox, Quartermaster 3rd Class
Jay Williams, Ordinary Seaman

USTB Ericsson

Lieutenant Nathan R. Usher
Ensign John R. Edie
Ensign John J. Hannigan
Jacobus J. Corino, Chief Machinist

Clarance M. Wingate, Chief Machinist

David Hepburn, Chief Gunner's Mate

James H. Agnew, Fireman 1st Class

John Hill, Fireman 1st Class

Leonard Roll, Gunner's Mate 1st Class

Tanaka Shosuke, Ship's Cook 1st Class

Emile Van Castern, Quartermaster 1st Class

Daniel J. Hollingsworth, Gunner's Mate 2nd Class

Harry D. Rogers, Quartermaster 2nd Class

Alvah M. Smith, Gunner's Mate 2nd Class

Nicholas Calango, Water Tender

James K. Doherty, Oiler

John B. McNalley, Oiler

Shiroshi Otsuka, Cabin Steward

Robert H. Russell, Water Tender

James H.W. Center, Seaman

Albert O. Maywald, Seaman

Maurice C. Minster, Seaman

Also included in the 93 awards were two Naval personnel not assigned to ships in the area. They were to Lieutenant Victor Blue for "...locating the enemy's ships in Santiago Harbor, 12 June 1898" and Assistant Naval Constructor Richard P. Hobson for "...sinking the Merrimac in entrance to Santiago Harbor, 3 June 1898."

Bibliography

Regulations

ARMY	AR 672-5-1, Change 15 (October 1990) AR 670
NAVY	SECNAVINST 1650.1E NAVPERS 1566.5G ALNAV 74-43, (19 April 1943)
MARINE CORPS	MCO 1650.19 MCO P 1020.34
AIR FORCE	AFR 900-48 (15 March 1989) AFR 35-10
COAST GUARD	COMDINST M1650.25
USPHS	COMMISSIONED CORPS PERSONNEL MANUAL Subchapter CC27.1
NASA	NASA MANAGEMENT INSTRUCTIONS 3451.1

Books and Articles

Armed Forces Decorations and Awards (DoD Gen - 40), Department of Defense, 1989.

Awards and Decorations for Commissioned Officers, U.S. Dept. of Health and Human Services/Public Health Service.

The Congressional Medal of Honor - The Names, The Deeds, Forest Ranch, CA, Sharp & Dunnigan Publications, 1984.

Belden, Bauman L., *United States War Medals*, American Numismatic Society, New York, N.Y., 1916.

Brantly, CWO 3 Deborah, "Army Superior Unit Award," *Soldiers*, June 1987: Page 41.

Doria, Cristina, *National Aeronautics and Space Administration Honor Awards Program*, (Draft Report 21 August 1989), NASA.

Du Bois, Arthur E., "The Heraldry of Heroism," *The National Geographic Magazine*, Vol. LXXXIV, No. 4 (Oct. 1943): pp 409-444.

Gleim, Albert F., *The Certificate of Merit - US Army Gallantry Award* 1847-1918, Private publication, 1979.

Fischer, Ronald E., *United States Medals of Honor 1862-1989*, Planchet Press Publication 43, 1989.

Grosvenor, Gilbert, ET. AL., *Insignia and Decorations of The U.S. Armed Forces*, National Geographic Society, Washington, D.C., 1944.

Kerrigan, Evans E. *American Medals and Decorations*, Noroton Heights, Conn.: Medallic Publishing, 1990.

Kroulik, Alfred R., "Polar Awards of the United States: Jeanette Arctic Expedition Medal, 1879-1882," *The Medal Collector*, Vol. 39, No. 11 (Nov. 1988): pp 5-12.

Kroulik, Alfred R., "Polar Awards of the United States: Peary Polar Expedition Medal, 1908-1909," *The Medal Collector*, Vol. 39, No. 12 (Dec. 1988): pp 26-29.

Kroulik, Alfred R., "Polar Awards of the United States: The Byrd Antarctic Expedition Medal, 1928-1930," *The Medal Collector*, Vol. 40, Nos. 1-2 (Jan/Feb 1989): pp 5-10.

Kroulik, Alfred R., "Polar Awards of the United States: The Second Byrd Antarctic Expedition Medal, 1933-1935," *The Medal Collector*, Vol. 40, No. 3 (March 1989): pp 5-11.

Lelle, John E., *The Brevet Medal*, Springfield, Va.: Quest Publishing Company, 1988.

Lobdell III, LTC Harrisson, "Silver Star," *Soldiers*, September 1986: Page 17.

Lobdell III, LTC Harrisson, "Legion of Merit," *Soldiers*, January 1986: Page 16.

Lobdell III, LTC Harrisson, "Soldier's Medal," *Soldiers*, June 1986: Page 16.

Lobdell III, LTC Harrisson, "DFC and Air Medal," *Soldiers*, January 1987: pages 40-41.

Lobdell III, LTC Harrisson, "Bronze Star," *Soldiers*, October 1986: Page 20.

Lobdell III, LTC Harrisson, Purple Heart," *Soldiers*, August 1986: Page 40.

Lobdell III, LTC Harrisson, "Meritorious Service Medal," *Soldiers*, March 1986: Page 45.

Lobdell III, LTC Harrisson, "Army Achievement Medal, " *Soldiers*, May 1986: Page 17.

McDowell, Charles P., *Military and Naval Decorations of the United States*, Quest Publishing Co., 1984.

Miller, Ian A., "New Medals for the US Merchant Marine, " *The Medal Collector*, Vol. 42, No. 7 (July 1991): pp. 15-17.

Mullin, Fitzhugh, *Plagues and Politics*, Basic Books, 1991.

NASA Honor Awards Program, National Aeronautics and Space Administration, Personnel Policy Branch, Office of Human Resources and Education.

Warnock, Timothy A., *Air Force Combat Medals, Streamers, and Campaigns*, U.S. Government Printing Office, Washington D.C., 1990.

Wheatly, Todd, "The Oak Leaf Cluster," *The Journal of the Orders and Medals Society of America*, Vol. 43, No. 7, pp. 5-18.